ROY MORRIS, JR.

SHERIDAN

Roy Morris, Jr., is editor of the magazine *America's Civil War*. He has written numerous articles on the Civil War and other aspects of military history. He won the 1987 Authors Prize given by *Civil War Times Illustrated*. Mr. Morris is a native of Chattanooga, Tennessee, where he once lived in a house on Missionary Ridge at the exact site of Sheridan's breakthrough.

SHERIDAN

The Life and Wars of General Phil Sheridan

ROY MORRIS, JR.

Vintage Civil War Library
Vintage Books
A Division of Random House, Inc.
New York

First Vintage Civil War Library Edition, August 1993

Frontispiece photograph courtesy Chicago Historical Society

Cartography by Jacques Chazaud

Library of Congress Cataloging-in-Publication Data
Morris, Roy.
Sheridan: the life and wars of General Phil Sheridan/
Roy Morris, Jr. — 1st Vintage Civil War library ed.
p. cm. — (Vintage Civil War library)
Originally published: New York: Crown, 1992.
Includes bibliographical references and index.
ISBN 0-679-74398-7
1. Sheridan, Philip Henry, 1831–1888.   2. Generals — United States —
Biography.   3. United States. Army — Biography.   I.   Title.
II. Series.
[E467.1.S54M67   1993]
973.7'3'092 — dc20
[B]   92-50621
CIP

Manufactured in the United States of America
10 9 8 7 6 5 4

To my own Little Phil,
Philip Burton Morris

ACKNOWLEDGMENTS

ANYONE UNDERTAKING A NEW biography of so prominent an individual as Phil Sheridan must necessarily follow in the footsteps of those who have come before. Among those whose tracks may be found in this study are Richard J. O'Connor, Sheridan's last modern biographer, and Paul Andrew Hutton, whose work on Sheridan's western career is virtually definitive. I am also indebted to the late Stephen Z. Starr for his marvelous study of Union cavalry during the Civil War, and to Robert M. Utley for his many learned works on the American West. On Sheridan's postwar administration of Texas, William L. Richter's painstaking scholarship was invaluable. Roger Thomas Zeimet's doctoral dissertation on Sheridan's service in the western theater of the Civil War was also quite helpful. Special thanks go to my friend Jeffry Wert, whose book *From Winchester to Cedar Creek* is an exhaustive and entertaining study of Sheridan's valley campaign, and who was kind enough to share with me in manuscript parts of his since-published *Mosby's Rangers* relating to the dirty little war-within-a-war that haunted the Shenandoah Valley for years after the larger war was over. To all these writers, and to the many others cited at the back of this book, I gladly acknowledge a debt of gratitude.

I would also like to thank my agent, Robert Gottlieb, senior vice president of William Morris Agency, for his kind personal and professional interest, and my editor at Crown, James O'Shea Wade, for saving me on more than one occasion from myself. Special thanks to my friends and colleagues at Empire Press— Brian Kelly, Ken Phillips, Carl Gnam, and Bill Vogt—for giving me the opportunity to continue learning about the Civil War and, through our magazine, *America's Civil War*, giving others the opportunity to learn, as well. Thanks also to Delinda Hanley of Empire Press and Peter Harrington of Brown University for their much appreciated help with picture research.

Three other people I want to thank particularly for their contributions, not merely to this book, but to the ongoing quality of my life. First, my good friend Phil Noblitt, with whom I have walked many Civil War battlefields, refought many battles, and played—poorly, on my part—many Civil War songs on our guitars. Second, my father-in-law, G. Burton Pierce, without whose unfailing interest and continuing generosity I could never have finished this book. And finally, my wife, Leslie, who has always been, from the time I met her a dozen years ago—just yesterday, Plum—my closest reader, gentlest critic, and dearest friend.

—R.M.
Chattanooga, Tennessee

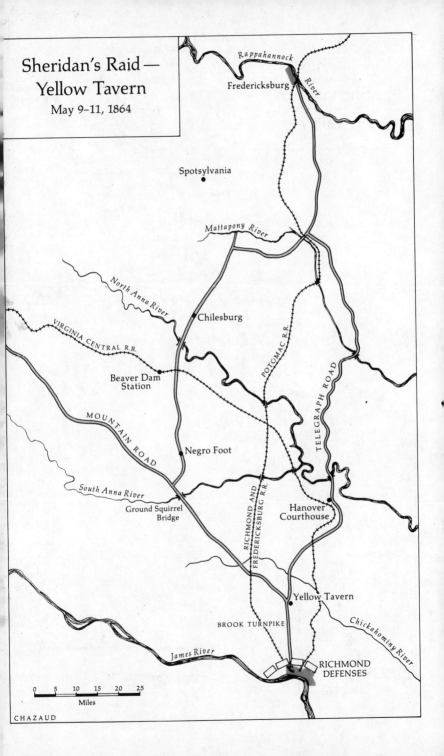

Sheridan's Raid— Yellow Tavern

May 9–11, 1864

Rappahannock River

Fredericksburg

Spotsylvania

Mattapony River

North Anna River

Chilesburg

VIRGINIA CENTRAL R.R.

POTOMAC R.R.

Beaver Dam Station

TELEGRAPH ROAD

MOUNTAIN ROAD

Negro Foot

South Anna River

Ground Squirrel Bridge

RICHMOND AND FREDERICKSBURG R.R.

Hanover Courthouse

Yellow Tavern

BROOK TURNPIKE

Chickahominy River

James River

RICHMOND DEFENSES

0 5 10 15 20 25
Miles

CHAZAUD

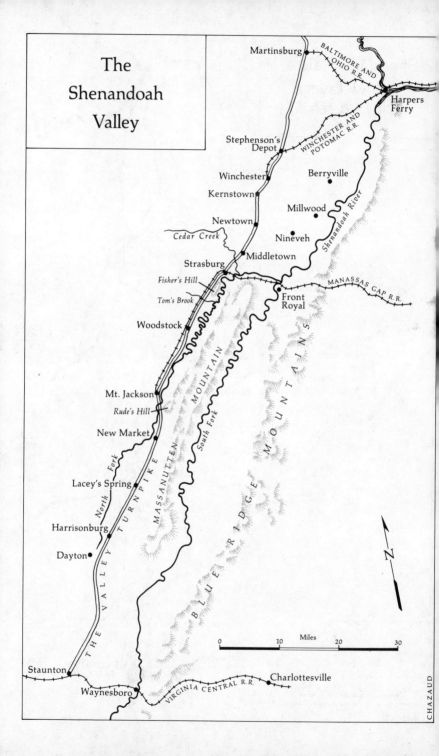

The
Shenandoah
Valley

Martinsburg

BALTIMORE AND OHIO R.R.

Harpers Ferry

Stephenson's Depot

WINCHESTER AND POTOMAC R.R.

Winchester

Berryville

Kernstown

Millwood

Newtown

Cedar Creek

Nineveh

Shenandoah River

Middletown

Strasburg

Fisher's Hill

MANASSAS GAP R.R.

Tom's Brook

Front Royal

Woodstock

MOUNTAIN

Mt. Jackson

South Fork

Rude's Hill

New Market

North Fork

MASSANUTTEN

B L U E   R I D G E   M O U N T A I N S

Lacey's Spring

THE VALLEY TURNPIKE

Harrisonburg

Dayton

N

Miles

0   10   20   30

Staunton

Charlottesville

Waynesboro

VIRGINIA CENTRAL R.R.

CHAZAUD

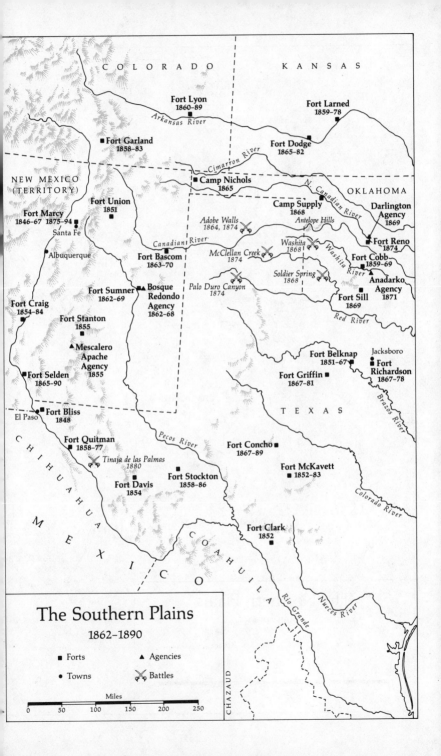

COLORADO

KANSAS

Fort Lyon
1860-89

Fort Larned
1859-78

Arkansas River

■ Fort Garland
1858-83

Fort Dodge
1865-82

Cimarron River

NEW MEXICO
(TERRITORY)

Camp Nichols
1865

N. Canadian River

OKLAHOMA

Fort Union
1851

Camp Supply
1868

Darlington
Agency
1869

Fort Marcy
1846-67 1875-94

Antelope Hills

Santa Fe

Adobe Walls
1864, 1874

Washita
1868

Fort Reno
1874

Albuquerque

Canadian River

McClellan Creek
1874

Washita River

Fort Cobb
1859-69

Fort Bascom
1863-70

Soldier Spring
1868

Anadarko
Agency
1871

Fort Sumner
1862-69

▲ Bosque
Redondo
Agency
1862-68

Palo Duro Canyon
1874

Fort Sill
1869

Fort Craig
1854-84

Red River

Fort Stanton
1855

▲ Mescalero
Apache
Agency
1855

Fort Belknap
1851-67

Jacksboro
■ Fort
Richardson
1867-78

Fort Griffin
1867-81

■ Fort Selden
1865-90

TEXAS

Brazos River

■ Fort Bliss
1848

El Paso

Pecos River

Fort Concho
1867-89

CHIHUAHUA

Fort Quitman
1858-77

Fort McKavett
1852-83

Tinaja de las Palmas
1880

Fort Stockton
1858-86

Colorado River

Fort Davis
1854

MEXICO

Fort Clark
1852

COAHUILA

Rio Grande

Nueces River

The Southern Plains

1862–1890

■ Forts   ▲ Agencies

● Towns   ⚔ Battles

CHAZAUD

Miles

0   50   100   150   200   250

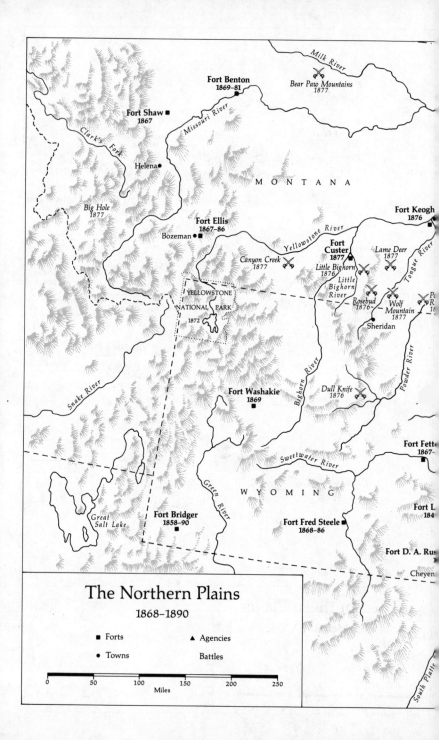

The Northern Plains

1868–1890

- ■ Forts
- ● Towns
- ▲ Agencies
- Battles

0   50   100   150   200   250
Miles

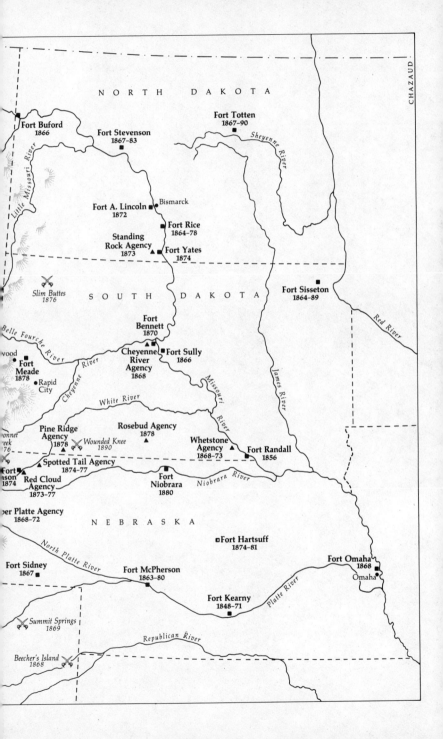

NORTH DAKOTA

CHAZAUD

Fort Buford
1866

Fort Stevenson
1867–83

Fort Totten
1867–90

Sheyenne River

Little Missouri River

Bismarck

Fort A. Lincoln
1872

Fort Rice
1864–78

Standing
Rock Agency
1873

Fort Yates
1874

Slim Buttes
1876

SOUTH DAKOTA

Fort Sisseton
1864–89

Red River

Belle Fourche River

Cheyenne River

Fort
Bennett
1870

wood

Fort
Meade
1878

Rapid
City

Cheyenne River Agency
1868

Fort Sully
1866

White River

Missouri River

James River

Pine Ridge
Agency
1878

Wounded Knee
1890

Rosebud Agency
1878

Whetstone
Agency
1868–73

Fort Randall
1856

onnet
eek
76

Spotted Tail Agency
1874–77

Fort
son
1874

Red Cloud
Agency
1873–77

Fort
Niobrara
1880

Niobrara River

per Platte Agency
1868–72

NEBRASKA

Fort Hartsuff
1874–81

North Platte River

Fort Sidney
1867

Fort McPherson
1863–80

Fort Omaha
1868

Omaha

Fort Kearny
1848–71

Platte River

Summit Springs
1869

Republican River

Beecher's Island
1868

PROLOGUE

HE WAS AN UNIMPRESSIVE little man, five feet five inches tall, with a large, bullet-shaped head and coarse black hair that looked, someone said, as though it had been painted on. Abraham Lincoln, himself no stranger to physical imperfection, described Phil Sheridan—with more wit than kindness—as "a brown, chunky little chap, with a long body, short legs, not enough neck to hang him, and such long arms that if his ankles itch he can scratch them without stooping." All his life, or at least until his feats on the battlefield had effectively transmogrified him beyond mere mortals, people looked down their noses at Sheridan and believed that they had taken his measure. It remained for that laconic realist, Ulysses S. Grant, to put the matter into proper perspective. Told one time too many that his bantam protégé was "rather a little fellow," Grant expounded, at some length for him, "You will find him big enough for the purpose before we get through with him."

Like all apparently simple men, Phil Sheridan was in fact the product of a complex mixture of elements, not least of which was a generous, if often challenged, self-regard. And if it is true, as Samuel Johnson maintained, that one hallmark of genius is an infinite capacity for taking pains, then Sheridan in his way was a sort of genius. Far from being the apotheosis of Celtic dash that northern newspapers made him out to be, he was instead the most deliberate and careful of commanders, with an army-wide reputation for having the best scouts—and sometimes the best spies—of any Union general in the Civil War. Not the least—one might even argue the greatest—of his talents was the one he learned first, as a fourteen-year-old shop clerk in central Ohio: moving merchandise and keeping records. In military parlance this is quartermastering, the careful marshaling of men and supplies. Sheridan may have thrown his troops into the hardest fighting once they reached a battlefield, but they were seldom hungry or ill-provisioned when they arrived there. Like another diminutive and low-born commander, Napoleon Bonaparte, he never forgot that an army travels on its feet and fights on its stomach. Nor did he ever get too grand to share a wagon or a meal with his men. "Put your faith in the common soldier," he was fond of saying, "and he will never let you down."

He knew, because he was, himself, a common soldier. Of all the North's preeminent generals, Phil Sheridan came farther, on less, than anyone, not excluding his two great mentors, Grant and Sherman. Grant's father, a wealthy tanner, was mayor of his Ohio village; Sherman's foster father was a United States senator and cabinet official. Sheridan's father, an Irish immigrant, was a simple laborer on the National Road. By 1853, the year his son graduated from West Point, he was also bankrupt. Small wonder that Sheridan embraced the soldier's life, with its close fraternal values of duty, loyalty, order, and endurance, so completely and unreflectively. Unlike Grant and Sherman, both of whom abandoned the peacetime army for the softening influence of hearth and home, the squat, ungainly Sheridan, a bachelor till the age of forty-four, was never anything more, or less, than a soldier. Nor did he ever want to be.

Like his childhood hero Zachary Taylor, Sheridan was a gruff, informal, no-nonsense fighter, who, while capable of a certain battlefield magnetism, had none of the elegant manners of a Stuart or a Lee. Instead, by way of compensation, he projected a nervous, tightly coiled energy that occasionally crossed into frontier-style violence. Once, when a southern railroad conductor treated him with less than adequate respect, Sheridan wordlessly interrupted a tête-à-tête with fellow general George H. Thomas, beat the offending party insensible, kicked him off his own train, and casually returned to his seat, picking up the thread of conversation with no explanation given and none required. The western farm boys and big-city easterners who served under him in his various commands may have called him "Little Phil," but they did so with affection, and they did so behind his back.

He was brusque, demanding, profane, and unforgiving. He was also hardworking, patriotic, uncomplaining, and brave. He favored, like most West Pointers of his era, the tactical offensive, as propounded for them by academy professor Dennis Hart Mahan in his legendary first-year class on tactics. But one of his greatest accomplishments, perhaps the finest fighting retreat of the Civil War, came while withdrawing from the field at Stones River. ("Here we are," he offhandedly told commanding general William Rosecrans, "all that are left of us.") His only arguable battlefield failure, not rallying his troops at Chickamauga, was more than redeemed at Missionary Ridge; and his subsequent performance in the Shenandoah Valley, heartless though it may have been, nevertheless helped to shorten the war. He never evaded command or responsibility, and he had little patience with those who did. Like Grant he knew how to politick for promotions and preferrals, while appearing to be above such tawdry self-interest. This subtle task he accomplished, again like Grant, by knowing how and when to keep his mouth shut—a commonsense expedient in such short supply during the Civil War as to appear the rarest of virtues and almost, though not quite, its own reward.

He sent hundreds of men to violent death—a friend once estimated that Sheridan had seen more dead bodies than any man alive—yet was himself wounded only once, at the beginning of his career, when a Yakima Indian bullet grazed the bridge of his not-inconsiderable nose and killed the less fortunate private standing beside him. He never shied from combat, either personal or professional; neither did he seek it out for the mere love of fighting. He is reported to have to told a squeamish infantry colonel, "Go in, sir, and get some of your men killed," and he certainly ordered a fractious cavalry brigadier to "attack with necessary casualties, before you retire." But he also forsook an open road to Richmond and all the cheap glory such a raid would have won, for the simple reason that it would have served no larger purpose and would have lost him thereby the respect of his men.

The sheer magnitude of his success in the Shenandoah Valley has sometimes made it appear that the outcome there was preordained. But while it is true that Sheridan enjoyed vast numerical and logistical advantages over his Confederate counterpart, Jubal Early, it is also true that superior Union numbers did not always result in Union victories, as Stonewall Jackson had already demonstrated more than once in that same valley. And while it goes without saying that Early was no Jackson, one might also add that he was no Sheridan, either. It is impossible to believe, had the situation been reversed, that Phil Sheridan would have called off the attack at Cedar Creek with a cavalier shrug of his shoulders and a foolish joke that he had won "glory enough for one day." On the other hand, it is perhaps equally unlikely that he would have made such an attack, outnumbered better than two to one, in the first place. The former stock clerk and quartermaster knew how to read numbers and, more important, how to interpret what they meant.

He did not say, as is commonly believed, "The only good Indian is a dead Indian," however much he may have believed it in his heart of hearts. What he did say, "The only good Indians I ever saw were dead," is less aphoristic but also less ruthless, more a joke than a philosophy. On the western prairies after the war he sought, perhaps obtusely, to employ the same large-scale cavalry tactics he had used to such advantage in the valleys of Virginia. It led, on both sides, to heartbreaking tragedies, for the Cheyenne at the Washita and for their chief tormentor, George Armstrong Custer, at the Little Bighorn. Still, if success is measured strictly by results, Sheridan was eminently successful in pacifying the West. By the year that he died, 1888, no tribe was willing, or even able, to undertake hostilities against the white man's might. But progress, whose impersonal, implacable agent Sheridan always envisioned himself to be, eventually would have crushed the Indian, no matter who functioned as its leading edge. Indeed, it could be argued that his cold-eyed endorsement of buffalo slaughter, rather than any particular military decision, was the decisive factor in the war on the plains. If so, it would have been of a piece with the gourmand's negative interest he habitually evinced in an enemy's empty stomach.

A lifetime of soldierly adventures and accomplishments ended in a muddle of bureaucratic infighting, the one type of battle Phil Sheridan was least equipped to wage. By then he had been in service to his country for exactly forty years, from the plains of West Point to the Pacific Northwest, a career suitably continental in breadth and scope. He died an irrelevancy, as soldiers in peacetime usually are, and thus missed the next war by a decade or so. Had he lived, he would have enjoyed it—or at least its outcome—immensely. For, like his other wars, it too was concerned primarily with power. And power, more than anything—its getting, keeping, wielding, and extending—was what Phil Sheridan was all about.

1

SOLDIER-MAKING

THE CROWD GATHERED EARLY around the flag-draped statue at the intersection of Massachusetts Avenue and Twenty-third and R streets in northwest Washington, D.C., on the day before Thanksgiving, 1908. Three sets of grandstands, painted red, white, and blue, held what *The New York Times* would later describe as "one of the most brilliant [assemblages] seen in Washington in months." President and Mrs. Theodore Roosevelt were there, along with assorted cabinet members, Supreme Court justices, high-ranking army and navy officers, foreign diplomats, society lions, clergymen, relatives, and invited guests. Special seats had been set aside for the white-haired mavens of the Grand Army of the Republic, that once-omnipotent veterans' organization whose chief function now was attending funerals. All had come to witness the long-anticipated unveiling of Danish-American sculptor Gutzon Borglum's bronze simulacrum of General of the Army Philip Henry Sheridan, two decades dead but about to make his capital reappearance on this, the forty-fifth anniversary of the Battle of Missionary Ridge, where he first caught the approving eye of Ulysses S. Grant and so ensured his meteoric and altogether improbable rise to glory.[1]

Regimental flags fluttered above the reviewing stands in the afternoon sun, supporting drapes of dark green laurel that lent the setting an incongruous Christmaslike air. White placards hung from the roofs of the bleachers, bearing the names of battles now nearly half a century old, but to the old men in the G.A.R. gallery as eternally present and evergreen as the sprays of laurel hanging above their heads: Perryville, Chickamauga, Stones River, Missionary Ridge, Fisher's Hill, Cedar Creek, Dinwiddie Court House, Yellow Tavern, Five Forks, Appomattox. First Lieutenant Phil Sheridan, Jr., of the Fifth U.S. Cavalry was there, along with his mother, Irene Rucker Sheridan; his uncle, Brigadier General (retired) Michael V. Sheridan; and his spinster sisters, Mary, Louise, and Irene. After brief introductory remarks by Secretary of War Luke Wright—himself, ironically, a former Confederate—Lieutenant Sheridan stepped up to his father's statue and pulled a sash unloosing two oversized American flags. Simultaneously, a light artillery battery boomed the seventeen-gun salute accorded a general of the army and the Marine Band furnished "The Star-Spangled Banner." A half-hour military parade, largely unseen by the crowd in the stands, followed smartly down Massachusetts Avenue, the president, like an excited child, going to the south end of the grandstand to watch.

T.R. was in fine fettle—when was he not?—pulling sculptor Borglum to his feet and pronouncing his statue "first-class." Approving shouts of "Right!" carried up from the veterans, and Roosevelt, canny politician that he was, played shamelessly to the crowd. "You—you men there, and there," he cried, pointing to the gray heads and polished medals, "are the men who did the deed! It is more important to have done a thing than to talk about it." Then, proceeding to talk about it, the president bent to his text. "It is eminently fitting that the nation's illustrious men, the men who loom as heroes before the eyes of our people, should be fittingly commemorated here at the national capital," he said, "and I am glad indeed to take part in the unveiling of this statue to General Sheridan. His name will always stand high on the list of American worthies. Not only was he a great general, but he showed his greatness with that touch of originality which we call genius. . . . His career was typically American, for from plain beginnings he rose to the highest military position in our land. We honor his memory itself; and moreover, as in the other great commanders of his day, his career symbolizes the careers of all those men who in the years of the nation's direst need sprang to the front to risk everything, including life itself, and to spend the days of their strongest young manhood in valorous conflict for an ideal."[2]

There was more of the same—the president spoke for twenty minutes—before the festivities concluded with a lively version of "Sheridan's Ride," the musical equivalent of Borglum's statue. Hundreds of people, groused the *Washington Post* the next day, "cheerfully climb[ed] over some thousands of others, whose dinner engagements did not take precedence of politeness." The rest stayed behind for a closer look at the artist's handiwork. The statue itself, twelve feet long, eight feet wide, and fourteen feet high, differed dramatically from other equestrian statues in the capital. Instead of depicting a dignified hero sitting astride a resting horse, Borglum had taken pains to show Sheridan and his mount, Rienzi, "in suddenly arrested motion" during the general's famous rallying ride from Winchester, Virginia, to Cedar Creek on the morning of October 19, 1864. Borglum's Sheridan, one and three-quarters times larger than life, was frozen in the act of reining in Rienzi, presumably to chide some skulkers to his right. His customary black plug hat was crumpled in his gloved right hand—an error, actually, since he was wearing a formal campaign hat that day, having just returned from a high-level strategy meeting in Washington. Borglum also erred in showing Sheridan with a smooth face and mustache; contemporary sketches showed the general with an uncharacteristic full beard at the time.[3]

The general's mouth, perhaps politicly, was closed. What he said in the course of his twelve-mile ride is a matter of some discrepancy. In his official report, Sheridan quoted himself as telling his men, rather mildly, "If I had been with you this morning, this disaster would not have happened. We must face the other way. We will go back and recover our camp." Others heard it differently. Army surgeon C. H. Parry probably came closest to the actual wording: "God damn you, don't cheer me! If you love your country, come up to the front! There's lots of fight in you men yet! God damn you! Come up!" For his money, Borglum favored the more economical "You will sleep in your tents tonight, or you will sleep in hell."[4]

But despite the slight errors of fact and the unreconcilable debate over words uttered in the heat of battle nearly half a century before, Borglum's statue was generally accorded a great success. From here the sculptor would go on to his gallery of presidential heads on Mount Rushmore and his incomplete frieze of the Union's great enemies, Robert E. Lee, Stonewall Jackson, and Jefferson Davis, at Stone Mountain, Georgia. Meanwhile, fixed in an immutable present, Phil Sheridan—hero of Cedar Creek, savior of the Union, scourge of Rebels, Indians, Democrats, Klansmen, communists, strikers, rioters, looters, and all other enemies of established order—continued to wave, is waving today, for his men to come up, to follow him forward, to win their famous victory.

HE WAS BORN ON or about March 6, 1831, somewhere along the wandering path his immigrant parents traced from their ancestral home in County Cavan, Ireland, to Somerset, Ohio, where he spent his childhood. The *Biographical Register of Officers and Graduates of the United States Military Academy*, his alma mater, accepts Albany, New York, as Phil Sheridan's birthplace, although a case could also be made for Ireland, Canada, Boston, or the high seas en route to or from all those places. His mother, who presumably would have had the final say in the matter, surprised the general late in life by allowing that he had been born in the New York capital, not small-town Ohio, as he had always assumed. But then, she also told the chairman of the Sheridan

Monument Association that her second son had been born at sea on the voyage over, an account supposedly confirmed by parish priests. Not surprisingly, Sheridan himself showed little regard for hagiological niceties, variously claiming as his birthplace all the American locations and several of the conflicting dates. It has been suggested that he purposely obscured his foreign birth to protect his putative presidential aspirations, in which case he must have been unusually ambitious, since by this reasoning he began to lie when he was seventeen, and unusually persistent, since he stood by the story in his posthumous memoirs, long after he had passed beyond such transient glories. Probably, he just never knew. Such questions of provenance aside, he manifestly considered himself American, which, in all things save possibly the place of his birth, indisputably he was.[5]

He was the third of six children (his older sister, Rosa, died at sea on the trip over) born to John and Mary Meenagh Sheridan, second cousins who had lived as tenant farmers on the Cherrymount estate in northern Ireland before staking their future on the New World's haven. The others, in order, were Patrick, Rosa, Mary, John, and Michael. John Sheridan's uncle, Thomas Gainor, had preceded his nephew to America, settling in Albany and sending back for domestic consumption a somewhat roseate picture of emigrant life. Taking Gainor at his word, or else anticipating their country's ruinous potato famine of a decade later, the Sheridans made their way to the Empire State, only to find that the Gainor version of Albany economics had edged, perhaps, into boosterism. There was nothing for them there, but construction gangs were hiring on the National Road, the great mid-American thoroughfare then in the process of inventing itself westward from Chesapeake Bay to the Mississippi River. Somerset, Ohio, with its large Catholic population and crossroads location, seemed as good a place as any to put down roots.[6]

The village, population 1,400, sat athwart a high ridge between the Hocking and Muskingum rivers, forty-three miles southeast of Columbus. For local reasons now lost to time, the boys living on the west side of town were called Pig Foots, those on the east were dubbed Turkey Foots, and the two factions warred ceaselessly for playground supremacy. Somerset boasted the oldest Catholic church in Ohio, the Church of St. Joseph, whose bells tolled a sober-sided 6:00 A.M.-to-6:00 P.M. working day, as well as several dry-goods stores, the obligatory one-room schoolhouse, a blacksmith's, a tinsmith's, a tavern, a courthouse, and a smattering of houses along the town's three main roads. The Sheridans lived in a three-room frame house on the southernmost street, Happy Alley. Phil and his brothers were Pig Foots.[7]

With the help of a sympathetic engineer named Bassett, John Sheridan rose from common laborer to subcontractor, earning a sufficient though by no means luxurious living as a free-lance roadbuilder and canal-digger before going bust in the failure of the Sciota and Hocking Valley Railroad in 1853. With her husband absent much of the time, Mrs. Sheridan inevitably inherited the task of raising their brood. Neighbors found her "clearheaded, resourceful, honest, and industrious," traits she bequeathed to her five children by both precept and example. Phil, though generally considered the most Meenagh-like of her offspring, apparently was not his mother's favorite. That distinction went to Patrick, the family's shining light, a diligent, dutiful, serious-minded youth who traveled with his father on the National Road and eventually bought into a local dry-goods store before dying suddenly at twenty-one, his promise tragically unfulfilled. All the boys worked; Phil clerked in a succession of Somerset stores, John and Mike found jobs in the town printing shop.[8]

In her own quiet, undemonstrative way, Mrs. Sheridan was something of a community leader. Once, when her husband was gone—as usual—a fight broke out between local railroad workers and a gang of roustabouts from a traveling circus. The call went out for all Somerset men to join ranks with their fellows; but Mrs. Sheridan, acting quickly, summoned her husband's employees and persuaded them not to take part in the trouble. The state militia ultimately had to be called out to quell the disturbance, but

Sheridan's workers dutifully held back in deference to the formidable Mrs. Sheridan.[9]

The family home looked across the Hocking Valley toward St. Mary's Female Academy, located on a hillside a half-mile away. One of the young ladies there, Ellen Ewing, daughter of United States Senator Thomas Ewing of nearby Lancaster, Ohio, was being courted by her foster brother, William Tecumseh Sherman, then a cadet at the United States Military Academy at West Point. The Ewings were Catholic and frequently came up to Somerset to attend mass at St. Joseph's. Mrs. Sheridan, as a pillar of the church, undoubtedly knew the Ewing family, but there is no evidence that the two future Union generals were boyhood friends—for one thing, Sherman was eleven years older. Nevertheless, Sheridan's youthful companion, Henry Greiner, later claimed that he and Sheridan had once interrupted a game of hopscotch to watch Sherman, resplendent in cadet gray, talking with his fiancée in a neighbor's doorway. If so, Sheridan promptly forgot all about it; he makes no mention of the episode in his memoirs.[10]

Sheridan's childhood was entirely typical of his time and place, small-town America in the mid-1800s. He larked about, skipped school, stole apples, bedeviled his teachers, teased the town tramp. It pleased him to say in later life that "the little white schoolhouse of the North" had given the Union an invincible edge over the presumably uneducated South. But by his own testimony and that of his fellows, Sheridan the student spent about as much time beneath a desk as Tom Sawyer did—or, for that matter, Tom's creator, Samuel Clemens, whose rough-and-tumble Missouri upbringing closely mirrored Sheridan's own. From a succession of glum, solitary bachelor teachers (whose chief professional recommendation seems to have been the speed with which they could wield a switch), Sheridan and his schoolmates attained a passing acquaintance with the English language and a rough approximation of arithmetic. The rest, in the time-honored tradition of American education, was left up to them.[11]

More fertile ground for learning was Finch's Tavern on the

town square, where rope-wristed, tough-talking Conestoga wagon drivers broke from their journeys on the National Road. Rambunctious, prideful, and competitive, these hardy teamsters, or "land pilots," as they preferred to style themselves, were homespun individualists who were not shy about mixing it up with whips and fists. Their creative way with the mother tongue was legendary, and Sheridan in his time would honor their craft. But except for occasional tavern brawls and the boisterous and competitive political campaigns that at this time in the nation's history frequently resembled them, patriotic celebrations provided the main recreational diversions in Somerset. Each Fourth of July the area's one surviving Revolutionary War veteran, a wizened coot named Dusenberry, was trundled out for a command appearance on the courthouse steps. Sheridan and his friends would follow him about, dreaming of glory in a war of their own. With a tin sword fashioned for him by an obliging smith, young Phil precociously drilled the town's youth in the profession of arms. His appearance, unfortunately, worked against him: his short legs, long arms, and large, oddly shaped head were distinctly simian. Still, he could and would fight. By the time he left Somerset, it was generally accepted that Sheridan could whip any boy there.[12]

The Mexican War, in 1846, provided a focus for his compensatory aggression. Too young to join the fighting, with its exotic, far-away-sounding names, Sheridan became instead a sort of self-appointed local authority on the conduct of the war, poring over newspaper accounts of the fighting and chairing informal strategy debates at Finck & Dittoe's dry-goods store. From the shop's windows he enviously watched the town militia, the Keokuk Rifles, kicking up dust in the village square. At the same time a plan was forming in the back of his mind. "The stirring events of the times so much impressed and absorbed me," he later wrote in his memoirs, "that my sole wish was to become a soldier, and my highest aspirations to go to West Point as a cadet from my congressional district."[13]

Here he got lucky. For the past three years, since quitting school, Sheridan had been clerking in the town's general stores, his brush with higher education seemingly a thing of the past. Industrious, honest, and willing to serve, he had advanced from lowly stock boy to head clerk and bookkeeper at Finck & Dittoe's. In this latter capacity he had become acquainted with the district's resident great man, U.S. Representative Thomas Ritchey. Like Sheridan's father and older brother, Ritchey was a Whig. When Ritchey's most recent appointee to West Point, a boy named Lewis, flunked out of school, the victim of mathematical deficiencies and "a poor attitude," Sheridan took it upon himself to approach the congressman about the vacancy. Remembering him from the dry-goods counter—and not wanting to offend another pair of local magnificos who were busily pushing their own sons for the post—Ritchey selected Sheridan as a compromise candidate. In March 1848, the mails arrived with his appointment papers. [14]

With characteristic energy and thoroughness, Sheridan spent the next several months painstakingly augmenting his meager education. The current schoolmaster, Mr. Clark, assisted as tutor. Natural uneasiness about the entrance exam was soon compounded by the arrival of an official-looking circular detailing the required attire for incoming cadets. Among the items listed was "one pair of Monroe shoes," a style of footwear unknown in Somerset. For a time Sheridan despaired, but his brother Pat had seen such shoes in Baltimore, and assured Phil that the local brand was suitable. Thus reassured, Sheridan left for West Point in June 1848. He would not see Somerset or his family for the next two years, and except for infrequent visits (and one year-long, self-inflicted exile) would never live there again after this first epochal departure. Aboard a steamboat crossing Lake Erie from Cleveland to Buffalo, he made his first comradely contact with a would-be fellow cadet, David S. Stanley of Cedar Valley, Ohio. Comparing notes, Sheridan was pleased to learn that Stanley did not have the requisite pair of Monroe shoes. Stanley, for his part, sized up the homely, ill-shaped Sheridan as "the most insignificant-looking little fellow I ever saw." In time the two future Union generals would modify their youthful first impressions.[15]

After a dutiful visit to his great-uncle Thomas in Albany, Sheridan arrived at West Point in early June along with the other sixty-three prospective cadets of the class of 1852. The long-dreaded entrance exam proved absurdly—and misleadingly—easy: candidates had to read and write a few sentences of prose and work a simple arithmetic problem. They had to be at least sixteen and not more than twenty-one years old, in good health, of suitable moral fiber, and over four feet nine inches tall. That was all. Lawmakers had purposely kept entrance requirements modest to avoid excluding "many young men of worth whose early education has been neglected"—young men whose fathers, it went without saying, might be made unhappy by their boys' failure to gain admittance. Sheridan met the minimal standards, gave his age as eighteen years and one month, and was duly enrolled as a provisional cadet.[16]

The would-be cadets were relieved of all money and personal possessions by the academy adjutant and issued minimal furniture and supplies for their Spartan living quarters: blankets, a chair, a slop bucket, a tin washbasin, a lump of soap, a slate for working arithmetic problems, a water dipper, stationery, and a few candles. But merely passing the entrance exam and drawing supplies did not make the new arrivals West Point cadets, as Sheridan and his fellow plebes quickly learned. To begin with, there was summer encampment, a two-month lark for the older cadets but a galling test of endurance for dewy-eyed newcomers. Here for the first time they experienced the rigid class system overarching the academy. As "mere conditional things," the plebes were supervised by second-year upperclassmen who considered it part of their supervisory duty to acquaint their young charges with the time-honored tradition of hazing. Each summer the entire cadet contingent, with the exception of third-year men away on furlough, moved into tents on the wide plain above the

Hudson River for hands-on training in the practical side of soldiering. For the older cadets this included infantry tactics, artillery drill, horseback riding, marksmanship, and swordsmanship. For the newcomers it consisted mainly of trying to keep their new white trousers clean on the dusty parade ground and learning how to get by without adequate sleep.[17]

Contrary to later practices at West Point and private colleges and universities, hazing in the 1850s was not so much physically punishing as mentally irritating. Older cadets cut their victims' tent ropes, stole their clothes, and pulled them out of bed by their ankles while they slept. Sheridan, according to fellow classmate John L. Hathaway, bore his part of the hazing manfully, although forty years later he was still denouncing it as a "senseless custom." More difficult to accept was the verbal abuse; to one of his classically Gaelic nature, being yelled at by strangers was hard to take. On at least one celebrated occasion later in his cadetship, he quite publicly and violently would not tolerate it. But for the time being he swallowed his pride and kept out of trouble until formal classes began in September.[18]

The first hurdle for incoming cadets was the midterm examination in January. Fewer than half of all candidates admitted to the academy in the 1850s managed to graduate, with those who did not often falling prey to the dreaded "January fever." Sheridan, with the example of young Lewis fresh in his mind, applied himself to his studies with a will. All too clearly he recognized his educational shortcomings, particularly in algebra and mathematics. Once again he got lucky. His roommate, a slight, scholarly New Yorker named Henry Slocum, was an excellent student who, conveniently enough, had been a schoolteacher before entering West Point. At night, long after taps had signaled lights out, the two cadets would hang a blanket over their window and continue their studies, Slocum serving as volunteer tutor. At the end of the probationary period, Sheridan managed to place fortieth in his class in mathematics, not particularly high, but high enough to survive.[19]

Life at West Point settled into a drab, monotonous routine. Each cadet theoretically was allowed thirty dollars a month in pay, but the money could only be drawn upon at the commissary, and then only to purchase such dull essentials as soap and razors. Even so, most cadets soon found themselves hopelessly in debt. Living quarters were purposely rough: cadets shared an eight-by-ten-foot room containing mattresses, blankets, a table, a straight-backed chair, a lamp, a washstand, and a mirror. Heat, such as there was, came from a small fireplace. The corps dining room featured a barely digestible fare of boiled meat, boiled potatoes, boiled pudding, stale bread, and weak coffee. It was not uncommon for cadets to find mice, roaches, and combs in their food. Butter was often rancid, molasses sour. The overworked, underfed young men were driven to such expedients as stealing fruit from neighboring orchards or purchasing contraband supplies from civilian sutlers who loitered openly outside academy grounds.[20]

In addition to drinking, smoking, gambling, and dueling, cadets were forbidden to cook in their rooms—so of course virtually every cadet drank, smoked, gambled, fought, and smuggled food into his room to cook during midnight "hashes" around the fireplace. (William Tecumseh Sherman, class of '42, was accounted the finest hash-maker ever to grace the academy.) Three hundred four separate regulations governed cadet behavior, with each breach of discipline resulting in a varying number of demerits, or "criminalities," as they were known in cadet slang. Demerits were assessed for everything from keeping an overdue library book to disobeying an order on the parade ground. More-serious offenses, such as fighting, resulted in a correspondingly greater number of demerits. Two hundred demerits in a given year resulted in automatic dismissal from the academy, as did getting caught at Benny Havens's notorious off-limits tavern. Even the use of outdoor latrines was proscribed by regulations. To circumvent this last stricture, cadets adopted the elemental expedient of relieving themselves from their barracks windows, much to the disgust of fellow cadets walking guard duty below.[21]

Wearing the uniform, the famous "cadet gray," was itself a daily ordeal. Heavy ankle-high shoes cut into the leg, while the seven-inch-high black leather hat, with its additional eight-inch plume, weighed a full five pounds and gave many cadets a severe headache. At least one, a slender, ringleted Virginian named George Pickett, flatly refused to keep his on his head, and came dangerously close to being dismissed for a resultant excess of demerits. For someone as oddly shaped as Sheridan, the stiff, bulky uniform was a sweaty discomfort. Even such a congenital stoic as Ulysses S. Grant found voice to complain: "My pants sit as tight to my skin as the bark to a tree . . . if I bend over quickly or run, they are very apt to crack with a report as loud as a pistol."[22]

Then there were the classes. The West Point curriculum at midcentury included mathematics, physical sciences, civil and military engineering, English composition, French, Spanish, rhetoric and ethics, history, constitutional law, and—almost as an afterthought—military tactics. A typical mathematics course included algebra, geometry, trigonometry, applied algebra, and mensuration. A 390-page mathematics textbook would routinely be covered in five weeks of study. By academy mandate, each student received a daily recitation grade in every subject. Sheridan, like most midwesterners and southerners, found himself at a distinct disadvantage to eastern cadets when it came to studies. Contrary to the popular image of a West Point dominated by aristocratic southerners, most of the faculty and highest-ranking cadets came from the East, where better schooling gave them a long head start in the academy's stifling classrooms.[23]

Within each class there was a self-contained democracy of shared struggles and competition. Here again, the widely held notion of a domineering southern clique has been greatly exaggerated. Small-town midwesterners like Grant, Sherman, and Sheridan were far more typical of the West Point of their day than the patrician Virginian, Robert E. Lee. Far from being an elite university of privileged scholars, the academy was a practical-minded school for engineers, whose skills at roadbuilding, canal-laying, railroad-grading, and bridge-throwing were in much greater demand than soldierly attributes and martial bearing. The most accomplished cadets were reserved for the engineering corps, the lowest-ranking for the cavalry. Despite its remarkable showing in the just-concluded Mexican War, the army and its professional officer corps were held in low esteem by the American public. "Soldier, soldier, will you work?" was a common schoolboy taunt for men in uniform.[24]

The academy curriculum reflected this imbalance. Only one course, in a cadet's senior year, dealt with the broader implications of military education: Dennis Hart Mahan's celebrated seminar on the science of war. Mahan, an eccentric, charismatic teacher who always sported a furled umbrella, had made West Point his entire life (he would die, perhaps a suicide, when forced into retirement in 1871). A devotee of France in general and Napoleon in particular, he founded the academy's Napoleon Club and preached the little corporal's doctrine of *toujours l'audace*. "Successful warfare is almost always offensive warfare," Mahan wrote in his influential *Elementary Treatise on Advanced-Guard, Out-Post, and Detachment Service of Troops, and the Manner of Posting and Handling Them in Presence of an Enemy*. The slender booklet, shortened to *Out-Post* by generations of cadets, would find its way into many an officer's saddlebag during the Civil War. Mahan's approach to war stressed the indirect offensive, the concentration of massed forces on an enemy's weakened flanks, the need to harry a foe without rest, and the then-revolutionary idea that an enemy army, not a strategic point on a map, was the great object of any campaign. Mahan also taught that commanders should attempt, whenever possible, to carry the war into the heart of the enemy's homeland as a way of making him share the misery. In time, a few of his more pragmatic cadets—Grant, Sherman, and Sheridan, in particular—would have cause to remember Mahan's teachings.[25]

For now, Sheridan had all he could do to keep up his grades. Diligence aside, he was not much of a student. Unlike the surprisingly bookish Grant, who whiled away a large amount of his time at West Point lost in the imaginative novels of Bulwer-Lytton, Frederick Marryat, and Washington Irving, Sheridan confined his reading to the required texts. The only exceptions were four studies of Napoleon's campaigns, a couple of books of poetry, and a handful of biographies, including those of Samuel Johnson, Lord Byron, and Mohammed—three men who were, in their separate ways, about as far from Phil Sheridan as he was from the moon. Perhaps he should have read more; it might have taken his mind off the painfully obvious fact that he was something of an outcast among his more favored fellow cadets. Not only was he short, unattractive, argumentative, and poor, he was also obviously Irish Catholic—at a time when the Irish potato famine had just sent hundreds of thousands of his parents' distressed countrymen pouring into the United States. Sheridan was not long off the boat himself—literally or figuratively—and it may have been that his bristling Irishness acted as a goad to certain cadets. Whatever the case, on September 9, 1851, at the beginning of his first-class year at West Point, "a quarrel of a belligerent nature" came within a whisker of ending his career before it started.[26]

On that day, Cadet Private Sheridan (he was still a private after three years in the corps) was given a peremptory order by Cadet Sergeant William R. Terrill, of Bath County, Virginia, to "dress," or close, with the next man in line. Something about Terrill's tone offended Sheridan. Crying, "God damn you, sir, I'll run you through!" he lowered his rifle and lunged his bayonet toward the flabbergasted cadet. At the last second he regained his self-control, lowered his weapon, and returned to line, where he continued to bombard Terrill with oaths and threats. A shocking breach of discipline had been committed before dozens of reluctant witnesses, and Terrill had no choice but to put Sheridan on report.[27]

The next afternoon Terrill was sitting alone on the front steps of his barracks when Sheridan—accidentally or not—happened by. Again something snapped. "God damn you!" Sheridan shouted, striking Terrill a wallop on the side of the head. The two slugged it out, the much-larger Terrill quickly gaining the advantage, until they were separated by a passing officer. This time Sheridan was placed under house arrest. Both parties were required to submit written explanations of their conduct to academy superintendent Henry W. Brewerton. Terrill, for his part, maintained with some justification that he had acted "altogether in self defence." Sheridan said only that he had been provoked by the Virginian's "improper tone" and his oppressive habit of speaking "improperly, unnecessarily, and continually" to the cadets in line. Brewerton, a generally unpopular superintendent then in his last year at the academy, reviewed the incident and recommended, rather leniently, that Sheridan be suspended for a year. Secretary of War Charles M. Conrad went along with his recommendation. An unrepentant Sheridan, decrying the suspension as "a very unfair punishment," returned to Somerset and Finck & Dittoe's dry-goods store.[28]

Nine months later he was back at West Point. In the interim his original class had graduated, taking with it his good friends John Nugen and George Crook. He made others, particularly a small-faced fellow Ohioan named Joshua Sill. By this time the academy had a new superintendent, the *beau idéal* of the army, Colonel Robert E. Lee. Sheridan's months in exile had not noticeably improved his disposition; he received more demerits in his last year than he had totaled during the previous three. It was not a particularly well-behaved class; of the fifty-one graduates besides Sheridan, twenty had as many or more demerits. Sheridan had 189, eleven shy of automatic dismissal. (He did not, as legend has it, exceed the limit and graduate only by official sufferance.) An Illinois cadet named John Schofield, who one day would succeed Sheridan as general of the army, had 196, as did a tall, muscular, blond-haired Kentuckian, John Bell Hood, whose destiny would take a different path. In all five of his graded subjects, including infantry tactics and artillery, Sheridan ranked in the bottom half of his class. Still, he had managed to graduate, which was more, perhaps, than most people had expected, himself included. His name was thirty-fourth in the roll of graduates recited by Superintendent Lee, who charitably certified the fractious new brevet second lieutenant as "well qualified for all corps" of the army. Graduating first in his class was a handsome, magnetic cadet from upstate Ohio, James B. McPherson, of whom great things were universally expected.[29]

Sheridan's low class ranking disqualified him for duty in the more prestigious branches of the service. Instead he was assigned to Company D, First Infantry Regiment, then garrisoned at Fort Duncan, Texas. After the decidedly mixed hospitality of West Point, even Fort Duncan, the most out-of-the-way posting on the entire frontier, must have seemed welcome. He had now entered the ranks of the regular army, from whose comradely embrace he would never stray. It was, given the scope and complexity of its tasks, a decidedly small organization. Since the successful conclusion of the war with Mexico six years earlier, the army had reverted to its peacetime size of 13,821, as congressionally mandated down to the lowliest commissary clerk. President James K. Polk, the author and instrument of Manifest Destiny, had decreed in July 1848 that the old army, as it existed before the war, was large enough for the nation's needs—this from a president whose aggressive administration, by fighting one war and threatening another, had enlarged the people's birthright by more than 1 million square miles in three years' time. In 1853, during the annual budgetary wrangles with Congress, Secretary of War Jefferson Davis felt constrained to point out that since the turn of the century national territory had doubled, the white population had increased by 18 million, and the indigenous Indian population (of whom he estimated some 40,000 to be "inimical warriors") had also doubled to 360,000, while the size of the army remained the same. Fewer than 7,000 soldiers now manned the fifty-four garrisons west of the Mississippi River.[30]

Congress resisted enlarging the army for three politically motivated reasons: opposition from the southern states whose elected representatives still tenuously held the reins of power and who feared that a large national army would be unduly coercive, i.e., antislavery; traditional American resistance to a standing army; and the prohibitive cost of supporting a larger force, when money might better be spent on such vote-seining internal improvements as roads and bridges. With the nation relentlessly expanding westward, the army turned to its primary task, making the frontier safe for democracy, with a minuscule constabulary and an annual turnover rate—from discharge, desertion, and death—of twenty-eight percent.[31]

The officer corps, of which Brevet Second Lieutenant Sheridan was now one of the most junior, had the usual mixture of promising young turks, old-line professionals, dedicated careerists, deadbeats, martinets, and out-and-out drunks. Promotion was strictly by seniority—and glacially slow. With no provision for retirement pensions, high-ranking officers often remained in uniform for life. As late as 1860, some were still veterans of the War of 1812. It was not unusual for an otherwise qualified officer to need thirty years to attain a major's rank, by which time many long since had opted to trade their soldier blue for civilian mufti. During the 1850s alone, such talented West Point graduates as George B. McClellan, William Rosecrans, Thomas J. Jackson, Braxton Bragg, Henry Halleck, Ulysses S. Grant, and William T. Sherman resigned their commissions and entered private business. Slow advancement was accompanied by low pay, twenty-five dollars a month for a second lieutenant, and the concomitant slackening of officers' morale was further aggravated by President Franklin Pierce's ill-considered decision in 1855 to fill half of the 116 officer vacancies in newly created regiments with civilian appointees, termed "Davis creatures" by disgusted professionals.[32]

The enlisted men serving under such officers on the army's far-flung western posts were, for the most part, poor soldier material. Many were fugitives from the stews of large eastern cities, poor, out-of-work, foreign, ill, or simple-minded. For eleven dollars a month they were expected to lead lives of crushing monotony and intermittent danger on remote outposts where living conditions were—to be charitable—uncomfortable, uncongenial, and unsafe. Quartered in drafty barracks, leaky tents, or clammy mud huts, wracked by periodic outbreaks of cholera, dysentery, yellow fever, and the soldier's wan companion, venereal disease, a ranker in the 1850s had a one-in-thirty-three chance of dying before his term of enlistment was up. Diversions were few, running mainly to crackpate whiskey and penny-ante cards. Small wonder that many chose to take "French leave," deserting in droves whenever the opportunity presented itself. Those who were caught faced a sentence of death, although in practice few deserters were executed prior to the Civil War. Instead, an unlucky miscreant would be stripped to the waist, tied to a pole, and given fifty lashes with a rawhide whip. His head would be shaved, he would be branded on the hip with an indelible *D*, and, to crown his mortification, he would be waltzed off the post to the mocking strains of "The Rogue's March." It was not a risk to be taken lightly. Still, in 1856 alone, over 3,200 enlisted men deserted.[33]

Into this squalid Spencerian environment, so different from small-town Somerset and picturesque West Point, Phil Sheridan advanced in the winter of 1854. His arrival was anything but auspicious. A "blue norther," howling across the plains from Canada, tumbled him headlong into Laredo, tearing down the newly erected sand walls of Fort McIntosh for good measure. A six-mule quartermaster's wagon relayed him westward to Fort Duncan, on the east bank of the Rio Grande across from the Mexican border town of Piedras Negras. No sooner had he arrived than he was sent back in the same direction he had come, to Camp La Pena, to scout for Lipan and Comanche Indians. These "savages," he was told, were in the habit of depredating about the vicinity, and two companies were usually detailed to watch for them and to interfere, whenever possible, with their sport.[34]

At first, all Sheridan found to interfere with was an abundance of deer, antelope, and wild turkeys. In the company of an enlisted man named Frankman, a butcher in his previous life,

Sheridan freely indulged a new-found passion for hunting, slaying small game in such staggering numbers that he was able to relieve the camp of its dependence on beef, "much to the discomfiture of the disgruntled beef contractor." But soon he had his first brush, albeit by proxy, with the Native Americans of the Southwest. Out hunting one afternoon, he spotted smoke on the horizon and moccasin prints in the sand. Beating it back to camp, he ran into Captain M. E. Van Buren at the head of a mounted rifle contingent. Van Buren was in pursuit of a band of Comanches; Sheridan eagerly put him on their trail. A few days later, outside Corpus Christi, the Indians stopped running and made a stand. Although outnumbered two to one, Van Buren impetuously attacked, receiving a Comanche arrow through the belt buckle for his troubles. Nine days later he died. Sheridan's introduction to western Indians, compliments of the late Captain Van Buren, taught him that—savages or not—they were not to be underestimated.[35]

Most of his time at Fort Duncan was not so divertingly spent. His arrival had given him a healthy respect for western weather. Unlike his brother officers, he scorned the post's existing quarters, tents pitched under an improvised shed, and painstakingly constructed a one-man hut from wooden poles and bits of tarpaulin. A stone fireplace and thatched roof completed the rude habitation. What the other officers thought of such industrious individualism is unrecorded. Sheridan said only that he was "more comfortably off than many of the officers, who had built none." One of the presumably hut-less lieutenants wintering alongside him that season was Richard W. Johnson of Kentucky. Johnson, who had graduated four classes ahead at West Point (and who would cross paths with Sheridan again a few years hence at Stones River, Tennessee), remembered him as "an active, enterprising young officer," but no more promising than a dozen other young lieutenants at the post.[36]

With the others, Sheridan attended a number of well-chaperoned balls at the home of the Mexican *comandante* in Piedras Negras—quaint, decorous affairs whose civilizing influence he rather ungraciously termed "undoubtedly beneficial . . . in softening the rough edges in a half-breed population." Intermingling with Comanches, Sheridan decided, had cost the Mexicans everything except their graceful manners and a residual fanatic Catholicism that expressed itself mainly by the placing of crosses at spots where one of their number had been slain. Since the Comanches in these parts were "bloodthirsty savages," there was no shortage of crosses on either side of the Rio Grande. Still, though their men were regularly cut down and their women and children carried off or ravished, the Mexicans somehow managed to retain a "reverence for the emblems of Christianity [which] was always uppermost in the mind of even the most ignorant."[37]

That winter Sheridan had the opportunity to see firsthand the effects of an Indian raid. This time it was Lipans, not Comanches, on the warpath. Swooping down on an animal herd within sight of the fort, the Indians killed a young herder, a former drummer boy at the post, but not before he had taken two of them with him and seriously wounded a third with the three shots he managed to get off before being riddled with arrows. Sheridan and a company of mounted riflemen gave chase, but the Lipans managed to cross the river into Mexico, from whose sanctuary they impudently taunted the Americans to come on and fight. That night Sheridan and another officer attended a dance in Piedras Negras and saw, to their surprise and disgust, two of the same Indians they had been chasing all afternoon. Sheridan, for his part, was ready to shoot them down, but the Indians were hustled out before shots could be exchanged.[38]

That brief encounter, and an uncharacteristically mild-mannered interest in, of all things, ornithology, represented the extent of Sheridan's service at Fort Duncan. In November 1854 he was promoted to second lieutenant and transferred to Company D, Fourth Infantry Regiment, at Fort Reading, California. Owing to the tardiness of the mails and the necessity of a roundabout trip to Bedloe's Island, New York, to take temporary charge of a con-

tingent of new recruits, it was July before Sheridan arrived at his
new post at the northern end of the Sacramento Valley. Conditions there were very different from the backwater posting at Fort
Duncan. Gold had been discovered along the upper Columbia
River in northeastern Washington, and unruly, opportunistic
miners, many of them hard-bitten veterans of the California gold
rush of 1849, thronged into the virgin territory. The path they
took to the new gold fields led directly across the ancestral lands
of the Yakima Indians, a somewhat morose, unfriendly tribe that
already had more than ample cause to be chary of whites—
especially those bearing picks and shovels.[39]

The Yakimas and the other Indians of the region—Walla
Wallas, Umatillas, Klikitats, Spokanes, Cayuses, Palouses, Nez
Percé, Kittitas, and Salishans—were still smarting from the rough
handling they had recently received at the Walla Walla Valley
peace talks. The two-week-long talks had been, in reality, a monumental filibuster by Washington Governor Isaac I. Stevens, a
bluff, domineering, self-impressed little man whose energy and
intellect compensated for a sickly, diminutive physique. A de-
scendant of New England Puritans, Stevens had graduated first in
his class at West Point, serving with distinction as a member of
Major General Winfield Scott's field staff in the Mexican War,
where he was twice breveted for bravery. He owed his present
sinecure as territorial governor to his tireless campaign efforts on
behalf of President Pierce, a personal friend. Stevens's aims were
multifold: to gain title to all Indian lands in the region; to remove
the inconvenient natives to reservations where they would be
taught, improbably, to farm; to encourage white immigration
into the territory; and to promote a northern route for the much-
bruited transcontinental railroad. It was an ambitious agenda,
only slightly complicated by the fact that the Indians in question
did not share its progressive goals.[40]

For two long weeks—they must have seemed endless to the
Indians—Stevens held forth, blustering, cajoling, and bullyrag-
ging his listeners, whom it pleased him to call "my children."

(One Coeur d'Alene chief pointedly told him, "We have not yet made friends. All Indians are not yet your children.") Finally, with a mixture of relief and foreboding, the chiefs gave in, signing the indecipherable scraps of paper thrust before them. Few if any understood the terms of the treaty, fewer still intended to abide by them. When the *Puget Sound Courier* prematurely published official notice of the treaty—not to be legally ratified for four more years—miners and homesteaders flocked to the area. The Yakimas, already warned by their principal chief, Kamiakin, to beware the white man's coming, reacted in a predictable way— they went to war.[41]

The war's first victims were a trio of luckless prospectors named Mattice, Eaton, and Fanjoy, whose ordinarily praiseworthy dispatch in moving into the territory proved, under the circumstances, to be their undoing. When news of the killings filtered back to the settlements, Indian agent A. J. Bolon rode out to talk sense to Kamiakin. On the way, he was relieved of both his scalp and his life by three other Yakimas who were, presumably, tired of such talk, one holding him down while the others slit his throat. They even killed his horse. With the Rogue River Indians to the south already acting up, Pacific Division commanding general John E. Wool was suddenly faced with a two-front war.[42]

Sheridan was blissfully unaware of all this. Upon arrival at Fort Reading, he was directed to replace his old academy classmate John Bell Hood, in command of a small group of dragoons then accompanying Lieutenant Robert S. Williamson's topographical expedition into the Willamette Valley. Williamson's task was to determine the feasibility of a railroad connecting Sacramento and the Columbia River, which happened to be the very tract of land over which the Yakimas and Stevens now were contending. If Sheridan envied the strapping Hood his new assignment—he was on his way to join Jefferson Davis's elite new Second Cavalry Regiment in Texas, along with such stalwarts as Robert E. Lee, Albert Sidney Johnston, George Thomas, Earl Van Dorn, J. E. B. Stuart, and other soon-to-be-famous officers—he managed not to show it. He was preoccupied just then with establishing order in his own command, which comprised "the most troublesome and insubordinate individuals" in the regiment, and with avoiding the real or imagined swarms of hostile Indians said to be operating in the vicinity. He was successfully coping with both tasks (the only Indians he saw were in a group of "naked, hungry and cadaverous" Pit Indians, wretchedly trailing the expedition, begging for food), when he was summoned to join Major Gabriel J. Rains's hastily organized autumn campaign against the Yakimas. [43]

From the outset the expedition was a laughable fiasco. To begin with, Rains, a North Carolina graduate of West Point who later would attain a certain ghoulish notoriety in the Civil War as the originator of land mines—"subterra shells," he called them—was now styling himself "General" Rains, a dubious paper promotion courtesy of Acting Governor Charles H. Mason of Washington. (Stevens was off powwowing with other luckless Indians east of the Rockies.) This "hocus-pocus" did not sit well with Sheridan or other army regulars, nor did they appreciate having to camp alongside six hodgepodge companies of Washington and Oregon volunteers. On Halloween, appropriately enough, the expedition marched north from Fort Dalles, intent on recovering the honor—if not the howitzer—lost a few weeks earlier when Major Granville Haller's two companies of regular troops ran afoul of five hundred Indians led by the ubiquitous Kamiakin. Haller's subsequent ignominious defeat, further emboldening the Indians, made Rains's task even more difficult. [44]

With customary enthusiasm, Sheridan was riding point with his dragoons when, on the second day out from the fort, they ran into a small band of hostiles. The Indians got away, but not before Sheridan, ever the store clerk, had relieved them of their pitiful cache of winter food: dried salmon, huckleberries, and camas roots. The next day, chasing another group of laggards, Sheridan's small party suddenly found itself cut off from the main body of troops by an unknown force concealed in a column of acrid alkali dust. Determined to cut their way through the attackers, the dragoons charged, only to discover they were counterattacking a regiment of Oregon volunteers who had, in turn, mistaken them for Indians. It was that kind of campaign.[45]

After another comic interlude that found the frustrated soldiers chasing the Yakimas up and down a range of hills in a day-long game of "king of the mountain," the expedition reached the Catholic mission of Father J. Charles Pandosy. Here they were rejoined by their guide, an unsightly, unsavory Indian called Cut-mouth John, so dubbed because part of his mouth had been shot away during a previous encounter with Indians. John had taken it upon himself to run down and kill an aged Yakima whose escape had been hampered by the lameness of his horse. In a surly mood from their insolent handling, the soldiers bedded down for the night. The next morning they were awakened by an impromptu one-man parade featuring Cut-mouth John decked out in priest's vestments he had stolen from the mission, dangling his hapless victim's scalp from his bridle and singing a somewhat inappropriate victory song. His "revolting personal appearance" and less than stirring triumph (not only was the slain Yakima an old man, but his ancient flintlock pistol could not even be fired) made John's performance less than a critical or popular success; he was quickly yanked off his horse and told to behave.[46]

The soldiers next turned their dour attention to Father Pandosy's deserted mission. The priest was not entertaining visitors just then, having already been carried off by the Indians, but the soldiers made short work of his pigs, his garden-grown potatoes, and his cabbages. In the course of their spadework they also turned up a buried keg of gunpowder, which, by a tortuous inversion of logic, they convinced themselves the good father had left for the Indians' use. Revengeful, they burned the mission to the ground.[47]

By now Rains had seen enough. With a sudden snowstorm raging through the mountain passes and threatening to maroon them in waist-high drifts, the dispirited expedition trudged back to Fort Dalles, the scalp of one old Indian and the ill-gotten booty from Father Pandosy's burned-out mission all it had to show for three weeks in the field. "Almost everyone connected with the expedition voted it a wretched failure," wrote Sheridan. Rains, professing himself somewhat disappointed, preferred charges against Captain Edward O. C. Ord of the Third Artillery, hilariously claiming that the captain had stolen Father Pandosy's shoes. Ord responded by charging Rains—not illogically—with incompetence. The long-suffering General Wool ignored both charges, pointing out that he had too few officers to staff one court-martial, much less two.[48]

Sheridan and his dragoons wintered at Fort Vancouver, on the Columbia River, while Wool waited for spring to resume the offensive and carried on, in the meantime, an acrimonious war of words with the territorial governors of Oregon and Washington. These "would-be military chieftains," Wool complained to commanding general Winfield Scott, had started the Indian trouble to "promote their own ambitious schemes," and appeared to be running a race "to see who can dip deepest into the treasury of the United States." If they would only cease their depredations, Wool continued, peace would be quickly forthcoming. In the meantime, Oregon volunteers under Lieutenant Colonel James F. Kelly made matters worse by seizing the extravagantly named Walla Walla chieftain Pio Pio Mox Mox under a flag of truce, then shooting him down when he tried to escape. The fact that he was a long-time friend of the white man and had assisted Colonel John C. Frémont in the opening of California did not appear to argue persuasively in his favor. His ears and scalp were carried back to the settlements in triumph.[49]

Such acts persuaded other northwestern Indians to help the Yakimas wage war on the rapidly proliferating "Bostons." (English members of the neighboring Hudson's Bay Company were called "King Georges.") Wool's nightmare of a unified Indian offensive became a reality. On both sides of the Cascade Mountains, bands of Yakima, Walla Walla, Spokane, Umatilla, Klikitat, Nez Percé, and Chinook warriors attacked farms, villages, and blockhouses along the Columbia River. On March 26, 1856, one hundred Yakimas and their allies attacked settlements at the Cascades, a six-mile stretch of rapids and portages linking eastern and western Oregon, seized the Lower Cascade landing, and laid siege to the Middle and Upper Cascades. Coincidentally, Colonel George Wright, at the head of the newly arrived Ninth Infantry Regiment, had marched east from Fort Dalles that same day with 250 regulars to come to grips with the Indians. Survivors of the surprise attack took refuge in a military blockhouse guarding the Middle Cascade. Others straggled into Fort Vancouver, thirty-six miles away.[50]

Sheridan mounted forty dragoons and set out at once to relieve the Middle Cascade, while the main force hastily back-tracked from Fort Dalles. Placing his men on the steamboat *Belle*, he augmented his firepower with a ceremonial brass cannon from a San Francisco steamer then conveniently in port. Early the next morning he reached the Lower Cascade, sending the steamboat back to Vancouver for reinforcements. With a handful of volunteers, Sheridan set off to scout the landing. Suddenly the main force of Indians, concealed in deep grass between the river and the blockhouse, opened fire, and Sheridan's first independent combat command very nearly became his last. A bullet grazed the bridge of his nose and caught one of his men, an orderly named McGrew, squarely in the neck, breaking his spinal cord and killing him instantly. The show cannon was brought to bear on the under-brush where the Indians were hiding, "with the effect," Sheridan remarked drolly, "of considerably moderating their impetuos-ity." Neither side wanting to risk a frontal attack, the rest of the day was spent in long-range sniping.[51]

Remembering Mahan's preachments on being prepared, Sheridan kept back a twenty-man Hudson's Bay bateau for pos-sible use. The next morning, after a few more cannon rounds, he and the others slipped down to the riverbank and crossed to the opposite shore, hoping to circle behind the Indians. Finding the channel too rough to float upstream, he decided to take the boat across to Bradfort's Island, in the middle of the river, and man-handle it to a point opposite the blockhouse. First, however, he looked to see what was distracting the enemy. Against all logic, the Indians seemed to have forgotten the soldiers; they were now enjoying a series of horse races. On the island, Sheridan stumbled on a group of old squaws left there for safekeeping. Thinking quickly, he compelled them to help tow the boat through the rapids. It was a near thing—had the Indians discovered the soldiers on the island, they could have cut them off from the mainland and destroyed the two groups separately. As it was, Sheridan's chancy maneuver worked. Linking up with the party in the blockhouse, he soon was joined by an advance column from Wright's relief force. After a few rounds from the soldiers' mountain howitzer, the Indians fled, Yakimas and Klikitats to the nearby mountains, the heretofore friendly Cascades back to their camp on the island.[52]

Abandoned by their erstwhile allies, the Cascade tribesmen professed their innocence. Sheridan thought otherwise. Having the warriors form a line, he personally examined each man's rifle to see if it had been fired recently, sticking his finger into the muzzles to check for fresh powder stains. Thirteen Indians failed this rather cursory test, and Sheridan turned them over to Wright for trial. Subsequently, nine were found guilty of participating in the "Cascade Massacre" and hanged for the murder of sixteen men, women, and children at the blockhouse. In the absence of a suitable gallows, the condemned were made to climb onto two empty barrels placed beneath a cottonwood tree while the noose was adjusted and the bottommost barrel kicked away. The hangings, Sheridan believed, "had a most salutary effect" on the other hostiles. A few weeks later the uprising ended.[53]

Not long after the battle of the Cascades, an old frontiersman named Meeks entered Sheridan's camp and inquired after a friend of his named Spencer, a Chinook chief who had served the army as an interpreter and scout. Spencer had sent his family ahead to Fort Vancouver for safety; they were now several days late in arriving. Sheridan immediately organized a search party. What he found, a few miles from his camp, sickened him. In a clearing about a mile from the main road Spencer's wife, two sons, three daughters, and an infant boy lay in a semicircle, strangled to death with the same long piece of rope—all except the baby, who had been strangled with a red silk handkerchief taken from his mother. Thirty years later Sheridan was still calling the murders "an unparalleled outrage which nothing can justify or extenuate." The fact that the killers were white, as subsequent investigation revealed, seems genuinely to have shocked him.[54]

The Spencer murders removed much of the luster from Sheridan's first campaign, but his exemplary conduct at the battle of the blockhouse made a favorable impression on his commanders. In a general order congratulating the army for putting down the rebellion, General-in-Chief Scott specifically cited Sheridan for "gallant conduct." It was the first formal notice anyone had taken of him.[55]

With Indian resistance winding down, Sheridan was sent west to Fort Yamhill, near the Pacific coast, to relieve Lieutenant William B. Hazen at the Grande Ronde reservation. It was a brief first meeting for the two prickly Ohioans who later would serve side by side in some of the heaviest fighting of the Civil War, and would keep up a private war of words for the rest of their lives. Hazen had begun construction of a permanent fort at the reservation, a project Sheridan completed successfully despite "parsimonious appropriations" by the government. Next he was sent south to Fort Hoskins with a portion of the 1,500 Coquille, Klamath, Modoc, Rogue River, and Chinook Indians already subjugated by the army. That summer a group of Coquilles quartered at Yaquina Bay, faced with starvation when their government food ration was late, grew increasingly restive. Alarmed, their civilian agent barricaded himself in a log hut; once again Sheridan led a relief column to the rescue. Thoughtfully, he had brought along a few head of cattle for the Indians, who descended on the slaughtered beef before it could be equally divided. The Indians were in a nasty mood, and Sheridan and the four troopers he had posted as guards were soon surrounded by dozens of knife-wielding braves. With some difficulty their principal chief, Tetootney John, succeeded in defusing the situation. In gratitude, Sheridan saw to it that John and his family were surreptitiously supplied with extra coffee and sugar rations.[56]

With the Indians still grumbling about their empty stomachs and, not without reason, blaming their agent for the breakdown in supplies, Sheridan determined to build a bigger blockhouse for the agent's protection. The only available level ground was already in use as a burial place for the resident Yaquina Bay Indians, a branch of the Flathead tribe who bound their heads with two long boards until, Sheridan claimed, "there probably was nothing in the form of a human being on the face of the earth that appeared so ugly." Aesthetics aside, the Yaquinas were understandably loath to disturb their ancestors' sleep for another white man's building. ("There is nothing more painful to an Indian than disturbing his dead," Sheridan the budding ethnologist observed.) As usual, however, they were given no choice. In partial recompense, the soldiers promised to push the rotting burial canoes out to sea to speed the dead to the happy hunting grounds. Here, at least, Sheridan saw an opportunity for amusement: the canoes were infested with gray wood rats, and much fun was anticipated watching the rodents attempt to escape from the sinking craft. The next day came, but no rats were anywhere to be found. The Indians reasoned that the animals had heard them talking and, having no wish to trade this world for the next, had simply disappeared. Sheridan preferred to believe that all the unusual activity had disturbed them. In any event, they were gone.[57]

In the spring of 1857, Sheridan was back at Yaquina Bay to supervise the transfer of the Indians to a new reservation on the Siletz River. Understandably, his charges were less than thrilled about being uprooted again. Sheridan placated them by agreeing to let them keep a few old guns for hunting purposes. The chiefs, for their part, promised to "live in peace forever" at the new reservation. But Robert B. Metcalf, the agent at Siletz, had different ideas. He demanded that the Indians be disarmed, or else he and the other civilian employees would walk off their jobs. Sheridan refused. A promise was a promise, he said; the Indians had come to Siletz "with the best of intentions of not only remaining peaceable but of regarding this as their future home." Metcalf was adamant. Until the Indians surrendered their arms, he declared, he would withhold their food supplies and "kill as many as he could" when they finally were driven by hunger to attempt to take their rightful supplies by force. In a long war of words, Sheridan managed to avert bloodshed until a new contingent of soldiers arrived at the reservation and relieved Metcalf's fears. Up and down the chain of command, Sheridan's actions—this time in the interests of peace—won official approval. No less a personage than General Scott commended "the calm temper and views of Lieutenant Sheridan."[58]

A part of Sheridan's untypical sympathy for the Indians may have stemmed from his new living arrangements. Like other lonely young officers at distant posts, he had found himself a female companion. Her name was Sidnayoh—Frances to her white friends—the daughter of Chief Quately of the Willamette Valley Klikitats. She had begun living with Sheridan at Fort Hoskins the previous summer. There was nothing unusual about the arrangement, although Sheridan chastely refrained from mentioning it in his memoirs. (A short time after the Civil War, Frances visited him in Washington before returning to Oregon to marry a Canadian fur trapper. A few years later, Sheridan implored his friend, President-elect Grant, not to send him back to the Pacific coast, "for many reasons some of which are personal.") She was with him now when he returned to Fort Yamhill for the thankless task of overseeing the chronically obstreperous Rogue River Indians. The Rogues had fought and lost their own war with the army at the same time their Yakima neighbors were losing theirs. The Rogues, however, were given to boasting that they had merely been overwhelmed by superior numbers; they could still "whip the soldiers" and "did not wish to follow the white man's ways." For the next four years, Sheridan would have his hands full dealing with them.[59]

To begin with, the Rogues observed a number of "absurdly superstitious" religious practices which, for the life of him, Sheridan could neither understand nor eradicate. When mourning their dead, of which there was no lack, owing both to the white man's diseases and their own ineffable "melancholy," the affected relatives would destroy all their household belongings, kill their horses, and chop off their hair, covering their heads with a thick hood of clay, charcoal, and resin which they allowed to stay in place until it fell off naturally. Even more barbaric, to Sheridan's mind, was their somewhat conditional belief in the efficacy of their own witch doctors. These "doctors" ministered to the ill with a bevy of mystical incantations designed to prove, somewhat contradictorily, that their own powers had both caused the illness and alone could cure it. If successful, the doctors claimed a standing fee of all the victim's horses. If unsuccessful, the deceased's family had the right to kill the attending physician. In practice, few of the doctors willingly remitted their fees, depending instead on the speed with which they could flee to the safety of the fort. One particularly adept practitioner, improbably named Sam Patch, frequently found refuge in Sheridan's cellar; he "seemed to know intuitively when the time had come to take leg-bail."[60]

Sheridan attempted to dissuade the Indians from the practice by challenging the shamans to make him sick or kill him. The magic would not work on white men, he was told. One female doctor, slower on the uptake than Patch, lost a particularly prominent patient, then lost the ensuing race to the fort, as well. Sixteen of the victim's relatives caught up with her on the parade ground and shot her, with a precise sense of Indian justice, sixteen times. Sheridan set out at once to punish the offenders. Accompanied by a single trooper, he rode into the Rogue village and demanded that the murderers be surrendered to him. The conversation grew heated; at the climax, Sheridan reached for his pistol—only to find it had been stolen from his holster. Modifying his tone to a more diplomatic level, he made a somewhat sheepish withdrawal from the camp. To his parting riposte that the murderers and his six-shooter be handed over immediately, the Rogues responded with "contemptuous laughter."[61]

Determined to regain both his pistol and his soldierly self-respect, Sheridan planned to march on the camp at dawn with fifty men. That night, however, he was warned by a friendly Indian that the tribe intended to waylay him along the road into camp. Repeating his tactics from the blockhouse fight, Sheridan ferried his men to the rear of the camp by boat and fell on the Indians from behind. Capturing the tribe's principal chief in the very act of putting on his warpaint, Sheridan repeated his demand for the doctor's murderers. After a parlay with the chief's brother, it was decided that fifteen of the culprits would be handed over, while the army "could kill the sixteenth man, since the tribe wished to get rid of him anyhow." At a prearranged signal the fifteen leaped to one side and the sixteenth, suddenly exposed, was brought down by rifle fire. While the encounter was taking place, other tribes on the reservation were watching from surrounding hills. Sheridan had his prisoners lay their weapons, "including my six-shooter," at his feet, then placed them all in ball-and-chain and worked them at hard labor "until their rebellious spirit was broken." The incident effectively ended the Rogues' troublemaking; they had permanently lost face with the other Indians. Soon Sheridan had the entire reservation farming, attending church, and sending their children to the white man's school. Great strides had been made, he said, in civilizing "these crude and superstitious people."[62]

By the spring of 1861, Sheridan had been a shavetail second lieutenant for nearly eight years. He had "seen the elephant," as the phrase then had it, from the Rio Grande to the Pacific Northwest, commanded small numbers of men in battle, gotten himself wounded and a few of his subordinates killed for his trouble, taken some Indian losses in return, and learned by good and bad example how an officer of the army ought to conduct himself. In the process he had impressed his superiors with his industry, ingenuity, and, on at least one occasion, his diplomacy. He was thirty years old, in the prime of health, and could properly expect to be promoted in due time, which, for a young officer like himself with no social or political connections, still meant years at his present rank. But two thousand miles away, on the opposite side of the continent, a great storm was gathering, and Second Lieutenant Phil Sheridan, U.S.A., like millions of his fellow countrymen, would wake one quiet April morning to find that the world, and his own unheard unremarkable life, had changed forever while he slept.

2

"WORTH HIS WEIGHT IN GOLD"

THE ATTACK ON FORT SUMTER, like all great catastrophes, was stunning and dismaying, but not entirely unexpected. In the tumultuous five months since Abraham Lincoln had been elected president of the United States with an uneasy minority of his country's votes, seven Deep South states had seceded from the Union; four of their neighbors would follow in the wake of the shelling at Charleston harbor and Lincoln's subsequent—some said provocative—call to arms. Dozens of southern army officers were resigning their commissions to follow their home states into rebellion, among them Phil Sheridan's old West Point superintendent, Robert E. Lee; his fellow classmate, John Bell Hood; and virtually all the southern-born officers in Jefferson Davis's elite First and Second Cavalry regiments. Among the regiments' highest-ranking officers, only George H. Thomas, who had married a New Yorker, remained true to his oath of allegiance—or else turned his back on his country, depending on who was telling the story.

For Sheridan and other young officers who had languished for years at the same frozen rank, the blizzard of resignations was a professional godsend. After having gone nearly eight years without a promotion, he was abruptly raised to first lieutenant in March 1861, and given his captain's bars two months later. If the current state of affairs would only last long enough, he told a friend, "perhaps I may . . . earn a major's commission."[1]

The war would certainly last long enough, though neither Sheridan nor any of his quarrelsome countrymen could have known it at the time. Soldiers stationed on the West Coast had all they could do to decipher the badly garbled, ridiculously exaggerated news from the front. First reports after the Battle of Bull Run, for instance, had Union casualties alone exceeding forty thousand. Unlike so many of the southern-born officers, however, Sheridan personally was untroubled by the larger issues of the struggle. A northerner, a midwesterner, and politically (if he was anything) a Whig, he never questioned his deepest loyalties. "Isolated as I had been through years spent in the wilderness," he wrote, "my patriotism was untainted by politics, nor had it been disturbed by any question out of which the war grew, and I hoped for the success of the Government above all other considerations." West Point had freed him from the dry-goods store and its dusty, penurious ledger books. At the age of thirty, he knew no other profession.[2]

The outbreak of the war and the military needs of the government back east occasioned numerous departures from western posts. Among the first to leave was Sheridan's commanding officer at Fort Yamhill, Captain David A. Russell, under whom he had served as company quartermaster for the past four years. Russell, a native New Yorker and fellow academy graduate, was ten years older than Sheridan and a veteran of the Mexican War. The two shared something of a mutual admiration society, with Russell praising the younger man's "energy, zeal and uniform good judgment," and Sheridan honoring his captain's "true manliness, honest and just methods [and] warm-hearted interest he took in all that pertained to matters of duty." They would meet again, three years later, in northern Virginia—but then it would be Russell serving under Sheridan.[3]

Russell's departure left Sheridan temporarily in command at Fort Yamhill, pending the arrival of Captain James J. Archer, a sad-faced, dark-haired Marylander who Sheridan had heard was planning to "go south." In a scene destined to be repeated many times that spring, Sheridan the northerner refused to relinquish command to Archer the southerner, "for fear he might commit some rebellious act." A tense few days ensued before word arrived that Archer had tendered his resignation from the army and had been granted a final leave of absence to send him on his way. Archer did indeed go south, taking command of a Texas regiment under Sheridan's classmate Hood, and served with distinction in the Army of Northern Virginia's early campaigns. On the first day at Gettysburg, in July 1863, he and most of his brigade were captured while spearheading the initial Confederate attack. A year in prison at Johnson's Island, Ohio, shattered his already feeble health, and Archer died a few weeks after being exchanged in early 1864.[4]

Fort Yamhill received mail only once a week. On that blessed day, Sheridan would climb a nearby hillside and maintain an anxious vigil on the road to the post. The war had been under way for nearly five months now and Sheridan, like other vigorous, ambitious, and combative young officers, feared that it would end before he had a chance to make his mark. At last, in September 1861, orders came calling him east to Jefferson Barracks, Missouri, where he was to join the newly created 13th Infantry Regiment, commanded on paper by his old Ohio neighbor, Brigadier General William Tecumseh Sherman, now off fighting Rebels in western Kentucky. After a roundabout journey from Portland to San Francisco, across the Isthmus of Panama and then north to New York, Sheridan made his way to Somerset—his first homecoming in over eight years. The family was no longer living in Happy Alley; after John Sheridan's bankruptcy they had removed to a small farm a few miles out of town. With Bull Run still fresh in everyone's mind, old friends and neighbors wanted Sheridan's professional assessment of the war's likely outcome. "This country is too great and good to be destroyed," he declared firmly. As for his own role in the drama, he had no clue, "but if you ever hear from me, I want you to hear that I am doing my duty to the best of my ability."[5]

En route to his new post, Sheridan paid a courtesy call on Major General Henry W. Halleck in St. Louis. Although merely a routine visit, something about Sheridan must have impressed the owlish Halleck. A few days later he summoned Sheridan back to St. Louis. "Old Brains," as Halleck was somewhat derisively called, had a problem he wanted Sheridan to help him with. That problem was money—or more precisely, what had happened to some $12 million in government funds mislaid during the madcap hundred-day reign of his immediate predecessor, flamboyant, charismatic Major General John Charles Frémont, the famed "pathfinder" of western exploration.

Frémont had been relieved of command in November for myriad administrative and military sins, not least of which had been his embarrassing and potentially catastrophic arrogation of presidential authority in issuing a self-anointed emancipation proclamation the previous August. Besides placing the entire state of Missouri under martial law, Frémont's unauthorized proclamation summarily freed any slaves held within the state. Reaction was predictable: northern abolitionists, whose banner Frémont had already carried to defeat in the presidential election of 1856, were delighted; men living in border states, even those still tenuously bound to the Union like Missouri, were mortified. Lincoln himself, although professing "in general no objection" to the document, nevertheless insisted that it be modified to conform to an earlier Act of Congress freeing only those slaves forcibly required to bear arms against the Union.[6]

Frémont's high-handed proclamation, coupled with his Ruritanian military airs and conversely inept handling of troops in battle, led Lincoln to sack him in favor of Halleck. By then, three separate investigative commissions—one civilian, one congressional, and one presidential—had begun looking into the extraordinary purchasing practices of Frémont's erstwhile chief quartermaster, Brigadier General Justus McKinstry. For months Washington had been hearing complaints about the blatant way in which government contracts were being awarded in St. Louis.

Illinois Congressman Elihu B. Washburne, one of Lincoln's closest associates and the chairman of the congressional subcommittee
investigating the matter, flatly declared that "a gang of California
robbers and scoundrels rule, control and direct everything."[7]

At the center of the scandal was McKinstry, a West Point
graduate, Mexican War hero, career soldier, and, from January
1860 to November 1861, chief supply officer at the St. Louis–
based headquarters of the sprawling Department of the West.
McKinstry was a textbook example of the corrupting influence of
money. In his position as head purchasing agent for the department, he had used his contacts in the local business world to buy
cheaply and sell dearly the mountains of food, clothing, and animals needed to adequately supply a growing army. It was common practice for unscrupulous purchasing agents to buy horses at
forced low prices, then turn around and sell them to the army for
twice as much. Coats, blankets, and shoes were so poorly made by
a McKinstry-favored company that they quickly became known
by the inferior type of wool used in their uniforms, shoddy, which
in turn came to represent any inferior equipment. Those who
questioned the practice or balked at extortion, bribes, and kick-
backs, were threatened, cajoled, and in some cases summarily
arrested and thrown into jail. Frémont, dreamy and incorruptible
himself, was preoccupied with his own troubles; McKinstry was
given free rein in all purchasing matters.[8]

Now Frémont was gone and McKinstry occupied a cell at
Jefferson Barracks, while Halleck and his staff attempted to restore order to what was called "a system of reckless expenditure
and fraud, perhaps unheard of before in the history of the world."
This was where Sheridan came in: as an experienced quartermaster and commissary, he was wanted by Halleck to preside over a
comprehensive audit of the department's accounts. It was a
lengthy, laborious assignment, but Sheridan attacked it with his
usual energy. He had, after all, kept the books at Finck & Dittoe's
while still a teenager, and even though he faced a mountain of
requisitions, vouchers, bills, and receipts, he found the duty "not

distasteful." His careful performance, in conjunction with the special three-man Commission on the Debts of the Western Department appointed by Lincoln and the congressional subcommittee already investigating the "stupendous frauds" rampant in the quartermaster corps, eventually led to the court-martial of McKinstry and his subsequent dismissal from the army "for neglect and violation of duty, to the prejudice of good order and military discipline"—the only Civil War commander to be so cashiered. More important, from the standpoint of Sheridan's future career, his uncomplaining attention to duty won him his first highly placed ally in Halleck. It would not be long before he would need such a friend.[9]

On the day after Christmas, 1861, Sheridan completed his auditing work and was assigned to serve as chief commissary for the fifteen-thousand-man Army of Southwest Missouri, then organizing at Rolla for a drive against Major General Sterling Price's homegrown Confederate troops. At once Sheridan went to Halleck and asked to be named chief quartermaster as well, arguing that as quartermaster he could "obviate all possible chances of discord between the two staff departments" by personally controlling the means of transporting supplies to the front. Halleck, though worrying that Sheridan was taking on too much, at length relented, and his new-found assistant set out for Rolla to assume his duties.[10]

Commanding the Army of the Southwest was Brigadier General Samuel R. Curtis, a West Point graduate, Mexican War veteran, and three-term congressman from Keokuk, Iowa. Prior to his entrance into politics, Curtis had managed the not-inconsiderable task of successfully balancing dissimilar careers as a practicing lawyer and civil engineer. Now, at age fifty-six, he had the stern-visaged look of a man accustomed to having his every pronouncement, however trivial, regarded as gospel by a worshipful flock. His thrusting appearance was made even more formidable by salt-and-pepper muttonchops squared off below his chin and thick, bushy eyebrows that gave his face, beneath balding pate and domed forehead, a peculiarly framed-in effect. Having actively colluded in Frémont's downfall, Curtis was well aware of the pressure from Washington for an unambiguous military victory. St. Louis and other Missouri cities remained under Union dominance, but Price's army had decisively bested a smaller northern force at Wilson's Creek in August, killing the Union's first certified war hero, Brigadier General Nathaniel Lyon, in the process. Increasingly emboldened Confederate guerrillas operated freely in the interior of the state. Curtis intended to follow Price to the death, but his task was complicated by the need to carry supplies across hostile, poorly roaded countryside that he described, with some justification, as a wilderness.

Sheridan, in his voluntary dual role, did what he could to alleviate Curtis's daunting supply problems. First he set out to reorganize the various regimental wagon trains. Some regiments had as many as fifty wagons, others fewer than four. Laboring day and night, Sheridan and his assistant, Captain Michael P. Small, effected a more equitable distribution of wagons—at the cost of much ill will from irate regimental commanders who typically complained that the new chief quartermaster was bypassing their authority and giving orders directly to their teamsters. The commanding general upheld Sheridan's organizational moves, but less-exalted officers painted the new quartermaster as a bullet-headed regular army detail-stickler with no sympathy or feel for volunteer soldiers. Brigadier General Franz Sigel, for one, flatly refused to cooperate with Sheridan, consistently withholding his men from work details and bombarding headquarters with outraged complaints.

Once again, as he had done in the past and would continue to do throughout his career, Sheridan found a much-needed ally at exactly the right moment. Colonel Grenville M. Dodge of the Fourth Iowa Infantry, post commander at Rolla, saw the necessity for Sheridan's actions and made sure that other regimental commanders complied with his requests. It was the beginning of a lifelong friendship between the two like-minded men. Each was quick, nervous, intense, active, and result-oriented; each was direct and practical; and neither was particularly squeamish about the rights of civilians in wartime, especially those in Rebel-leaning southwestern Missouri. To keep the army fed and moving, Sheridan confiscated all available livestock and corn from the few hardscrabble farms in the region and put blue-clad soldiers to work running flour mills seized along the line of march. As Dodge remembered in his postwar book, *The Battle of Atlanta and Other Campaigns*: "The punishment that he gave to some of the people to make them tell where their horses, forage and sweet potatoes were hidden would astonish those of our people who have been so horrified at the mild persuasions used for similar purposes in the Philippines." Sheridan, after all, had trained in a very hard school in the Pacific Northwest; now he was beginning his postgraduate study.[11]

The expedition continued ponderously south, its progress hampered by late-winter rains that swelled creek crossings and turned already bad roads into impassable quagmires. A few miles outside of Springfield, where Price's army was thought to be holed up, Curtis deployed his troops in line of battle, telling Sheridan to arrange his wagons behind the men as a last-ditch defensive position in case they had to fall back. Sheridan, said Dodge, considered the order "a very singular one" and shuddered to imagine his civilian wagon-drivers flying off at the first false report of trouble. Luckily, the teamsters' warrior resolve was not tested; Price's troops had quietly abandoned Springfield the preceding day. Curtis's failure to close the noose around Price's neck troubled Sheridan, as did his strange obsession with salt supplies. Curtis, he said, "made a hobby of this matter of salt. He impressed me deeply with his conviction that our cause would be seriously injured by a loss which would inure so greatly and peculiarly to the enemy's benefit." About all the Confederates had left behind in Springfield, Sheridan deadpanned, was salt.[12]

Despite his increasing reservations about Curtis's fitness to command, Sheridan continued to labor manfully to keep the army supplied with food. With a corps of millwrights, machinists, and millers recruited from the Fourth Iowa and 36th Illinois regiments, he kept the mills around Springfield running overtime to provide flour and meal for the troops. A visiting correspondent for the *New York Herald* found Sheridan "a modest and agreeable gentleman, whose private excellence was only equaled by his energy in the performance of his official duties." The army had no supply worries, the journalist felt, so long as Sheridan remained on the job.[13]

Thus provisioned, Curtis continued his dogged pursuit of Price, which culminated in the Battle of Pea Ridge, Arkansas, on March 7–8, 1862. Price had withdrawn into the Boston Mountains, just across the Missouri border, to link up with Brigadier General Ben McCulloch's Texas, Arkansas, and Louisiana troops. McCulloch, a crusty Tennessean who had followed his storied neighbor Davy Crockett to Texas and had later become a leader of the Texas Rangers, had materially assisted in winning the Battle of Wilson's Creek by personally leading two Louisiana infantry companies in routing Sigel's forces, capturing five Yankee guns for good measure. A seasoned frontier fighter, he had little use for formal military tactics and normally disdained a regular uniform for a black velvet suit in the field. This time, however, he was decked out in powder blue pants and dove gray jacket.

All in all, it was a decidedly colorful Rebel force that now arrayed itself against Curtis's army. Besides Price's Missouri home guard and McCulloch's rangy southwesterners, there were several thousand Creek and Cherokee Indians, organized into more or less formal regiments by three-hundred-pound Brigadier General Albert Pike. Pike, a Mexican War hero, ex-newspaperman, internationally known poet, and practicing lawyer, had recently endeared himself to the Creeks by winning a large lawsuit for them against the same government they were now planning to fight. At the head of the Cherokee Mounted Rifles was Colonel Stand Watie, a three-quarters Cherokee who had narrowly escaped assassination some years earlier for his role in signing the treaty that yielded the tribe's Georgia homeland to the whites. Now, with the tribe divided in its loyalties—or at any rate unde-cided about which tribe of white men it wished most to lose—Watie was the leader of the pro-South faction; he intended to demonstrate the quality of his support on the battlefield.[14]

Confederate Major General Earl Van Dorn, fourteen months away from meeting his fate at the hands of a jealous Tennessee husband, had arrived to take charge of all Rebel forces in the vicinity. Ill with fever and unfamiliar with the countryside, he nevertheless devised a plan to envelop the smaller Union army by sending Price's Missourians north on a risky night march around the enemy rear, while the rest of his ragtag army wheeled west to support the expected dawn attack. It might have worked, had Curtis not been alerted to it at the eleventh hour by his irregular band of scouts, chief among them a young, long-haired frontiers-man with flat gray-blue eyes and a killer's languid gaze named James Butler Hickok. "Wild Bill" (or "Duck Bill," as he was then more commonly if surreptitiously known) had just returned from a week-long foray behind enemy lines. The Rebels, he told Curtis, were even now moving behind Pea Ridge to position themselves for an attack at Elkhorn Tavern, sentinel to the vital road leading back to Springfield.[15]

Curtis, to his credit, knew death when he saw it and abruptly about-faced to meet the enemy head-on. Price's infantry roared down the valley toward the tavern, having completed an all-night, fifty-five-mile march around the Union flank in driving snow. Three times they attacked Colonel Eugene A. Carr's division; twice they drove it back; the third time it held southwest of the tavern. Meanwhile Pike's native Americans overran German-born Colonel Peter J. Osterhaus's flabbergasted division, pouring from the woods, all feathers and tomahawks, chanting their death songs and screaming for scalps. (Thirty Federals subsequently were re-ported scalped in the battle, but it was never proven beyond a reasonable inference who, if anyone, had done the deed.) The Indians were so busy celebrating, however, that Pike had great difficulty getting them to act like disciplined soldiers instead of marauding bucks. While they were cavorting about in horse collars taken from slain artillery horses, their allies on the left were being roughly handled by Colonel Jefferson C. Davis's Union division. The formidable McCulloch, whose troops had vowed to follow him to hell if that was where he led them, had been toppled from his horse by a sharpshooter's bullet to the heart—not, as legend had it, Wild Bill Hickok's bullet, but one fired by the even more improbably named Peter Pelican of the 36th Illinois. With McCulloch gone where no man could follow, his soldiers lost their battle fire and the Confederates' plan of all-out attack rapidly fell apart.[16]

After a short, restless night spent within shouting distance of each other, the two sides exchanged artillery fire at dawn. The Rebels, who had badly depleted their ammunition the day before, did little damage; but Union cannoneers unleashed a devastatingly accurate barrage, followed closely by an uncharacteristically spirited attack by General Sigel's two divisions. A similar charge on the Union right drove the Rebels from Elkhorn Tavern. The usually taciturn Curtis galloped along behind the lines, swinging his cloth hat over his head and shouting "Victory!" at the top of his lungs.[17]

Back at Springfield, Sheridan was in charge of the military telegraph when word arrived of the Union triumph. The first reports were hand-delivered by a special messenger sent by Sigel, who now exhibited rather more industry in advancing his own cause than he had in assisting Sheridan with his. Whether his personal dislike of Sigel colored his actions, or whether as a professional soldier he simply felt that a commanding general was entitled to announce his own victories, Sheridan held back Sigel's vainglorious account and waited instead for Curtis's official report, telegraphing him in the meantime that "the whole country is rejoicing at your victory." For all the gratitude it gained him from Curtis, he might just as well have sent Sigel's message first.[18]

Fresh from his triumph over the forces of rebellion, Curtis returned to headquarters intent on quashing a second, albeit smaller, uprising centered entirely upon his pugnacious young quartermaster. He and Sheridan had been at odds since shortly before the battle over the somewhat hazy ethics involved in acquiring fresh horses for the army. In the best tradition of Justus McKinstry, some of Sheridan's subordinates had been stealing horses from local farmers and selling them back to the army at a profit. Sheridan, in his position as quartermaster, controlled the army's purse strings, and immediately put a stop to their sport by declaring such horses captured property, branding "US" on their flanks, and refusing to pay the thieves a penny. "Misled by the representations that had been made, and without fully knowing the circumstances," Curtis ordered Sheridan, in essence, to shut up and pay the men. In a letter to Major Thomas J. McKinney, Curtis's adjutant, Sheridan pointedly refused, adding somewhat injudiciously that "I will not jayhawk or steal on any order, nor will I acknowledge the right of any person under my supervision in this district to do so." Quartermasters did not ordinarily use such language to their commanding generals, particularly one who had just preserved the entire state of Missouri for the Union. Curtis came back from the front in high feather, immediately had Sheridan placed under arrest, and drew up a lengthy and self-justifying bill of particulars, charging among other things that Sheridan had disobeyed a standing order to provide horses and supplies for the army, had remained behind "where he was not needed," and—this was the real bone in Curtis's craw—had been disrespectful.[19]

Although in later years he sought to downplay the incident as "the culmination of a little difference that had arisen between General Curtis and me," Sheridan at the time was mortified and furious. Ever afterward he believed that the trouble had been started by an assistant quartermaster from Iowa named Winslow, who had secretly coveted his position as chief. Prior to the war, Sheridan said, Winslow had been an unsuccessful banker back home, and "as chief quartermaster of the army in Missouri, there would be opportunities for the recuperation of his fortunes which would not offer to one in a subordinate place; so to gain this position he doubtless intrigued for it while under my eye." Curtis, who may also have gotten wind of Sheridan's less-than-admiring opinion of his generalship, wasted little time in naming Winslow to the post. In his memoirs Sheridan clearly relished recounting his successor's subsequent career: "The war over he turned up in Chicago as president of a bank, which he wrecked; and he finally landed in the penitentiary for stealing a large sum of money from the United States Treasury at Washington while employed there as a clerk." It was something of a point of pride with Sheridan never to forget a slight.[20]

Curtis went to some pains to explain to Halleck why his young protégé, who had so noticeably distinguished himself in the four months he had been in Missouri, had suddenly and culpably become a drag on the service. With tortured logic he blamed the jayhawking on Sheridan himself, noting to Halleck's assistant adjutant general that if quartermasters would only furnish adequate supplies, such extracurricular stealing could be controlled. Sheridan, he said, had left his troops the unpalatable choice of stealing or starving.[21]

Grenville Dodge and other concerned officers went to Curtis in Sheridan's behalf, a move that gained Sheridan nothing and won for his defenders the unsubtle warning that they, too, "might possibly go to the rear with the over nice Quartermaster who must be learned what *war was*." By now Sheridan had seen enough of Curtis to realize that his own usefulness to the victor of Pea Ridge was finished, regardless of the outcome of any future trial. He may also have realized that the war for Missouri likewise was finished, and that any subsequent service there would merely involve the same boring, if occasionally dangerous, sort of garrison duty he already had endured for eight years out west. Not only was his usefulness to Curtis concluded; Curtis was equally useless to him. Seasoned paper-shuffler that he was, Sheridan played his one trump card: he petitioned Halleck for a transfer. It was rather hastily granted, as much perhaps to preserve the semblance of departmental unity as to placate Sheridan, and he returned to St. Louis "somewhat forlorn and disheartened at the turn affairs had taken," but nonetheless relieved to be away from Curtis.[22]

Preoccupied just then with a major battle taking shape in nearby west Tennessee, Halleck had little time for his down-at-the-mouth former quartermaster. Still, more to get him away from Curtis's reach than for any pressing administrative need, he sent Sheridan—with no apparent awareness of the irony involved—on a horse-buying swing through Wisconsin and Illinois. The governors of those great states had been pressing the army to dispense a little government largesse their way, and in the course of a month Sheridan dutifully bought four hundred Wisconsin and Illinois horses—none of which, presumably, had been jayhawked from their Union-loving owners.[23]

He was still in Chicago, having made it the center of his horse-buying activities, when the first reports arrived of the terrible battle at Shiloh, Tennessee, on April 6–7, 1862. There, newly promoted Major General Ulysses S. Grant had been surprised and nearly overwhelmed by Confederate General Albert Sidney Johnston's 44,000-man army. Six weeks earlier Grant had wrecked the South's plan for an east-west defensive cordon along the Tennessee-Kentucky border by capturing Forts Donelson and Henry, becoming in the process (much to Halleck's chagrin) the North's newest military hero. But at Pittsburg Landing on the Tennessee River, twenty-two miles north of the Rebel railroad center at Corinth, Mississippi, Grant had been caught napping by Johnston's unexpected attack. The general in charge of Grant's lead division, William Sherman, likewise had been surprised by the Rebels' early-morning drive. "My God, we're attacked!" he had shouted as a skirmisher's bullet killed the even more surprised orderly standing next to him. Eventually, however, Sherman and Grant managed to rally their inexperienced troops long enough for Major General Don Carlos Buell's Army of the Ohio to reach the field with reinforcements.[24]

On the second day the battle degenerated into a bloody stalemate around Shiloh church, and Confederate General P. G. T. Beauregard (Johnston had carelessly bled to death from a minor leg wound on the first day of fighting) withdrew to Corinth to lick his wounds. Shiloh's astonishing casualty lists, nearly 24,000 killed or wounded, stunned both soldiers and civilians alike. In two days of fighting, more Americans had shot, stabbed, blasted, and clubbed each other to death than the British and Mexican armies combined had managed to slaughter in the nation's first three wars. The ever-phlegmatic Grant, who could count headstones as well as the next man, gave up the notion that the war could be won quickly. Complete conquest, he now saw, was the only way for the Union to save itself.[25]

Inflamed by reports from the battlefield, Sheridan hastened back to St. Louis, intent on asking Halleck for yet another favor. ''The desire for active service . . . uppermost in my thoughts,'' he rushed into army headquarters, only to discover he was five days too late. Halleck had steamboated downriver to Pittsburg Landing immediately after the battle to personally take command of the still-shaken Union forces. With fifteen divisions—more than 120,000 men—massed for a renewal of the springtime bloodletting, Halleck somewhat grandly intended to march on Corinth, crush the rebellion, and restore peace to the entire country before April was out. Marooned in St. Louis, Sheridan importuned Halleck's assistant adjutant general, Colonel John C. Kelton, to send him to the front, and Kelton, who had been at West Point with him for three years, consented. On April 15 he issued an order directing Sheridan to report in person to Halleck in Tennessee. That comradely bit of circumvention Sheridan would always consider the turning point in his military career, which is to say, his life.[26]

Wangling a ride on a hospital boat, Sheridan arrived at the front ready and eager to kill some Rebels. He had previously told his friend Dodge that "if I could get into line duty I believe I could do something." He had, after all, led troops into battle with hostile Indians, and been mentioned by the general-in-chief himself for gallantry. But Halleck, who had more on his mind than his perennially supplicating quartermaster, took one look at Sheridan and turned him over to Colonel George Thom, chief of topographical engineers. Curtis and his charges notwithstanding, Sheridan's record with the Army of the Southwest had typed him as an unusually energetic and efficient problem-solver. With a huge army preparing to advance against the Confederates, he would be more useful to the Union cause coordinating supplies than practicing heroics.[27]

Thom put him to work expediting supply trains from Pittsburg Landing, a dirty, thankless job that involved laying corduroy roads across swampy bottomland. As always Sheridan focused his entire energy on the task at hand, although he considered it "rough, hard work, without much chance of reward." This went on for two weeks, while Halleck developed his grand advance. Grant and Sherman had been disastrously surprised at Shiloh; Halleck did not intend to be similarly caught. Consequently, the spade and shovel became more important than the rifle or sword. Inching forward through the Mississippi delta, the exhausted Federals entrenched each night. It had taken the Confederates two days to march from Corinth to Shiloh; it would take the bluecoats nearly a month to reverse the feat. In the meantime, an increasingly downtrodden Grant, reduced to the ineffectual role of Halleck's second-in-command, despairingly considered resigning from the army. Only Lincoln's residual fondness for any general who would demand and receive the enemy's unconditional surrender, as Grant had done at Donelson, saved his services for the Union cause.[28]

Halleck had begun the advance by bravely telegraphing Washington: "I leave here tomorrow morning, and our army will be before Corinth tomorrow night." Soon, however, he was disabused of that notion. Heavy rains, clinging heat, and swampy

roads kept extending his travel time. Fantastic rumors of enormous Confederate reinforcements at Corinth—one prisoner told
the Yankees, presumably with a straight face, that there were
146,000 Rebels already there, with another 50,000 or so en route
even as he spoke—did nothing to induce the fussy Halleck to
hurry. Each night, after an average advance of less than a mile,
the men were put to work digging ditches. Then, an hour before
daylight, they were rousted out of their blankets to stand watch
against a repeat of the Rebels' apparitional attack at Shiloh. It
was physically and mentally sapping, and it literally sickened
many of the troops. In the Second Michigan Cavalry alone,
nearly two-thirds of the regiment's 1,200 members were unfitted for duty by camp fever. The weather itself seemed allied
against Halleck.[29]

Circumstances being what they were, Halleck was grateful
for any blessing, however small. One worry, at least, had been
taken from him: his own care and feeding. Someone had suggested he appoint Sheridan to look after his equipment and
transportation needs. Having grown heartily tired of supervising
road crews in the Mississippi heat, Sheridan himself was glad
for the change. Halleck, he found, "did not know much about
taking care of himself in the field." In short order he had the
general's camp running as efficiently as his supply trains had
run to the Army of the Southwest. "General Halleck was delighted with the improvements," he noted. But, as with Curtis
two months before, Sheridan allowed his punctilious construction of military procedure to get him embroiled in a fruitless
dispute. A hitch had developed over the supply of fresh beef for
Halleck's mess. Colonel Joseph McKibben transmitted to Sheridan a direct order from Halleck to find the beef and get it to his
table. Sheridan refused; he was not a caterer, he told the colonel. Besides, the responsibility for obtaining the general's food
was beyond his duties as quartermaster. McKibben attempted to
persuade him, for once, to bend the rules—he even brought in
Colonel Thom to aid negotiations—but Sheridan was adamant.

Rather than report him for insubordination, McKibben went and got the beef himself. The next day, without comment, Halleck formally added the title of commissary to Sheridan's official résumé, thus ensuring that he, Halleck, would not have to go hungry again.[30]

The army's stately procession continued, leaving Sheridan with ample time on his hands. Active and impatient by nature, he filled his days riding around the countryside with his tentmate, Major John H. Brinton, Halleck's staff physician. Together they amused themselves by watching Sherman's division, guarding a flank, skirmish with Rebels on the struggle south. Sheridan took this opportunity to renew his slight acquaintance with the rust-bearded general, whose wife and family he had known from childhood. The two Ohioans were much alike— more so, in fact, than Sherman and Grant, Grant being altogether quieter and less profane. Sherman had just been promoted to major general, and whether from wanting to share his good fortune, or as a personal favor to an old neighbor, he wrote to Governor David Tod of Ohio, recommending that Sheridan be given command of a state volunteer regiment. Tod respectfully declined Sherman's recommendation, feeling that regular army officers were too severe in their methods to command unseasoned volunteers, but Sheridan was grateful nonetheless for Sherman's good intentions.[31]

Tod was not traveling with the army in the field, but a number of other governors were. Indiana's formidable Oliver P. Morton was there, ostensibly to buoy the spirits of his Hoosier troops, but chiefly (so it seemed to Washington) to send gloomy predictions of impending doom. Also on hand was Michigan Governor Austin Blair, an activist chief executive who had personally raised funds to recruit and equip much-needed regiments for the Union cause and who, just now, was in the market for a new colonel for the Second Michigan Cavalry. The regiment's former colonel, Gordon Granger, had recently been promoted to brigadier general in the Army of the Mississippi. Unlike his Ohio counterpart, Blair actually wanted a regular army man to lead the regiment, and

Sheridan's name was brought to his attention as an energetic and talented young officer eager for field command.[32]

Sheridan also had the curious advantage, in this case, of not being from the governor's own state. Regional jealousies had divided the Second Michigan between urban and rural factions, and Blair wanted to avoid taking sides by choosing a colonel from out of state. Sheridan never knew who first proposed his appointment, although he was later told it was Granger. More likely, however, a young captain in the regiment, Russell A. Alger of Detroit, was his secret champion. Alger, who was destined for a long and ultimately disastrous political career as postwar governor of Michigan, favorite-son candidate for president, and secretary of war under William McKinley, was good friends with regimental quartermaster Frank Walbridge, who knew Sheridan well. The two officers took it upon themselves to ride all night from camp to Pittsburg Landing, where Blair was preparing to board a riverboat for home. After successfully presenting their case, they galloped back to camp—it killed Alger's horse—and with a flourish handed Sheridan a telegram on the morning of May 27, 1862: "Captain Philip H. Sheridan, U.S. Army, is hereby appointed Colonel of the Second Regiment Michigan Cavalry, to rank from this date. Captain Sheridan will immediately assume command of the regiment."[33]

Delighted with the news, Sheridan hurried to Halleck's tent, brandishing his appointment. If he expected the commanding general to share his joy, he was quickly disappointed. By now Halleck had grown used to Sheridan's frequent changes of scenery, but he had also become accustomed to his efficient quartermastering. He told Sheridan that any appointment would have to be approved by the War Department. Sheridan was savvy enough to know that Washington, as a consequence of intense hand-wringing by state governors after Shiloh, had come around to the view that regular officers were too strict for the tender feelings of volunteer troops.[34]

Returning downhearted to his tent, Sheridan told Alger and

Walbridge what Halleck had said. They urged him to go back. Halleck, who seems to have had a true soft spot for Sheridan, at length agreed to let him go without formal approval. He somewhat casually passed along the word that Sheridan's new regiment was preparing to leave that very night on a raid below Rebel lines at Corinth. Sheridan had just enough time to accept a hurried congratulatory toast at headquarters, turn over his quartermaster's property to his successor, and pin a pair of Granger's "well-worn" cavalry colonel's eagles to his infantryman's coat. Catching up with the regiment at Farmington, he tossed a hastily packed haversack onto his saddle, introduced himself to the officers in his command, and rode to war, exactly thirteen and a half months after the first predawn explosion had shattered the quiet at Charleston, South Carolina.[35]

The new brigade commander, replacing Granger, was Colonel Washington Lafayette Elliott of the Second Iowa. The son of a naval captain, Elliott had sailed to France with his father aboard the USS *Constitution*, visited the West Indies, attended West Point for three years without graduating, served with the Mounted Rifles in the Mexican War, and patrolled the Indian frontier prior to the Civil War. He was the sort of active, positive soldier Sheridan always favored, and together they set out on the first important cavalry raid of the war. After a month of hesitant groping, Halleck had finally come into contact with the Confederates' forward defense at Corinth. He wanted Elliott to swing wide of the enemy's right flank and cut the lines of the Mobile & Ohio Railroad at Booneville, a station twenty-two miles due south of Corinth. At midnight on May 27 the expedition set out, nine hundred troopers of the Second Michigan and Second Iowa regiments. The Michiganders, for their part, were getting their first look at the short, dark officer at their front, but in the hubbub surrounding the advance neither Sheridan nor his command had time to introduce themselves properly. The men were traveling light, carrying only sugar, coffee, and salt. For other staples they would have to depend on the countryside.[36]

At Iuka, southeast of Corinth, the brigade arced west toward Booneville. Sheridan's typical good luck with provisions held true to form. Credulous Mississippians, supposing the dust-covered Yankee horsemen to be some of their own, freely supplied them with livestock and produce. Still it was hard going. The weather, as far as the northerners were concerned, was purgatorial, the roads rough and ill-marked, and not even Elliott had a clear idea where they were headed. At 2:00 A.M. on May 30 Sheridan's regiment, in the lead, reached the outskirts of Booneville. Elliott brought up a line of skirmishers, and at first light they swept into the village, brushing aside a handful of surprised Confederates.[37]

Moving quickly, Elliott sent Sheridan south to destroy a railroad bridge supposedly located a short distance from the station. With half his regiment Sheridan followed the railroad for a mile or so without finding a bridge or culvert along the route. The nearest bridge was nine miles farther south, at Baldwin—as were three Rebel infantry regiments and an artillery battery. Under the circumstances, Sheridan opted to forget the bridge and concentrate instead on the railroad itself. Rails and ties were manhandled from their beds, turned upside down, and fired with torches from burning fences. The softened iron was then bent into unusable shapes. It was an early demonstration of the sort of Yankee ingenuity Sherman's troops would develop into an art form on their excursion through Georgia two years hence. As the destruction was being carried out, a squadron of Confederate cavalry made a dash for Sheridan's flank and rear. Captain Archibald P. Campbell, commanding the reserve, handsomely blunted the assault with a volley from his men's Colt repeating rifles. Meanwhile, to the north, Lieutenant Colonel Edward Hatch had discovered some two thousand convalescent Confederates, as well as a supply train bulging with artillery, small arms, and ammunition. Alarmed by the unmistakable signs of a general enemy withdrawal from Corinth, Elliott ordered Sheridan back to Booneville.[38]

The woods and fields around the station were filled with Rebel soldiers, ill with a variety of ailments, who were being evacuated from Corinth. Unsanitary conditions and contaminated water had combined to place some eighteen thousand southerners—over a third of Beauregard's total force—on regimental sick lists. Dysentery, measles, and typhoid fever raged in epidemic proportions through their camps. Sheridan and his troopers rode among the stricken enemy with the blithe disregard of the well, and here he heard the not entirely welcome news that Corinth was being evacuated. On the morning after Sheridan's departure Halleck had initiated a day-long bombardment of the town preparatory to an all-out attack. Such an attack, however, had not been necessary. Beauregard and his subordinates had no intention of risking a major battle so soon after Shiloh, with a third of the army too sick to hold a gun. Instead, under cover of darkness, they had simply melted away, shielding their retreat with dummy guns and straw-man artillerists, while empty trains steamed noisily into town bringing phantom reinforcements and a regimental band serenaded them with false hurrahs. By the time Halleck's advance guard entered Corinth, at dawn the same day, the entire Rebel army was moving south—in the precise direction of Elliott, Sheridan, and the Second Brigade.[39]

Back at Booneville, Elliott ordered Hatch to move the sick Confederates away from the railroad and set fire to the supply train. The exact degree of northern solicitude is a matter of some dispute. Colonel William R. Bradfute, commander of the Rebel cavalry at Booneville, later claimed that "6 corpses and 3 live soldiers, who were too sick to help themselves, were burned on the train and in the depot house." And Beauregard himself, in an open letter to the *Mobile Evening News*, accused Elliott of committing "an act of barbarism scarcely credible and without precedent . . . in civilized warfare." Sheridan, who was not at the scene when the train was burned, said merely that "the captured cars had been fired, and . . . their complete destruction was assured by explosions from those containing ammunition." The amount of damage done by the raiders was also in dispute. Elliott estimated damages at $250,000 to $500,000 in lost supplies and ammunition, while Beauregard put it at about one-tenth that much. Most of the Confederate supply trains had already passed through Booneville prior to Elliott's surprise arrival, and the Federals did not have time to round up or parole their bedraggled prisoners, whom Sheridan scrupulously conceded could fairly reenter active service as soon as their comrades caught up with them.[40]

Still, from the Union standpoint the raid had been an important success, if for no other reason than that a correspondent from the widely read *Cincinnati Commercial* had been on hand to publicize it as "a feather in the cap of every man in the army that rides a horse." Sheridan's old Missouri comrade Grenville Dodge later characterized the episode as little more than "a picket affair," but Halleck himself deemed it "splendid," and promised that Elliott would be duly rewarded. In less than four days the brigade had traveled nearly two hundred miles behind enemy lines, destroyed a trainload of supplies and a valuable stretch of railroad, and returned to camp in Farmington virtually intact, the only losses being nine members of the Second Iowa who had been ambushed by Rebels while unaccountably riding a handcar north of Booneville. The lost troopers not belonging to his regiment anyway, Sheridan termed their loss "insignificant," which, in a military sense at least, it was.[41]

Whatever the brightness of its accomplishment, the brigade had little time to rest on its laurels. The Rebels were in full retreat toward Tupelo, fifty miles south of Corinth, and the Union army was following after, a little like a yard dog following a hobo: snapping at his heels, baring its teeth, then yipping backward whenever the vagrant wheeled around. General John Pope was of the opinion that a portion of Beauregard's rear guard could be captured by a quick, concerted movement. Accordingly, after one short day of rest, the brigade was back in the saddle on June 2, moving south through Corinth along the track of the railroad. Two days later the horsemen passed through Booneville, where the still-smoldering embers from the burned supply train were viewed "with much satisfaction" by Sheridan and the others.[42]

Taking his regiment southwest toward Blackland, Sheridan encountered Rebel pickets near a small stream called Wolf's Creek. Hoping to gobble up the main body of pickets, he sent the regiment's saber battalion, together with the revolving rifle contingent, flashing across the shallow stream. On the other side, however, the Federals suddenly found themselves confronted by a sizable body of artillery and infantry. Not liking the odds, Sheridan gave the order for a hasty retreat. Fortunately for him, the Confederates had been so surprised to see a relative handful of Union riders tearing through their camp that they had allowed them to escape without a fight. The move had the mixed results of confirming Pope's suspicions regarding the Rebels' rear position, while at the same time accelerating the speed of their retreat.[43]

Two days later Sheridan was sniffing farther south, this time toward Baldwin, fifteen miles above Tupelo, when he ran into a regiment of gray-clad cavalry and a company of Georgia Mounted Dragoons led by Captain Isaac W. Avery. This time he had the numbers on his side, and vigorously attacked with his five companies, driving the Rebels for two miles. Avery, en route to find help for his wounded orderly, took a wrong turn and found himself in the midst of Sheridan's entire regiment. He had the immediate and wholly understandable urge to remove himself from their company, but was dissuaded from doing so by a Union officer who advised him to surrender instead of being shot to pieces. Sensibly selecting the first option, Avery was taken to Sheridan, who gave him parole with the offhand observation that some southern officers considered being paroled an insult. Avery, who given the alternative had no qualms about the process, had about decided he liked the short, long-armed Union colonel when Sheridan abruptly demanded to know how much infantry the Rebels had in the vicinity. Avery refused to say, which led to a brief argument between the two, an argument Sheridan quickly terminated with a rueful smile and the not entirely accurate justification that he had the perfect right, as Avery's captor, to demand such information. The ride back to Booneville was uneventful, Sheridan's bluff having been effectively called, and Avery found him "a most intelligent and courteous gentleman, a social man of the world and a most charming companion." Avery apparently made less of an impression on Sheridan, who did not mention him in his memoirs.[44]

After a second reconnaissance to Baldwin on June 9–10 to determine whether the Confederates had abandoned the town (they had), Sheridan was ordered back to Corinth, where Halleck and the entire army had hunkered down, Micawber-like, to see what would turn up next. For Elliott, Sheridan, and Hatch, what turned up was promotions, Elliott to brigadier general, Sheridan to brigade commander, and Hatch to full colonel. Less than six weeks after joining the brigade, Sheridan now was leading it, Elliott having been appointed Pope's chief of staff. This was all to the good from Sheridan's point of view, but he shared with others a disgruntled wonderment at the way Halleck had allowed the enemy to withdraw unmolested, except for whatever desultory damage Sheridan and the cavalry had managed to inflict on the sick, the lame, and the laggard. Somewhat immodestly, Halleck called his walkover at Corinth "a victory as brilliant and important as any recorded in history." Newspaper correspondents, as is their wont, were considerably less impressed. "One of the most barren triumphs of the war," said the *Chicago Tribune.* "Beauregard [has] achieved another triumph," seconded the *Cincinnati Commercial.* For his part, Sheridan could not understand why an energetic pursuit had not been ordered after Corinth. Occasional flare-ups between the Confederate rear guard and his own brigade might serve to get a few men killed, wounded, or captured, but apart from adding a few more northern and southern families to the undifferentiated ranks of the bereaved, they accomplished nothing—with the personal exception, modestly unmentioned, of gaining oneself a quick promotion.[45]

The rest of the month was uneventful; Halleck was more concerned with not provoking a Confederate counterattack than with maintaining pressure on the enemy. All he wanted, he said, was for the Rebels to stay away from the railroad, and "there is no object in bringing on a battle if this object can be obtained without one." Meanwhile his own army languished in camp, pestered by fleas, chiggers, ticks, and lice, amusing themselves as best they could with homemade recipes for a kind of giant-sized cobbler composed of several pounds of hardtack, great gouts of sugar, and the region's one saving grace—fresh blackberries. "The gods never ate a better dish," one Indiana soldier fondly remembered.[46]

Sheridan, as usual, continued his habit of personally seeing to his men's supplies. "Men who march, scout, and fight, and suffer all the hardships that fall to the lot of soldiers in the field must have the best bodily sustenance, and every comfort that can be provided," he believed. This he took pains to provide, much as he had hunted game for his messmates in Texas and constructed his own cabin as a stay against northers. He had, in fact, a true epicure's interest in food and drink, a trait that later would manifest itself in the negative industry with which he would seek to deny such staples to the enemy, while at the same time indulging himself to such a degree that it would, from early middle age on, soften the lines of his campaign-hardened body.[47]

Residual quartermastering aside, Sheridan spent the rest of June scouting and mapping the countryside. Mapmaking had never been his best class at West Point—what had been?—but he had picked up enough rudimentary knowledge to produce rough sketches of the surrounding roads, streams, woods, and swamps for himself and his regimental commanders. These sketches would soon prove helpful. Vainglorious John Pope had been summoned east by Lincoln to take command of the newly created Army of Virginia; his replacement at the head of the Army of the Mississippi was the brilliant but erratic Major General William Starke Rosecrans of Cincinnati. The fire-scarred Rosecrans (the result of a bungled prewar lab experiment) was a fervent Catholic who traveled with a priest, eschewed vulgarity, and seemed to take as much pleasure in jousting with the War Department as he did in hunting Rebels. For the next fifteen months his fate and Sheridan's would be inextricably linked, in ways neither man could yet foresee.[48]

For the present, Rosecrans sent Sheridan's brigade back to Booneville to act as a sort of glorified tripwire for the rest of the army. Understandably ill at ease operating eight miles in advance of the rest of the army, the brigade made camp a mile above Booneville, and Sheridan deployed pickets around the clock to prevent a Shiloh-like visitation by the enemy. On the morning of July 1, his *dies mirabilis*, just such a visitation occurred, in the form of a Rebel cavalry contingent under the adoptive Mississippian, Brigadier General James R. Chalmers. Chalmers was that rarity among officers, particularly at this stage of the war: a political appointee who actually showed some fighting ability. Even rarer, he was personally liked by Confederate General Braxton Bragg, a notoriously hard-to-please martinet who had recently taken over command of the Confederate army from the ill, exhausted Beauregard. Bragg was now in the process of rearranging his forces; to cover the transfer of an infantry division to Ripley, twenty-five miles west of Booneville, he instructed Chalmers to feint attack on Sheridan's brigade.[49]

Around eight-thirty that morning Chalmers's advance guard made contact with Union pickets along the Blackland Road, three and a half miles west of Booneville. The commander of the pickets, Lieutenant Leonidas S. Scranton, immediately notified Sheridan, who dispatched four additional companies under regimental captain A. P. Campbell. Withdrawing slowly through a thick stand of timber, Scranton's pickets linked up with Campbell at the point where the Blackland and Booneville roads converged a mile west of town. Here, fighting dismounted, they forced Chalmers to show his hand. Two Rebel regiments deployed on either side of the road; it soon became apparent, Sheridan said, that Chalmers "meant business." So, too, did Sheridan. He directed Campbell to hold where he was; if forced to retreat, he was to do so as slowly as possible. Rosecrans, from headquarters, sent much the same order to Sheridan himself. But Sheridan's stubborn fighting spirit, until now more frequently directed at his superiors than at the enemy, had been aroused. In a dispatch to Brigadier General Alexander S. Asboth at nearby Rienzi, he flatly declared, "I will not give up my camp without a fight."[50]

Sheridan had in hand a somewhat under-strength brigade of 827 troopers, against whom the enemy arrayed at least twice as many. Much was made later—by Sheridan as well as others—of the disparate numbers involved in the fight. Sheridan estimated Confederate strength, with less than his usual precision, at "between five and six thousand." Other Union estimates ranged as high as seven thousand. No Confederate reports of the battle are known to exist, but one authority on Union cavalry has ventured the educated guess that Rebel strength was between twelve hundred and three thousand men, and was far more likely to have verged on the smaller number. Moreover, Sheridan was holding some aces that Chalmers lacked. In the first place, he had the always-handy advantage of knowing the terrain far better than the enemy. He had, after all, become practically a full-time resident of Booneville in the last few weeks, while Chalmers was new to the neighborhood. Then, too, he could count Confederate noses as they appeared in the open, while the Rebels were never sure how many bluecoats were lying in wait for them in the woods. Finally, several of the Second Michigan's companies were armed with six-shot Colt repeating rifles and pistols, giving them many times the firepower of the attacking force. What seemed, on paper, an unequal match turned out to be a much more even fight—which Sheridan, to his credit, apprehended from the start.[51]

While Chalmers's Confederates deployed on either side of the road for a frontal assault on Campbell's position, Sheridan brought up the Second Iowa to act as reserve. Attacking across an open field, the Rebels were met by withering fire at a distance of less than thirty yards. The shower of bullets from the Colt revolvers staggered the attackers, allowing the Yankees to fall back toward Booneville. Chalmers had foreseen the difficulties of attacking head-on; double columns of mounted men were left on either flank. After a second frontal attack was beaten back—literally—by Campbell's defenders, Chalmers commenced a flanking movement, attempting to intersperse his cavalry between the Union defensive line and Sheridan's camp. A more panicky commander might have wilted under pressure. Sheridan did not. Instead, remembering the long-ago fight at the Cascades, he "determined to take the offensive."[52]

Here his mapmaking efforts paid off in spades. A concealed road led through the woods on Chalmers's left. Quickly selecting two saber companies from each of the regiments, Sheridan charged his old sponsor, Captain Russell Alger, with what he admitted was "a forlorn hope." While Sheridan brought up his last reserves and occupied the Rebels with a full-bolt advance, Alger was to circle to their rear and charge in column down the Blackland Road, making as much commotion as possible. A turncoat Mississippian named Beene, whom Sheridan had fortuitously put on his payroll a few days earlier, would guide Alger and his ninety-man force into position. Sheridan gave him an hour to cover the distance before he commenced a general attack.[53]

Although ill with camp fever on the day of the battle, Alger performed admirably his part in the charade. Passing undetected around the enemy, he moved into position at exactly the moment that Sheridan sent the Second Iowa forward against the Confederate left. At the same time, a two-car supply train steamed into Booneville with grain for the brigade's horses. The men in the ranks knew that Sheridan had called earlier for reinforcements; believing, as men will, that their deliverance was at hand, they sent up a cheer. Cannily, Sheridan augmented the noise by having the engineer blow his whistle to let the enemy know that a train had arrived. The combined cacophony of train whistles, enemy yells, rapid-fire rifles, and, presently, the ominous swish of sabers at their backs produced in the Rebels a profound sense of disquiet. In "the utmost disorder," they broke and ran. Throwing aside rifles, knapsacks, coats, and anything else that could slow them down, they hastened west down the Blackland Road.[54]

In the meantime, Alger and his phantom horde had also turned around, unable to penetrate the enemy rear. The stampeding Rebels, it soon developed, were headed in exactly the same direction. For a time, according to one of the Federals on hand for the fun, the north Mississippi countryside was the scene of "some of the best horse racing you ever saw." Alger himself engaged in a running gunfight with a Confederate officer riding alongside him. The two emptied their revolvers at a distance of a few feet without noticeable effect except perhaps the necessary discharge of nervous energy. The duel ended abruptly when Alger's horse sideswiped a tree, tumbling him backward and breaking his ribs. Stunned, he lay unnoticed in the underbrush as skedaddling Rebels passed on either side. Others from the raiding party straggled back into camp, hatless, winded, and in many cases riding double, but "none the worse for wear except for a few scratches and bruises." Sheridan, who earlier that afternoon had telegraphed Asboth for reinforcements, saying he was "considerably cut up," now boasted, "I will not want any infantry supports; I have whipped the enemy today."[55]

It remained to tally the cost of the engagement. Sheridan assessed his casualties at forty-one—twenty-four wounded, sixteen missing, and one killed. One of those missing was Alger. Fearing he was dead, Sheridan sent a contingent of the Second Iowa to look for the captain's body. They found him sitting up, a little foggy-headed and sore-ribbed, to be sure, but still drawing the breath of life. Sheridan met him at the edge of camp, clapped him on both shoulders, and declared, "Old fellow, you have done well." It was the first great step in a long and ultimately disappointing career for Alger, a distant cousin of Horatio Alger, the "pluck and luck" novelist of the Gilded Age. He would live through the war, emerging as a brigadier general, and return to make his fortune as a lumber magnate in upstate Michigan. Inevitably, politics would beckon; he would serve as Republican governor of Michigan and twice would be the state's favorite-son candidate for president before being appointed secretary of war to President William McKinley. In this last position he would so bungle his part of the Spanish-American War that he would be hauled before a government investigating commission chaired by Sheridan's longtime associate Grenville Dodge, and ultimately resign in disgrace after the commission returned a finding that the department had indeed been grossly mismanaged, which any number of the army's ill-clothed, underfed, yellow-fever-ridden privates could have told the commissioners free of charge.[56]

But for the time being Alger could bask in his glory, as could the delighted Sheridan. Disdaining Rosecrans's panicky order to retreat, he had demonstrated in his first independent command a coolness and resolve that were rare commodities in any officer, let alone one so new to the job. And if his assessments of enemy strength and losses were weighted perhaps toward the high end of the scales (fifty-four years later Chalmers's aide-de-camp was still complaining that Sheridan's report of the "insignificant skirmish" was so much "fiction"), there was no gainsaying the totality of his triumph, especially as viewed by his immediate superiors. The day after the battle, Rosecrans issued a general order praising "the coolness, determination, and fearless gallantry displayed by Colonel Sheridan and the officers and men of his command." Division commander Granger chimed in three days later, noting "the excellent management of the troops by Colonel Sheridan." More to the point, Rosecrans recommended to Halleck, Sheridan's loyal benefactor, that his erstwhile quartermaster-commissary be made a brigadier general, adding pointedly, "He would not be a stampeding general." Halleck wasted little time in passing along a similar recommendation to Secretary of War Edwin Stanton. "I respectfully recommend Colonel Sheridan for promotion," he wrote to Stanton on July 6. No immediate action was taken; the mills of the gods grind slowly, but at least the wheels had been set into motion.[57]

In the meantime, Sheridan was ordered to withdraw from his "too much exposed" position at Booneville and make camp with Asboth's infantry division at Rienzi, seven miles northeast. He did so reluctantly, fearing that Asboth's somewhat relaxed attitude toward discipline might spread to his own brigade. He also worried that his independence as a commander might be usurped by the higher-ranking Hungarian-born general. There were no problems, as it turned out, with the easygoing Asboth, but Gordon Granger was a different matter. Sheridan was grateful to the rough-talking New Yorker for his role in gaining him a field command, and readily conceded that "Granger had many good qualities, and his big heart was so full of generous impulses and good motives as to far outbalance his shortcomings." Still, the division commander was something of a fussbudget, with an "uncontrollable propensity to interfere with and direct the minor matters relating to the command." Sheridan found himself spending half his time soothing the ruffled feelings of various subordinates miffed at Granger's "ill-judged meddling" and "freaky and spasmodic efforts to correct personally some trifling fault that ought to have been left to a regimental or company commander to remedy." Sheridan was neither the first nor the last Union officer to find Granger a pain in the neck; and he was glad for the occasional opportunity to escape the general's smothering attention by going out on patrol.[58]

Sheridan's pickets roamed from Jacinto, nine miles east of Rienzi, to the Hatchie River, eleven miles west. Not much was going on militarily, now that the campaign for Corinth was over. Still Sheridan kept busy, regularly sending his troops out on scout. It was not in his nature to relax, even in the strength-sapping heat of a Mississippi summer. Late in July his activity paid off. Colonel Hatch, at the head of a four-hundred-man force, raided the town of Ripley, where the 26th Alabama Regiment was reported to be staying. The Rebels, hearing news of the raid, withdrew from town just ahead of Hatch's minions, leaving behind a cache of their letters. What the letters revealed was enough to set off alarms among the Union high command. Ten days after the fall of Corinth, Halleck had divided his swollen army, sending Major General Don Carlos Buell east along the track of the Memphis & Charleston Railroad toward Chattanooga, Tennessee, a vital junction town whose capture would put the North in the luxurious position of being able to sever the only railroad linking Virginia to the lower South. It would also—and this was at least as important a consideration, from the career standpoint of all concerned—make Abraham Lincoln happy.[59]

From the beginning of the war, the president had cherished the concept of liberating the Union-loving mountaineers of East Tennessee from the malign embrace of their Confederate neighbors. Once in Chattanooga, Buell would be in a position to do just that. Unfortunately, his pace had been maddeningly slow. Every mile of railroad had been contested, torn up, or sniped at by southern guerrillas. Despite pointed warnings from Halleck, newly installed in Washington as Lincoln's general-in-chief, that the president was finding Buell's progress unsatisfactory, that much-put-upon general had still not reached the Tennessee border by the end of July. And now, as Halleck had warned, time had run out.

Back in Mississippi, Sheridan had divined from the captured letters that the Confederates were moving large numbers of troops eastward to intercept Buell at Chattanooga. This information he immediately forwarded to Granger, who raced it to Rosecrans, who hurried it to Grant, Halleck's successor as western commander. In actuality, the Rebels were not planning to stop at Chattanooga—Braxton Bragg had a larger, more ominous strategy in mind—but Sheridan's prompt handling of the captured letters nevertheless added more luster to his rising reputation. The day after he alerted his superiors to the enemy's dangerous intentions, five of them, Generals Rosecrans, Granger, Elliott, Asboth, and Jeremiah C. Sullivan, telegraphed Halleck in Washington: "Brigadiers scarce. Good ones scarcer. . . . The undersigned respectfully beg that you will obtain the promotion of

Sheridan. He is worth his weight in gold. His Ripley expedition has brought us captured letters of immense value." The wheels of preferment were turning faster. And at army headquarters U. S. Grant, who forgot very little, had been given good cause to remember Phil Sheridan.[60]

His general's star was on the way, but there was still some unfinished business with the Rebel cavalry in Mississippi. Throughout the month of August, Sheridan continued his harrassing raids on camps and villages, capturing handfuls of prisoners and whatever livestock and armory his hard-riding troopers could carry off. On August 26 the Rebels decided to return the favor. That afternoon, while half the brigade was out reconnoitering and the rest were sleeping or lounging in their tents, an estimated eight hundred Confederate irregulars led by Colonel William C. Falkner tore into camp without a word of warning from the posted pickets. The men spilled from their tents, grabbing their rifles, while the Rebs rode among them, snapping off a few desultory rounds.

Falkner was a legendary figure in northern Mississippi, a self-taught lawyer and journalist who had killed two men—one of them his friend Robert Hindman, brother of future Confederate general Thomas Hindman—in street-corner scuffles before the war. (Falkner never knew why Hindman had attacked him; apparently it stemmed from a misunderstanding about a club Falkner belonged to that Hindman wanted to join. Somehow Hindman was given the false impression that Falkner had blackballed him. Instead of asking Falkner about it, Hindman tried to shoot him, and he was fatally stabbed for his misapprehension.) It was said Falkner possessed a charmed life: Hindman's pistol, fired at point-blank range, had thrice failed to discharge; his brother's post-trial attempt at assassination similarly misfired when he dropped his pistol while taking dead aim at Falkner's heart. Falkner's second victim, a man named Morris, attacked him after his acquittal for Hindman's death. A slight, dark-eyed, furiously self-contained little man, Falkner had raised two regiments for the southern cause. This was the second, newly gathered from among his hometown neighbors in Ripley when the first voted him out as colonel for excessive irascibility. These "raw levies,".as Sheridan accurately called them, had attacked the Union camp under the mistaken impression that it had been left undefended. When a few shots from a supporting artillery battery rudely disabused them of this notion, they turned and fled, leaving behind— Colonel Falkner's among them—their hats. Sheridan sent Hatch's veterans galloping after them; they soon returned "loaded down with plunder in the shape of hats, haversacks, blankets, pistols, and shotguns."[61]

William C. Falkner left behind something else: a great-grandson and namesake who, after adding a dandified *u* to his surname, would relive and refight, through the scope of his imaginative genius, his great-grandfather's long series of duels with Yankees, carpetbaggers, land barons, and, ultimately, himself. This William Faulkner would rechristen his forebear John Sartoris, but the bare bones of his hero would remain W. C. Falkner of Ripley, Mississippi, whose own ration of miracles would run out for good in 1889 when his former business partner, Richard J. Thurmond (he always had bad luck in his friends), would shoot him down on a Ripley street corner without a word of warning, explanation, or regret following Falkner's election to the state legislature.[62]

Back at Rienzi, Sheridan counted his losses, six wounded and four or five missing, "some of whom I think will come in." Eleven prisoners were brought back by Hatch, "unfortunately," in Sheridan's eyes, since he had given orders not to take any of them alive. The problem of differentiating between honestly raised irregulars and bushwhacking guerrillas would always be a thorny one for Sheridan and his compatriots. "There must be some definite and fixed policy on our part to combat and break up this most infernal guerrilla system of theirs," Granger worried after the attack at Rienzi; "it is bound soon to waste our entire army away and for no equivalent. We must push every man, woman, and child before us or put every man to death found in our lines. We have in fact soon to come to a war of subjugation, and the sooner the better." Sheridan himself was mute on the issue, but a time would come when he would confront it again, even more urgently, in northern Virginia.[63]

For the present he contented himself with the fine response of his men to the surprise attack—Captain William W. Eaton, the officer in charge of the pickets, pointedly excepted and presently court-martialed for dereliction of duty. A few days later he happily received from Captain Campbell a three-year-old black gelding that the city-bred captain considered too high-spirited for his own use. Sheridan renamed the horse Rienzi in honor of the recent skirmish and rode it for the remainder of the war, at the close of which it would be, under its new name, Winchester, nearly as famous as Sheridan himself.[64]

Meanwhile, the war in Mississippi had become a drab sideshow to events now developing farther north and east. Braxton Bragg, as Sheridan had warned in July, had raced his army past Buell into Chattanooga. Not stopping there, he had prepared a two-pronged assault, in concert with General Edmund Kirby Smith's eighteen-thousand-man army in East Tennessee, on the enemy's heartland, after first liberating "loyal" Kentucky from the Union yoke. "My army has promised to make me military governor of Ohio in ninety days," Bragg rather atypically joked to fellow general John C. Breckinridge, and events in the field tended to bear him out. Cavalry raiders Nathan Bedford Forrest and John Hunt Morgan were rampaging freely through Middle Tennessee, threatening Buell's supply depot at Louisville, and making the enemy hold on Nashville increasingly tenuous.[65]

From Washington to Corinth, and at all points in between, the War Department's telegraph lines crackled with an urgency just short of panic. Lincoln himself queried Buell: "What degree of certainty have you that Bragg with his command is not now in the valley of the Shenandoah, Virginia?" Buell was certain because he was now in the process of racing him, mile for mile, into central Kentucky, calling over his shoulder for reinforcements and hoping against hope to reach Louisville first. With proper dispatch, if not exactly enthusiasm, Grant complied with Buell's breathless request. On September 4 he directed Gordon Granger to take a division to Kentucky and rescue Buell from Bragg—and from himself. One of those rescuers, although Grant did not yet know it, was Phil Sheridan.[66]

3

INFANTRY BRIGADIER

THE RAILROAD STATION AT CORINTH was already teeming with Union soldiers, horses, artillery, and supplies when Sheridan led his division-strength relief column onto the crowded loading platform on the afternoon of September 7, 1862. Earlier that day he had relinquished command of the now-depleted Second Cavalry Brigade to Colonel A. L. Lee and marched north with the Second Michigan Cavalry and four infantry regiments, the Second and 15th Missouri and the 36th and 44th Illinois, the veteran "Pea Ridge Brigade." His orders, courtesy of the ubiquitous Gordon Granger, were to transport the regiments to Louisville or Cincinnati, depending on which city was more grievously threatened by Bragg's invading Confederates. Sheridan, for one, was delighted to go. As he had seen following Curtis's Missouri campaign six months before, the war in Mississippi was winding down, while "the chief field of usefulness and opportunity was opening up in Kentucky." Having won his spurs—and, so it was rumored, his general's star—in ninety days of furious activity in the fetid scrublands of Mississippi, he now welcomed a change of scene.[1]

An unhappy onlooker at the railroad station was Major General Ulysses S. Grant. After the near-fatal blow to his reputation at Shiloh and a subsequent disheartening few months in Henry Halleck's smothering embrace, Grant had succeeded to command of the Department of the Mississippi, only to find his eighty-thousand-man army steadily whittled away by demands from other, more active fronts. Now, despite some last-minute foot-dragging, he was being compelled to send away yet another veteran division to help save Buell from his own mistakes. To make matters worse, he was losing some of his best troops; the Pea Ridge Brigade had literally won a name for itself with Curtis in Arkansas, and here, suddenly, was Phil Sheridan, with the best cavalry regiment in Mississippi, preparing to board the train for Kentucky. It was almost more than the general could bear.

Soft-spoken and diffident to the point of shyness, Grant was in many ways Sheridan's opposite. While the latter had spent his time at West Point brawling and cursing, Grant had been in the library, reading romantic European novels and sketching somewhat wooden pastoral scenes of dusky Indian maidens and dainty horses. Sheridan had actively sought an army career; Grant's overbearing father had enrolled him at West Point without even bothering to tell him about it. They had served in the same regiment (though not at the same time), but Sheridan had eagerly broken lances with the outmanned, overrun Indians of the Pacific Northwest, while Grant, a decorated Mexican War hero, had looked upon the Indians' plight and pitied them for "generally acquir[ing] some of the vices of civilization, but none of the virtues." With a bankrupt father, a priest-fearing mother, and three younger siblings he had scarcely seen twice in a decade back home in Ohio, Sheridan had grimly soldiered on through the fifties. Grant, adoring his wife and missing his children, had taken to his room with a bottle and resigned his hard-won captain's commission almost as soon as he received it, preferring, it seemed, the county poorhouse to an officer's tent.[2]

Now, yet again, their careers were taking divergent tracks. Sheridan was leaving behind an enviable reputation as a self-sufficient, aggressive cavalry commander whose fighting spirit was sure to win him greater renown. Grant, his own star still in eclipse after shining so briefly following the fall of Fort Donelson, was relegated to commanding a paper army in backwater Mississippi while Sheridan headed east to join the inevitable battle for control of Kentucky. Sidling over to Sheridan, Grant said he was surprised to see him in Corinth; he had not expected him to leave. Sheridan replied—"somewhat emphatically, I fear"—that his orders directed him to take his troops to Kentucky. Rather wistfully, Grant said he preferred for him to stay in Mississippi. Sheridan, afraid his orders would be countermanded at the last moment, made it clear he would rather go. Resignedly, Grant let him do just that, "a little nettled at his desire to get away." It was not, all things considered, the friendliest of partings.[3]

Sheridan and his men went by train to Columbus, Kentucky, where they boarded five steamboats for the trip upriver to Cincinnati. The voyage was uneventful, despite warnings from a panicky Union gunboat captain that the Rebels were in sufficient force at Caseyville to prevent the safe passage of enemy boats. Offloading his soldiers outside of town, Sheridan advanced on the supposed southern stronghold, only to be greeted by a spontaneous outpouring of loyal Caseyvillians exuberantly waving the Stars and Stripes. They had tried earlier to show the gunboat captain their love for the Union, but he had not stayed around long enough to find out. Three miles below Cincinnati, Sheridan was ordered to take his men south to Louisville and assist in fortifying the imperiled river town. He arrived one week to the day after leaving Corinth and immediately reported to the ranking general on the scene, the fearsome Major General William "Bull" Nelson, headquartered at the prestigious Galt House hotel.[4]

Neither Louisville, in general, nor Nelson, in particular, was in the best of moods when Sheridan arrived. The city, in fact, was in a state of panic following the overwhelming Confederate victory at Richmond, Kentucky, a week earlier, where Kirby Smith's gray-clad invaders had trampled Nelson's two green divisions, killing or wounding more than 1,000 men and capturing or driving off another 4,300. Most of these were Indiana Hoosiers hastily sent to the front by their formidable governor, Oliver P. Morton, a self-impressed Republican politico who, needless to say, was less than enthralled by Nelson's leadership qualities. Six feet five inches tall and over three hundred pounds in weight, Nelson had reached Richmond at the height of the debacle, recklessly exposing himself to Rebel bullets in a futile effort to inspire his recruits. "If they can't hit me they can't hit anything!" he had roared at the top of his foghorn voice—and immediately had taken two hits to the thigh in painful and contradictory example. Now he lay in bed on the second floor of the Galt House recovering from his wounds while Kirby Smith was off occupying Lexington, Frankfort, Cynthiana, Georgetown, and Paris, and menacing with his cavalry—for the sheer hell of it—Louisville, Indianapolis, and Cincinnati.[5]

Even lying down, as he was when Sheridan entered his room, Nelson was a larger-than-life character. A native Kentuckian and a personal friend of Abraham Lincoln (his brother Tom was Lincoln's minister to Chile), he had served twenty-one years in the U.S. Navy, seeing action in the Mexican War and acquiring along the way a sailor's salty manners and wounding tongue. Personally commissioned a general of volunteers by Lincoln to oversee the organization of a Unionist army in their home state, Nelson had led Buell's first reinforcements onto the field at Shiloh, winning a second star for his troubles, and was now the logical choice to organize the defense of Louisville, Kentucky's largest and most strategic city. Coarse, profane, and physically imposing, Nelson rubbed many people the wrong way, neither noticing nor caring what impression he left in his bullish wake.

Sheridan was not afraid of any man, even one a foot taller and nearly three times as heavy as he. Still, he was thrown off balance by Nelson's opening salvo. Why, thundered Bull, was Sheridan not wearing the proper shoulder straps? Nonplussed, Sheridan replied that he was wearing the appropriate markings for a colonel of the Second Michigan Cavalry. Not so, said Nelson, enjoying his little joke; Sheridan should be wearing a general's star. His promotion, rumored since early July, had finally come through, helped along by yet another telegram to Halleck from Granger and Major General Horatio Wright, department commander at Cincinnati, repeating the now-clichéd message that Sheridan was "worth his weight in gold." His appointment, endorsed by Halleck and Secretary of War Stanton, had been backdated to July 1, 1862, in honor of Booneville.[6]

Nelson's second piece of good news concerned the makeup of Sheridan's brigade. He would retain command of the Pea Ridge Brigade and Hescock's battery, and would also be in line to receive new regiments of volunteers rushing to the city following Lincoln's call for more troops. For the present, Nelson directed him to position his men below the city and assist in preparing a defense against the Rebels.[7]

Louisville was ablaze with rumors of impending invasion. The editor of the *Louisville Journal*, George D. Prentice (whose two sons, ironically enough, were off serving in the Confederate Army), postured apocalyptically: "Your wives and children and your hearthstones are imperiled, and to protect them you must, if necessary, confront the foes with bare breasts and impale yourself upon their murder-spotted bayonets." Brigadier General J. T. Boyle, district commander at Louisville, wired Lincoln: "We must have help of drilled troops unless you intend to turn us over to the devil and his imps." Martial law was imposed throughout the city, taverns were closed, and every available man between the ages of eighteen and forty-five was ordered to enroll for military drill. Black inmates from the county jail were pressed into service digging entrenchments alongside soldiers. Sheridan's men, in one night of Herculean labor, dug five miles of rifle pits.[8]

Meanwhile, the devil and his imps—or at least their southern-born familiars—had advanced unchecked into central Kentucky. Bragg, as he had predicted, had won the race to the Kentucky border. In seventeen days his army had marched more than 150 miles from Chattanooga, in southernmost Tennessee, to Glasgow, Kentucky, 110 miles south of Louisville. Upon arrival Bragg issued a grandiloquent proclamation advising Kentuckians that "I have entered your state with the Confederate Army of the West, and offer you the opportunity to free yourselves from the tyranny of a despotic ruler. We come not as conquerors or as despoilers, but to restore to you the liberties of which you have been deprived by a cruel and relentless foe." It was a very pretty document; the trouble was that Kentuckians in the main favored neither side. What they wanted, against all probability in a civil war, was to be left alone. Failing that, they wanted to sit out the first round of fighting and see how things developed. The fifteen thousand extra muskets Bragg carried with him into the state would remain, by and large, untouched in their crates.[9]

While Bragg pontificated, Buell kept moving, albeit tardily, toward Louisville. His rate of progress displeased everyone, from the president of the United States to the lowliest private. There were rumors—untrue—that he was Bragg's brother-in-law, and that the two opposing generals had secretly arranged to avoid fighting each other. There was also widespread dissatisfaction at Buell's earlier efforts to prevent looting of southern civilians and to prosecute Brigadier General John B. Turchin and other offending officers for their roles in the brutal sack of Athens, Alabama, that May. Halleck, now in Washington, had taken to delivering thinly veiled threats that Buell was in danger of being sacked himself. Still the obdurate general continued his plodding, insensible to either threats or demands. When at last he wired Halleck that he was moving against the enemy in central Kentucky, Halleck replied with one crushing sentence: "Go where you please, provided you find the enemy and fight him."[10]

When Bragg inexplicably turned away from Louisville, Buell marched grandly into the city. Many of his subordinates, however, considered his conduct something less than an unqualified triumph. Observant as always, Sheridan noted: "There was among the officers much criticism of General Buell's management of the recent campaign . . . he was particularly censured by many for not offering battle to General Bragg while the two armies were marching parallel to each other and so near that an engagement could have been brought on at any one of several points." Denunciations of Buell, he wrote, "were open, bitter, and almost universal, from the lowest to the highest."[11]

Inside the city, nerves remained taut. Not knowing that Bragg had declined the gambit, so to speak, Louisvillians expected full-scale fighting in the streets. Bull Nelson, like the good sailor he was, ordered all women and children evacuated across the river to Indiana. The *Louisville Journal* proclaimed breathlessly: "Before this article meets the eyes of our readers, this city may be attacked by rebels and its streets reddened with blood." Uncomfortably aware that he was living on borrowed time—which even now was running out more quickly than he knew—Buell spent the last days of September reorganizing his recruit-swollen army. Then, on the same ill-starred day, September 29, two hammer blows fell on Buell and his army, the first before he had even had time to go down to breakfast from his second-floor room at the Galt House.[12]

Shortly before eight that morning, Bull Nelson, armed only with his stinging tongue, had been shot and killed by fellow Union general Jefferson C. Davis. A few weeks earlier Nelson had ordered Davis out of town after arguing over army affairs. At the prompting of his close friend, the ubiquitous Governor Morton, Davis had approached Nelson that morning and demanded an apology. "Go away, you damned puppy," Nelson said in a loud voice. "I don't want anything to do with you." Davis, who had been nervously balling up a calling card, angrily flipped it into Nelson's face. Nelson responded by backhanding him halfway across the room. With the imprint of Nelson's hand still visible on his cheek, Davis borrowed a pistol from an obliging bystander and shot Nelson once in the chest. "Tom, I am murdered," were Bull's last words to his stricken friend, General Thomas Crittenden.[13]

News of Nelson's death raced across the city. Sheridan was camped outside the city when word came of the killing; he grabbed a horse and rode to the hotel, arriving at about 10:00 A.M. In the general melee inside the hotel, it was impossible to get an accurate account of events. Generals James S. Jackson and William R. Terrill, Sheridan's old West Point nemesis, were openly vowing revenge on Davis; others took the gunman's side. Sheridan himself had no opinion on the matter. The bald facts were bad enough: Nelson was dead, Davis was under house arrest, and the already fragmented Army of the Ohio was split into factions on the eve of its most important campaign.

Meanwhile, Buell had absorbed a second blow. By order of the president, he was directed to relinquish command of the army to Major General George H. Thomas, the Virginia Unionist who had taught Sheridan artillery tactics at West Point. Buell accepted the news without protest, perhaps even with relief. But a contingent of bluegrass politicians protested to Lincoln, warning that Buell's removal would be "dispiriting to the people and to the army." The stolid Thomas, whether through loyalty to Buell or owing to a natural aversion to taking command, wired Halleck that he was "not well enough informed" to command the army. With Lincoln's tacit assent, Halleck suspended the order pending further instructions. For the time being Buell retained command, with an enemy army scratching at the gates and his best subordinate general lying dead in the morgue.[14]

Looking about for a replacement for Nelson, Buell's eyes lit on his former inspector general, Charles C. Gilbert, a "major general" by virtue of a recent paper appointment and a man with no battlefield experience whatsoever. In fact, Gilbert was a mere captain—his general's appointment was never confirmed—and if Buell was somehow unaware of this, other officers knew it only too well. One was Sheridan. Under Buell's plan, Sheridan was to command a brigade in Gilbert's corps. But, well skilled by now in intraservice jousting, Sheridan went instead to Buell's chief of staff, Colonel James S. Fry, and informed him of Gilbert's bogus promotion. "I considered it somewhat unfair that I should be relegated to a brigade, while men who held no commissions at all were being made chiefs of corps and divisions," he later recounted, no doubt in milder terms than those he employed on Fry. Buell, at the end of the longest day in his life, placated Sheridan by giving him command of an entire division; Gilbert was left in charge of the corps.[15]

This was more like it. Less than a month after leaving Mississippi as a cavalry colonel in charge of a brigade, Sheridan now found himself commanding three infantry brigades—twelve regiments in all—and two artillery batteries. The division included the 35th Brigade, comprising the 44th Illinois, Second and 15th Missouri, and 73rd Illinois; the 36th Brigade, consisting of the 85th, 86th, and 125th Illinois, and 52nd Ohio; the 37th Brigade, with the 36th and 88th Illinois, 21st Michigan, and 24th Wisconsin; Battery G, First Missouri Light Artillery; and Battery I, Second Illinois Light Artillery. There were roughly 6,500 men in the division, more than three times the number Sheridan had previously commanded. His inexperience would soon evidence itself on the battlefield.

On October 1 the army left Louisville, moving southeasterly toward Bardstown, where Bragg's Rebels were bivouacked. Buell's plan was to feint toward Frankfort with two divisions of troops, thereby giving the impression that Smith's army, not Bragg's, was his main target. Then, while Bragg rushed to Smith's defense, Buell would take the rest of his army, nearly sixty thousand men, and interpose himself between the Confederates and their line of retreat. Heavy skirmishing began almost as soon as the Federals left Louisville. Confederate cavalry led by Colonel John A. Wharton slowed the Union advance to a walk—which it would have been anyway, since the inexperienced regiments had so encumbered themselves with knapsacks, frying pans, coffee pots, skillets, boots, blankets, and canvas ponchos that they tottered along in the scorching heat like French legionnaires in the Sahara Desert. Wharton's cavalry snapped alongside the marchers, picking off unwary recruits, killing twenty-five on the second day alone. In light of Nelson's recent murder, it was ironic that Wharton was the first Rebel commander the army encountered;

three days before Appomattox he too would be shot dead in a Texas hotel room by a disgruntled Confederate colonel who, like Davis, would escape prosecution for his crime.[16]

Rebel cavalry was not the only problem dogging Buell's advance. The state was in the grip of a summer-long drought; creeks had dried up, rivers had shriveled into stagnant pools. Clouds of dust choked the soldiers as they marched along the unpaved roads. The new recruits, overburdened with their knapsacks and unused to such exertions, fell by the wayside in increasing numbers. Buell's threadbare veterans, who had been taunted by volunteers in crisp blue uniforms when they arrived in Louisville from Alabama, enjoyed the satisfaction of a last long laugh. During halts in marching, they lay in the grass beside the road as limping stragglers labored to keep pace. "Hay foot, straw foot," they would taunt. "How do you like it, as far as you've got?" At a rare water hole, Sheridan's Illinois troopers spread their handkerchiefs over the stagnant, scum-covered pool to filter the brackish water while they drank. Others drank from ponds fouled by dead mules and cows.[17]

Straggling and foraging were endemic in both armies, and experienced commanders usually found occasion to look the other way, so long as such breaches of discipline did not occur during battle. Gilbert, however, perhaps feeling the need to reinforce his authority, issued strict orders against such free-lance activities. Sheridan dutifully seconded the orders, directing his brigade commanders to put a stop to the "dangerous and unsoldierly practice." Whether he actually enforced the strictures is debatable; he was too smart a leader to test his authority on such minor infractions. But Gilbert, with all the rank and none of the qualities of a major general, determined to stop it. The worst offenders, or at least the most blatant, were the veterans in the 36th Illinois.[18]

Twice these Pea Ridgers openly defied their corps commander. On the first occasion the regiment had halted beside an apple orchard. Some of the men were busily stuffing their pockets when Gilbert happened by. Outraged, he ordered his escort to fire on the soldiers. Immediately, fellow regiment members sprang to their feet, rammed home cartridges, and waited. Gilbert demanded to speak to the ranking officer; Captain (later Colonel) Silas Miller was pointed out. Gilbert lambasted him for dereliction of duty until Miller coolly noted: "General, one word from me will bring the boys out of that orchard a damn sight sooner than you can shoot them out, and should it come to that, I . . . assure you, General, that my boys never allow themselves to be outdone in a shooting business." There the matter rested.[19]

The second incident concerned the use of a rare spring of clear water near Gilbert's camp. The general had posted guards around "the sacred precincts," but the 36th, after marching all day without water, disregarded the guards and rushed the spring. A staff officer attempted to shoo the soldiers away and received a gun butt to the head for his intervention. Gilbert then ordered his guards to drive the regiment away. Miller, who was now making something of a career of defying Gilbert (thereby winning a permanent place in his men's affection), ordered the soldiers to fix bayonets and skewer the first man who tried to stop them. "My men are going to have all the water they want, before marching another foot," he warned. "If you want to die, come on." The twice-chastened Gilbert retired to his tent.[20]

Another of Sheridan's regiments faced a different problem on the march. The 73rd Illinois, the so-called Preacher Regiment, was a new levy, having entered the service earlier that summer. Ten Methodist ministers, including the regimental colonel, James F. Jaquess, the lieutenant colonel, a major, and six captains, belonged to the unit, as well as a number of younger men active in the Illinois Methodist Episcopal Conference. Like other new regiments, the 73rd entered the field with an abundance of equipment. Fellow soldiers in other units did what they could to help the regiment lighten its load, making off with large numbers of blankets, canteens, and cookery while the 73rd was conducting its regular morning and evening prayer services, a practice the churchmen soon abandoned as an unforeseen casualty of war.[21]

For the next three days Bragg and Buell struggled to concentrate their forces in near-total ignorance of each other. Bragg, having now written off Kentucky as a losing proposition, was more concerned with getting back to Tennessee with the enormous stores of grain, cattle, horses, sheep, and clothing Smith had stockpiled during his sojourn in the Bluegrass. To that end he ordered his far-flung forces to concentrate at Versailles, twelve miles southeast of Frankfort, where it was a straight shot down to the Cumberland Gap. If the enemy threatened, he would fight; otherwise he would retreat. Buell's three corps, twenty miles apart, were ordered to meet at Perryville, a small hamlet nine miles southwest of Harrodsburg on the banks of the Chaplin River.

On the afternoon of October 7 Gilbert's corps reached the outskirts of Perryville and was turned away by Confederate snipers on a low range of hills immediately east of a Chaplin River tributary known as Doctor's Creek. A few pools of stale water lay along the rocky creekbed within easy range of the Rebels' guns. The frustrated Federals bedded down for the night, thirsty, hot, and bone-tired, the coveted water in Doctor's Creek tantalizingly close but dangerously far away. Shortly before midnight Union skirmishers got near enough to Doctor's Creek to see pools of water shimmering in the bright autumn moonlight. Encouraged by their report, Buell ordered Gilbert to seize the hill overlooking the creek. Gilbert gave Sheridan the job. Sheridan in turn selected Colonel Dan McCook's 36th Brigade to carry out the general's wishes. The twenty-eight-year-old McCook, one of the Union's seventeen "Fighting McCooks" (his older brother, Alexander, commanded Buell's I Corps), had been William Sherman's law partner prior to the war. At 2:00 A.M. McCook deployed two regiments, the 85th Illinois and 52nd Ohio, on either side of the Springfield road and advanced on the Rebel unit, the Seventh Arkansas, that was picketing Peters Hill just east of Doctor's Creek. A short, sharp firefight ensued; flashes from muskets flared in the dark. The Confederates, outflanked by the 52nd Ohio, retreated to their main line on Bottom Hill, half a mile away.[22]

At a cost of six killed and twenty-seven wounded, McCook had gained possession of Peters Hill. He brought up a battery of artillery and part of the 125th Illinois, sent back word that he had taken the objective, and waited for further orders. It was now daylight. For the next hour a spirited artillery duel took place between the two sides. Anticipating an infantry assault, McCook ordered his men to lie down during the barrage. The Confederate commander on the scene, Brigadier General St. John Liddell, ordered the Seventh Arkansas, supported by the Fifth Arkansas, to retake the hill. These two veteran units, which had distinguished themselves at Shiloh, advanced crisply through the woods toward the Union position, but at a range of two hundred yards McCook's raw recruits opened a galling fire. The Seventh, which was not having a very good day, immediately fell back. The Fifth, on its right, made another drive for the crest, but likewise retreated to the base of the hill.[23]

From the crest of the hill McCook watched clouds of dust rising through the mist on either side of him. The Rebels, obedient to Bragg's wishes, were preparing to attack. The young colonel urgently requested reinforcements to hold the hill. Sheridan arrived in person a few minutes later with the division's other two brigades and Hescock's battery. Taking stock of the situation, Sheridan had the men scoop out a strong line of rifle pits along the heavily wooded hillside. Soon Gilbert reached the site, conferred with Sheridan and McCook, and gave orders that under no circumstances was the division to advance any farther. He hastened back to notify Buell of the early-morning developments.[24]

Gilbert may have thought his orders were clear enough, but he failed to take into account Sheridan's aggressive spirit. From the beginning of his career fighting Indians in the Northwest through the winning of his general's star at Booneville, Sheridan had been governed by his primary instinct to attack. It had always worked in the past, and he had no reason to believe it would fail now. At 7:00 A.M. Captain Ebenezer Gay, Buell's cavalry commander, arrived at Peters Hill with 1,350 riders, including Sheridan's old unit, the Second Michigan. Gay wanted McCook to help him drive the Rebel infantry into the woods beyond. McCook refused and Gay attacked alone. Meanwhile, Sheridan brought forward the 37th Brigade, consisting of the Second and 15th Missouri and 44th and 73rd Illinois, and massed it in two lines along the crest of the hill.

Gay's troopers ran into galling fire—seventeen men from the Second Michigan alone were felled by bullets—and Sheridan sent the two Missouri regiments down the eastern slope of the hill to support Gay's attack. In his memoirs (which fail to mention Gay), Sheridan maintained that the assault had been undertaken to clear the woods of "annoying" sharpshooters, which implied that he was merely doing a little judicious skirmishing. In fact, the Rebels were still in force at the base of Peters Hill, and it took a second charge by Sheridan's Missouri regiments, supported by their two Illinois counterparts and artillery fire from friendly batteries, to dislodge them. Brigadier General Speed Fry, a native of the area serving as Gilbert's officer of the day, opportunely brought up two more regiments and Sheridan threw them into the fray as well.[25]

With six Union regiments streaming down the hillside and across the narrow valley between the two hills, and with Sheridan's two batteries raining a hail of shot onto his own exposed artillery, Liddell withdrew his guns and urged his skirmishers back to the main line. Gilbert cantered back to the foot of Peters Hill to oversee the placement of two more brigades on the heights. Hearing the unmistakable sounds of heavy firing to the front, he signaled Sheridan not to bring on an engagement. It was too late. Sheridan's men had already crossed a small tributary between the two hillsides and were in the process of climbing Bottom Hill. Sheridan replied in a masterpiece of sangfroid that he "was not bringing on an engagment, but that the enemy evidently intended to do so, and that I believed I should shortly be attacked."[26]

Something about the reply did not sit well with Gilbert, and he rode to the front to personally enforce the order. "I observed, visiting General Sheridan's ground, that a part of it was vacant," Gilbert reported. It was vacant because, as Gilbert could see, Union soldiers were swarming about the crest of Bottom Hill, half a mile away. Locating Sheridan, Gilbert repeated his order about not starting trouble, explaining, as if to a troublesome child, "that General Buell was particularly solicitous that nothing be done to bring on a general engagement until after the junction of the flank corps." Sheridan shrugged; it was all a misunderstanding, he said.[27]

The assault had succeeded without too many casualties—154 in all—but the false impression it gave Buell about enemy strength led to several crucial misconceptions. To begin with, the capture of Bottom Hill had been accomplished in large part because Liddell's Confederates had been ordered to fall back and take their place in a grand attack column massing northeast of the hill. Buell, misled into thinking that the enemy had fallen back in disarray and that he had the luxury of taking his time, decided to postpone further action until the next day. By doing exactly what he had been told not to do, Sheridan had unwittingly contributed to a general relaxation of tension among the Union high command at the very moment that Bragg's Confederates were assembling to launch a devastating frontal assault on Alexander McCook's unwary corps, moving into place a mile to the north.

Back on Peters Hill, Sheridan watched aghast as Brigadier General Lovell Rousseau's division stacked its arms and sauntered casually down to Doctor's Creek to fill its canteens with brackish water, blissfully unaware of the Rebel tornado about to swirl down on them. First to reach the creek were the men of the 42nd Indiana, in Colonel William Lytle's brigade. Sheridan attempted by signal flag to warn them away from the creek, but it was too late. No sooner had they reached the water than three Confederate batteries opened fire. "Now they show themselves," Rousseau exclaimed.[28]

From his position overlooking the Chaplin River, Alexander

McCook could see no enemy troops except for a few cavalrymen cantering toward his left. The countryside around Perryville was unusual; abrupt mounds of hills rose and dipped in close formation, like a rug pushed into a corner. Behind these folds three divisions of Confederate veterans had massed unseen. Concerned—but not overly—about the cavalry on his left, McCook ordered Terrill to take his brigade and advance toward the river. "I'll do it, and that's my water," Terrill responded. A few days earlier, in Louisville, Terrill had run into a familiar, if not necessarily welcome, figure from his past—Phil Sheridan. The two had not seen each other since their slugfest at West Point ten years earlier. Now, allies again, they impulsively shook hands and buried their grudge. They did not, as romantic versions of the story maintain, bump into each other the night before the battle. Sheridan was busy arranging Dan McCook's assault on Peters Hill that night, and Terrill was camped several miles away, idly discussing with Brigadier General James S. Jackson and Colonel George Webster how little chance officers like themselves had of being killed in battle.[29]

Terrill's lead regiment, the 123rd Illinois, was brand-new. Organized only a month before, the men had received little in the way of formal training. After today, many never would. At about 2:30 P.M., Brigadier General George Earl Maney's Confederate brigade suddenly rose up from one of Perryville's sheltering ravines and poured a devastating volley point-blank into the astonished midwesterners. To survivors of the battle it appeared that the Rebels had simply sprung from the ground like dragon's teeth. Inexplicably, Terrill ordered his men to charge. Down the hillside the regiment dashed, then just as quickly dashed back again, leaving behind the crumpled bodies of 180 fallen comrades, including Jackson and Terrill, whose Virginia-born father had warned that he would never revisit his native state except to die. Two years later, when Terrill was joined in death by his younger brother, Confederate Brigadier General James Terrill, the family put up a joint headstone that read: "God alone knows which was right."[30]

From their vantage, Sheridan and his men watched in horror as wave after wave of Rebels swept the Union left. Rousseau's division, separated from them by a steep ravine, was roughly handled by three successive Confederate brigades. Colonel Lytle, a spruce young lawyer from Cincinnati who had become famous before the war for his poem "Antony and Cleopatra," was unhorsed by a shell fragment that left him sitting dazed and bloody on a rock, his sword unnoticed in his hand. Lytle would live to fight another day, under Sheridan, but for now he had fought all he could. So, too, had Webster, the last of the unlucky trio who had tempted fate the night before. Like Jackson and Terrill, Webster was killed trying to stem the rout of the Union left.[31]

Shortly after 3:00 P.M., a message arrived for Sheridan from General McCook, urging him to protect McCook's right flank. Sheridan did what he could, directing Hescock's battery to shell the oncoming Rebels from the north end of the hill. Hescock had barely found the range, however, when Confederate batteries began shelling Peters Hill in return. Sheridan turned both of his batteries toward the enemy cannon, personally directing their fire on foot. The cannonading echoed across the valley between the two hills. Three miles away at Union headquarters, Buell had just finished a leisurely lunch with Gilbert when the artillery duel commenced. Incredibly, he still had no idea that a major battle was under way. Owing to a natural phenomenon known as "acoustic shadow," the roar of battle could not be heard at headquarters. Only after Sheridan's batteries opened directly to his front did Buell realize, albeit dimly, what was taking place. "It sounds like a fight," he said.[32]

Riding toward the front, Gilbert was stopped by a messenger from Major General Thomas Crittenden, commander of the II Corps, who wanted to know what all the heavy firing was about. Gilbert, true to form, replied that he had met some little resistance, but "that his children were all quiet and by sunset he would have them all in bed, nicely tucked up." A very different message soon arrived from Sheridan, describing the gruesome disaster on the Union left and warning that he was about to be attacked himself and needed reinforcements to hold his position. Gilbert sent Brigadier General Albin Schoef's division to cover Sheridan's left and do what he could for McCook's shattered corps.[33]

On Sheridan's front, the Rebels had ceased their artillery fire. After a short lull, four gray-clad regiments trotted across the narrow valley separating the two sides. Battle flags waving, the Confederates advanced toward Sheridan's line, "yelling like fiends broke loose from pandemonium." The attackers crossed to within musket range of the forward regiment, the 36th Illinois, which greeted them with a withering blast. At the base of a small rail fence they rallied, tying a flagstaff to the fence and flaunting their defiance at the enemy above. "Never did troops display more courage and determination," one of Sheridan's men recalled. But the combined fire from the Union batteries and the well-placed infantry soon brought the Rebels up short. To the mocking cheers of the Federals they retreated down the hillside, wracked by fire from Peters Hill. Sheridan's men had held their position.[34]

To their right, Colonel William P. Carlin's 31st Brigade swung into action, driving the battered Confederates back toward Perryville. With the pressure to his front relieved by Carlin's timely attack, Sheridan swung his artillery toward the left in a belated attempt to relieve McCook. Gilbert, alarmed by the sudden change of direction, dispatched an aide to see what, exactly, Sheridan was doing. He had driven the enemy, Sheridan told the messenger, adding characteristically that he had "whipped them like hell." It was bold talk, and even accurate, as far as it went. But it failed to point out that not only had Sheridan enjoyed the advantage of holding the high ground, but he also outnumbered the Confederates in his vicinity four to one. While Carlin continued to the outskirts of Perryville, Sheridan waited atop Peters Hill, concerned that another enemy force might present itself. At length the ever-nervous Gilbert recalled Carlin's men from Perryville, where they had been lobbing cannonballs over the roofs of the town at the retreating Rebels, and formed his line on Sheridan's position. It was now past sunset and the Battle of Perryville was over.[35]

Pleased with the performance of Sheridan's troops, Gilbert relaxed his order regarding the division's supply trains. The night before, despite Sheridan's best persuasive efforts, Gilbert had refused to allow the men to visit their food wagons, forcing them to fight a day-long battle with nothing in their stomachs. Now, on his way to supper with Buell, Gilbert graciously permitted them to eat. It was, said Sheridan, "a great boon"—although many of the men were now too exhausted to hold a fork.[36]

At Gilbert's invitation, Sheridan accompanied him to Buell's headquarters for supper. Like the rest of his division, Sheridan had had nothing to eat all day, and he "enjoy[ed] the meal with a relish known to a very hungry man." Buell, who seemed to be running a restaurant more than a headquarters, betrayed a very hazy understanding of the day's events. "The conversation indicated that what had occurred was not fully realized," Sheridan noted—rather mildly, in view of the circumstances. The fact was that Buell could not bring himself to admit that he had allowed one-third of his army to absorb a frightful beating while Gilbert's corps had been content to defend itself against sporadic attacks by a single brigade of enemy troops, and Crittenden's corps had scarcely been used at all. Sheridan returned to camp believing that Buell was "unconscious of the magnitude of the battle that had just been fought."[37]

But if Buell was unaware of the day's importance, his counterpart on the other side of the river was not. That evening, for the first time, Braxton Bragg belatedly realized that he was facing the entire Union army, not just parts of it. With his own army shot to pieces after a day of gallant but uncoordinated frontal assaults, he decided to make a virtue of necessity and retire from Perryville with what spoils he could carry. He had no intention of risking another battle for the dubious honor of Kentucky sovereignty. By three-thirty the next morning, all the Confederates were gone.

For both sides, the Battle of Perryville had been tragically indecisive. Southern losses totaled 3,396 killed, wounded, or missing. Union losses were even more severe, at 4,211. Sheridan's part of the bill was an even 350 casualties, including 44 killed, 292 wounded, and 14 missing. Several northern newspapers erroneously reported that Sheridan himself had been killed, leading him to remark, somewhat dryly, that the false reports "had been corrected before my obituary could be written." A Rebel private succinctly summarized the battle in his diary: "Both sides claim the victory—both whipped," he wrote.[38]

Inevitably, there were recriminations following the battle. The whispering campaign against Buell grew ever more vocal. He was either a fool or a traitor, some said. Sheridan did not believe the general a traitor; he would not vouch for his foolishness. Perryville had been, in his eyes, "an example of lost opportunities." Even taking into account the acoustic quirk that had prevented Buell from hearing the roar of the guns, Sheridan could not excuse his ignorance of the true situation facing the army. "Had a skillful and energetic advance of the Union troops been made, instead of wasting precious time in slow and unnecessary tactical manoeuvres," he said, "the enemy could have been destroyed before he quit the State."[39]

As it was, Buell was content to provide the enemy with an armed escort back into East Tennessee—which was where Abraham Lincoln wanted Buell to be. When Buell left off following— one could scarcely call it pursuing—Bragg's army and doubled back toward Bowling Green, the thoroughly exasperated president summarily removed him from command, naming as his replacement Sheridan's old commanding general in Mississippi, William Starke Rosecrans. "The army as a whole did not manifest much regret at the change of commanders," Sheridan noted coolly, "for the campaign from Louisville on was looked upon generally as a lamentable failure."[40]

Sheridan himself was pleased with the change. Like most of Buell's subordinates, he had never really warmed to the distant Ohioan. The aggressive, excitable Rosecrans—also from Ohio and a fellow Catholic, although much more actively religious than Sheridan—was closer to his type of soldier. Moreover, Sheridan could not forget the helpful role Rosecrans had played in securing his promotion to brigadier general. With his own shortcomings at Perryville overshadowed by the more glaring mistakes of his superiors, Sheridan could turn the page on a frustrating but nevertheless instructive battle and look ahead to his next encounter with the enemy—an encounter that, under Rosecrans, was coming sooner than anyone might expect.

Rosecrans arrived in Bowling Green on November 2, taking over for the dejected Buell, who told him weakly, "I have done my best, if not *the* best." It went without saying that his best had not been good enough. Lincoln was tired of generals afflicted by "the slows." He had skipped over Buell's three corps commanders, each of whom technically outranked Rosecrans, because he believed Rosecrans had the necessary spunk to be a successful general. In this belief, he was fully supported by the men in the field, who regarded "Old Rosy" with a warmth and affection enjoyed by few other Union commanders, then or later. In the words of a popular soldier ditty: "Old Rosy is the man, Old Rosy is the man / We'll show our deeds where'er he leads / Old Rosy is the man."[41]

But if Rosecrans could count on support from the highest and the lowest, he could also number many powerful enemies who fell somewhere in between. "Subserviency to men in power is not one of my distinguishing virtues," he observed, in an understatement of monumental proportions. War correspondent Whitelaw Reid, who knew him well, drolly remarked that Rosecrans "never omitted an opportunity to do himself an injury." Proud, obstinate, and talkative, he had never learned to keep his own counsel. Men as varied and influential as Stanton, Halleck, and Grant had all felt the sting of Rosecrans's lash. For the present, with Old Rosy installed in the chill bosom of Lincoln's always contingent favor, they could do nothing more than hold their tongues and wait for him to make a mistake.[42]

Sheridan's division arrived at Bowling Green a day before its new commander. Although it had suffered only eight percent of the army's losses at Perryville, the division was nevertheless "much reduced" by fatigue and disease. Particularly hard hit were the eight new regiments, whose members had not yet become accustomed to hard campaigning, and thus were easy prey for the same insidious diseases that had so weakened the army in Mississippi earlier in the year. Rosecrans's first task, as he saw it, was rebuilding and reinvigorating his downtrodden army. This would take time; but Lincoln, after months of prodding Buell, was disinclined to patience. To the president's immense frustration, however, Rosecrans would not be hurried to his tasks. He had no more intention of invading East Tennessee than Buell had demonstrated six months earlier. Instead he began transferring his army to Nashville to counter the Confederate force that Bragg was reassembling thirty miles away. East Tennessee would have to wait. "It was apparent to everyone," wrote Sheridan, "that a battle would have to be fought somewhere in middle Tennessee . . . notwithstanding the pressure from Washington."[43]

To indicate the direction he intended to take, Rosecrans renamed his command the Army of the Cumberland—the Cumberland being the river that wound through Nashville. (The Confederate Army of Kentucky had also undergone a recent name change reflecting its geographical destiny; it was now the Army of Tennessee.) One result of the reorganization was the transfer of Sheridan's division from the center to the right wing of the army. Henceforth he would serve under his old West Point classmate McCook, "a chucklehead" in the words of one Union colonel, but potentially an improvement over the unlamented Gilbert, who now had vanished into the well-papered wilderness of a rear-echelon desk, from which he had so briefly and ingloriously emerged.

Sheridan's division moved down to Nashville the first week in November, encamping across the river from the state capitol, whose graceful porticos bristled with cannons placed there by

jittery military governor Andrew Johnson. After nine months of
Union occupation, the self-styled "Athens of the South" had lost
its Grecian elegance. The town was now crowded and filthy, its
streets disfigured by cotton-bale barricades and earthen parapets,
its normally busy wharves empty and neglected. Prostitutes and
whiskey peddlers, by contrast, did a booming business; drunken
soldiers wandered the streets preying on civilians—those whom
Johnson had not thrown into jail for refusing to sign a loyalty
oath. The number of prostitutes plying their trade in "Smokey
Row" eventually swelled to such proportions that the army provost marshal had 1,500 of the "soiled doves" rounded up and
shipped to Louisville, with strict instructions not to come south
again.[44]

Sheridan, as he had done in Mississippi, set up his own private intelligence-gathering network in the person of an itinerant
Tennessee preacher and Bible peddler named James Card, who had
offered his services to the Union cause "in any capacity which
might be useful." Like Sheridan, Card was a small, active man; he
had traveled widely through Tennessee and Georgia hawking his
wares. With the help of his two brothers, the erstwhile evangelist
was soon bringing back detailed information on the size, strength,
and location of the enemy, information the always-inquisitive
Sheridan considered "of inestimable value."[45]

In all the reshuffling, Sheridan acquired new brigade commanders. Brigadier General Joshua Sill, his roommate during
their last year at West Point, had been demoted from division to
brigade status and supplanted by Brigadier General Richard W.
Johnson, with whom Sheridan had served in Texas before the
war. Sill promptly requested transfer to Sheridan's division. Although delighted to see his old roommate, Sheridan was reluctant
to replace Colonel Nicholas Greusel, whom he felt had "already
indicated much military skill and bravery, and at the battle of
Perryville had handled his men with the experience of a veteran."
Still, military protocol had to be followed, and Greusel reverted to
command of the 36th Illinois Regiment. Other organizational

changes soon followed. Colonel Frederick Schaefer, a native of Baden, Germany, and a veteran of the unsuccessful revolution of 1848, returned to the division after missing the Kentucky campaign due to illness. By virtue of seniority he assumed command of the 35th Brigade from Lieutenant Colonel Bernard Laiboldt. A follower of fellow German general Franz Sigel, Sheridan's old Missouri nemesis, Schaefer was tall and slender, with a student-like appearance. Excitable and nervous before a battle, he was cool and deliberate during a crisis.[46]

The third new brigade commander, completing a clean sweep of Sheridan's subordinates, was Colonel George Roberts of the 42nd Illinois. Roberts's brigade had been garrisoned in Nashville prior to Rosecrans's arrival; by pulling strings, Roberts had induced the commanding general to let him change places with Colonel Dan McCook's brigade, much to the action-loving McCook's dismay. Sheridan pronounced Roberts "an ideal soldier both in mind and body," and admired his tall good looks and gallant dash. All in all, he believed himself fortunate to have such accomplished new assistants.[47]

November dwindled into December with the usual round of drills, parades, and picket duty. Sheridan pushed his officers hard, believing that good habits in camp made for good leadership on the battlefield. One Wisconsin subaltern witnessed a display of Sheridan's displeasure when an officer performed unsatisfactorily on picket duty. Grabbing the offender's sword and tossing it to his cook to use as a toasting fork, Sheridan declared that "it would be a better use than that man could put it to." With the enlisted men, however, Sheridan sometimes displayed a lighter touch. A private of the 73rd Illinois, mistaking the casually dressed general for a fellow ranker, demanded none too deferentially where he might find the quartermaster. "Who the hell are you, anyway?" Sheridan wanted to know. "I'm a high private of respectable parentage like yourself," the soldier replied with some heat. When an officer arrived and addressed the little man as "general," the private belatedly realized his mistake, but Sheridan merely "turned to me with a quizzical smile and said . . . he was never too busy to give any information he possessed."[48]

The same could not be said for Rosecrans, at least insofar as Washington was concerned. The telegraph wires hummed with increasingly angry messages from Lincoln to his commanding general. With an army of nearly eighty thousand men assembled at Nashville and an insolent Rebel army said to be dancing— literally—on the American flag at holiday balls less than thirty miles away, Rosecrans still refused to be budged. "To threats of removal or the like," he magisterially informed superiors, "I must be permitted to say that I am insensible."[49]

In fairness to Rosecrans, he had good reasons for biding his time. The Cumberland River was too low to bring supplies down- stream from St. Louis, and the railroad between Nashville and Louisville had been torn up by Rebel cavalry. From Lincoln's point of view, however, the continued inaction of his second- largest army was cause for great anxiety. The British parliament was to reconvene in January, and pressure was growing for Great Britain to intervene in the quarrel on the side of the South. France, with an eye toward Mexico, continued to urge a joint European intervention. The terrible Union debacle at Fredericks- burg, Virginia, in mid-December further deepened the president's gloom. "Things will be ripe soon," Rosecrans assured him. Until then Lincoln and the rest of the world would simply have to wait.[50]

At last, on Christmas Eve, Rosecrans issued orders for a general advance. At a late-night meeting with his generals, he grabbed a mug from a tray of hot toddies, slammed it on the table, and announced: "We move tomorrow, gentlemen. . . . Press them hard! Drive them from their nests! Make them fight or run! Fight them! Fight them! Fight, I say!" Sheridan, sitting by the fireplace watching cedar shavings curl into flames, said nothing. The time for talk was over.[51]

On the day after Christmas, the army moved south. Sheri- dan's division marched along the Union right, behind the lead division of Jefferson C. Davis, newly sprung from house arrest after paying five thousand dollars' bail to a Louisville court. (Davis would never be tried for Nelson's murder: Oliver Morton had powerful friends in Washington, including Lincoln's future attorney general, James Speed, who had the case removed from the docket.) Rosecrans counted about 44,000 effectives in his three advancing corps. The rest of the army was left behind, like spume from a flood, at Nashville and along the line of march, garrisoning each water crossing and railroad spur. Nevertheless, Confederate cavalry raided around the army, carrying off McCook's entire supply train and capturing close to seven hundred prisoners.

The weather, like the news, was bad. Drenching rains turned the roads into swamps; wagons had to be pulled from the muck by hand. Prohibitions against campfires forced the soldiers to sleep in wet clothes, without even a hot cup of coffee to fight the chill. The landscape echoed the gloomy weather. Many homes had been burned in the region; blackened chimneys, like gaunt tombstones, dotted the dreary countryside. Refugees fled the Union advance, their pitiful belongings loaded onto rickety wagons, driving their livestock before them.

Skirmishing between the two sides was steady. On December 30, Sheridan's division, with Roberts's brigade in the lead, drove to within three miles of Murfreesboro. Through information obtained from a Rebel deserter, Sheridan reported that "Bragg is fully posted in regard to our movements" and intended to make a stand north of Murfreesboro. Rosecrans's hope of surprising the enemy before it could concentrate was already shattered. Bloodied Union cavalry, riding into camp after yet another clash with Confederate horsemen, grimly taunted Sheridan's troops with warnings of the "fun" lying just ahead of them.[52]

That night Rosecrans finalized plans for a morning attack. While McCook held the Union right, Crittenden's corps would initiate battle on the far left, fording shallow-running Stones River to strike the enemy right, then wheeling north to roll up the line as George Thomas's center corps advanced to cut off their retreat. Like most of Rosecrans's plans, this one was complex and problematic, depending on two equally doubtful variables—that McCook could hold his position for the three hours needed to drive the enemy right, and that the always aggressive Bragg would passively acquiesce in his own destruction by staying on the defensive all that time.

To increase the odds of this happening, Rosecrans had McCook extend his lines by building a string of untended campfires beyond his flank. This seemed like a good idea at the time, but it was too clever by half. Bragg was indeed fooled by the phony fires, but instead of being frozen into inaction by the sight, he simply moved another division into place and shifted his own lines farther to the west. When Bragg attacked, as he fully intended to do at dawn, his legions would strike McCook's flank at an even more oblique and advantageous point. Rosecrans, in effect, had outflanked himself.

Despite McCook's personal guarantee that he could hold the right, the situation still troubled Rosecrans. "I don't like the facing so much to the east," he told McCook. "If you don't think your present the best position, change it." Sheridan, too, entertained doubts. The low rumble of moving men and equipment emanating from behind enemy lines made him restless with worry. Several times during the night he inspected his line, visiting each of his twelve regiments "to remedy any defects that might exist, and to let the men see that I was alive to their interests and advantages." Sill, commanding the far-right brigade, also heard the rumblings. The Rebels were so close he could make out the jingling of canteens and the metallic clashing of rifles. Along with an aide, Sill rode to Sheridan's headquarters, a small campfire beside a fallen tree in the rear of the reserve brigade. Together, the former roommates walked over to the picket line on the extreme right of Sill's position, listened a while longer, then went to see McCook, whom they found sleeping on some straw beside a fence. The enemy, they warned, was massing on the right.[53]

The sleepy-eyed McCook was not impressed. Rosecrans was planning to attack so strongly on the enemy right that the Rebels would be forced to withdraw troops from the left to meet the challenge, he told them. Meanwhile, Johnson would take care of the Union right. Sheridan and Sill rode back to the front, but unlike McCook they did not go back to sleep. Instead, Sheridan sent two reserve regiments forward to augment Sill's brigade, and had the rest of the division assemble before daylight in battle formation. Roberts's brigade held the left, south of Wilkinson Turnpike, Sill was on the right, and Schaefer's brigade was in reserve. Between the reserves and the frontline troops Sheridan unlimbered his batteries.[54]

The other divisional commanders in the area, Johnson and Davis, were not so scrupulous. Both ignored an eleventh-hour warning from McCook to watch for a dawn attack. Johnson's artillery horses were being watered at a small creek several hundred yards to the rear, and his men were moving about in the misty half-light, making breakfast and drinking coffee. Rosecrans had fixed on 7:00 A.M. as zero hour to give the soldiers time to eat. Sheridan's men had eaten in the dark, two hours before. Suddenly, wordlessly, ten thousand Confederate troops broke for Johnson's unsuspecting division at a dead run, two lines of gray-coated infantry stretching as far as the eye could see. The Federals never had a chance. A Tennessee private in the first wave of attackers said his brigade "swooped down on those Yankees like a whirl-a-gust of woodpeckers in a hailstorm."[55]

With terrifying suddenness the Union right disintegrated. Brigadier General Edward Kirk, upon whose brigade the onslaught first fell, dropped mortally wounded in the battle's first minutes. Fellow brigadier August Willich, another veteran of the failed German revolution of 1848, rode up to a body of dark-coated soldiers, shouting for them to rally, only to be rendered speechless in two languages by a Confederate officer who pointedly observed that they were wearing different uniforms. In the abandoned Union campsite, frying pans sizzled with breakfasts no one would eat. One dead soldier still clutched his coffeepot. A keening refrain carried down the line: "Sold again! We are sold again!" Rosecrans, hearing the gunfire three miles away, believed it was merely the preliminary skirmishing he had ordered to confuse the enemy. "It is working right," he assured his staff.[56]

The Confederate attackers, after driving Johnson from the field, pivoted north to strike Davis's flank. Others charged across a shallow cottonfield toward Sill's brigade and that of Colonel William E. Woodruff, holding Davis's left. Dozens of jackrabbits, flushed from cover by the onrushing Rebels, led the charge. Sheridan's artillery opened fire, tearing great gaps in the enemy line; musket volleys from fifty yards forced the attackers into stumbling retreat. Sill, buoyed by the successful stand, led a counterattack through the blood-spattered cotton. Leaning across his horse's neck to tell artillery captain Asahel Bush to double-shot his guns, he suddenly pitched headlong to the ground, struck in the face by a minié bullet. Staff officers carried the dying general off the field in a blanket. Rosecrans, told of Sill's death, said grimly, "We cannot help it. Brave men must be killed."[57]

Sheridan, likewise, had no time to mourn for his friend. Woodruff, on the right, had been overrun, leaving the division vulnerable to being flanked. Sheridan receded Sill's brigade and ordered Roberts to cover the withdrawal by charging the Rebels in the woods to the south. At the same time, Schaefer and Greusel, now commanding Sill's brigade, were directed to form a new defensive line on the high ground behind their artillery batteries. Roberts's men charged forward across an open field, sunlight glinting off their bayonets. The Rebels fell back behind their artillery; canister splintered in the trees above them. The charge bought Sheridan time to cobble together a new position at a right angle to his original line. He also attempted, without notable success, to rally Davis's badly demoralized men. William Carlin, who previously had come to Sheridan's aid at Perryville, again caught his eye, his pipe-smoking calm contrasting favorably with

Davis, "who seemed overpowered by the disaster that had be-
fallen his command."[58]

A similar disaster now threatened Sheridan. The two enemy
divisions that had overrun Johnson and Davis now wheeled ominously toward his line. The distinctive "sip-sip" of bullets clipped
through the branches of mangled cedar trees. Sheridan held as
long as he could, then withdrew deeper into the woods to link up
with Brigadier General James S. Negley's unbloodied division.
Calmly chewing an unlit cigar, he stationed his men at a ninety-
degree angle to Negley, facing south-southwest—almost exactly
opposite the direction they had faced a few minutes before. The
enemy pressed them on every side.

It was now 9:00 A.M. McCook's corps had been under devastating attack for almost three hours; of his sixteen thousand
troops, only Sheridan's division remained in the fight. As he had
done at Perryville, McCook failed to take charge of the situation.
"The right wing is heavily pressed and needs assistance," he reported to Rosecrans. Then, on the heels of his first report: "The
right wing is being driven. It needs reserves." Rosecrans, hearing
the steady thump of artillery, blanched at the news. "So soon?"
he asked. He dispatched a message to Sheridan telling him to hold
where he was. Sheridan had no illusions about the order—it
"would probably require a sacrifice of my command."[59]

He prepared to make that sacrifice, but he wanted to force the
Rebels to pay dearly for it. His new position was formidable: huge
slabs of limestone covered the ground like a poorly shuffled deck
of cards. Fissures and crevices gave the men a semblance of cover,
while towering cedars grew straight up through the rocks, ob-
scuring the sun and giving the woods an almost Grimmsian air of
gloom. Against these natural advantages, the division faced an
insuperable obstacle; after two hours of constant firing, the men
were nearly out of ammunition. Worse yet, the ammunition train
had been moved to a new position in the rear of the army. Lovell
Rousseau's division, coming into line beside them, gave them a
handful of extra cartridges, but with the enemy teeming through

the trees in a constant angry swarm, they were understandably loath to diminish their reserves.[60]

Three times the Confederates charged Sheridan's line, each time presaging their attack with knee-buckling artillery fire. The fire was fearful in its effect; ricocheting shells rattled over the limestone slabs like bowling balls, knocking down whole rows of Union defenders. The noise itself was deafening and continuous. Through it all Sheridan moved calmly about, directing artillery, shifting his lines, giving orders "as quietly as though sitting in his tent." Studiedly insouciant, he lit his cigar. Rousseau, among others, marveled at his comportment. "I knew it was hell in there before I got in," Rousseau said later. "But I was convinced of it when I saw Phil Sheridan, with hat in one hand and sword in the other, fighting as if he were the devil incarnate."[61]

Finally, after two hours of unremitting fire, Sheridan yielded to the inevitable. As the Rebels prepared another assault, he ordered Roberts—"an ideal soldier both in mind and body"—to cover the retreat. Meanwhile, Union gunners labored to bring their artillery off the field. The crashing bombardment had taken a huge toll on the batteries' horses, and the field pieces had to be hauled away by hand. Eight of the division's eighteen guns were reluctantly left behind. Roberts's brigade, the only one of the three with any ammunition left, deployed north of the Wilkinson Turnpike while the rest of the division withdrew under fire through the shattered trees. Roberts, on horseback, rode the line, shouting encouragement to his thinned-out ranks. A perfect target, he toppled from the saddle with three bullet wounds. Gasping in pain, he ordered his men to put him back on his horse; he died as they were hoisting him up. Advancing Confederates buried his body beneath a stone, carving his name on the rock with a bayonet.[62]

Command devolved to Colonel Fazilo Harrington of the 27th Illinois, but he too fell quickly, a piece of whirring shrapnel carrying away his jaw and killing him instantly. Lieutenant Colonel Luther Bradley assumed command. Meanwhile, Sheridan and the rest of the division completed an orderly retreat through the jagged rocks and splintered trees. Despite constant pressure, Sheridan reported, "the division came out of the cedars with unbroken ranks, thinned by only its killed and wounded."[63]

In the clearing north of the woods, his face blackened by gunsmoke, Sheridan ran into his commanding general. "Here we are," he told Rosecrans, "all that are left of us." He spoke the truth; in four hours of furious combat, culminating in one of the bravest fighting retreats of the war, he had lost more than 1,600 men, including three brigade commanders. Sill, Roberts, and Harrington were dead; soon Schaefer would join that terrible list. Sheridan was cursing, not so much from despair as from frustration. "Watch your language," Rosecrans ordered. "Remember, the first bullet may send you to eternity." With a third of his division heaped among the rocks and cedars behind him, Sheridan scarcely needed a lecture on the destructive capabilities of bullets. He shrugged. "Unless I swear like hell the men won't take me seriously," he said.[64]

Rosecrans dashed away on his gray charger, Boney, trailing his aides behind him. Sheridan's men, after refilling their cartridge pouches, withdrew to a clump of timber behind a newly formed defensive line. Rosecrans continued riding recklessly from place to place. "This battle must be won," he kept repeating, as though words alone could make things right. With his own men temporarily out of the fray, Sheridan joined Rosecrans's party. Rebel artillerists, recognizing the horsemen as Yankee officers, unleashed another volley. An unexploded shell whizzed past Rosecrans in a hot gust of wind and, to the horror of all, plucked Colonel Julius Garesche's head from his body as quickly and neatly as a gardener snips a flower. Blood and brains spattered Rosecrans's face. The headless body rode another twenty paces before sliding limply to the ground. Sheridan, as stunned as the others, noted a "momentary expression of horror" on Rosecrans's face.[65]

Buoyed by their success on the Union right, the Confederates redoubled their efforts to break the center. Rosecrans's lines had been forced back nearly three miles, bent into a narrow V, the two flanks almost touching. At the confluence of the two, in another clump of cedars, Rosecrans had collected some fifty cannon, which now told on the Rebels with killing effect. Again and again the southerners charged. "The dreadful splendor" of the Confederate attack could only be imagined, wrote Union Colonel William Hazen, "as all description must fall vastly short." The Rebel effort was magnificently brave, but, as at Perryville, it was not enough. By 5:00 P.M. their attacks had ceased. The Union line had held at last, with nowhere else to bend. The Confederates had simultaneously driven the Yankees too far and not far enough. Night fell, as it had at Perryville, on a southern army that had won the day—but not the battle. Seven thousand Federals, and an equal number of Confederates, lay dead or wounded on the awful field.[66]

At Union headquarters, a dilapidated log cabin alongside the railroad, Rosecrans convened a meeting of his corps commanders. Thomas and Crittenden urged him to remain where he was; McCook, unsurprisingly, favored retreat. Rosecrans concluded with a melodramatic flourish, "Go to your commands and prepare to fight and die here." With the blood of his close friend Garesche still staining his tunic and the extra-military importance of the battle fresh in his mind, Old Rosy decided to send back to Nashville for resupply and wait to see what Bragg would do. The next morning, after a night of unparalleled suffering—it was so cold that the wounded were stuck to the ground by their own frozen blood—Bragg was shocked to find Rosecrans still standing between him and Nashville. The Confederates moved forward cautiously. On Sheridan's end of the line a midafternoon sortie resulted in the capture of nearly a hundred prisoners, many of them wearing Union overcoats they had stripped from the dead. Their easy repulse convinced Sheridan that the Rebels had depleted their strength. The arrival of a much-needed artillery train, escorted by Sheridan's old brigade commander, Dan McCook, lifted Union hopes. An ill-advised attempt by Bragg the next day to break the Union left ended with a deafening roar from Rosecrans's well-placed artillery. In the space of an hour, 1,700 Rebels were killed or wounded.[67]

The Battle of Stones River was over, although it took Bragg another day to admit it. Nearly 25,000 soldiers had fallen in the fighting; Sheridan's losses totaled 1,633, or forty percent of his division, his highest casualty rate of the war. Still, "though our victory was dearly bought, yet the importance . . . was very great, particularly when we consider what might have been the result." From a purely personal standpoint, Stones River had been a triumph for Sheridan. He had, with the help of the much-lamented Sill, correctly perceived the danger looming on the night before the battle. Alone among division-level commanders on the Union right, he had prepared for an attack that, once it was launched, had quickly overwhelmed other, more unwary divisions. With the help of outstanding subordinates, whose worth he had recognized long before the battle, he not only had withstood the initial attack, but had also managed to delay the enemy's advance for two crucial hours, enabling Rosecrans to cobble together a new position. As a fighting withdrawal, his division's performance at Stones River ranked among the very best in this, or any other, American war. No less an expert than Ulysses S. Grant would later say: "It was from all I can hear about it a wonderful bit of fighting. It showed what a great general can do even in a subordinate command; for I believe Sheridan in that battle saved Rosecrans' army."[68]

Grant was not alone in his praise of Sheridan. McCook commended his "gallant conduct and attention to duty," and Rosecrans reported that "the consistency and steadfastness of [Sheridan's] troops . . . enabled the reserves to reach the right of our army in time to turn the tide of battle and change a threatened rout into a victory." He urged that Sheridan be promoted to major general. For someone who, a mere seven months earlier, had been a lowly commissary captain wrangling over the quality of beef for his general's table, Sheridan's rise had been truly remarkable. Furthermore, it had been achieved on the battlefield, not in some drawing room or rear-echelon tent. His men—those who had not been left behind on the viney hills of Perryville or in the winter-stricken woods at Stones River—knew his worth as a fighting general; their steadfastness and courage had helped him prove it. Soon the rest of the country would know it, too.[69]

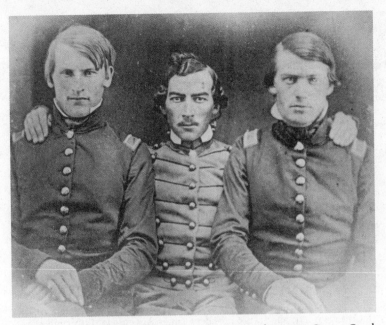

West Point cadet Phil Sheridan, center, with former classmates George Crook, left, and John Nugen. This is the earliest known photograph of Sheridan.
UNITED STATES MILITARY ACADEMY ARCHIVES

Brigadier General
Phil Sheridan as he
looked at the Battle of
Stones River.
UNITED STATES ARMY MILITARY
HISTORY INSTITUTE

Sheridan, seated far right, with Major General William S. Rosecrans, seated fourth from left, and future president James A. Garfield, fifth from left.
USAMHI

Major General William S. Rosecrans commanded Sheridan at Stones River and Chickamauga.
LIBRARY OF CONGRESS

Brigadier General William H. Lytle of Cincinnati died leading one of Sheridan's brigades at Chickamauga.
CINCINNATI HISTORICAL SOCIETY

Sheridan about the time he took over the Army of the Potomac's cavalry corps.
NATIONAL ARCHIVES

Secretary of War Edwin Stanton opposed Sheridan's promotion.
LIBRARY OF CONGRESS

Confederate cavalry legend J. E. B. Stuart, killed by Sheridan's forces at Yellow Tavern.
ELEANOR S. BROCKENBROUGH LIBRARY, MUSEUM OF THE CONFEDERACY

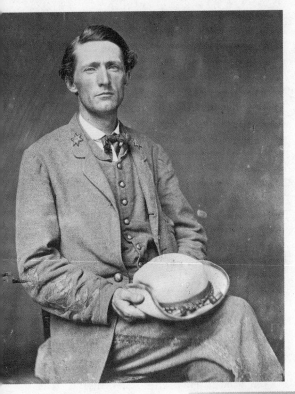

Confederate Colonel
John Singleton Mosby.

Lieutenant General Jubal
Early, Sheridan's nemesis
in the Shenandoah.

Sheridan, standing with sword, and his staff during the Shenandoah Valley campaign. James W. Forsyth is seated at far left on steps.
USAMHI

Sheridan and his cavalry commanders. From left: Wesley Merritt, David M. Gregg, Henry Davies, James Wilson, and Alfred Torbert.
USAMHI

Artist James E. Taylor sketched Sheridan's dramatic arrival at Cedar Creek.

Ill-fated puppet emperor
Maximilian of Mexico.

George Armstrong Custer at
the end of the Civil War.

This was Custer's favorite
photograph of himself.
NATIONAL ARCHIVES

Sheridan at the heigh
of his power
CHICAGO HISTORICAL SOCIET

4

THE VALLEY AND
THE HEIGHTS

IMMEDIATELY AFTER THE BATTLE of Stones River, William Rosecrans took to his bed, officially a victim of "lung fever," but more likely suffering from nervous collapse. The battle had worn on everyone, from commanding general to lowly private. Even so inexhaustible a spirit as Phil Sheridan felt the need for "recuperation, reinforcement, and reorganization" before going after the wounded Rebels. Strictly speaking, Stones River had been a draw, though the Union army could claim, by virtue of holding the ground, a somewhat qualified victory. Farther reaching was its political impact. The Emancipation Proclamation had passed into law on January 1, while the armies at Stones River were still bleeding and dying. After the North's crushing defeat at Fredericksburg three weeks earlier, Rosecrans's triumph—however contingent—at least ensured that the president's gesture would not be discounted in European capitals. And though U. S. Grant was still grumbling two years later that "Stones River was no victory," Lincoln himself was well aware of the battle's import. Months later, after relations between the president and his tart, prideful general had soured irredeemably, Lincoln could still write to Rosecrans, in all sincerity: "I can never forget, whilst I remember anything, that about the end of last year and beginning of this, you gave us a hard-earned victory, which, had there been a defeat instead, the nation could scarcely have lived over."[1]

The practical effect of the battle, however, was to render Rosecrans virtually immobile for the next six months, during which time Lincoln, Stanton, and Halleck all attempted without notable success to get him moving again. As he had done after taking command, Rosecrans dug in his formidable Dutch heels and refused to be hurried, if "hurried" is the right word for a six-month convalescence. To the very real problems of logistics and supply confronting any general in enemy territory, Rosecrans added an exaggerated wariness and respect for an opponent who had demonstrated twice within two months' time an unnerving knack for throwing the first—and heaviest—punch. The near loss at Stones River had undeniably given him pause.

Sheridan, with his usual restless energy, spent the winter months drilling, foraging, and nosing about. Although his division had done remarkably little straggling during its desperate withdrawal through the cedar woods, one of his first tasks nevertheless was to make an example of four regimental officers who had deserted their colors during the heat of battle. Forming the division in a hollow square, Sheridan marched the miscreants into the center and, telling them he "would not humiliate any officer or soldier by requiring him to touch their disgraced swords," directed his black servant to cut off their shoulder straps before having them drummed out of camp to the mocking strains of "The Rogue's March." This "mortifying spectacle" had the desired effect; no other division officer abandoned his troops.[2]

With the army two hundred miles away by railroad from the Union supply base at Louisville, rations were cut and freight loads limited. Fruits and vegetables were scarce in the picked-over countryside around Murfreesboro; scurvy became epidemic in camp. One regiment, finding a field of overlooked potatoes, broke ranks and pulled the humble delicacies from the ground, eating them raw, dirt and all. In an effort to lighten the teamsters' loads, Rosecrans lodged some of the soldiers in lightweight pup tents, an ill-advised expedient that never failed to bring derisive "bow-wows" from the occupants whenever the general passed in review.[3]

Sheridan did his part to keep the army supplied, sending out as many as 150 wagons at a time to gather grain from neighboring farms. The wagonloads of corn and grain brought back to camp were almost incidental to the reconnaissance reports Sheridan gleaned from his officers, "the real nature of these excursions." One report brought more news than he bargained for. Colonel Joseph Conrad of the 15th Missouri, presumably with a straight face, reported that the foraging had gone all right, except for the misconduct of the two women attached to divisional headquarters, who had gotten drunk on applejack and fallen into Stones River. "To say that I was astonished at his statement would be a mild way of putting it," Sheridan confessed. It seemed the two women had enlisted independently a few months before and had since developed a sisterly regard for each other. One was "coarse and masculine" and had little trouble passing for a man. The other, though "bronzed and hardened by exposure," was attractive enough that Sheridan wondered whether she had really fooled all her tentmates, after all. Whatever the case, the two were removed from the ranks, given more-suitable clothing, and shipped north to Louisville, that convenient repository of fallen females.[4]

Less amusing was the fate of one of Sheridan's scouts, the younger brother of James Card. With time on his hands, Sheridan had devised a plan of his own for interrupting train traffic between Chattanooga and Tullahoma by burning bridges behind enemy lines. Card and his brother, with three other East Tennessee Unionists, set out from headquarters early that spring. Two weeks went by without a word from Card or his compatriots; another brother volunteered to go to their father's home to see what he could learn of the venture. Some days later, Card turned up at Sheridan's tent with a hair-raising account of his capture, imprisonment, and escape from the Rebels. Sheridan gave him the bad news that his younger brother was also missing. "They have caught him," Card said heartbrokenly. "The poor fellow is dead." As usual, the scout's instincts were correct. Confederate guerrillas had captured the younger Card at his father's farm and summarily lynched him. It took all Sheridan's formidable persuasive powers to convince Card to remain with the army through the upcoming campaign. The next winter he formed a band of like-minded Tories and sought bloody revenge for his brother's death.[5]

In early March, Sheridan's division was chosen to spearhead the army's first offensive operation since Stones River. Goaded by a telegram promising a major generalship in the regular army to the first northern general who won "an important and decisive victory," Rosecrans devised a joint operation, infantry and cavalry, to destroy Confederate Major General Earl Van Dorn's pestiferous cavalry, now wintering at Columbia, Tennessee, thirty miles south of Murfreesboro. Sheridan was to march west to Spring Hill, twelve miles north of Columbia, with Colonel Robert H. Minty's cavalry brigade and link up with Colonel John Coburn's three-thousand-man force coming down from Nashville. Once united, they were to attack Van Dorn's presumably unsuspecting stronghold.[6]

In practice the plan failed utterly. Sheridan and Minty managed to capture an insignificant number of prisoners (Sheridan noting with detached professional interest the exceptionally large incidence of saber wounds suffered by both sides), but Coburn's column was quickly gobbled up by the vigilant Van Dorn and his accomplished subordinate, Brigadier General Nathan Bedford Forrest. Belatedly Sheridan pursued Van Dorn to the banks of the rain-swollen Duck River above Columbia, "with a view to making some reprisal" for Coburn's debacle, but the Confederates fell back across the river, frustrating Sheridan's hopes of revenge and confirming Rosecrans's reservations about venturing too far from camp. Two months later a jealous husband walked into Van Dorn's headquarters and shot the young general in the back of the head for his ungallant attention to the gentleman's wife.[7]

The botched campaign did not reflect badly on Sheridan—it had not been his idea in the first place. Instead, on April 10, he received word that he had been promoted to major general of volunteers, postdated to December 31, 1862, in honor of Stones

River. Rosecrans had recommended him for the honor along with six other generals including, incredibly, Jefferson C. Davis, whose division had splintered during the first hour of battle. For some reason the Senate was slow to act, leading Sheridan to remark a little sourly of his promotion that "a long time elapsed between the promise and the performance." Nevertheless, he was delighted to receive his second star. A few days later the officers of the division pooled their money and bought him a jeweled dress sword, a pair of revolvers, and a glass and silver wine set valued at two thousand dollars to commemorate his new rank.[8]

The division was quartered a few miles southwest of Murfreesboro at Camp Schaefer, named in honor of Sheridan's fallen colonel. In late April a freshly minted brigadier general arrived in camp, William Haines Lytle of Cincinnati. Lytle had served under Rosecrans in West Virginia early in the war, and had been seriously wounded at the Battle of Carnifex Ferry. He was wounded again at Perryville, fighting on the Union left (indeed, his wound may have come from Sheridan's own cannon, firing at the Rebels from Peters Hill). Courtly and diminutive, Lytle became an immediate favorite of everyone. A member of one of Cincinnati's first families, he had been groomed from birth for leadership. At twenty he had captained volunteers in the Mexican War. In the ensuing years he had been a successful lawyer, a member of the Ohio legislature, a losing candidate for lieutenant governor, and a major general of the state militia. He had also found time to write an irresistibly sentimental poem, "Antony and Cleopatra," which brought him national fame in 1858. The poem, with its Shakespearean opening line, "I am dying, Egypt, dying," quickly became a favorite of after-dinner recitalists on both sides of the Mason-Dixon Line and made Lytle, at thirty-six, one of the best-known generals in either army.[9]

Lytle wasn't the only well-connected Ohioan to join the Cumberlanders that spring. Rosecrans's new chief of staff, replacing the luckless Garesche, was Brigadier General James A. Garfield, a shambling, big-headed protégé of Treasury Secretary

Salmon P. Chase. Glib and gregarious, with a hearty handshake that seemed to say, a fellow-officer thought, "Vote early, vote right," Garfield had managed to parlay two insignificant victories in eastern Kentucky into election to the U.S. House of Representatives. Since Congress did not convene until December, he had chosen to remain in the army, serving most recently as a member of the court-martial that had convicted Major General Fitz-John Porter of disloyalty and misconduct. That celebrated trial had been widely viewed as a blatant Republican political vendetta— Porter was a Democrat and one of Major General George McClellan's closest supporters—and many of the officers on Rosecrans's staff rightly regarded Garfield with suspicion. But the guileless Rosecrans (who was not immune to flattery, particularly if it confirmed his own generous view of himself) welcomed Garfield as a confidant, and henceforth the newcomer rode at the general's elbow, his pale blue eyes focused carefully on Rosecrans's every move.[10]

April passed uneventfully into May, with Rosecrans remaining the only army commander not taking the offensive. In Virginia, "Fighting Joe" Hooker fought and lost the Battle of Chancellorsville to Robert E. Lee. Farther south, Rosecrans's old nemesis U. S. Grant began a complex, month-long campaign to capture the Rebel bastion of Vicksburg, Mississippi. Settling into a brutal, civilian-killing siege, Grant worried that a sizable force of Confederates now gathering under General Joseph E. Johnston might fall upon him from the rear. These concerns were passed along to Washington. Once again Lincoln went to the telegraph office. "I would not push you to any rashness," he advised Rosecrans, "but I am very anxious that you do your utmost, short of rashness, to keep Bragg from getting off to help Johnston against Grant." "I will attend to it," Rosecrans replied.[11]

On June 2 the army broke camp. Rosecrans intended to advance on Bragg in Middle Tennessee while Major General Ambrose Burnside moved down from Cincinnati to capture Knoxville. The army was well under way when Washington abruptly ordered Burnside to send eight thousand reinforcements to Grant at Vicksburg. Consequently, Rosecrans halted his advance. A few days later he circulated a memo among his seventeen corps and division commanders asking them three questions: First, had Bragg been so weakened by detachments to Mississippi that their own army had a reasonable chance of winning a battle? Second, if the army now advanced, was it likely to prevent additional Rebel reinforcements from being sent against Grant? And, third, was an immediate advance therefore advisable? On all three questions at least thirteen of the generals answered no, including a unanimous negative response to the third. In his answer Sheridan reasoned logically that Bragg would simply fall back before any advance, making it impossible to prevent him from reinforcing Johnston and greatly complicating the task of feeding their own army. Characteristically, he sidestepped the first question—whether the army had a reasonable chance of winning the battle. That, in Sheridan's always careful construction of his duties, was not for him to say.[12]

Rosecrans sent the results of his poll to Washington, adding that it would be better to wait a little while to ensure success. To do otherwise, he argued, would merely violate the "great military maxim not to risk two great and decisive battles at the same time." Halleck, who had authored a standard textbook on military theory before the war, noted with acerbity that "there is another military maxim, that 'councils of war never fight.' " The gibe finally did the trick. On June 23, 1863, 170 days after the Battle of Stones River—and 169 days after Lincoln wanted it done—Rosecrans at last moved south.[13]

The great objective was Chattanooga, the same bugbear that one year earlier had led Don Carlos Buell on his exhausting parabola from Alabama to Kentucky to professional oblivion. The frontierlike little town, with its rutted dirt roads and wooden-planked sidewalks, held an exalted military importance far beyond its scruffy appearance. Here crossed two of the Confederacy's most important railroads, the East Tennessee & Virginia, running north-south, and the Memphis & Charleston, running east-west. Any invasion of the Deep South would necessarily have to start from Chattanooga. As if to underline the town's importance, nature herself had ringed Chattanooga with dominating mountains, steep-sided ridges, and a notoriously turbulent and often-unnavigable river. The city's five thousand residents—less several hundred Unionists run out of town since the start of the war—understandably considered themselves safe from attack.

Braxton Bragg had spent the winter constructing a formidable defensive line, seventy miles wide, from Columbia to McMinnville. His Tullahoma headquarters was ringed by breastworks six hundred yards deep. As added protection, a high ridge blocked the northern approaches. Four gaps, all fortified, cut through the ridge. The Union army would have to come through somewhere; logic dictated the less-rugged terrain on the Confederate left. But Rosecrans had not spent the past five months in complete idleness, Washington opinion notwithstanding. He feinted instead toward both flanks, while driving through the two eastern passes. Indiana Colonel John T. Wilder's mounted infantry brigade, armed with new seven-shot Spencer repeating rifles, brushed past startled enemy pickets at Hoover's Gap and held off numerically superior forces until the main body of Federal troops could catch up. On July 1, with Sheridan's division in the vanguard, the Army of the Cumberland entered Tullahoma. In one carefully thought-out week of bluff and maneuver, Rosecrans had driven the Rebels entirely out of Middle Tennessee.

Had it not been for uncommonly heavy rains, Rosecrans might well have gotten into Bragg's rear and forced a decisive battle at Tullahoma. As it was, Bragg fell back toward Chattanooga, closely pursued by the dogged Federals. Typically, Sheridan's division led the way, chasing the Rebels all the way to Sewanee Mountain, thirty miles away. Sheridan himself took two infantry regiments and a cavalry force and climbed to the mountaintop hamlet of University, where Confederate Bishop-General Leonidas Polk had founded the University of the South before the war. Saddle-weary from his ride, Sheridan ordered a railroad handcar sent up to him. It never got there; soldiers bringing it up the mountain took a wrong turn and fell into enemy hands. Sheridan and his traveling companion, Colonel Francis Sherman, stumbled eleven bone-jolting miles down the mountain in the dark. "I had reason to remember for many a day this foolish adventure," Sheridan recalled ruefully, "for my sore bones and bruised muscles caused me physical suffering until I left the Army. . . . I have never ceased to regret that I so thoughtlessly undertook to rejoin my troops by rail instead of sticking to my faithful horse."[14]

Bragg reached Chattanooga on July 4, 1863. With almost literary irony, Independence Day was marked by three major Union victories: at Vicksburg, at Gettysburg, and in Tennessee, where Rosecrans's virtuoso maneuvering had carried his army to the very outskirts of the town Lincoln himself had called "fully as important as . . . Richmond." But if Rosecrans expected to be congratulated for his feat, he was quickly disabused of that notion. In a curt telegram announcing the victories at Gettysburg and Vicksburg, Secretary of War Stanton pointedly ignored Rosecrans's accomplishment. "Lee's army overthrown; Grant victorious," he wired. "You and your noble army now have the chance to give the finishing blow to the rebellion. Will you neglect the chance?" Rosecrans, who never let an insult pass unchallenged, fired back: "You do not appear to observe the fact that this noble army has driven the rebels from Middle Tennessee. . . . I beg in behalf of this army that the War Department may not overlook so great an event because it is not written in letters of blood." As usual, Rosecrans proved to be his own worst enemy; not only did his injudicious telegram destroy any vestige of support from the terrible-tempered Stanton; it also meant that future pleas for reinforcements would fall on deaf ears, with consequences too dire to imagine.[15]

Each step the army took toward Chattanooga brought it one step farther from its base of supplies. The Confederates, falling back, had severely damaged the railroad below Tullahoma. The mountainous countryside made wagon trains impractical, and army engineers labored around the clock to repair the broken tracks. Sheridan's division, at Cowan, was given the critical task of patrolling the rail lines as the engineers advanced. By the end of July the railroad was open all the way to Stevenson, Alabama. Ten miles away, at Bridgeport, a partially destroyed bridge spanned the Tennessee River. There Rosecrans intended to cross the unfordable river and fall on Bragg's rear. Sheridan was ordered to save the bridge.

On July 29 Sheridan occupied Bridgeport with two brigades, leaving the third at Stevenson to guard the army's supply depot. As the stores of food and ammunition mounted, so did the pressure on Rosecrans to take the offensive. The slowness of his advance, Halleck said, had caused great disappointment in Washington. "The patience of the authorities here has been completely exhausted," he warned, "and if I had not repeatedly promised to urge you forward, and begged for delay, you would have been removed from command." Typically, Rosecrans thanked Halleck for his troubles and declared that "whenever the Government can replace me by a commander in whom they have more confidence, they ought to do so." He did not intend to move until the last wedge of hardtack had been added to the pile. Even a private letter from the president, assuring his recalcitrant general that "I am not watching you with an evil eye," failed to hurry the proceedings. Finally, on August 4, Halleck relayed to Rosecrans a "peremptory order" to advance. Not only that; he was to report his movements every day until he had crossed the Tennessee River.[16]

Sheridan, at the tip of the army's cautious advance, was unconcerned with Rosecrans's bureaucratic problems, although as a former quartermaster he no doubt recognized the difficulties involved in the care and feeding of fifty thousand men in enemy territory. Something of his own mounting frustration was revealed in a run-in he had at the time with a civilian railroad conductor. Escorting Thomas on an inspection tour of the newly reopened rail line between Cowan and Bridgeport, Sheridan was irked by a long and unexplained delay. The conductor, "a great, burly six-footer," was gruff and noncommittal to Sheridan's questioning. Finally, after the general ordered him to get the train moving again, the conductor replied airily that he took his orders from the military superintendent. By the time the last words were leaving his mouth, Sheridan had jumped up from his seat, slugged the railroader two or three times, and kicked him off his own train. Then he returned to his seat beside the unflappable Thomas and casually resumed their conversation. Rosecrans learned of the incident and somewhat avuncularly cautioned Sheridan, for the sake of safety and regularity, not to interfere with railroad employees "except in very extreme cases." Sheridan explained that the man had been "saucy and impertinent in language and manner," and that, besides, the conductors on the line were "dishonest and worthless." There the matter rested.[17]

After fending off Washington for another few days while a second rail line was opened north of Chattanooga, Rosecrans put the army in motion on August 16. He intended to maneuver Bragg out of Chattanooga the same way he had forced him from Tullahoma. While the left wing of the army demonstrated openly above Chattanooga, the larger portion would cross the river at Bridgeport, southwest of the city, where Sheridan was guarding the railroad bridge. Unfortunately, Rebel sappers had set fire to their side of the bridge the night before, sending it sagging into the water below. Sheridan informed Rosecrans of the incident and offered—embarrassment compounding necessity—to build him another one. Fifteen hundred men from the Third Brigade hurried into the surrounding woods with axes and draft horses, and by nightfall they returned with enough logs for a new trestle bridge. Plank flooring for the bridge was in short supply, so Sheridan simply made up the difference by helping himself to the floors and walls of nearby buildings. On September 2 the division marched across the new bridge; other Union troops crossed by pontoon bridges and log rafts. Enemy resistance was negligible.[18]

Convinced that the Yankees would attack from the northeast, particularly after Wilder's men had shelled the town from that direction, Bragg had neglected to defend the crossings farther south. Unchallenged, Rosecrans's three corps crossed the river and clambered, troll-like, up and down the steep sides of Lookout, Raccoon, and Sand mountains. Bragg, envisioning a siege uncomfortably like Vicksburg's at Chattanooga, abandoned the town on September 8, falling back toward LaFayette, Georgia, twenty miles south. The next day lead elements of Crittenden's corps entered Chattanooga.

At that point, with the raising of the Stars and Stripes above the city's best-known landmark, the Crutchfield House, Rosecrans's military career had attained its zenith, though no one realized it at the time. Since taking command of the army at Louisville eleven months before, he had occupied Nashville, fought and won the Battle of Stones River, maneuvered the Confederates out of Middle Tennessee, and now taken Chattanooga, gateway to the lower South. He might have rested with some justice on his laurels, as stolid George Thomas advised him to do. But with Thomas's former Mexican War captain, Bragg, in full retreat, Rosecrans determined to continue his pursuit. Directing Crittenden to garrison Chattanooga and then follow from the north, Rosecrans sent his other two corps eastward through Stevens and Winston gaps in Lookout Mountain. The three Union columns were now too far from each other for rapid concentration, in the event such a move should become necessary.

Alarming signs began trickling in about the whereabouts of Bragg and his army. Once again it was Sheridan, with his practiced nose for scouting, who sounded the first disquieting note. Growing uneasy about "the disjointed situation of our army," he instructed the ubiquitous Card to select a willing local man to pass through enemy lines and "bring me such information as he could gather." Card chose an Alabama Unionist from Sand Mountain who knew the country well and who wanted, for his troubles, a small grubstake to get safely away once his usefulness had ended.

Sheridan duly agreed to buy the man's livestock, and the spy set out for the Rebel camp. His unpracticed stealth soon got him captured, but by crawling on his stomach through enemy lines, grunting and rooting like a wild hog, he managed to make his way back to camp. There he told Rosecrans that the enemy was preparing for a major fight and, worse than that, was being secretly reinforced by Lieutenant General James Longstreet's corps from the redoubtable Army of Northern Virginia.[19]

Rosecrans might have shrugged off the warning of one unlettered hillbilly, except that similar reports were coming in from all three corps commanders. Crittenden, to the north, reported that Bragg's rear guard seemed to have halted near Lee and Gordon's Mill, a dozen miles south of Chattanooga; Wilder's brigade had skirmished heavily when it tried to brush past. McCook, twenty-five miles farther south at Alpine, advised that he was no longer able to communicate with Thomas, since Confederates were swarming over each intervening road. Most alarming of all, Thomas's lead division, under Major General James S. Negley, had been strongly attacked as it emerged from Dug Gap, west of LaFayette. With some difficulty, Negley had managed to extricate his men from the trap and retrace his steps out of McLemore's Cove, but it had been a near thing.

In the midst of growing uncertainty, an unexpected visitor arrived at Rosecrans's headquarters: Assistant Secretary of War Charles A. Dana. He was there, Dana told Rosecrans ambiguously, "for the purpose of conferring with you upon any subject which you may desire to have brought to the notice of the department." Either his visitor's phlegmatic attitude or the mere mention of Stanton's name set Rosecrans off, and he proceeded to unburden himself of a year's worth of pent-up anger at the War Department in general and Stanton and Halleck in particular. Dana heard him out—what else could he do?—then replied, somewhat inscrutably, that he had "no authority to listen to complaints against the government," but had merely been sent "for the purpose of finding out what the government could do to aid

you." In typical Rosecrans fashion, the general soon recovered
from his flash of temper and extended a more cordial welcome to
Dana. He could not know it, but the sandy-bearded bureaucrat
slouching before him represented a far graver threat to Rosecrans's career than all the hard-eyed Rebels now stirring like fire
ants in the north Georgia woods.[20]

With Dana at his side, Rosecrans left Chattanooga on September 13. Already he had issued orders to McCook and Crittenden to concentrate their troops on Thomas's position. Late—
very late—he had come to the realization that Bragg's
Confederates were not retreating after all, and that his army,
dispersed as it was across forty miles of Georgia hills, was in
immediate danger of being cut to pieces, one wing at a time.
Along with the rest of McCook's corps, Sheridan's division began
retracing its steps over Lookout Mountain toward Winston Gap.
A correspondent for the *Cincinnati Commercial*, James W. Miller,
had accompanied the division from Tennessee. As the men
trudged up the mountain in the hot September sun, Sheridan
beckoned to Miller from a roadside log. He pointed back toward
the east, where great clouds of dust were visible above the tree
line. "Is our cavalry over there?" the inexperienced Miller asked.
"Our cavalry can't get there," Sheridan said with the trace of a
smirk. He looked searchingly at the writer, then added, "There
will be tremendous work." Miller thought Sheridan was somewhat disappointed in him for not realizing what was afoot.[21]

The entire army was sidling northward toward Chattanooga
along a six-mile front, taking care not to poke the sleeping dog,
Bragg. Two parallel roads led back to Chattanooga, Dry Valley
Road through McFarland's Gap and LaFayette Road through Rossville Gap. If Bragg succeeded in cutting these escape routes, the
Union army would have to fight for its life. Between the two sides
ran a sluggish, rather deep creek with abrupt, rocky slopes. Its
name, Chickamauga, was a Cherokee word meaning stagnant or
bad water. The Indians who once lived along its banks had named
it for the smallpox spores that swam in its waters and infected

their bath. It was a dark, ominous stream, shadowed by over-hanging branches and rippled by the occasional water moccasin. Romanticizers would later call it, with good reason, the "River of Death."

Bragg did indeed plan to turn the Union left and get between it and Chattanooga, but he failed to take into account the greater mobility of the enemy. He believed that Rosecrans's left was still at Lee and Gordon's Mill. In fact, Sheridan's division was now posted there as rear guard for the army's extreme right. Merely by marching, Rosecrans had succeeded—although he did not realize it—in outflanking Bragg. By nightfall of the eighteenth, the Confederates had managed to cross the creek after a stubborn defense by the always-stubborn Wilder and Sheridan's old brigade commander at Perryville, Dan McCook, but the initiative had passed for the time being into Rosecrans's hands.

At daybreak on September 19 the Battle of Chickamauga began, ironically initiated by George H. Thomas, the most defensive-minded general in either army. Receiving reports that a single unsupported Confederate brigade was across the creek, Thomas had sent Colonel John T. Croxton's brigade chasing after it. Croxton was met by Nathan Bedford Forrest's cavalry and a full division of Rebel infantry. The startled Croxton notified Thomas that he would be glad to bring in an enemy brigade, if only Thomas would tell him which one he wanted.

The commanding generals' initial responses were in keeping with their antipodal characters: Rosecrans excited and optimistic, Bragg petulant and irritable. Like the other 100,000 men on the field, they were dumbfounded by the sheer hellborn fury of the fast-developing battle. The dense woods and vine-littered thickets obscured much of the fighting from the naked eye, but no one within earshot could mistake the virtually unbroken musket and cannon fire for anything other than a battle of seismic disproportion. It would be, both sides realized, a battle of total annihilation.[22]

Sheridan's division, at the southern end of the battlefield, was not immediately engulfed by the fighting. Rosecrans was using McCook's corps as his reserve, sending one division to Thomas on the Union left and one to Crittenden in the army's center. Sheridan was ordered to anchor the right, reflecting his hard-won reputation as a "stayer." Moving up to Lee and Gordon's Mill to relieve Brigadier General Thomas J. Wood's division, Sheridan discovered that Wood had already left, leaving the critical crossing unguarded. He immediately sent Lytle's brigade into action, driving the enemy across the stream and preventing a beachhead in the Union rear. It would not be the last time at Chickamauga that Wood would force Sheridan to fend for himself.[23]

Leaving Lytle to watch the ford, Sheridan hurried north to reinforce the army's center. En route, he and his staff rode through a covey of Union infantry, scattering them with the cry, "Make way for Sheridan!" Getting word that the enemy was present in force in the woods below Rosecrans's headquarters at the Widow Glenn cabin, Sheridan personally led Colonel Luther P. Bradley's brigade in a costly afternoon assault. At the price of nearly three hundred casualties, including the twice-wounded Bradley—a brigadier under Sheridan did not have the safest job description—he managed to halt the Confederate advance and stabilize the Union line. Driven back by greater numbers, the brigade passed through the same weary foot soldiers it had scattered ingloriously a few moments before. "Make way for Sheridan!" the soldiers jeered.[24]

Sheridan bedded down his brigade near the Widow Glenn's. The rough handling he had suffered that afternoon led him to recall Lytle's brigade from Lee and Gordon's Mill. Putting the men to work improvising barricades, he rode over to the Glenn cabin around midnight to learn what he could of the day's results. Most of the army's ranking officers were there, including the three corps commanders, chief of staff Garfield, and the ever-present Dana, whose eleven brief telegrams to Washington during the course of the day represented something of a new standard in self-contradiction. At 2:30 he had wired that "decisive victory seems assured." At 4:00 P.M. he was maintaining, "Everything is prosperous." Thirty minutes later he began changing his tune: "I do not dare to say that our victory is complete, but it seems certain." An hour later: "Now appears an undecided contest."[25]

Dana was not the only one befuddled by events. Rosecrans seemed in a state of nervous exhaustion, alternately cajoling and browbeating his weary subordinates. Thomas, usually his strong right hand, dozed in the corner, rousing himself only to advise strengthening the left—his own position. For his part, Sheridan was struck by the prevailing sense of anxious depression, notwithstanding the fact that the Rebel attack that day had been largely unsuccessful. Thinking of Bragg's track record at Perryville and Stones River, Rosecrans directed Thomas to hold his position, while McCook eased toward the right and Crittenden floated in reserve behind their two corps. It did not seem unlikely that Bragg would break off the fight. Orders were copied and read aloud and coffee served to the gathering. For some reason, McCook availed himself of the opportunity to burst into song, regaling his fellow generals with verse after verse of a lugubrious ballad, "The Hebrew Maiden's Lament." Troubled and exhausted, Sheridan returned to his tent, where he was soon joined by McCook and Crittenden. The three loudly denounced the predicament they were in, and Sheridan paced the floor the rest of the night.[26]

Sunday, September 20, dawned smoky and cold. A heavy mist hung low to the ground, while a haze of undissipated gunsmoke gave the sun a reddish hue. At Union headquarters Garfield looked skyward and intoned dramatically, "This will indeed be a day of blood." Rosecrans, as was his custom, rode restlessly from one end of the field to the other, his pasty, puffy-eyed appearance unnerving at least as many men as it inspired. At the Widow Glenn's, Sheridan had his troops back at work strengthening the breastworks begun the night before. He was still troubled by his exposed position on the extreme right, which was uncomfortably similar, both in location and numbers, to his near-fatal position at Stones River. Rosecrans shared his uneasiness, ordering McCook to tighten his lines and giving that star-crossed corps commander a "severe rebuke."[27]

After a confused delay of nearly three hours, during which time Bragg waited impatiently for his own generals to act and Rosecrans continued tinkering with his lines, the battle reopened on the Union left. Division after division of Confederates grimly assaulted Thomas's position. The attacks, although ably beaten back, provoked Thomas into a renewed flurry of demands for more reinforcements. Rosecrans responded by recklessly stripping units from the center. The thunderous gunfire on the Union left, coupled with Thomas's hectoring, played on the general's troublesome nerves. At 10:30 A.M. Captain Sanford Kellogg, Thomas's nephew by marriage, galloped up and reported, to Rosecrans's consternation, that there was a large gap in the right-center of his line. Unseen by Kellogg was an intervening division, hidden from view by a thick stand of trees.[28]

Without bothering to double-check the report, Rosecrans hastily dictated an order to Wood to "close up on Reynolds as fast as possible, and support him." In military terms this was an impossibility, requiring two entirely dissimilar movements. But Wood, having felt Rosecrans's lash already that morning, moved with understandable alacrity to carry out the new order, even though it meant pulling his own division out of line and marching it to the rear in the face of the enemy.[29]

Rosecrans's habitual fiddling had dangerously disarranged the Union right. Sheridan's reserve brigade, under Laiboldt, had been shifted toward the left, behind Jefferson C. Davis's division. His other two brigades, Lytle's and Bradley's, were ordered to move to Thomas's aid. They had just left their breastworks and wheeled northward, parallel to the LaFayette Road, when a devastating enemy assault column, eleven thousand strong, burst from the woods across the way and fell upon them like the judgment of God.

Into the gap left by Wood's departed troops stormed five Confederate divisions, spearheaded by Ohio-born Brigadier General Bushrod Johnson's Tennesseans. The spectacular assault, by an even more spectacular coincidence of timing, had fallen at the worst possible moment for the Union. A few minutes' difference either way and the gap would have been closed. As it was, the Rebels poured unchecked through the enemy line, a great gray hemorrhage spilling over both exposed flanks and lapping against the long, low hill ahead. The attack shattered Laiboldt's and Davis's three brigades and bore them rearward like flecks of foam. Davis's men had suffered the same fate at Stones River; now, as then, some shouted as they fled, "See you in Ohio!"[30]

All that remained of the Union right were Sheridan's division (minus Laiboldt's departed brigade) and Wilder's Lightning Brigade on the far end of the battlefield. With the Confederates swarming up the gentle incline toward the Widow Glenn's, Sheridan attempted, through Lytle, to stanch temporarily the gaping wound. From his vantage point on the crest of the hill, Lytle could see at a glance that the situation was hopeless. Pulling on a pair of dark kid gloves, he said softly, perhaps to himself, "If I must die, I will die as a gentleman." Then, turning to the nearest regiment, the 88th Illinois, he added, "All right, men, we can die but once. This is the time and place. Let us charge." To the 24th Wisconsin he added, in meager encouragement, "Boys, if we can whip them today we will eat our Christmas dinner at home."[31]

Lytle's counterattack—gallant, quixotic, and doomed— bought little time for Sheridan and the rest of the division. Almost as soon as it was undertaken it was smashed; the Rebels were already in among them. At the crest of what is now Lytle Hill the two sides collided in "a veritable tornado of battle." Bayonets, muskets used as clubs, even rocks picked up from the ground, were put to deadly use in hand-to-hand combat. Lytle, sitting atop his horse, was an easy target. Hit first in the side by a Rebel bullet, he turned to say something to an aide and was struck simultaneously by three more shots, one smashing him squarely in his handsome face, knocking out several teeth and exiting through his neck. He died, a poet gagging on his own last words ("brave, brave, brave boys"), a few minutes later.[32]

Somehow Sheridan managed to organize a second defensive line three hundred yards to the rear, but it too was quickly overwhelmed. The damage was simply irreparable. Rosecrans, sitting calmly—or in shock—at the north end of the hill a few hundred yards away, watched the Confederate assault with bullets zinging around his ears. "If you care to live any longer," he told his staff laconically, "you had better get away from here." Heeding his own advice, he rode for the rear, stopping occasionally to shake his sword at other, less exalted fugitives. Like them he was headed toward Chattanooga.[33]

Thinking perhaps of Stones River and the stand that Sheridan had made there, Rosecrans sent word that he wanted to see him, but Sheridan was preoccupied just then with forming his short-lived second line. By the time he had a moment to spare, Rosecrans had already ridden on. "It is to be regretted that he did not wait till I could join him," Sheridan lamented, "for the delay would have permitted him to see that matters were not in quite such bad shape as he supposed."[34]

Instead, Rosecrans rode up the Dry Valley Road toward Rossville, accompanied by the ever-present Garfield. There, at a point where the road divided, one branch leading to Chattanooga, the other back to the battlefield, the two men arrived at the literal crossroads of their lives. Dismounting and putting their ears Indian-style to the ground, they could hear heavy firing on the Union left. Rosecrans hesitated, torn between riding back to the field and continuing on to Chattanooga. To his everlasting regret he chose the latter. Afterward, Rosecrans maintained that he had fully intended to return to the battlefield, but that Garfield had persuaded him to go to Chattanooga. Garfield said merely that he had offered to go and see what had happened to Thomas's corps. Whatever the case, Garfield's ride back to the battlefield started him on the road to the White House (and ultimately to an assassin's bullet), while Rosecrans's disastrous decision, however well-intentioned, planted the seeds of his professional undoing.[35]

It was now early afternoon, and Thomas was in the process of winning undying—if not entirely deserved—fame as "the Rock of Chickamauga." In the wake of the enemy breakthrough and the subsequent disintegration of the Union right, a new defensive line had been cobbled together a few hundred yards behind Thomas's position on the heavily wooded spurs of Snodgrass Hill. Throughout the early afternoon individual units, carried backward like flotsam in a heavy sea, had come to rest on these anchoring hills. Here Thomas and the others were making the fight of their lives, while the rest of the army continued its headlong flight. Rosecrans telegraphed Lincoln from Chattanooga: "We have met with a serious disaster; extent not yet ascertained."[36]

Conspicuously absent from this last-ditch defense was Sheridan. After failing to rally the various fragments of his command on the far side of Lytle Hill, he had joined the panicky retreat toward Chattanooga. In his official report of the battle, as well as in the revealingly truncated account in his memoirs, he maintained that he had been prevented from linking up with Thomas by an intervening column of enemy troops. This column, he said, had advanced parallel to his own men and turned captured Union cannons on his flank. But Sheridan exaggerated both the speed and the depth of the Confederate penetration. The onrushing Rebels had indeed broken the Union line, with fatal consequences for Lytle and scores of other Third Division members lying dead on his namesake hill; but the Confederate advance had soon bogged down, a victim of its own successes. Ammunition had been used up, and men were panting like dogs after a mile-long run. Sheridan's old classmate John Bell Hood, the ranking southern general on the scene, had gone down with a minié bullet in the leg, and precious time was lost while subordinate generals debated the finer points of commission dates and protocol. Longstreet, the overall wing commander, had paused to eat a quick bite of lunch, then gone off to find Bragg. It was nearly 3:00 P.M. by the time the Rebels gathered themselves sufficiently to attack again—more than enough time, in the view of some critics, for Sheridan to have made his way to Snodgrass Hill.[37]

Fellow Union general John B. Turchin, who stood with Thomas that day at Snodgrass Hill, later castigated Sheridan for his alleged lack of initiative. "It is surprising," Turchin wrote in his postwar study, *Chickamauga*, "why, as the senior officer, he did not assume the command of those troops and have handled them as he was eminently able to do. By taking the Crawfish-Spring road, he could have reached Vidito's [*sic*] house, and there have fallen upon the left flank of Longstreet's troops when they were out of breath from their exertions, and have then knocked the last of the Southern dash out of them."[38]

Something of the sort, in fact, was suggested to Sheridan by Wilder, whose mounted infantry had slowed but not stopped the Confederate advance at the Widow Glenn's. By way of Lieutenant Colonel Gates P. Thruston, McCook's assistant adjutant general, Wilder proposed that Sheridan join him in counterattacking the enemy flank. Sheridan responded that he could not rally his men, and recommended instead that Wilder "get out of there." Undaunted, Wilder was preparing to attack alone when he was interrupted by—of all people—Dana, who had gotten separated from the others in the unprecedented hurly-burly following the breakthrough. Hatless and winded, Dana demanded that Wilder personally escort him to Chattanooga so he could telegraph the news to Washington. By the time Wilder had sent Dana safely on his way with a civilian guide, the chance to counterattack the enemy already had been lost. For the rest of his life, Wilder maintained that such an attack would have succeeded, saying, "I would have struck them in flank and rear with five lines of Spencer rifles in the hands of the steadiest body of men I ever saw."[39]

In the meantime, Thruston overtook Sheridan, who was riding up the Dry Valley Road with Jefferson C. Davis amid the wreckage of their divisions. "General Phil was furious," Thruston observed. "Like the great Washington . . . he was swearing mad, and no wonder. The devoted Lytle and the truest and bravest had fallen in vain resistance around him. His splendid fighting qualities and his fine soldiers had not had half a chance. He had lost faith.'' Thruston offered to ride over to Thomas's position and ascertain the situation. Leaving the road and cutting diagonally across a field, he easily managed to reach Snodgrass Hill. Not surprisingly, Thomas immediately sent him back to fetch Sheridan and Davis, but by the time he reached them again, they had proceeded to the entrance of McFarland's Gap.[40]

At the mouth of the gap, Sheridan, Davis, and Negley stopped to discuss their next moves. They decided that Davis would stay there to protect the army's wagon trains, while Sheridan proceeded to Rossville and then doubled back to the battlefield along the only reasonably secure route, the LaFayette-Chattanooga Road. Negley would split the difference, going to Rossville to await further developments. Thruston arrived about this time, conveying Thomas's verbal order for Davis and Sheridan to join him on Snodgrass Hill. The excitable Davis immediately turned back, but Sheridan held fast to the original plan. His roundabout line of march, north to Rossville, then east and south to the battlefield, brought him into contact with Thomas's left about dusk, but by then Thomas had already begun withdrawing.[41]

Years later, supporters of Thomas made much of Sheridan's supposedly dilatory march, one going so far as to label a chapter in his worshipful biography of Thomas "Sheridan Deserts the Field." But the downgrading of Sheridan, dependent to a great degree on the unconfirmed testimony of Thruston, failed to take into account the fact that, as Sheridan noted, Confederate artillery occupying the ridge between Snodgrass Hill and the Dry Valley Road had effectively prevented a direct approach. And while Sheridan's subsequent return to the battlefield was not the remarkable feat of arms that Archibald Gracie, Jr., declared it to be in his 1911 study, *The Truth about Chickamauga*, it was nevertheless a more than adequate refutation of the spurious charge that he had quit the field.[42]

Given the chaotic situation following the Confederate break-through and the commanding general's precipitous abandonment of the battlefield, Sheridan's actions were professionally competent, if not necessarily valorous. At the very least, he managed to rally his shattered division, collect a substantial number of abandoned artillery, ammunition trains, and caissons, and bring his force into position to cover Thomas's subsequent retreat to Chattanooga. It was not, after all, Sheridan's army at Chickamauga, it was Rosecrans's. At the divisional level on which Sheridan functioned, responsibility principally involved, in the absence of direct orders to the contrary, one's own division. Neither the commanding general, Rosecrans, nor Sheridan's corps commander, McCook, remained on hand to provide alternative directions. Left to his own devices, Sheridan discussed the situation with the only two generals of equal rank remaining in the vicinity, decided upon a course of action, and duly implemented it. Revealingly, no official criticism of his conduct was ever voiced after the battle; on the contrary, Sheridan was praised by both Rosecrans and McCook, and in Washington the ever-helpful Halleck called his efforts "gallant." Sheridan's return to Chickamauga, late and unavailing as it was, saved his career from the professional ruin soon to be visited on Rosecrans, McCook, and Crittenden for their real or imagined failures that day.[43]

But that lay still in the future. Now, riding toward Rossville through the most melancholy evening of his life, Sheridan gave way to admittedly gloomy reflections. Not only had he lost 1,517 officers and men in a shockingly short time, but "it did not seem to me that the outlook for the next day was at all auspicious, unless the enemy was slow to improve his present advantage." He and Thomas, sitting together on a roadside fence, shared a drink of brandy, then parted for the night. Sheridan bedded down beneath a tree after a supper of coffee and bread provided by a sympathetic private. By his own admission, he was "very tired, very hungry, and much discouraged by what had taken place since morning."[44]

But Sheridan, in his despondency, underestimated Braxton Bragg's amazing knack for frittering away victories. Before the last Rebel yell had died away on Snodgrass Hill, Bragg was totting up his damages and turning aside suggestions that he chase the Union army out of Chattanooga. He responded to such importuning with a statement of fact couched as a question: "How can I? Here is two-fifths of my army left on the field, and my artillery is without horses." Bragg's general demeanor was anything but that of a man who had won a great, if somewhat incomplete, victory. At a time when speed was even more than usually essential, he temporized and equivocated, counting dead horses and captured equipment. And on the night of the day that he won Chickamauga, Bragg effectively lost Chattanooga.[45]

The disorganization of the Union army was so complete that a fresh demonstration of hostile intent likely would have driven it from Chattanooga. The majority of Bragg's subordinates certainly believed that to be the case. Longstreet, accustomed to Lee's aggressiveness, urged Bragg to follow up his victory, bypass Chattanooga, and move on Knoxville. Nathan Bedford Forrest also implored him to attack again, noting that "every hour is worth ten thousand men." Bragg opted instead to besiege the town. To the badly routed Union army, worn out by months of marching, fighting, and fleeing, such enforced immobility was a kind of mercy, a space in which to catch its breath.

On September 23, the day the Rebels invested Chattanooga, Abraham Lincoln convened an emergency session of his cabinet to hurry relief to the threatened town. Two corps from Major General George G. Meade's Army of the Potomac were dispatched to Chattanooga under the command of "Fighting Joe" Hooker, now professionally rehabilitated after his rout at Chancellorsville. As the Confederates had done prior to Chickamauga, the reinforcements were secretly transported by train. Meanwhile, Major General William T. Sherman was directed to bring four additional divisions east from Vicksburg. Soon, Union forces at Chattanooga would outnumber their besiegers.

For the time being, the Federals inside Chattanooga were engaged in the usual backbiting and fault-finding typical of a routed army. Coming in for a lion's share of the blame were the two luckless corps commanders, Crittenden and McCook. The ubiquitous Dana—a "loathsome pimp" in Gordon Granger's pungent phrase—informed Washington a week after Chickamauga that "a very serious fermentation" had taken place within the army owing to the "desertion" of the two at the height of the battle. Other generals, he said, had openly refused to serve under either man again. Worse yet, the army's respect for Rosecrans had "received an irreparable blow," the men in the ranks no longer cheering as their leader passed among them. "Under the present circumstances," Dana concluded direly, "I consider this army very unsafe in [Rosecrans's] hands."[46]

Lincoln resisted firing Rosecrans, although he conceded ruefully that, since Chickamauga, the hitherto indomitable general had been acting "confused and stunned, like a duck hit on the head." Political considerations, never far from the president's heart, argued against removing Rosecrans, at least until Ohio elected a new governor in October—Cincinnati-bred Rosy was one of the state's most popular officers. Then, too, Lincoln still felt a personal debt for Rosecrans's opportune victory at Stones River. Besides, it mattered less that Rosecrans had lost a tactical battle at Chickamauga than that he still held Chattanooga, whose loss Lincoln called a thorn in the Confederate vitals.[47]

Meanwhile, the situation inside Chattanooga worsened daily. Food for the forty thousand remaining Union troops had to be carted sixty backbreaking miles over treacherous mountain passes north of town. Torrential rains made the road nearly impassable; exhausted by the long slog, horses and mules died by the thousands. Confederate cavalry raided at will, burning supply wagons and sabering teams. Mobs of bluecoats trailed supply wagons into town, picking through the mud for scraps of food. Moldy crackers brought a dollar apiece on the open market, a cow's tail fetched ten times that much. One Kansas outfit even caught and ate a dog.

Sheridan's men fared better than most. A company of the Second Kentucky Cavalry, temporarily without orders, had attached itself to his division. Not one to miss an opportunity, he sent the Kentuckians foraging deep into the countryside, the result being that "I carried men and animals through our beleaguerment in pretty fair condition."[48]

By mid-October Rosecrans was gone, a victim of his own transgressions and Dana's malevolent pen. It was no secret to anyone that Dana was actively lobbying for a change of commanders. But while Rosecrans ignored well-intentioned warnings about "traitors from Washington now in camp," the Washington paper-shuffler kept up a steady jeremiad of telegrams alleging Rosecrans's unfitness for duty and even questioning his sanity. Alarmed and dismayed by the ongoing stalemate, Lincoln gave Grant command of the newly created Military Division of the Mississippi, comprising all major Union armies in the west. Grant was permitted the option of retaining Rosecrans as head of the Army of the Cumberland or replacing him with Thomas. Like countless others, Grant had crossed swords with Rosecrans in the past. He was not overly fond of Thomas, either, but "I accepted the latter."[49]

Once inside the encircled city, Grant went directly to Thomas's headquarters. There was a noticeable chill, not just of weather, in the air. Grant had unintentionally irritated the Rock of Chickamauga by sending him a somewhat panicky telegram advising him to hold Chattanooga at all costs—to which Thomas had snapped back famously, "I will hold the town till we starve." Now, met by a studied lack of hospitality, Grant did not concern himself with social niceties. Instead he demanded a detailed explanation of Rosecrans's reported plan to open a new supply route into town. Major General William F. Smith, who had helped think up the plan, was put in charge of the operation and given two days to carry it out.[50]

On the night of October 26–27, 1,500 handpicked Union soldiers floated around the toe of Moccasin Bend on specially constructed pontoon boats. Another 3,500 marched overland toward the ferry from Chattanooga. From Bridgeport, Hooker brought up his Potomac veterans. The surprise was complete, the Federals storming ashore like latter-day Marines, and by 10:00 A.M. the key river crossing at Brown's Ferry was in Union hands. Seventy-two hours after arriving at Chattanooga, Grant had opened the "Cracker Line." Fresh supplies and ammunition poured into town. Now it was only a matter of waiting for Sherman to arrive from Vicksburg before the Union army went back on the offensive.

Although Sheridan did not realize it, the successful assault at Brown's Ferry kept him from returning to a quartermaster's desk. Recalling Sheridan's role during the Pea Ridge campaign—and his own well-stocked table during the Corinth excursion—Halleck had suggested that Grant put Sheridan in charge of transporting supplies over the mountains. The Cracker Line made this unnecessary. Instead Sheridan retained his combat division, passing the long autumn weeks with the myriad mundane tasks of command. The monotonous days were interrupted by two unusual diversions, one pleasant, one not. The first involved a Cincinnati thespian named James E. Murdock, who had come to Chattanooga to retrieve his dead son, lost in the holocaust at Chickamauga. While in camp, Murdock kept busy—no doubt as therapy—giving impromptu patriotic recitations. "He never failed to excite intense interest in the breasts of all present," Sheridan recalled, "and when circumstances finally separated him from us, all felt that a debt of gratitude was due him that could never be paid." A year from now Murdock would find himself reciting a famous ode to Sheridan, in the wake of another desperate battle.[51]

Less diverting was the fate of three soldiers who had deserted after Chickamauga. As he had done at Murfreesboro, Sheridan had the division form a square to watch the execution. "It was the saddest spectacle I ever witnessed," he wrote, "but there could be no evasion, no mitigation of the full letter of the law; its timely enforcement was but justice to the brave spirits who had yet to fight the rebellion to the end."[52]

A day later Sherman arrived with reinforcements. Following the Cracker Line into Chattanooga, he met with Grant, who explained his plans for driving the enemy from the surrounding heights. Sherman's men were given the honor of spearheading the attack on Missionary Ridge, the main Rebel stronghold. Thomas's soldiers, Grant whispered, were too demoralized by their defeat at Chickamauga to leave their breastworks. This was unfair, and also untrue, but Grant had in mind Thomas's reluctance a week earlier to attack the ridge with only his four divisions. By urging Grant to wait until Sherman arrived, Thomas had saved him from a colossal error, but that did not prevent the commanding general from complaining darkly to Washington about "the fixed and immovable condition of the Army of the Cumberland."[53]

Conditions in the Rebel camp were at least as bad as those inside Chattanooga. Boredom, hunger, frostbite, and disease combined to make life miserable for the victors of Chickamauga. A day's rations frequently amounted to nothing more than a few hard crackers and a tablespoon of sugar. Many of the southerners were too hungry to sleep at night. Even worse was the slow decline of Confederate morale in the weeks following Chickamauga. Thrilled and emboldened by their army's great day, the men in the ranks had fully expected to drive the Yankees from Chattanooga and march unchecked to the Ohio River. Instead, to their near-unanimous disgust, Bragg had done nothing—worse than nothing, since they could clearly see the enemy strengthening his forces below. The common soldiers' contempt for Bragg was more than matched by that of their officers. In their eyes, the dour North Carolinian had once again frittered away victory and unavailed himself of his army's sacrifice. Mutual recriminations flew back and forth between Bragg and his subordinates, until Jefferson Davis himself felt called upon to visit Bragg's headquarters in a fruitless attempt to settle the matter.[54]

On November 22 a Rebel deserter came into Sheridan's camp with a report that two more divisions had left Missionary Ridge to support James Longstreet's ill-conceived drive on Knoxville. Sheridan passed the word to his superiors. Grant, sensing a trap, ordered Thomas to determine Bragg's true intentions. Thomas sent Wood's division toward Orchard Knob, a small hill occupied by the Rebels midway between the town and the ridge. Sheridan's division moved behind Wood in reserve. Believing the advance was merely a review, southern troops on Orchard Knob were stunned when the Federals kept coming toward them. As Grant and Thomas watched from nearby Fort Wood, the blue-clad soldiers fought their way into the enemy breastworks and soon secured the salient. Sheridan's division began throwing up rifle pits and bringing forward artillery batteries. Even the hard-to-please Grant was impressed. "The troops moved under fire with all the precision of veterans on parade," he reported to Halleck.[55]

That same night Sherman's men crossed the Tennessee River directly opposite the north end of Missionary Ridge, preparatory to their planned assault on the enemy-held heights. In Grant's overall scheme, Thomas would menace the ridge from the center, while Hooker would advance from Lookout Valley, threaten Lookout Mountain, and, if practicable, move forward to the south end of the ridge. Sherman's crossing went well at first, but when he brought his troops into position at the north end of the ridge, he was mortified to discover that he was atop a separate spur, more than a mile away from the Confederate flank. Worse yet, the steady sound of digging and scraping indicated that the enemy, far from being surprised by the move, was busily entrenching on the heights beyond.

The next morning, while Sherman pondered his unhappy position, Hooker's troops assaulted Lookout Mountain. Three divisions, one from each of the three armies now on the scene, made the climb up the steep, rocky cliffs. Through the smoky haze, eager onlookers inside Chattanooga watched as blue-jacketed figures advanced steadily upward amid orange flashes of gunfire and puffs of cannon smoke. By early afternoon the greatly outnumbered Rebels had been routed. At dawn the next morning members of the Eighth Kentucky Volunteers planted the American flag on a prominent outcropping as thunderous cheers rang out from the Union garrison below. "Impregnable" Lookout Mountain had fallen in a day.

Now it was Sherman's turn. To Brigadier General Hugh Ewing, his brother-in-law, Sherman said with studied casualness, "You may go up the hill if you like." That presupposed a certain freedom of movement not actually available to Ewing or his soldiers. Grant's sortie against Orchard Knob two days earlier had induced Bragg to recall Major General Patrick Cleburne's superb fighting division and place it on the far right of his line, directly across from Sherman's jumping-off point. As Ewing's lead division advanced across the intervening hollow and began climbing the ridge side, Cleburne's troops stopped them with a storm of fire. Rebel cannoneers depressed the muzzles of their guns and bowled cannonballs down the hill at the Yankees; others rolled large rocks onto the bluecoats where they lay.[56]

Sherman, watching from the heights beyond, kept signaling, "Where is Thomas?" Imperturbable to the last, the Rock of Chickamauga responded, "I am here." "Here" was beside Grant on Orchard Knob, where the unsmiling Union commander watched the proceedings silently, an unlit cigar clamped tightly in his mouth. Not only had Sherman failed to take his end of the ridge, but Hooker's column had been delayed crossing rain-swollen Chattanooga Creek and was late moving into place at the far end of the ridge. At 3:00 P.M. Sherman signaled Grant that he had done all he could do for one day. Grant responded frostily, "Attack again."[57]

Sherman tried once more, to no good effect, then hunkered down for the duration of the afternoon, thoroughly whipped by Cleburne's single division. It was now close to four in the afternoon. Grant turned to Thomas and asked, "Don't you think it's about time to advance against the rifle pits?" Thomas wordlessly motioned for the prearranged signal—six guns fired in rapid succession—to be given. Gordon Granger, who had been annoying everyone on Orchard Knob by personally lobbing cannonballs at the ridge with a small fieldpiece, eagerly carried out the order. Half a mile away the 23,000 men in the Army of the Cumberland moved forward as one, their destination the bristling enemy rifle pits at the base of Missionary Ridge.[58]

Sheridan's division was third in line. On his left was Wood's division, which had let the Rebels through the gap at Chickamauga; on his right was Richard Johnson's, which had fractured so badly at Stones River. Except for some early-morning picketing, no one had done anything all day. That was the rub. To a man, the Cumberlanders smoldered at the implication they were fit only for reserve duty, while Sherman's men presumably rolled down Missionary Ridge and politely freed them from their self-imposed trap. They watched with a certain bitter satisfaction as Sherman, instead, was stopped in his tracks. They had their own score to settle with the Rebel army. The last thing Sheridan said to his division before it moved out was "Remember Chickamauga." All down the line men were shouting the name of the battle, as though it were an incantation, or a spell to be exorcised only with blood.[59]

The army moved over an open plain, battle flags in the forefront, regimental bands blaring away in the rear. All eyes in both armies were trained on the advance. Rebel artillerists opened on the approaching horde, red-black explosions flowering the sky. The men in the front ranks broke into a dead run, heading straight for the enemy. Sheridan, riding at the front of Colonel Charles Harker's brigade, looked back to see his soldiers grimly lowering their bayonets as they came. All along the line Union attackers poured into the Rebels at the base of the ridge. Resistance magically melted away. Some Confederate units had been told to fall back at the first enemy contact; others, ignorant of the battle plan, thought their comrades were simply deserting and hastily joined them. Southern sharpshooters in a second line of pits halfway up the ridge had to hold their fire while their mates pulled back. As more and more Federals reached the works, they began to bunch up, milling about in confusion as enemy fire rained down from above. The rifle pits quickly became, in one survivor's words, "a hideous slaughter pen." The men at the front soon realized they could not stay where they were—they must either go forward or die.[60]

Sheridan, for one, had anticipated as much. Before the advance he sent an aide back to Granger to ask whether they should stop at the pits or continue up the ridge. Now, without waiting for Granger's answer—or Sheridan's either, for that matter—the men began climbing Missionary Ridge, advancing in small V-shaped clusters behind their regimental flags. Before them disorganized Confederates stumbled backward. Sheridan's messenger returned with Granger's answer: they were only to carry the base of the ridge. It was too late for that now, even if Sheridan had wanted to recall them. Seizing a flask from his orderly, Sheridan raised it to a group of Rebel officers outlined clearly against the crest. "Here's at you!" he shouted. An exploding shell sprayed him with dirt. "That's damn ungenerous! I shall take those guns for that!" he cried.[61]

Everywhere along a two-mile front, Union soldiers scrambled upward; individual units raced each other to the top. Grant, watching in disbelief from Orchard Knob, demanded to know who had ordered the charge. "I don't know," said Thomas. "I did not." The excitable Granger, although also disowning responsibility, could not resist adding, "When those fellows get started, all hell can't stop them." Grant, unconvinced, warned that someone would suffer if the attack should fail.[62]

Sheridan, aboard Rienzi, followed a winding dirt path toward the crest. Frantic Rebels, their artillery too poorly sited to fire directly into the enemy, lit shell fuses and rolled cannonballs down the ridge; others attempted to drag their guns away. All along the crest Confederate resistance was crumbling. The dramatic, impetuous charge had proven too much for the dispirited Confederates. With Yankees crashing in on them from all sides, pouring a deadly enfilading fire down their flanks, the long-suffering veterans of Shiloh, Perryville, Stones River, and Chickamauga did something they had never done before, and would never do again in such great numbers. They ran.

Sheridan reined Rienzi through a low place in the Rebel entrenchments and joined his delighted comrades on the crest. Colonel Joseph Conrad of the Second Missouri, who had drolly reported the presence of the two female troopers at Murfreesboro, rushed up to urge Sheridan to dismount before he was struck by a stray shot. "I accepted his excellent advice," Sheridan reported, "and it probably saved my life." Conrad was not so lucky; he went down with a serious thigh wound at the instant of his solicitude. The ridge was swarming with Union victors, the last Confederates fleeing down the opposite side. "My God," cried one Indiana private, "come and see them run!" Sheridan leaped astride one of the cannons that had showered him with dirt a few minutes before. Wrapping his banty legs around the barrel, he swung his hat and cheered. Harker followed suit, but mistakenly chose a newly fired gun and scorched his rear end so badly that he couldn't ride a horse for weeks. Granger appeared on the scene and rode happily among the men, good-naturedly threatening to court-martial them for "disobeying orders." Cheers and laughter rang from one end of the ridge to the other; hats and knapsacks sailed through the air. In less than an hour the siege of Chattanooga had been broken.[63]

Back at Orchard Knob, Grant and the others watched, transfixed. Dana, whose ceaseless vilification of Rosecrans had undermined that gifted but flawed general and brought Grant to Chattanooga in the first place, was nearly beside himself with joy. "Glory to God!" he wired Washington. "The day is decisively ours. Missionary Ridge has just been carried by a magnificent charge of Thomas's troops." Grant was less sanguine; things had not worked the way he planned. "Damn the battle," he was alleged to say. "I had nothing to do with it."[64]

The charge had indeed been astonishing, but the most important part of the battle, from Sheridan's standpoint, was still to come. Half a mile away, on the far side of the ridge, the Confederates were attempting to bring away what was left of their artillery. Sheridan cut short his victory celebration and ordered Harker and Colonel Charles Wagner to pursue the enemy to Chickamauga Station, where Bragg had his supply depot. Colonel Francis Sherman's brigade would follow in reserve. Wagner's pursuit gobbled up another nine pieces of Rebel artillery before he and Harker ran into stout resistance a mile east of Missionary Ridge. Sheridan sent the 15th Indiana and 26th Ohio regiments around the enemy right, their ranks silhouetted against the early-rising moon. Flanked on either side, the southerners fell back, leaving behind another two cannons and a number of wagons. Sheridan now called a halt to the pursuit, uncomfortably aware that his division was the only northern unit still actively engaged. Hurrying back to Missionary Ridge, he begged Granger for more troops. Granger, however, thought they had done well enough for one day, although he allowed Sheridan to continue his pursuit. At 2:00 A.M. Sheridan reluctantly stopped for the night, having single-handedly orchestrated the only effective follow-up to the smashing victory at Missionary Ridge.[65]

His bulldog tenacity was not lost on the army's commander. "To Sheridan's prompt movement," Grant reported, "the Army of the Cumberland and the nation are indebted for the bulk of the capture of prisoners, artillery, and small-arms that day. Except for his prompt pursuit, so much in this way would not have been accomplished." As it was, Sheridan claimed more than 1,700 prisoners and seventeen artillery pieces, at a loss of 1,346 men, one-tenth of whom were killed outright on Missionary Ridge. In all, Sheridan's casualties accounted for nearly half of the Army of the Cumberland's total. For the first time since Perryville, however, he had managed not to lose a brigade commander—Harker's scorched bottom notwithstanding.[66]

Sheridan did lose eleven of the cannons his men had captured on Missionary Ridge. These, he said indignantly, "were hauled off the field and appropriated by an officer of high rank." That officer, Brigadier General William Hazen, had commanded the brigade nearest to Sheridan in the climb up the ridge. When Sheridan's men left to pursue the enemy to Chickamauga Creek, Hazen blithely added the fieldpieces to his booty. Despite Sheridan's demands that the guns be returned to their rightful captors, Hazen refused to give them up. What was more, Hazen also claimed that his unit had been first to the top of Missionary Ridge, an honor Sheridan hotly disputed. Twenty years later the two generals were still fighting over that hour of glory.[67]

But what counted most was the approval of the army's commanding general, and in this regard Sheridan clearly triumphed. With his bold and quick-thinking conduct at Missionary Ridge he had put to rest any lingering doubts concerning his uncharacteristic performance at Chickamauga. Like the much-maligned army in which he served, he had redeemed his honor and avenged his losses. Under the unforgetting eye of Ulysses S. Grant he had helped to win a mighty victory at Chattanooga, one that confirmed Grant's unrivaled status as the North's preeminent man-at-arms. Crowned by such laurels, Grant would soon head east to even greater renown. And in his wake, shining with reflected glory, Phil Sheridan would follow, tugged by the force field of Grant's inexorable rise.

5

CAVALRY COMMANDER

ON THE LAST DAY of February, 1864, Abraham Lincoln signed into law a bill reviving the rank of lieutenant general of the army. The rank had remained vacant since the passing of George Washington, the only previous holder of the title, a generation before. Like so much else the Father of His Country touched with his giant hands, the rank had entered a near-mystical realm of superstition, reverence, and awe. Now, with one swish of Lincoln's pen, it succeeded into the waiting grasp of the least prepossessing candidate for greatness anyone could imagine: U. S. Grant of Galena, Illinois.

Grant advanced on the capital the way he advanced on the enemy—with the same saturnine implacability he habitually trained on a disappointing world. Summoned to the White House, he simply appeared at the door of the East Room, where the president's weekly reception was being held, and waited silently until Lincoln caught sight of him in the crowd and declared, "Why, here is General Grant. Well, this is a great pleasure." The next day, at a special cabinet meeting, he officially received his lieutenant general's commission. Despite the presence of certain unconvinced doubters—Pennsylvania Congressman Thaddeus Stevens, for one, archly observed that even saints are not canonized until after death—the vast majority of Washingtonians, like the rest of the war-weary nation, turned to Grant as their appointed savior.[1]

In truth, Grant did have a plan to save the Union, but it was a harsh prescription for a serious illness. With the war now entering its fourth spring, the North had roughly twice as many men-at-arms as the South, a preponderance not nearly as decisive as it seemed, since even the most obtuse of generals now realized they needed such an edge whenever they had to mount an attack. Grant proposed, with deceptive simplicity, to improve those odds by seeing to it that there was no rest, anywhere, for anyone—he would send the various Union armies attacking simultaneously on all fronts, and keep them attacking until something broke. The Confederates, thrown off balance by unremitting pressure, would be unable to concentrate at any particular point. Lincoln assured Grant that he would have all the men he needed for the job, which amounted to the simple arithmetic of subtraction, one by one, of the enemy's dwindling defenders. When enough Rebels had been subtracted, the North would win. That was Grant's plan.

Phil Sheridan, who had learned his mathematics in a Somerset, Ohio, dry-goods store, was not privy to Grant's Olympian ciphering. In fact, at the moment of Grant's ascendancy, he was not even with the Union army in Tennessee, having taken advantage of the winter lull in fighting to go on his first extended leave of the war, visiting the Ohio homeplace, Chicago, and Milwaukee. The forty-day furlough was a much-needed break for Sheridan, who, besides fighting Rebels for the past two years from Mississippi to Missionary Ridge, had been engaged most recently in what he termed "a series of blunders, lasting through the entire winter," involving the relief of supposedly imperiled Knoxville, Tennessee.[2]

Immediately after the battles for Chattanooga, Lincoln (who had something of a one-track mind when it came to Union-loving East Tennessee) had insisted that Grant send a relief force to Knoxville, then being menaced by Confederate General James Longstreet's twelve-thousand-man force. Accordingly, Grant had dispatched his mercurial confidant, William Sherman, on a forced march to the garrisoned town a hundred miles away. By the time

Sherman arrived, the Federals had already withstood a gruesomely mismanaged Rebel attack on Knoxville's Fort Sanders, then settled back for a post-Thanksgiving feast in honor of their would-be deliverers. Sherman was so disgusted by the stark contrast between his own sore-footed, half-starved troops and Major General Ambrose Burnside's well-fed headquarters staff that he immediately turned around and headed back to Chattanooga, leaving behind an unhappy Gordon Granger to guard against Longstreet's unlikely return.

Sheridan, commanding one of Granger's two divisions—T. J. Wood of Chickamauga's "fatal order" fame had the other—spent the next several weeks attempting mainly to feed and clothe his weatherbeaten regulars in the picked-over countryside of East Tennessee. Few of his men had overcoats, tents, or heavy clothing suitable for the chilly Tennessee winter; hundreds were reduced to wearing "a sort of moccasin, made from their blankets" in place of shoes. At one point a much-needed supply train arrived from Chattanooga with a consignment of new clothing for Sheridan's men, but the department commander at Knoxville, Major General John G. Foster, had the cargo distributed equally among all the Union divisions, much to Sheridan's chagrin.[3]

With bad weather setting in and campaigning at a standstill, no one wanted to be stuck in out-of-the-way East Tennessee, least of all the army's recalcitrant commanders. Burnside had already taken his leave, citing exhaustion from his official duties, which some cynics felt had consisted mainly of resisting any and all calls for help from his hard-pressed comrades in Chattanooga prior to that city's dramatic deliverance. Next to leave was Foster, who decided that his old war wound—from the Mexican War—was acting up again. He was followed by Major General John G. Parke, Burnside's former chief of staff, who in turn passed the baton to Granger. "By this time," Sheridan noted dryly, "the transmission of power seemed almost a disease. At any rate it was catching." Just as quickly, Granger unloaded on Sheridan, who already knew there was little responsibility, and less authority, in the temporary command of the Army of the Ohio. Brigadier General August Willich, a German-born veteran of the punctilious Prussian army, archly observed that the way things were going, a corporal would soon command the entire Union army.[4]

Granger's eventual reappearance forestalled that piquant spectacle, and Sheridan took advantage of his superior's return by going immediately on extended leave. He had just returned to his headquarters at Loudon, Tennessee, on the evening of March 23, 1864, when he was handed a telegram from Washington: "Lieutenant General Grant directs that Major General Sheridan immediately repair to Washington and report to the adjutant-general of the army."

Sheridan did not know what to make of the order, although he may have supposed he was going to be given Granger's corps in reward for his aggressive showing at Missionary Ridge. It was no secret that Grant had become disgusted with Granger's rather antic behavior during the past few months, and indeed had considered giving Sheridan his old benefactor's command. For now, all Sheridan knew was that the order meant a severing of relations with the Second Division, which he had led, in its various incarnations, since Bull Nelson's death in Kentucky in October 1862.[5]

Sheridan left Loudon by train the next day. He had intended to make his exit without undue fanfare, much as Rosecrans, in very different circumstances, had departed Chattanooga the previous autumn. "The bond existing between them and me," Sheridan recalled, "had grown to such depth of attachment that I feared to trust my emotions in any formal parting from a body of soldiers who, from our mutual devotion, had long before lost their official designation, and by general consent within and without the command were called 'Sheridan's division.' " News of the general's departure inevitably filtered down to the men in camp, and he was greeted at the railroad station by a spontaneous turnout of the entire division, which ringed the hillsides above the station "and as the cars moved out for Chattanooga . . . waved me farewell with demonstrations of affection."[6]

In Chattanooga, George H. Thomas, still commanding the Army of the Cumberland, told Sheridan the staggering news—he was to be given charge of the cavalry corps in the Virginia-based Army of the Potomac. This was not at all what Sheridan had expected. Not only had he exclusively commanded infantry since leaving Mississippi nearly two years earlier; now he was to head an entire corps, in a different army and a different theater of war. Nor would he have been reassured to know that the presiding spirit of his advancement, Grant, had wanted someone else instead. When intramural pressures mediated against Grant's first choice, Major General William B. Franklin, Henry Halleck somewhat laconically suggested Sheridan for the post—"How would Sheridan do?"—and Grant acceded, with what actual measure of enthusiasm it is impossible to say, although Grant professed in later years that Sheridan had been the very man he wanted for the job.[7]

For a soldier as concerned with the lay of the land, literally and figuratively, as Sheridan, the notion of going to Virginia to fight on the enemy's home soil was distinctly unsettling. What he needed, first of all, was someone who was familiar with both the Army of the Potomac and the alien countryside over which it had fought. He found just such a man in Captain James W. Forsyth of Ohio, a former colleague from academy days and the Pacific Northwest. Forsyth had been George B. McClellan's inspector general during the Peninsula and Antietam campaigns and thus knew most of the ranking officers in the east. He readily agreed to serve as Sheridan's chief of staff, initiating a close personal and professional relationship between the two men that would last for over two decades, ending only with Sheridan's death and Forsyth's controversial role as commander of the vengeful Seventh Cavalry at the Wounded Knee massacre in 1890.

With Forsyth, brother Michael Sheridan (newly arrived to serve as Phil's headquarters aide), and Lieutenant Thomas W. C. Moore in tow, Sheridan left Chattanooga for Washington on March 29, arriving six days later and checking into the landmark

Willard Hotel, one block from the White House. Immediately he went to report to Halleck (Grant was away from the city for the day), and Halleck just as quickly escorted him to the office of the formidable secretary of war, Edwin M. Stanton, scourge of unsuccessful generals and importunate office-seekers everywhere. Sheridan, by his own account, was now less than physically prepossessing, having been worn down to a wraithlike 115 pounds, and his legs had not gotten any longer in the interim. He had the distinct impression that Stanton was less than taken by his appearance, and "if I had ever possessed any self-assertion in manner or speech, it certainly vanished in the presence of the imperious Secretary, whose name at the time was the synonym for all that was cold and formal."[8]

Last stop on his list of duty calls was the White House, where Abraham Lincoln shook his hand, exchanged a few pleasantries, and hoped aloud that Sheridan would somehow be able to meet Grant's expectations. The president quoted back to him, verbatim, Grant's dissatisfied critique of the Army of the Potomac's cavalry, and concluded the somewhat mutually disappointing interview with the stale joke, "Who ever saw a dead cavalryman?" If Lincoln had intended to stiffen Sheridan's resolve, he needn't have bothered; Sheridan had seen enough dead cavalrymen to know they died as suitably as the next man when a bullet found them, or a saber thrust. Glum and dispirited, he returned to Willard's for a last night's sleep on clean linen before joining his new command in the field.[9]

Canny professional that he was, Sheridan doubtless understood that he was stepping into a difficult situation. His immediate predecessor, Major General Alfred Pleasonton, had been exiled to that repository of disgraced commanders, the Department of the Missouri, owing to "jealousy and ill feeling" within the Army of the Potomac. Brigadier General Henry Davies, who had commanded a brigade under Pleasonton and would continue to do so under Sheridan, attributed Pleasonton's downfall to a difference of opinion with terrible-tempered George Gordon Meade, the army's titular commander, over the proper use of cavalry. Grant's explanation for the move, that he was "dissatisfied with the little that had been accomplished by the cavalry so far in the war," pointedly ignored the fact that at Brandy Station, Virginia, in June 1863, the Union cavalry under Pleasonton had risen up and given Major General J. E. B. Stuart's vaunted Confederate horsemen the fight of their lives.[10]

In fact, Pleasonton's downfall seems to have stemmed from two entirely different causes. First, as head of the cavalry, he had complained loudly and bitterly about the newly created Cavalry Bureau's inept handling of his demands for horses. The staggering number of mounts needed to replace those lost to combat or disease—some six thousand a month—would have strained any government agency's abilities, but Pleasonton made few friends with his abrasive demands. Equally damaging to his position was his disapproval of the so-called Dahlgren-Kilpatrick Raid in February 1864, a crackpated, unsavory scheme to raid Richmond, free Union prisoners, and assassinate southern leaders. Pleasonton had argued against the raid, the brainchild of division commander Judson Kilpatrick, but Meade had approved it. Worst of all, insofar as Pleasonton's job security was concerned, the raid had been an abysmal failure. Being right had not endeared him to the vinegary Meade.[11]

News of Pleasonton's downfall raced through the cavalry before Sheridan's arrival at the corps' Culpeper, Virginia, headquarters on April 5. His advent was "not received with much cordiality" by the officers or men of his new command. Few, if any, knew about his brief but auspicious stint as a cavalryman in Mississippi two years earlier. Hearing only that he was an infantry commander, they naturally resented being handed over to a humble foot-slogger. The easterners also disliked the fact that Sheridan had served exclusively in the western theater of the war. Previous experience with the likes of blowhard Major General John Pope, who had led the army to disaster at the Second Battle of Bull Run, "had not induced the belief that the West was the point of the compass from which the advent of wise men bringing rich gifts of victory and success was to be confidently expected," as Davies observed archly.[12]

But Sheridan rapidly disarmed his critics by his matter-of-fact assumption of command and his politic retention of Pleasonton's former staff. In contrast to his punctilious predecessor, Sheridan seemed refreshingly down to earth. "He would as soon borrow a light from the pipe of an enlisted man as from the cigar of an officer," one low-born trooper remarked approvingly. Major Benjamin W. Crowninshield, a grateful holdover from Pleasonton's staff, was pleased to note that the corps' new commander "had no favorites but the men who best carried out his orders."[13]

It was well that Sheridan managed, early on, to engage his officers' loyalties. There was much work to be done, and not much time in which to do it. Riding down to headquarters on the same train as Grant, Sheridan heard firsthand the plan for the upcoming campaign. On or about the first of May the various Union armies, from Virginia to the Rio Grande, would begin a concerted offensive aimed at seizing control of the war from the South. In the west, their old friend Sherman would drive into Georgia from his hard-won base in Chattanooga, with orders to "get into the interior of the enemy's country as far as you can, inflicting all the damage you can against their war resources." Meanwhile the Army of the Potomac, with Grant in position at Meade's elbow, would move against Robert E. Lee's fabled army, making it, rather than the enemy capital of Richmond, its main objective. Sheridan's role, as cavalry commander, would be to spearhead the crossing of the Rapidan River, secure the vital fords, and assist the infantry in transiting, as quickly as possible, the forbidding countryside known as the Wilderness, one hundred square miles of marshland and brambles, and flushing Lee's army into the open for a last gigantic fight to the finish.[14]

Grand strategy was fine for the general-in-chief, but Sheridan first had to consider the parlous state of his new command. After a long winter of riding picket, guarding trains, and escorting messengers, interrupted only by the poorly planned and embarrassingly executed Dahlgren-Kilpatrick Raid, the cavalry corps was grievously worn down. Men and horses had been overworked, underfed, and poorly sheltered. Captain F. C. Newhall, inspecting the state of the cavalry prior to the spring campaign, found "very large deficiencies of arms and horses," poorly located and badly maintained campsites, and a decided lack of supervision by regimental officers. All in all, said Newhall, the cavalry corps was "not in condition to perform active duty with credit. . . . I am convinced that both divisions cannot put into line of battle 5,000 efficient cavalry at the present time."[15]

The cause of such disarray, as Sheridan saw it, was Meade's hidebound use of cavalry. The army commander deemed his horsemen "fit for little more than guard and picket duty," Sheridan groused, and even expected his cavalry chief to camp at army headquarters—"practically as one of his staff, through whom he would give his detailed directions as, in his judgment, occasion required." While the Rebels wintered their cavalry in the rear, Meade had his weary troopers riding a sixty-mile picket line around the comfortably encamped, unthreatened infantry. Unless Meade reduced the frequency and length of picket duty, Sheridan warned, the horses and men would "be of but little service in the upcoming campaign."[16]

Meade agreed to lighten the load on the cavalry, but he was not so forthcoming on Sheridan's second proposal: that he be allowed to concentrate the hitherto scattered regiments and use the entire corps to fight the enemy cavalry en masse. It was Sheridan's hardly revolutionary idea that cavalry should fight cavalry and infantry fight infantry. Meade was "staggered" (Sheridan's word) by the brash proposal—who would protect the army's vulnerable supply trains and exposed flanks?—and not much convinced by his new chieftain's truculent guarantee that he would "make it so lively for the enemy's cavalry" that the army would not have to worry about the safety of its flanks. For the time being, Sheridan realized, he would have to bide his time. But not for long.[17]

In the meantime, he busied himself with the day-to-day responsibilities of his new command—drilling and inspecting the thirty-one regiments of the corps, refitting the men with better weapons and mounts, and getting to know his subordinate generals, none of whom had ever served with him before. Of the three divisional commanders, two were newcomers like himself. Delaware-born Brigadier General Alfred T. A. Torbert, commanding the First Division, had just been appointed to replace Brigadier General John Buford, hero of Gettysburg, who had died in Washington of typhoid fever four months earlier. Torbert, an 1855 graduate of West Point, had seen a great deal of action during the Peninsula Campaign and at Second Bull Run, South Mountain, and Antietam—but always as an infantry officer. His unexpected appointment to the cavalry sent promising young Brigadier General Wesley Merritt, the interim division head, back to command of the Reserve Brigade.

Less unexpected was the banishment of Kilpatrick from his post as commander of the Third Division. Known unaffectionately to his men as "Kill-Cavalry" for his reckless and aggressive ways, Kilpatrick had been in military eclipse since the failure of his Richmond raid. Without bothering to check with Sheridan, Grant transferred Kilpatrick to Sherman's army in the west, replacing him with twenty-six-year-old Brigadier General James Harrison "Dandy" Wilson, a former member of Grant's personal staff and most recently head of the embattled Cavalry Bureau. Sheridan, who would never much care for Wilson (the feeling was mutual), complained to Grant that he was "very much embarrassed" by Wilson's appointment, which created seniority problems between Wilson and his subordinate commanders, but the decision stood. Wilson would have a stormy six-month career with the Army of the Potomac before being transferred, like Kilpatrick before him, to the west, where his subsequent accomplishments—particularly his raid on Selma, Alabama, at war's end—would come to rival Sheridan's own.[18]

Brigadier General David McMurtrie Gregg, an experienced horseman from the old army, commanded the Second Division.

Quiet, competent, and well liked by both his fellow officers and the rank and file, the full-bearded Gregg was a welcome holdover from the Pleasonton regime. Also on hand was a young firebrand named George Armstrong Custer, a newly made general who commanded a brigade under Torbert, and Custer's fellow Michigander, Colonel Russell Alger, who had done so much to help Sheridan obtain his first command two years earlier in Mississippi. Altogether, the cavalry corps numbered about 12,500 sabers, plus another 860 gunners in eight flying batteries.

In the predawn hours of May 4, 1864, Grant's ambitious offensive began. Sheridan, who had been given advance word of the army's movement ten days earlier, had already sent Wilson ahead to scout the major fords across the Rapidan, which were found to be unguarded. At the same time he told his three division commanders to draw subsistence-level rations for the men, issue them 150 rounds of ammunition apiece, and be ready to move at a moment's notice. That notice came on the afternoon of May 3. Wilson's Third Division was to spearhead the crossing at Germanna Ford, Gregg's Second Division would cross at Ely's Ford, six miles downstream, and the two groups of horsemen would secure the vital crossings until Grant's four infantry corps had come up. Torbert's First Division was to remain behind the Rapidan, guarding the army's four-thousand-strong wagon train, until May 5, when it too would cross the river.[19]

The crossings went smoothly—too smoothly, perhaps. Less gifted strategists than Robert E. Lee might well have anticipated the Union moves; but Lee wanted the enemy to cross the Rapidan. Once across, Grant's army would pass into the evil-looking, evil-smelling Wilderness, where gnarled, vine-throttled trees grew out of the marshy underbrush, so close together that the entire landscape was swathed in a perpetual dusk. Lee planned to let the Yankees enter the Wilderness; he did not intend that they should leave it.

Avid topographer that he was, Sheridan already had foreseen that the benighted countryside of the Wilderness, with its nearly impenetrable thickets, haphazardly running streams, quicksand-spotted bogs, and intermittent, narrow roads, was poor ground for large-scale cavalry operations. Any fighting there would have to be done on foot, in small groups, along the fringes of the over-arching woods, since columns of horsemen using the cramped roadways were sure to invite a Rebel ambush. Not that Meade wanted his cavalry fighting; after effecting the river crossings, their principal assignment was to guard the trains and cover the army's left flank as it groped its way through the Wilderness. On May 5 Sheridan received a flurry of orders from Meade to draw in his cavalry and "take immediate dispositions for the protection of the trains." Unsurprisingly, he balked at such a passive role in the great battle now commencing. "I cannot do anything with the cavalry except to act on the defensive," he complained to Meade. "Why cannot infantry be sent to guard the trains and let me take the offensive?" Meade's response, that Sheridan was fully autho-rized to detach parts of his command for such secondary opera-tions as cutting the enemy's communications, did not placate his salty subordinate, who still wanted to go full-bore after the Rebel cavalry—and the devil take the hindmost.[20]

While Sheridan's troopers obediently guarded the wagon trains, the awful slaughter of the two-day Battle of the Wilder-ness exploded around them. Mindful of what had happened to the Union army at nearby Chancellorsville a year earlier, Grant had not wanted to fight Lee in the nightmare locale beyond the Rap-idan. Forty-eight hours was all he needed to get through the Wilderness and interpose himself between Lee's army and Rich-mond. An additional forty-eight hours, he joked, and he would be in Richmond itself—"That is, if General Lee becomes a party to the agreement. But if he objects, the trip will undoubtedly be prolonged." Grant proved to be a better prophet than comedian. Reacting swiftly to the Union advance, Lee sent his three infantry corps hurrying along parallel roads into the Wilderness, where they struck the overconfident Yankees with all the savagery they could muster. Grant responded in kind, and the carnival of killing known variously as the Overland Campaign or the Forty Days began in earnest.[21]

Despite Meade's best efforts, the cavalry corps inevitably was drawn into the fighting. On May 6 and 7 the action centered on Todd's Tavern, a key Wilderness crossroads guarding the junction of Brock and Catharpin roads two miles south of the Union left flank. Stuart's Confederate horsemen, attempting to get into the Federal rear, were first checked, then repulsed, and finally driven completely from the woods around Todd's Tavern by elements of the First and Second Divisions. Young Custer particularly distinguished himself in this running series of skirmishes, described by one of his Michigan officers as "sulky, stubborn, bulldog fighting" between dismounted horsemen racing to hold or carry hastily improvised breastworks.[22]

Sheridan sent Meade a flurry of messages detailing the "splendid" and "handsome" success of the corps. But Meade, understandably preoccupied by the mounting carnage of the Wilderness, took little notice of the seemingly secondary skirmishing between the two cavalries. All this would change dramatically when Grant, tired of battering against Lee's defenses, decided to take a different tack. He directed Meade to swing around Lee's right flank, a corps at a time, and hasten toward Todd's Tavern and Spotsylvania Court House, five miles southeast. Suddenly the crossroads at Spotsylvania became crucially important. If Grant got there first, he would be between Lee's army and Richmond. Lee would have no choice but to attack, despite the fact he had scarcely half as many men as Grant. Even given the current rate of exchange, 17,666 Federal casualties to 7,800 Confederates in the Wilderness, such enormous bloodletting still favored the North, which could more easily replace the men it lost. So long as Grant kept his nerve—and he showed no signs of losing it—he ultimately would win a war of attrition. He knew it, Lee knew it, and the armies they led were about to learn it.[23]

Sheridan, in furtherance of Grant's plan, devised a scheme of his own to take and hold Spotsylvania for the Union army. On the night of May 7 he directed Wilson to ride west by way of Fredericksburg to the strategic crossroads settlement, seize it, and establish a bridgehead on the western bank of the Po River at Snell's Bridge to contest any Rebel crossing. At the same time, he sent orders to Gregg and Merritt (who was temporarily commanding Torbert's division; Torbert was down with an abscessed spine) to ride at daybreak from Todd's Tavern and seize the other two river crossings, Corbin's Bridge and Blockhouse Bridge, to cover the move on Spotsylvania.[24]

There was nothing wrong with Sheridan's plan, but in the typical chaos of a night march made in the presence of the enemy through the inky gloom of the Wilderness, things predictably went awry. Wilson got to Spotsylvania easily enough, but by morning found himself confronting an ever-increasing force of Rebel cavalry and infantry. Unknown to Sheridan, Confederate Major General Richard H. Anderson, commanding Lee's I Corps in place of the wounded James Longstreet, had made a night march of his own to Spotsylvania, preceded by Major General Fitzhugh Lee's cavalry division. In the meantime, Gregg and Merritt, bivouacking at Todd's Tavern, six miles away, had run afoul—quite literally, as it turned out—of the army's commanding general and his lead infantry corps. The result was a delay that might have proved fatal to Meade's army, and would at any rate soon prove fatal to thousands of unfortunate foot soldiers who would pay with their lives for the confusion and disorganization of the night's advance.[25]

When Meade arrived at Todd's Tavern between midnight and 1:00 A.M. on May 8, he found Gregg and Merritt encamped in the fields and on either side of the only road leading directly to Spotsylvania. They were without orders, they said, so Meade gave them one—get out of the way. He told Gregg to head west down the Catharpin Road toward Corbin's Bridge; Merritt was to send one brigade to the Blockhouse Bridge, while the other led the infantry down the Brock Road toward Spotsylvania. Meade sent a courier in search of Sheridan to advise him of the new orders to his cavalry, noting pointedly that "they are in the way of the infantry." Sheridan's own orders, marked 1:00 A.M., presumably reached Gregg and Merritt some time after Meade's, but by then they had been superseded, and at any rate it was now too late to stop Anderson from crossing the Po.[26]

Fitzhugh Lee's troopers had moved northward along the Brock Road, felling trees and pulling apart fences to block the Union advance. Merritt's cavalry, in the vanguard of Meade's army, had the unenviable task of removing the obstructions from the roadway while being potshotted by Lee's dismounted riders. Sheridan arrived on the scene before sunup and was outraged by what he considered the profligate expenditure of his cavalry to clear the road for some uselessly milling infantry. He asked Major General Gouverneur K. Warren, commander of Meade's V Corps, for help in overrunning Lee's barricaded cavalry at Alsop. Whether something in Warren's demeanor irritated Sheridan, or whether the contingency of the situation played on Sheridan's already jangled nerves, the sharp-faced Warren made an inadvertent enemy that morning, one who did not readily forget such things.

For the time being, Sheridan had other things to worry about. He ordered Wilson to evacuate Spotsylvania at once, before he was swallowed by a pincerlike Rebel movement. Then he went in search of Meade. All the frustrations of the past five weeks swelled within him to a wrathy climax. At Piney Branch Church he located Meade's headquarters, and in short order there ensued one of the most famous arguments of the Civil War. Neither man had had much sleep the night before, and the pressures of campaigning, coupled with the mounting casualties within their respective commands, further enflamed the explosive situation. Colonel Horace Porter of Grant's staff was a reluctant witness to the quick-flaring confrontation. Meade, he said, "had worked himself into a towering passion regarding the delays encountered in the forward movement, and when Sheridan appeared went at him hammer and tongs, accusing him of blunders, and charging him with not making a proper disposition of his troops, and letting the cavalry block the advance of the infantry." This was true to a great extent, but Sheridan was never one to admit failure, or to return a soft answer in the face of wrath. To the charge that his cavalry was not doing all it should have done, Sheridan retorted that if that was true, it was Meade's fault, not his, since Meade had consistently interfered with his handling of the corps. In fact, said Sheridan, "since he insisted on giving the cavalry directions without consulting or even notifying me, he could henceforth command the Cavalry Corps himself . . . I would not give it another order."[27]

This was too much for the shaken Meade. He hurried off to find Grant, who was camped nearby. A few days earlier the general-in-chief had witnessed a similar argument involving Meade and another balky junior officer, Brigadier General Charles Griffin. Then Grant had suggested that Meade arrest Griffin for insubordination. But if Meade expected a similar reaction to Sheridan's outburst, he was quickly disappointed. Repeating Sheridan's boast that he could "thrash hell out of Stuart any day," Meade waited for Grant to pass judgment. "Did Sheridan say that?" Grant asked. "Well, he generally knows what he's talking about. Let him start right out and do it."[28]

The canny Meade could see which way the wind was blowing. Besides, now that the two armies were ensnarled again at Spotsylvania, there was no immediate need for cavalry. A raid behind enemy lines might at least unsettle the enemy. Orders were drawn by Meade's chief of staff, Brigadier General A. A. Humphreys, and were in Sheridan's hands later that same day. He was directed "to immediately concentrate your available mounted force, and . . . proceed against the enemy's cavalry." Once again, as at Perryville (and, to a lesser extent, Chickamauga), bluster and blarney had overshadowed command mistakes, and Sheridan had successfully avoided censure for his actions.[29]

He did not intend to fumble his opportunity. Assembling his three division commanders that night, Sheridan told them: "We are going out to fight Stuart's cavalry in consequence of a suggestion from me; we will give him a fair, square fight; we are strong, and I know we can beat him, and in view of my recent representations to General Meade I shall expect nothing but success." The men were to draw three days' rations, the horses only a half ration of grain. Mobility—though not haste—was to be the watchword. Unlike previous cavalry raids, this one would proceed at a measured walk. Sheridan did not want his horses or men exhausted by the time they met the enemy. Like Grant, he intended to make Rebel soldiers, not real estate, his primary target. "Our move," he explained to his officers, "would be a challenge to Stuart for a cavalry duel behind Lee's lines, in his own country."[30]

On the morning of May 9 the corps moved out in a single column, thirteen miles long, from Aldrich's Station near Fredericksburg. Sheridan hoped to draw Stuart after him by following the most direct route to Richmond, due south along the Telegraph Road. He had under him some ten thousand troopers and six batteries of horse artillery. Many of the men were armed with Spencer or Sharps repeating rifles, giving them an even greater edge in firepower. Morale was excellent; not only were the men delighted to be leaving the Wilderness behind, they were also buoyed by their strong showing in the recent series of skirmishes. The much-vaunted Confederate horsemen, in fact, had never recovered from their near-thrashing at Brandy Station or, to be more exact, from the enormous uplift in confidence that engagement had given to the Union troops. Now, in Phil Sheridan, they had a commander who personified such confidence in word and deed. Coming under fire an hour out of camp, Sheridan rode to the head of the column and asked whether they were facing infantry or cavalry. Told it was cavalry, he roared, much to the delight of nearby horsemen, "Keep moving, boys. We're going on through. There isn't cavalry enough in all the Southern Confederacy to stop us."[31]

Sheridan was more correct than he realized. Jeb Stuart, at

Spotsylvania, knew immediately when the Union cavalry moved; moreover, he had his entire command within easy range of consolidation. But for reasons that can only be guessed, he galloped after Sheridan with only three of his six brigades—some 4,500 men—in tow. It may have been that Stuart, so loudly criticized for losing touch with Lee's army before Gettysburg, wanted to keep half his command attached to the general at all times. Or he may have assumed that Sheridan, like other Yankee horsemen before him, intended merely to burn a few bridges and raid a few farms, then scamper back to the safety of his own lines. Finally, Stuart may have felt that a speedy pursuit, allowing him to get between Sheridan and Richmond, would be enough in itself to discourage the enemy and obviate any threat to the capital.[32]

Whatever Stuart's rationale, his decision to leave behind half of his command was a disastrous mistake, one that played directly into Sheridan's hands. While the long blue column continued southward at a leisurely pace, walking its way ever closer to Richmond, Stuart divided his already outnumbered force, sending one brigade to snap at the Yankees' heels while he attempted to circle ahead with the other two. Handicapped by worries that Sheridan might still turn north and get into the rear of Lee's army, Stuart lost valuable hours keeping his men between the two forces. This permitted Custer, spearheading Merritt's First Division, to ride unchallenged into Beaver Dam Station at dusk on May 9 and burn two supply trains and an estimated 1½ million rations and medical stores intended for use by Lee's beleaguered army at Spotsylvania. Nearly four hundred ecstatic Union prisoners just captured in the Wilderness were also delivered from their brief captivity.[33]

May 10 was more of the same, with Sheridan's troopers moving inexorably ahead and Stuart's ragged cavalry trailing in impotent pursuit. At Ground Squirrel Bridge on the South Anna River, halfway to Richmond, Sheridan camped for the night, content to let Stuart get around him by "urging his horses to the death," while Sheridan's contingent, man and beast, enjoyed a restful night beside the Anna's cooling waters. The next morning Sheridan received reports that Stuart had arrived at the crossroads hamlet of Yellow Tavern, six miles north of Richmond, and there was preparing a last-ditch defense. This was all Sheridan could have hoped for, and more. Not only had Stuart taken the gambit, so to speak, by offering combat to the much larger Union force; he had also run the legs off his horses and men in order to do so. Without hesitating, Sheridan made straight for Richmond down the same Mountain Road Stuart had gone up two years before on the first leg of his fame-making ride around George McClellan's besieging Union army. Merritt's division, led by Colonel Alfred Gibbs's Reserve Brigade, reached the outskirts of Yellow Tavern about 11:00 A.M. and found Stuart's two brigades already deployed in line of battle along two connecting ridges just east of the Mountain Road and directly north of the Brook Turnpike, which funneled southward into Richmond. Stuart, with little more than an hour in which to make his dispositions, had opted to strike Sheridan in flank as the Union troopers galloped, presumably, toward the southern capital.[34]

Once again Stuart was wrong. When Gibbs's horsemen ran into enemy fire from the east, they wheeled immediately to face the guns. Colonel Thomas Devin's brigade, right behind, reached the turnpike and likewise pivoted east, one regiment continuing to the outer defenses of Richmond, three miles south. Stuart had already alerted General Braxton Bragg, now that city's garrison commander, that Sheridan was heading his way with a large force. "If attack is made on Richmond," Stuart warned, "it will be principally as dismounted cavalry, which fights better than the enemy's infantry."[35]

Just now, Sheridan was not intent on Richmond; his slant brown eyes were focused on the legendary Rebel horseman whose flamboyant personal style—red satin-lined cape, yellow sash, and black ostrich-plume hat—was completely antithetical to his own, save for the powerful emotional response each elicited from his dazzled troops. Having promised Meade that he could "thrash hell out of Stuart any day," Sheridan had proceeded in less than three to run his peacock quarry to ground, even if the ever-confident Stuart still believed it was he who had set the better trap. As it was, Stuart had principally managed to ensnare himself. Against Sheridan's ten thousand men he could oppose only three thousand, and one-fourth of these had to remain, as horse-holders, in the rear. His third brigade, following in Sheridan's wake, was too far away to reach Yellow Tavern in time for the battle. In the meantime, Bragg's defenders (unsurprisingly, given their leader's dismal history) would not venture out of their fixed defenses. Stuart would have to fight alone. He sent a last, hopeful message to Bragg—"I cannot see how they can escape"—and prepared to meet the enemy.[36]

Sheridan brought Wilson's division and one brigade of Gregg's rear guard rapidly into line alongside Merritt. Indecisive but bitter fighting spilled over into the afternoon. At 4:00 P.M., after a two-hour lull in the firing, Sheridan sent Custer's Michigan brigade around to the left of Stuart's line, while the remainder of his force advanced dismounted against the Rebel center and right. Custer's charge, made by the First, Fifth, and Sixth Michigan regiments, broke Stuart's left, capturing two cannons from a well-served Rebel battery that had been making Yellow Tavern, in Sheridan's words, "an uncomfortably hot place" for his men.[37]

All along the line the Union troops drove forward irresistibly, while Stuart tried personally to rally his troops. Behind him, the First Virginia Cavalry made a spirited countercharge, and Custer's troops swirled back toward the disputed crossroads. Stuart, mounted behind a fence and snapping off rounds from his nine-shot LeMat revolver, was caught in the eddy. Earlier he had resisted pleas to remove himself from the center of the fight, shrugging, "I don't reckon there is any danger." Now, as Yankees dashed past him on every side, one paused and—almost as an afterthought—sent a .44-caliber pistol bullet crashing into the general's torso, just below his rib cage. Stuart reeled in the saddle; frantic aides helped him down from his horse and propped him against a tree. His assailant, a forty-eight-year-old private from the Fifth Michigan named John A. Huff, continued running. Huff had already served a stretch with Berdan's Sharpshooters, winning a prize as best shot in that notably dead-shot regiment, and his killing range from Stuart, less than fifteen yards, was almost too easy for one of his skill.[38]

While Stuart was taken on a jolting ambulance ride back to Richmond (he would die the next evening at his brother-in-law's house), Sheridan completed his rout of Stuart's command, scattering Rebels in three directions and sending a reconnaissance party clattering down the Brook Turnpike toward the city. It was now growing dark, and church bells within the capital tolled a steady alarm. After burying the dead and succoring the wounded, Sheridan followed his scouting party southeast through the outer defensive line toward the Mechanicsville Turnpike. It was the same route Kilpatrick had taken on his disastrous raid ten weeks earlier, and Sheridan was momentarily tempted to make for the enemy capital himself. He was convinced, he told aides, that he could take Richmond, but equally convinced that he could not hold it. Instead he turned left toward the old Fair Oaks battleground, intending to cross the Chickahominy River and link up with Major General Benjamin Butler's Army of the James, which he had learned was four miles south of Richmond in the direction of Haxall's Landing, the expedition's prearranged meeting place.[39]

The command moved out at eleven that night through pelting rain and howling winds. Inside Richmond the steeple of St. John's Church, a city landmark, was toppled by the storm. The eerie nightscape was not improved by the presence of Confederate land mines, called "torpedoes," which earlier had been sown along the line of march. The mines (actually buried artillery shells equipped with tripwires stretched across the road) were primitive but effective—particularly in the dark. After losing several horses and a number of wounded riders to the mines, Sheridan resolved the problem by bringing up a couple of dozen Rebel prisoners and making them feel for the wires on their hands and knees. Their captors found the ensuing spectacle—much shrinking and groping on the Rebels' part—rather droll. The decidedly unamused prisoners told Sheridan the owner of a nearby house had helped plant the mines, and the general had the shells dug up and placed in the man's cellar, primed for use if an enemy column passed that way.[40]

At daybreak the Union column approached Meadow Bridge, near Mechanicsville, where Sheridan intended to cross the rain-swollen Chickahominy and link up with Butler. Wilson's division, in the lead, ran headlong into a salvo of artillery fire from a battery inside Richmond's inner defenses. The division had been led, either intentionally or by mistake, into an ambush by its civilian guide. Colonel John B. McIntosh, one of Wilson's brigade commanders, had mistrusted the guide from the start, ordering him to stay close at hand. Now, with the advance abruptly taking fire in the streaky dawn, McIntosh calmly blew the man's brains out with his pistol.[41]

Wilson sent back word that the column could not pass safely between the battery and the south bank of the river. Sheridan dispatched Custer to Meadow Bridge to hold it for a crossing. To his alarm, Custer found that the enemy had set fire to the bridge the night before; worse yet, a strong contingent of Rebel artillery, infantry, and dismounted cavalry was waiting for them on the other side of the river. Sheridan hastened the rest of Merritt's division to assist Custer, with orders to repair the bridge at all costs. Meanwhile, other Confederate units were attacking the rear of the column. It was, thought one officer, "the tightest place in which the corps ever found itself."[42]

Sheridan remained calm. He faced Wilson and Gregg around to the rear to meet the new threat, while instructing Merritt to use fence rails to improvise a new bridge. Across the Chickahominy, Rebel marksmen peppered Merritt's engineers, but the previous night's rain had put out the flames before the bridge could be seriously damaged, and a passable span was quickly built. Timely fire from Captain James M. Robertson's battery of horse artillery enabled Wilson to turn the enemy flank, sending his attackers dashing back to the safety of Richmond's defenses, while Merritt crossed the Chickahominy and secured the vital bridgehead for the corps. By noon the firing had ceased and Sheridan was left in lone possession of the field.[43]

The rest of the afternoon was spent collecting the wounded and burying the dead. Sheridan later maintained that he was "perfectly confident" he could extricate himself from the sticky situation, either by defeating the enemy outright or by retreating across the Chickahominy at one of several fords below the bridge. "This means of getting out from the circumscribed plateau I did not wish to use," he explained with the wisdom of hindsight, "for I wished to demonstrate to the Cavalry Corps the impossibility of the enemy's destroying or capturing so large a body of mounted troops." Whatever his motive, Sheridan again showed a cool head in a crisis. "Surrounded!" he laughed at panicky subordinates. "Surrounded by a lot of war department clerks! Take it easy."[44]

Unchallenged by further Confederate attacks, the column proceeded to Haxall's Landing by way of the old killing ground at Gaines's Mill, arriving on May 14. Six days after leaving Spotsylvania on his first extended cavalry raid, Sheridan had made good on his promise to Meade. Not only had he thrashed Stuart, he had also killed him. The decisive Union victory at Yellow Tavern sent a message to both armies that the military equation in Virginia had changed dramatically. No longer would the romantic figure of the Confederate horseman, so strikingly personified by Jeb Stuart, loom larger than life in the popular imagination. It was a new war now—Grant's war—and the outcome, if not yet preordained, was beginning at least to come into focus. Stuart the gallant cavalier had died, gut-shot, in the southern capital, while church bells outside his window rang the alarm for a better-armed, better-horsed, and increasingly better-led Yankee cavalry now passing insolently near the seat of the Confederacy, its tough-talking little commander crowing that "if I could be permitted to cross the James River and go southward I could almost ruin the Confederacy."[45]

For the time being, however, Grant needed Sheridan and his troopers back with the rest of the army. After nearly two weeks of unparalleled bloodletting in the Wilderness and at Spotsylvania, the Union general-in-chief had decided to go back to his successful "sidling" tactic, moving south around Lee's right flank to draw him out of his formidable defenses. Grant wanted Sheridan's cavalry to act as both decoy and shield for the planned flanking movement. He explained as much when Sheridan arrived at army headquarters on May 24. "Now, Sheridan evidently thinks he has been clear down to the James River, and has been breaking up railroads, and even getting a peep at Richmond," Grant joked to his staff when Sheridan entered, "but probably that is all imagination, or else he has been reading something of the kind in the newspapers. I don't suppose he seriously thinks that he made such a march as that in two weeks." Delighted to be the target of one of Grant's infrequent jests, Sheridan gamely replied, "Well, after what General Grant says, I do begin to feel doubtful as to whether I have been absent at all from the Army of the Potomac."[46]

Getting down to business, Grant gave Sheridan his new assignment. Dandy Wilson would take his division north to the Union right to make Lee think his left flank was about to be attacked. Meanwhile, Sheridan's other two divisions, under Gregg and the newly returned Torbert, would lead the army's advance across the Pamunkey River at Hanovertown Ford. The cavalry made the crossing without undue difficulty on May 27 (Custer ostentatiously swimming his horse across the river in the face of Rebel sniper fire), but Lee had anticipated Grant's maneuver, and two divisions of dismounted horsemen were waiting for them behind formidable breastworks three miles west of Hanovertown at the crossroads village of Haw's Shop, so named for its landmark blacksmith shop. Commanding the southern force was Major General Wade Hampton, a massive, hearty South Carolinian who had replaced—as much as anyone could—the much-lamented Stuart as senior cavalry commander.[47]

The resulting firefight, lasting for well over five hours, took a heavy toll on Gregg's Second Division. Particularly effective was Confederate Brigadier General Matthew Butler's newly arrived brigade of mounted infantry, the Fourth, Fifth, and Sixth South Carolina. Armed with Enfield rifles instead of shorter, less accurate carbines, the Carolinians unleashed such a devastating fire that they were mistaken by Gregg's men for regular infantry. Sheridan sent word to Meade that he was facing Rebel infantry and asked for foot soldiers of his own. Unconvinced, Meade demurred, and Sheridan was forced to make do with his own dismounted troopers. Near dark, he sent Custer's brigade into the fight with orders to break the Confederate line. Custer typically wanted to lead the charge on horseback, but Gregg made him dismount. At the same time that Custer was arranging his Wolverines for a twilight attack, Hampton began pulling back, having captured enough Federal prisoners to learn that Union infantry was already across the Pamunkey within supporting distance of Sheridan's force. Custer's men, supported by Gregg's division, carried the thinned-out southern works, but at a disproportionately high cost. Gregg reported losing 256 officers and men, while Custer's troops suffered their heaviest loss of the entire campaign. Nevertheless, Grant now had a definite fix on Lee's intentions, which, as usual, almost supernaturally mirrored his own.[48]

Both armies headed in the direction of Cold Harbor, an aptly named, inhospitable village twelve miles southeast of Haw's Shop. Again, the Rebels got there first. Torbert's division drove to within a mile and a half of Cold Harbor on the afternoon of May 30, inflicting another round of casualties on Butler's white-gloved South Carolinians. The next morning Sheridan, Torbert, and Custer discussed plans for dislodging Fitzhugh Lee's dismounted cavalry from their fence-rail breastworks in front of Cold Harbor. Disregarding his hard-learned maxim that "combinations rarely work," Sheridan permitted Merritt and Custer to attack the Confederate line head-on while Devin's brigade circled left to attack the enemy flank. Devin failed in his task—an exasperated Torbert later charged that he had not made a serious attempt to carry it out—but the First Michigan managed to make a mounted saber charge late in the afternoon that struck Lee's troops just as they were falling back on their infantry support. The startled foot soldiers, thinking they were seeing a rout in progress, turned and ran the other way, making a reality of their fears and leaving a somewhat surprised Sheridan in abrupt possession of Cold Harbor.[49]

Captured Confederates informed Sheridan that Lee's entire army was now in the neighborhood of Mechanicsville, six miles away, and Sheridan deemed it advisable to withdraw to his original position. "I do not feel able to hold this place," he informed Meade. "I do not think it prudent to hold on." He was in the process of abandoning Cold Harbor that night when peremptory orders from Meade commanded him "to hold the place at all hazards." Sheridan obligingly reversed his march and put his now-exhausted troopers to work strengthening the same Rebel breastworks they had carried earlier in the afternoon. The men, said Captain Theodore Rodenbough, were "weary and disgusted, having been on duty for eighteen hours." Still, "the morale of the corps was so good and their confidence in Sheridan so great that when the order 'to hold at all hazards' was repeated, they never dreamed of leaving the spot."[50]

At daybreak the Confederates attacked, but Sheridan's men, utilizing their rapid-fire Spencer and Sharps carbines, easily beat back two separate attacks and held until Major General Horatio Wright's VI Infantry Corps arrived to relieve them three hours later. Sheridan, although admittedly "very apprehensive" about his predicament, had managed to hold the vital crossroads for nearly a day with only his three-thousand-man cavalry force. Whether he did his infantry comrades a favor, however, is debatable. Two days later, Grant, reacting perhaps to the disappointment of again having failed to outmaneuver Lee, sent his troops careening madly toward the heavily fortified southern works west of Cold Harbor. In less than eight minutes the Federals lost nearly seven thousand men—many of whom had pinned scraps of paper to their uniforms to simplify matters for the burial parties—with no visible effect on the Rebel line. "I regret this assault more than any one I ever ordered," a shocked Grant told his staff that night.[51]

Despairing of winning a decisive victory north of Richmond, Grant now began shifting his forces south of the city, intending to besiege the critical railroad junction at Petersburg, thirty miles below Richmond. To deny supplies and reinforcements to Lee, he determined to send Sheridan's cavalry on another raid around Lee's army, this time in the direction of Charlottesville, with orders to tear up as much of the Virginia Central Railroad as possible. Besides disrupting Rebel supplies from the verdant Shenandoah Valley, the raid would have the effect of drawing off the enemy cavalry while Grant's army completed its crossing of the James River east of Richmond.[52]

Sheridan broke camp at daybreak on June 7, taking with him some six thousand men. Wilson's division once again had been left behind to handle whatever incidental cavalry needs the commanding general deemed essential. Of necessity the riders were traveling light—three days' rations per man, two days' grain for their horses. Cooking utensils amounted to a tin cup and half a canteen per man, which doubled as frying pan and stew pot. As it had done before Yellow Tavern, the column moved at a walk to conserve the horses. The countryside was enveloped in a heavy drought, and choking clouds of dust hung over the west-marching corps. By the end of the second day, numerous horses began giving out, forcing their erstwhile riders to trail the command on foot.[53]

Sheridan followed the north bank of the North Anna River, intending to strike the railroad first at Trevilian Station, twenty-eight miles due east of Charlottesville. The ever-vigilant Lee, hearing that Sheridan was moving in his rear, dispatched Hampton and Fitzhugh Lee in close pursuit. Taking a more direct route, the two southerners reached the vicinity of Trevilian Station ahead of Sheridan and bedded down for the night. The next morning, June 11, Sheridan sent Torbert and Merritt clattering down the road toward the station, supported by Devin's brigade. At the same time, Hampton had his gray-clad force in motion, planning to strike the Yankees at Clayton's Store, a strategic crossroads three miles northeast of Trevilian.[54]

While the two sides were closing with each other, tawny-haired Custer was marching his Michigan brigade around the Rebel right, screened from the enemy by thick-growing trees. Hampton had dismounted one of his brigades for the frontal attack, and eight hundred lightly guarded horses, as well as caissons, supply wagons, and ambulances, had been left behind at the station. Without hesitating, Custer sent Colonel Russell Alger and the Fifth Michigan Cavalry charging into the Rebel camp. Alger quickly snatched up all the horses, prisoners, and supplies he could find, then with "pardonable zeal" followed the remaining fugitives north toward Gordonsville. Meanwhile, Fitzhugh Lee's division, riding toward the sound of the guns, crashed into Custer from the east, separating him from Alger's men. Hampton rapidly disengaged a part of his attacking force and sent it hurrying back to Trevilian to help.[55]

Nearly surrounded, Custer pulled his men into a circle, frontier-fashion, and grimly held his ground. Lee's troops grabbed back everything Alger had seized, along with their would-be Union captors. Alger and a handful of men escaped, rejoining the command later that day. The battle swirled on in the staggering summer heat, Sheridan reinforcing his flanks and eventually breaking through the enemy front. Custer, who earlier had grabbed his regimental standard from a fallen color-bearer and concealed it inside his jacket, led his Wolverines forward to meet Sheridan, capturing some four hundred Rebels who had found themselves trapped between the two blue lines. Custer's longtime cook and servant, "Aunt Eliza" Brown, seized during the kaleidoscopic melee, stole home that night through enemy lines, proudly lugging the general's personal suitcase.[56]

Hampton broke off the engagement late that afternoon, going into camp west of Trevilian. Although he later claimed a victory in the fight, the fact that Sheridan now held the station, along with hundreds of Rebel dead and wounded left behind on the battlefield, effectively contradicted Hampton's boast. Nevertheless, by getting between the Union cavalry and Gordonsville, the South Carolinian had checkmated Sheridan from advancing farther west. Hearing from some of his prisoners that Major General David Hunter was moving his Federal infantry southward up the Shenandoah Valley, instead of east toward Charlottesville, as he had been led to believe, Sheridan concluded that he had done all he could under present conditions. He decided to break off the raid and return to the safety of the Union lines.[57]

The next morning Sheridan had his troopers out tearing up track between Trevilian and Louisa Court House, while Torbert's division felt for a way back across the North Anna River. At Mallory's Cross Roads, near the river crossing of the same name, Torbert's men attempted to budge the entrenched Rebels from their breastworks behind a railroad embankment, but instead left the ground littered with several hundred of their own. Low on ammunition and fearing an influx of enemy infantry, Sheridan grudgingly decided to leave the same way he had come, by way of Carpenter's Ford, farther east. The resultant retreat took twice as long to accomplish—eight days back, as opposed to four days forward—and was further complicated by the nearly eight hundred Rebel prisoners and Union wounded he was forced to take with him. The searing drought had not abated, and broken-down horses were mercilessly shot and left along the way (the Confederates, following at a distance, estimated the number at twelve per mile—some 1,200 in all). As always, Sheridan's men foraged at will among the civilian population, although not without risk. Enraged Virginians, "in the shape of guerrillas," picked off unwary stragglers, cut their throats, and left them hanging from trees along the Yankees' line of march, with signs proclaiming—no doubt redundantly—"Such will be the fate of every forager caught."[58]

Finally, on June 21, Sheridan reached the Union supply base at White House. Grant had already transferred the bulk of his supplies to City Point, across the James, and Sheridan's dog-tired troops were left the unpalatable task of escorting the remaining nine hundred supply wagons across the river to the new base. Hampton's cavalry, which had trailed Sheridan all the way from Trevilian Station, attacked the stretched-out convoy at Charles City Court House and St. Mary's Church on June 24, but a staunch rearguard defense by Gregg's division—coupled with the prostrating heat, which felled both attackers and defenders—saved the trains.[59]

Sheridan's state of mind, which had begun to darken in the swirling fight at Trevilian and had progressively worsened during the ensuing retreat, was not improved by the news that Wilson's division, left behind with the army outside Richmond, had been badly roughed up in an unequal fight with Rebel infantry and cavalry at Ream's Station, south of Petersburg. Sheridan was preparing, with noticeable ill will, to mount a rescue party when Wilson dragged into camp three days later. He had lost 815 men killed, wounded, or captured, as well as all his supply trains and artillery. Meade, who had sent Wilson raiding southward in Sheridan's absence, considered the losses small enough payment for what he styled a "brilliant success," but Sheridan himself was not so thrilled. He was further angered when Wilson told him that the always irascible Gouverneur Warren had once again complained about being delayed on his march by Wilson's (read Sheridan's) cavalry. While waiting to throw a pontoon bridge across the Chickahominy River, Wilson had received a verbal potshot from Warren to the effect that "if he can't lay that bridge . . . get out of the way with his damned cavalry and I'll lay it." That was twice now that Warren had loudly and publicly criticized Sheridan's men—the day was coming when Sheridan would return the favor, in spades.[60]

But the crowning blow came when Wilson showed Sheridan a dispatch from Meade demanding that Wilson defend himself from sensational charges made by the Richmond newspapers that Union cavalry had broken into churches and homes during the raid and that Wilson himself, "a highwayman, a wine-bibber and a modern Sardanapalus," had encouraged such looting. "Damn him," Sheridan said of Meade. "Give him hell." Wilson then proceeded to defend his men, although he was forced to concede that "there exists in our cavalry service an organized band of thieves, who are under no restraint whatever, and who have been skillful enough so far to elude every attempt to arrest."[61]

Sheridan felt no such compunction when it came to looting, which he preferred to style "foraging." In his subsequent report of the Trevilian raid, he set forth his own credo on the subject. "I do not believe war to be simply that lines should engage each other in battle," he wrote, "and therefore do not regret the system of living on the enemy's country. These men or women did not care how many were killed, or maimed, so long as war did not come to their doors, but as soon as it did come in the shape of loss of property, they earnestly prayed for its termination. As war is a punishment, if we can, by reducing its advocates to poverty, end it quicker, we are on the side of humanity."[62]

Sheridan would soon get the opportunity to enlarge upon his philosophy of Mongol-style humanitarianism. With the Union army settling into what would become a ten-month siege at Petersburg, he took his cavalry into camp for a much-needed period of rest and refitting. The only operation of note was a diversionary lunge back across the James River in late July in conjunction with the exploding of a giant mine under the Confederate defenses at Petersburg. The subsequent Battle of the Crater was a dismaying Union disaster, the main effect of which was to convince Grant firmly and finally that the war could not be won quickly, and so must be won slowly, in the rat-fouled trenches now snaking their way ineffaceably across the south Virginia landscape.[63]

Meanwhile, events in the always troublesome Shenandoah Valley again had taken a turn for the worse. Stonewall Jackson was long since dead, but the Rebels seemed to have located his approximate familiar in the crusty person of Lieutenant General Jubal A. Early, a hard-drinking, acid-tongued, irreligious old infantryman who had defeated Hunter's Union army at Lynchburg in mid-July and then proceeded, in Early's own words, to "scare Abe Lincoln like hell" by tearing down the Valley Turnpike all the way to Maryland and Pennsylvania, raiding, looting, and burning to the very outskirts of Washington itself. "Early's Washington Raid," as it inevitably became known, presented Grant with a political dilemma as well as a military one. In particular, the Rebel burning of Chambersburg, Pennsylvania, on the same day as the Union fiasco at the Crater, had stirred public opinion in the North at a time when Lincoln was preparing for a difficult reelection campaign against the former "savior of the Union," deposed Major General George B. McClellan, who seemed likely to be nominated by the Democratic Party in August. The administration could ill afford such open displays of weakness, especially now that the main thrust of the war effort had bogged down so conspicuously outside Petersburg.[64]

Awakening slowly to the psychological importance of the Shenandoah Valley—the "back door" to Washington, as it were—Grant determined to rectify the situation by merging the four overlapping military departments in the region into a single military division under one commander. Meeting with Lincoln on the last day of July, he went over his proposal and suggested again, as he had in April, that his old West Point classmate, William B. Franklin, be appointed to the post. Again Lincoln demurred, wondering instead if Meade was interested in taking the job. He was—and Grant seemed willing to rid himself of his difficult subordinate, who might at any rate render more useful service in an independent command. But after thinking it over that night, his gaze narrowed on someone else. The next morning he telegraphed Washington, "I want Sheridan put in command of all the troops in the field, with instructions to put himself south of the enemy and follow him to the death. Wherever the enemy goes, let our troops go also." Given the sort of flint-hearted campaign Grant now envisioned for the Shenandoah Valley, such a roughened soldier as Phil Sheridan, well schooled in the theory and practice of devastation, might prove more useful than a Philadelphia Main Liner in the fierce and flame-darkened days to come.[65]

6
''FOLLOW HIM TO THE DEATH''

GRANT'S CHOICE OF SHERIDAN to head the Army of the Shenandoah, more a product of personal taste than a reward for Sheridan's comparatively brief tenure as cavalry chief, made few people happy. Anticipating this, the general-in-chief went to some lengths to obfuscate matters. Ever-malleable David Hunter, the ranking general in the valley, could remain as administrative head of the new department, Grant said, with Sheridan merely commanding in the field. This, it was hoped, would forestall complaints that Sheridan was too young and inexperienced for the post by preserving the paper-shuffling status quo while still giving Grant what he wanted, a more aggressive presence at the front. Lincoln, though somewhat surprised by the decision—he thought they had settled on Meade—nevertheless telegraphed Grant a qualified endorsement of the change.[1]

"I have seen your dispatch in which you say, 'I want Sheridan put in command of all the troops in the field, with instructions to put himself south of the enemy, and follow him to the death,' " Lincoln wrote. "This, I think, is exactly right as to how our troops should move; but please look over the dispatches you may have received from here, ever since you made that order, and discover, if you can, that there is any idea in the head of anyone here of 'putting our army south of the enemy,' or of following him to the 'death' in any direction. I repeat to you, it will neither be done nor attempted, unless you watch over it every day and hour and force it."[2]

Preoccupied though he was by his own stygian efforts at Petersburg, Grant nevertheless took Lincoln's advice to heart, hurrying by train to Hunter's headquarters at Monocacy Junction, Maryland, thirty miles northwest of Washington. Meanwhile, pursuant to orders, Sheridan arrived in the capital for another disheartening conference, similar to the one he had suffered through in April, with the president and his doleful brain trust, Stanton and Halleck. Lincoln told him straight out that both he and Stanton had objected to the new assignment on the grounds that Sheridan was too young for the post, but that Grant had "ploughed round" the difficulties by retaining Hunter in formal command. How well Grant was plowing they were not yet aware; after the general concluded his visit, a conveniently exhausted Hunter would ask to be relieved of all further duties, and Sheridan would assume "temporary" command of the entire Middle Military Division.[3]

While in Washington, Sheridan also received a quick lesson in election-year politics. In the wake of the Crater fiasco, Early's raid on the capital, the knee-buckling casualties from the Wilderness, Grant's stalled offensive at Petersburg, and Sherman's molasses-like advance through Georgia, the administration could ill afford another setback. Sheridan, they knew, was aggressive, even impetuous. His main task, they now gave him to understand, was to avoid being beaten, since "the defeat of my army might be followed by the overthrow of the party in power" and inevitably lead, in Sheridan's curiously dainty phrase, "to the complete abandonment of all coercive measures."[4]

That Grant did not necessarily share the administration's squeamishness was immediately impressed upon Sheridan when he arrived at Monocacy Junction on August 6. Grant gave him a copy of the orders he had originally prepared for Hunter calling for an immediate concentration of forces around Harpers Ferry. Grant wanted a swift pursuit of Jubal Early, whether the Rebel raider was north or south of the Potomac River. More than that, he wanted Sheridan to carry out a new kind of warfare in the Shenandoah Valley. "In pushing up the . . . Valley, as it is expected you will have to go first or last, it is desirable that nothing should be left to invite the enemy to return," Grant instructed. "Take all provisions, forage, and stock wanted for the use of your command. Such as cannot be consumed, destroy. . . . [T]he people should be informed that so long as an army can subsist among them recurrences of these raids must be expected, and we are determined to stop them at all hazards."[5]

Grant's order, typically terse, was an elaboration of a new strain of music he had tried out on Hunter a few weeks earlier, urging him then to "make all the valleys south of the Baltimore and Ohio [Railroad] a desert as high up as possible. . . . [E]very particle of provisions and stock should be removed, and the people notified to move out." He had wanted Hunter's troops "to eat out Virginia clear and clean as far as they go, so that crows flying over it for the balance of the season will have to carry their provender with them." Hunter, accordingly, had burned the Virginia Military Institute to the ground, along with the homes of Virginia Governor John Letcher and other prominent Confederates, including several of his own apostate southern kinfolk, before running out of time and nerve. It was up to Sheridan to finish the job.[6]

The command Sheridan inherited from Hunter was something of a hybrid, comprising units already on the scene or en route by railroad from other fronts. The largest of these was the VI Corps, Army of the Potomac, under Major General Horatio Wright, the same Wright who, as department commander at Cincinnati prior to the Battle of Perryville, had made the unaccomplished Charles C. Gilbert a major general and thus occasioned Sheridan's out-of-character (and out-of-channels) complaint about the inequities of promotion, which had resulted in his first divisional command. A large, jolly, urbane man, Wright had replaced the much-lamented John Sedgwick as commander of the corps after Sedgwick's tragicomic death at Spotsylvania three months earlier. ("They couldn't hit an elephant at this distance," Sedgwick had joked of Confederate sharpshooters, immediately before one such underrated sniper sent a bullet crashing into his face from eight hundred yards away.) Commanding Wright's three divisions were Brigadier Generals David A. Russell, George W. Getty, and James B. Ricketts. All were West Pointers and veteran fighters; Russell had been Sheridan's post commander at Fort Yamhill, Oregon, before the war.[7]

The second infantry contingent was the two-division XIX Corps, newly arrived in Virginia from Louisiana, where it had recently taken part in Major General Nathaniel Banks's lamentable Red River campaign. Commanding the corps was Brigadier General William H. Emory, an old army veteran who had graduated from West Point the same year Sheridan was born, and subsequently had seen service in Mexico, on the western frontier, and in Bleeding Kansas prior to the Civil War. Called "Bold Emory" by his academy classmates, he was now "Old Brick Top" to the soldiers serving under him, in honor of his fiery red hair and temperament.[8]

Completing the alignment was the euphemistically named Army of West Virginia, closer in size to a corps than an army, commanded by Sheridan's oldest and dearest friend, Brigadier General George Crook. The two prickly Ohioans had entered West Point together in 1848, befriended each other during their schooling, and fought Indians together in the Pacific Northwest. They had then served under William Rosecrans in that ill-starred general's Tennessee campaign, mutually enduring the cauldron of Chickamauga, before their careers again diverged. Now, despite the fact that Crook's eight-thousand-man army had been routed by Early at Kernstown two weeks earlier, Sheridan still "placed implicit faith in his experience and qualifications as a general."[9]

In addition to three infantry corps and twelve attached artillery batteries, approximately 35,000 troops in all, Sheridan was to have three divisions of cavalry at his disposal. He had already told

Halleck at their meeting in Washington that "for operations in the open country of Pennsylvania, Maryland, and Northern Virginia, cavalry is much better than infantry." Two of the divisions were his own, en route from the Army of the Potomac and commanded by Brigadier Generals Alfred T. A. Torbert and James Harrison Wilson. The third, already on the scene in the Shenandoah Valley, was headed by Brigadier General William W. Averell.[10]

Organizing the cavalry into an unofficial corps, Sheridan surprised everyone by naming Torbert to be its chief. His reasons for bypassing Averell, who was senior to Torbert and, many thought, his superior as a soldier, were never spelled out. It may have been a desire on Sheridan's part to entrust the corps to an officer who had already served under him, as Averell had not. Or he may have intended it as a message to his new command that things were going to be different now, with Sheridan at the helm. It is also possible that he might have heard from Crook or others that Averell had performed badly at Kernstown, refusing to commit his horsemen to the fight and thus allowing the Rebels to turn Crook's flank. Whatever the case, Torbert was duly installed as cavalry chief, and the disappointed Averell was brusquely told to follow orders.

Taking over a "small and very dilapidated hotel" at Harpers Ferry, Sheridan resumed his career-long habit of steeping himself in the topography of a region before commencing a new campaign. His teacher, a young man he quickly grew to like, was Lieutenant John R. Meigs, eldest son of United States Quartermaster General Montgomery Meigs. Young Meigs, at twenty-two, had achieved great success at West Point, graduating first in his class of 1863 after briefly interrupting his studies to serve as volunteer aide at the First Battle of Bull Run. His subsequent service on the staffs of Hunter and Major General Franz Sigel had given him a personal knowledge of the Shenandoah Valley that Sheridan found immediately helpful. But Meigs, although undeniably brilliant, had a dark side to his nature, one that eventually would cost him his life. At the Battle of New Market, he had chopped down a Union straggler with his own saber; a week later he personally led a party that burned the home of a Virginia civilian suspected of killing northern soldiers. Nor was he overburdened with scruples—when Hunter leveled the Virginia Military Institute that June, Meigs helped himself to an expensive set of mathematical instruments, which he carried with him until the day he died.[11]

That day was coming sooner than anyone expected. But for now, Sheridan listened carefully as Meigs traced the roads, mountains, farms, and streams crisscrossing the usually lush—though now drought-baked—valley. From Union scouts he learned that Early was in force at Bunker Hill, twelve miles west of the forward Union camp at Halltown. Accordingly, on August 9 he ordered a general advance the next morning in the direction of Berryville, a village that lay another twelve miles east of the important crossroads town of Winchester. It was his intention to steal a march on Early and gain his right flank and rear in a single day's march. Not that Sheridan planned on making the campaign "a race-course"; he wanted nothing less than "to destroy, to the best of my ability, that which was truly the Confederacy—its armies."[12]

The advance to Berryville went without a hitch, the infantry reaching its destination late that afternoon. Early, as expected, withdrew south to Winchester, then south again to Fisher's Hill, a prominent outcropping of Massanutten Mountain immediately below the village of Strasburg. Without firing a shot, except for the odd skirmisher's round, Sheridan had managed to maneuver the Confederates completely out of the lower valley. (The valley ascends in height from north to south, so one marched *up* the Shenandoah Valley by moving south, *down* the valley by moving north—a confusing bit of directional legerdemain.)

After taking up position at Cedar Creek, a tributary four miles north of the high ground at Fisher's Hill, Sheridan began to grow increasingly anxious. "The enemy," he told Halleck, "have made some show of resistance in front of Strasburg. I am yet unable to determine its character, and could not get my command sufficiently in hand to attack him this evening." One of Emory's late-arriving XIX Corps divisions had not yet reached the front, nor had Wilson's cavalry. The army's cumbersome supply train, too, was some distance to the rear, although it was expected to arrive the next day. There were also troubling reports that Lieutenant General James Longstreet's much-vaunted I Corps was on its way to Early's aid from the trenches around Petersburg. If so, the odds in Sheridan's favor would be dangerously reduced. "I am exceedingly anxious to hear whether Longstreet has left to come here or not," he implored.[13]

The next morning the army suffered an unexpected body blow when Confederate Lieutenant Colonel John Singleton Mosby's partisan rangers waylaid the tardy supply train outside Berryville, burning most of the wagons and making off with two hundred prisoners and three times as many horses. It was the opening sortie in what would rapidly become a dirty little war-within-a-war, pitting Rebel rangers against northern cavalry that considered them mere "guerrillas," outside the bounds of formal warfare and therefore subject to being shot down or strung up without the niceties of military protocol.

For the time being, Sheridan was less concerned about Mosby's raiders than about the loss of supplies for his vulnerable army and the ever-looming threat of a major Rebel reinforcement in the area. On August 14 a special messenger arrived from Washington with a warning from Grant that it was "now certain" that two divisions of Rebel infantry, along with cavalry and artillery, had been dispatched to Early's aid. Sheridan, he advised, "must be cautious and act now on the defensive until movements here force them to detach to send this way." Early's force could not possibly exceed forty thousand men, Grant reassured him, but it was still too many for Sheridan to risk attacking head-on. In point of fact, only one division of Confederate infantry and another of cavalry had been sent to the Shenandoah from Lee's army at Petersburg. Sheridan still retained a numerical advantage of better than three to one, but even that was not considered enough to offset continued uncertainty about Early's intentions or repeated calls for caution from Grant, the White House, and the War Department. Deciding that his current position was altogether too vulnerable, Sheridan accordingly ordered a two-part strategic withdrawal toward Winchester and Berryville. Early, watching contemptuously from Fisher's Hill, decided that Sheridan, like his predecessors, was "without enterprise" and "possessed an excessive caution which amounted to timidity." It would prove to be a hasty—and costly—misapprehension.[14]

Sheridan left behind the First Cavalry Division, commanded by young Brigadier General Wesley Merritt, with orders to implement the second part of Grant's strategy: to seize or destroy all livestock and grain in the area. Meanwhile, the bulk of the army marched all night through heavy rain to the outskirts of Winchester, where Sheridan learned upon arrival that the cavalry had skirmished heavily with elements of Longstreet's I Corps at Cedarville—concrete proof that Early had indeed been reinforced by Lee and ample reason to continue withdrawing to Halltown, the jumping-off point for the roundabout trip to Cedar Creek.

Neither the northern public nor the press understood the political exigencies of the moment. It seemed to them, as it seemed to Early, that Sheridan was merely the latest in a long line of pusillanimous Union commanders who flinched from combat as soon as they entered the Shenandoah Valley. Cries were heard again for more vigorous prosecution of the war, particularly from loyalists living on the outskirts of Washington, where the Rebel threat struck uncomfortably close to home. Even some of Sheridan's own men, veterans who did not ordinarily go looking for a fight, grumbled at the apparently motiveless marching. One joker dubbed the army "Harper's Weekly," in honor of the length of time it had been gone. But Grant, who represented a constituency of one insofar as Sheridan's job security was concerned, remained satisfied with his careful course—at least for the time being. Still, if Early returned his current reinforcements, he wanted Sheridan to "push with all vigor [and] give the enemy no rest."[15]

For the next two weeks the opposing armies engaged in an

elaborate game of cat-and-mouse, the Confederates alternately advancing or retreating, striking at the Union flanks and making threatening gestures toward the Potomac River. Early justified his gadfly posture by noting that "my only resource was to use my forces so as to display them at different points with great rapidity, and thereby keep up the impression that they were much larger than they really were." But Sheridan, with Grant's continued backing, did not rise to the Rebel bait. Federal cavalry blocked the approaches to Maryland and raided around the enemy rear, while the rest of the army hunkered down behind formidable lines of breastworks, waiting for Early's reinforcements to leave.[16]

Meanwhile, events beyond the Shenandoah Valley were changing the political, and hence the military, equation of the war. On August 23, with Grant bogged down outside Petersburg, Sherman lost in the wilds of Georgia, and Sheridan hugging the Potomac River, a despondent Abraham Lincoln had asked his cabinet members to sign, unread, a presidential memorandum noting that "it seems exceedingly probable that this Administration will not be reelected" and pledging to cooperate with the new president-elect to "save the Union between the election and the inauguration; as he will have secured his election on such ground that he cannot possibly save it afterwards." Six days later, as expected, the Democratic Party, meeting in Chicago, nominated George B. McClellan for president on a plank calling for a negotiated peace. "After four years of failure to restore the Union by the experiment of war," said the Democrats, "justice, humanity, liberty, and the public welfare demand that immediate efforts be made for a cessation of hostilities . . . to the end that at the earliest practicable moment peace may be restored."[17]

Then, even as Lincoln's own political advisers were predicting defeat in November, an electrifying message arrived from Sherman: "Atlanta is ours, and fairly won." With one blow, the entire complexion of the war had changed. Lincoln sent the mercurial general a note of "national thanks" and proclaimed the following Sunday a day of prayer and thanksgiving for Sherman's "glorious achievements." Outside Petersburg, Grant ordered a one-hundred-gun salute (typically, for Grant, with *loaded* guns, to make the salute physically, as well as psychically, painful for the bunkered Rebels across the way). At a stroke, the fall of Atlanta had reversed the wave of pessimism and peace-hunger sweeping the North, and ensured that proponents of a so-called hard war—Lincoln, Stanton, Grant, and his generals—would remain in control of the Union effort.[18]

Grant, for his part, had never flinched. The week before, he told Sheridan, he had inflicted ten thousand casualties on Lee's army at Petersburg; he predicted that Lee would soon recall his reinforcements from the valley. "Watch closely," he advised, "and if you find this theory correct push with all vigor. Give the enemy no rest. . . . Do all the damage to railroads and crops you can. . . . If the war is to last another year, we want the Shenandoah Valley to remain a barren waste." The day after Atlanta fell, Sheridan moved south again to Berryville, Crook's corps inadvertently driving Early's reinforcements (who were in the process of leaving) back into Winchester. Sheridan put the men to work digging an eight-mile-long line of breastworks, while Early watched from behind Opequon Creek, four miles east of town, and decided to keep his reinforcements on hand a few more days to see what the enemy intended to do.[19]

Heavy rains set in a day later, limiting movement by either side. Sheridan, who had no intention yet of forcing the matter, took advantage of the weather to organize "an efficient body of scouts" to gather intelligence on Early's strength. Rhode Island Major Henry K. Young, a member of his headquarters staff, was given overall responsibility for the unit, which was drawn primarily from the 17th Pennsylvania Cavalry. Sergeant Joseph E. McCabe, an experienced trooper, served as second-in-command. Young's scouts—valley residents soon came to know them as "Young's Robbers"—numbered between fifty and sixty members. Sporting captured Rebel uniforms, they penetrated enemy lines in search of useful information, which they then brought directly to Sheridan's camp, receiving cash payments in return for their finds. It was a dangerous game, particularly with Mosby's rangers lurking about the countryside, but it soon paid handsome dividends.[20]

On the night of September 14, Young's men brought into camp a middle-aged black man named Thomas Laws who lived near Millwood, between the two armies, and had a signed pass from Early permitting him to travel back and forth to Winchester to peddle vegetables. From Crook, who had become acquainted with Winchester residents while occupying the town earlier that summer, Sheridan learned that a young Quaker schoolteacher living there, Rebecca Wright, was a Union loyalist who might be depended upon to aid the cause. After satisfying himself of Laws's fidelity, Sheridan sat down at his desk and wrote to Miss Wright. "I learn from Major-General Crook," he began, "that you are a loyal lady and still love the old flag. Can you inform me of the position of Early's forces, the number of divisions in his army, and the strength of any or all of them, and his probable or reported intentions? Have any more troops arrived from Richmond, or are any more coming, or reported to be coming?" He added as a postscript, "You can trust the bearer."[21]

The next day Laws took his vegetable cart back to Winchester. Inside his mouth, wrapped in a piece of tinfoil, he carried Sheridan's message, having been given careful instructions to swallow it if accosted by the enemy. Laws went straight to Wright's home and, despite the fact that he was "an entire stranger" to her, delivered the note. By sheer coincidence, Wright had entertained a Confederate officer the night before, and the two young people had discussed, purely by way of making conversation, the southern presence in Winchester. The officer had told her that Brigadier General Joseph Kershaw's infantry division had left for Richmond the previous morning, along with a battalion of artillery that had accompanied it to the valley the month before.[22]

Rebecca Wright discussed the situation with her mother, Rachel (although not with her sister, Hannah Ann, who was as pro-southern as Rebecca was pro-Union), and decided to chance answering Sheridan's message. She wrote: "I have no communication whatever with the rebels, but will tell you what I know. The division of General Kershaw, and Cutshaw's artillery, twelve guns and men, General Anderson commanding, have been sent away, and no more are expected, as they cannot be spared from Richmond. I do not know how the troops are situated, but the force is much smaller than represented. I will take pleasure hereafter in learning all I can of their strength and position, and the bearer may call again."[23]

That would not be necessary. When Laws returned to Union headquarters that evening with Wright's answer again concealed under his tongue, Sheridan began making immediate plans to attack Early at Newtown, southeast of Winchester, as soon as Kershaw was safely beyond recall. In the midst of his preparations, however, he received a peremptory summons to meet with Grant at Charlestown. One day earlier such a directive might have severely discomfited him; now, with Rebecca Wright's opportune message stuffed in his pocket (and Kershaw's crack infantry division safely on its way back to Richmond), he could meet the Union general-in-chief with renewed enthusiasm for the task at hand.

It was well for Sheridan that events were beginning to come together; the administration's patience, fairly or unfairly, was wearing thin. With Early still stomping about the lower valley, interfering with the daily operation of the Baltimore & Ohio Railroad, the politically influential president of the B&O, John W. Garrett, was complaining about the interruption of rail service into Washington from the West Virginia coalfields and warning of a crippling shortage of coal that winter. Halleck passed along the complaints to Grant, who already had received a suggestion from Lincoln that Sheridan be reinforced with "say ten thousand men" and encouraged to strike at Early to break the politically embarrassing deadlock.[24]

Hence Grant's hurried trip to Charlestown. His later explanation for the journey—that he was afraid Stanton and Halleck might interfere with his orders to Sheridan—has the ring of untruth about it; there is no evidence that either functionary ever tampered with his messages. More likely, Grant too had grown restive at Sheridan's uncharacteristic inactivity, especially in light of the recent reduction of Early's force, which Grant undoubtedly knew about prior to his visit. He later admitted that he went to Charlestown with a campaign plan for Sheridan stuffed in his coat pocket, and there is no reason to doubt that he fully intended to see it put into action before he left.[25]

As it was, he could have saved himself a trip; Sheridan had his own strategy already mapped out. In essence, it duplicated his advance up the valley five weeks before, with the same malign intent: to strike Early's right flank, get astride his line of retreat, and roll up the Rebel army in detail as it struggled to escape southward. Grant listened impassively to his young commander, his own hastily worked-out plan still buttoned inside his greatcoat. "Could you be ready to move by next Tuesday?" he asked when Sheridan had finished. "Oh, yes," Sheridan replied. "I can be off before daylight on Monday." Grant nodded. "Go in," he said.[26]

Grant had scarcely departed, satisfied that matters were well in hand, when Sheridan received an encouraging report from Averell's cavalry north of Winchester. Two divisions of Rebel infantry—over half of Early's existing force in the valley—were en route to Martinsburg, twenty miles away. Against the advice of worried subordinates, Early had rashly divided his little force, leaving only Major General Stephen Dodson Ramseur's 2,400-man division in place to guard the eastern approaches to Winchester. Brigadier General Gabriel Wharton, with an additional 1,600 men, was within striking distance, four miles northeast at Stephenson's Depot. Convinced that Sheridan was afraid to act, Early had taken his other two divisions north on what one disgusted aide later termed a "wild goose chase," intending again to disrupt repairs along the suddenly voguish B&O. But whatever enjoyment Early may have derived from his trip down the valley was quickly rendered unamusing by a telegram he happened to read at the local telegraph office, a copy of a Federal message describing Grant's just-completed visit with Sheridan. There was only one probable reason for the Union general-in-chief's trip to Charlestown—and it wasn't sightseeing. Hastily, Early ordered his divisions back to Winchester. It was now virtually certain the Yankees were planning to attack.[27]

"The disjointed state of the enemy," as Sheridan later described it, encouraged him to change his battle plan at almost the last minute. Instead of driving on Newtown and attempting to turn Early's right flank, he now intended to move directly on Winchester, envelop the two enemy divisions left in the vicinity, and splinter the other two divisions before they could reunite. Orders were given to march promptly at 2:00 A.M. on September 19. Ignoring again his maxim about combinations rarely working, Sheridan had devised for Early's benefit a complicated series of cavalry and infantry maneuvers aimed at achieving nothing less than a double envelopment of the entire Rebel force at Winchester. While Wright's VI Corps and Emory's XIX Corps attacked Ramseur's lone division from the east, Crook's VIII Corps would follow James Wilson's cavalry division south around the enemy's right flank, and Torbert's two other mounted divisions would swing northward around the enemy left and come in behind them above the town. Early's other divisions, attempting to escape down the Valley Pike, would be effectively bottled up by Crook's preset roadblock.[28]

The plan depended more on speed and surprise than on sheer numbers, the one battlefield variable Sheridan could personally control. Owing perhaps to his recent experience with the cavalry and his previous acquaintance with the loose-hipped farm boys of the Army of the Cumberland, he failed to allow for the ingrained slowness of the Potomac-bred Federals. Nor did the terrain around Winchester easily lend itself to large-scale movements. Berryville Pike, down which the central attack would come, cut through a two-mile-long canyon of steep-sided hills and thick, bushy woods before opening onto a cleared plateau two miles east of Winchester. Paralleling the road were two sizable streams, Red Bud Run on the north and Abraham's Creek on the south, both of which emptied into deeply running Opequon Creek, the de facto dividing line between the two sides, two miles farther east. In order to come to grips with the enemy, Wilson's cavalry would have to force a crossing at the Opequon, clear the roadway through Berryville Canyon, and slide quickly to its left to allow the infantry to debouch from the canyon, presumably in passable order, all the while under fire. Meanwhile, farther north, Torbert's other two divisions were directed to ford the heavily picketed stream, drive through the enemy at Stephenson's Depot, and wheel south for a sweep up the Valley Turnpike.

At 3:00 A.M. on the nineteenth, Wilson's horsemen crossed Opequon Creek and galloped up Berryville Canyon in total darkness, scattering startled Confederate pickets before them. Brigadier General John B. McIntosh's brigade, which six days earlier had surrounded and captured the entire Eighth South Carolina Regiment, 106 officers and men in all, in the same vicinity, led the charge. Quick-firing its redoubtable Spencer repeating rifles, the brigade fought through the western entrance to the canyon, wrenched a line of breastworks from the enemy, and fanned out across the open plateau. McIntosh himself went down with a severe leg wound (it would be amputated that night, invaliding him out of the war), but the Union horsemen dismounted and held the position in the face of a determined counterattack by Ramseur's lone division. Sheridan, aboard his black charger Rienzi, followed the cavalry into the canyon, reaching the battlefield at about 7:00 A.M. Stopping a moment to console the wounded McIntosh—"You have done nobly," he said—Sheridan spurred his horse up a hill near the mouth of the ravine and surveyed the open countryside with an eye toward positioning Wright's infantry corps.[29]

Behind him, in Berryville Canyon, things had already begun to go wrong, perhaps disastrously. Wright, in direct contravention of the order that "the utmost promptitude should be exercised" in passing through the canyon, had inexplicably brought his entire wagon train with him. The narrowness of the canyon forced the long columns of infantry to proceed one at a time through the jam-packed pass. With Wright's trains clattering along behind him, the XIX Corps was compelled to sit by the wayside and wait for the road to clear. It was after 10:00 A.M. before Emory's corps managed to extricate itself from the cramped canyon and emerged into the open land beyond.[30]

Meanwhile, in response to Ramseur's hasty message that the Yankees were attacking in force along the Berryville Road, Early rushed back to Winchester from Stephenson's Depot, after first starting Major Generals Robert Rodes's and John Gordon's divisions in the same direction. By 10:00 A.M. he had three of his four divisions in line across Berryville Pike from Red Bud Run to Abraham's Creek. His fourth, now under the personal direction of Major General John C. Breckinridge, was kept in place at Stephenson's Depot, along with a preponderance of the southern cavalry, with orders to fall back on the main line if pressed.[31]

By midmorning Sheridan's hopes of defeating the enemy in detail had effectively been ruined by three unexpected factors: the infuriating mix-up involving Wright's wagon train and Emory's foot soldiers, Early's prompt reaction to the Union attack, and Sheridan's own faulty plan in trying to shoehorn twenty thousand soldiers through one narrow pass. What had seemed a golden opportunity to destroy Early's army once and for all now threatened instead to become a full-blown Union disaster. Fuming at the unwonted delay, Sheridan aligned his infantry, a division at a time, on either side of Berryville Pike. Holding his friend David Russell's division in reserve, he hastily cobbled together an assault column from the emerging VI and XIX Corps. Shortly before noon the blue line went forward into a maelstrom of Confederate fire. On the right, Brigadier General Cuvier Grover's division burst through a stand of woods, huzzahed its way across a ripening cornfield, and drove Gordon's graycoats through a sec-

ond fringe of trees. Meanwhile, the VI Corps divisions of Brigadier Generals G. W. Getty and James B. Ricketts slammed forward
along Berryville Pike, scattering Ramseur's gallant but outgunned
division rearward toward Winchester.[32]

The initial assault had gone according to plan; unfortunately,
the plan was grievously flawed. Sheridan's orders had dictated
that the VI Corps, on the Union left, guide itself by Berryville
Pike. But for once his practiced eye for terrain had failed him: six
hundred yards from the mouth of the canyon the road turned
sharply south, carrying the VI Corps attackers ever farther away
from the XIX Corps on their right. A gap, easily visible to the
experienced eye, instantly appeared in the Union lines. Rodes and
Gordon, who were nothing if not experienced (their men, after
all, had once been Stonewall Jackson's), wasted little time in ex-
ploiting the gap. With a resounding thud, their two fire-tested
divisions smashed into Grover's spent attackers, sending them
howling back toward the sheltering woods. The tide of battle
shifted to the graycoats; Rodes, however, did not live to see it. A
steel splinter from a Yankee shell nicked him, almost gently,
behind the left ear, tumbling him backward from his horse, dead
at the age of thirty-five.

Sheridan, watching from his hill behind the army's center,
refused to panic. As the Rebel attack pressed forward, engulfing
the VI Corps' now-exposed right flank, Colonel Charles H. Tompkins's First New York and Fifth Maine artillery batteries held
their ground, slinging hatfuls of grapeshot into their guns and
firing over the heads of their retreating comrades at Rodes's onrushing Alabamians. Tompkins's stand bought Sheridan enough
time to summon Russell's division from reserve and send it forward to plug the gap in the Union right-center. Russell had complained earlier in the day about being put in the rear of the line,
but Sheridan had assured his old comrade that he was simply
trying to ensure that he had a dependable commander backing
him up. Now, rushing to the front, Russell's men rallied around
Tompkins's batteries on either side of the Berryville Road.[33]

For the next thirty minutes the two sides fired point-blank

into each other at killing range. Russell, already hit in the chest by a Rebel bullet, died instantly from a shell fragment through the heart. (''He was my captain and friend,'' Sheridan would remember in his memoirs, ''and I was indebted to him, not only for sound advice and good example, but for the inestimable service he had just performed and sealed with his life, so it may be inferred how deeply I felt his loss.'') At the moment, however, there was no time for good-byes. Before his death Russell had sent his third brigade, commanded by the extraordinary young military intellectual Colonel Emory Upton of New York, into the woods where the XIX Corps had fled. As the Confederates charged again toward Russell's position, Upton's brigade suddenly broke from concealment and shattered the enemy flank, plugging the gap in the Union line and dooming the Rebel counterattack.[34]

A lull now ensued in the fighting along the front. From his headquarters knoll just south of the pike, Sheridan waited impatiently for word from his cavalry commanders north of Winchester. Hearing nothing by midafternoon, he directed Crook to shift his VIII Corps from the Union left to the right, sacrificing as he did any hope of bottling up the Rebels inside Winchester. Crook immediately got his two divisions moving through Berryville Canyon, where they passed a long, melancholy line of walking wounded, professional skulkers, and overburdened stretcher-bearers heading the opposite way, out of the battle. After the war an acrimonious dispute—the first of many—arose between Sheridan and Crook over what next transpired. Sheridan maintained that he had directed Crook ''to act as a turning column, to find the left of the enemy's line, strike it in the flank or rear, [and] break it up.'' Crook, with the support of at least one witness, Captain Henry DuPont, claimed that Sheridan had merely told him ''to look out for our right''—hence the credit for the subsequent flanking maneuver was Crook's alone. Whatever the case (and it would not be the last time Crook denigrated Sheridan's accomplishments and expanded on his own), the resulting attack began the Confederate downfall at Winchester.[35]

Throwing one division forward into the woods occupied by

Emory's fought-out corps on the Union right, Crook personally led his other division across Red Bud Run, bringing it around beyond the Confederate left. The two divisions charged simultaneously, striking Gordon's hard-pressed legions in front and flank, driving them sullenly rearward. The Union left and center also pressed ahead, urged on by Sheridan, who had left the relative safety of his hillside vantage and, spurring Rienzi through a blizzard of rifle and artillery fire, rode the line from one end to the other, exhorting his weary but inspirited troops "to kill every son of a bitch" before them. In the meantime, Torbert's cavalry had fought its way through stiff enemy resistance northeast of Winchester and now formed in a single unbroken line, five brigades strong, across Martinsburg Pike two miles north of town. There, with the late-afternoon sun slanting golden off drawn sabers and upraised regimental standards, the troopers charged southward in what an admiring infantry officer later called "a sight to be remembered a lifetime."[36]

The Confederate line was now bent into an inverted L on the plateau east of Winchester. The Union horsemen, slowly at first, then faster and faster, clambered down the pike toward the enemy line. The Rebels here already had endured a frantic early-morning march to the battlefield, withstood numerous Federal infantry charges and virtually constant artillery shelling, and made their own gallant counterattack. Through it all they had comported themselves with the southern soldier's habitual good-natured valor. But the sudden apparitional descent of seven thousand sword-waving Yanks onto their flank, unchecked by any answering Confederate cavalry, was too much at last for them to bear. First singly, then in groups, then all together, they turned and ran for the illusive safety of Winchester.

The cavalry charge, as Sheridan had planned, completely buckled the Confederate left, sending shock waves down the enemy line. An erroneous report that Union troops had also gained his right flank—actually it was Ramseur's division, falling back in good order—persuaded Early to order a general withdrawal.

The southern forces raced through Winchester in the dusk, ignoring both their officers' shouted demands and the frantic supplications of the town's alarmed citizens, led by General Gordon's wife, Fanny, who, mindless of flying shells and whizzing bullets, took to the streets in a vain attempt to stem the rout. Colonel George S. Patton of the Second Virginia, grandfather of the fabled World War II commander, likewise exhorted his men to stand firm and died, the victim of a Federal sniper, in the jumbled alleys of Winchester.[37]

Suddenly it was over. Sheridan, in the company of Crook, cantered through Winchester's debris-littered streets. Three young girls, Jennie and Susie Meredith and a friend named Griffith, ran out to greet them with "the most unguarded manifestations and expressions." Crook warned the girls against displaying too much Unionist sentiment, lest the town change hands for a seventy-fourth time. They laughed off his warning; Early's army, they said, was so demoralized it would never reenter Winchester. Sheridan wanted to find a quiet place to compose a telegram to General Grant, and Crook took him to Rebecca Wright's home. She flung open the front door, shook hands with Crook, and received an enthusiastic greeting from the beaming, red-faced Sheridan, who impulsively cried, "Hurrah for this loyal girl!"[38]

Sitting down at a desk in Wright's private schoolroom, Sheridan wrote out his victory message. Headed "Winchester, 7.30 p.m."—itself a dead giveaway of the battle's outcome—the message informed Grant that he had attacked Early's forces "and after a most stubborn and sanguinary engagement . . . completely defeated him." The conduct of his officers and men had been "most superb," Sheridan reported, noting proudly that "they charged and carried every position taken up by the Rebels from the Opequon Creek to Winchester." A follow-up message from Chief of Staff James Forsyth, widely attributed to Sheridan himself, expanded on the day's success in a more lyrical and quotable vein: "We have just sent them whirling through Winchester,"

Forsyth wrote, "and we are after them tomorrow. This army behaved splendidly."[39]

The words "whirling through Winchester" captured the public's fancy, and the phrase soon echoed from one end of the North to the other. Abraham Lincoln sent along his personal blessing for the great victory Sheridan had won, Grant chimed in with a one-hundred-gun salute and a recommendation to Secretary of War Stanton that Sheridan be named a brigadier general in the Regular Army and given permanent command of the Middle Military Division. In the first warm glow of success, Sheridan neglected to mention that he had suffered more than 4,500 casualties at Winchester, twice as many as his men had inflicted on the greatly outnumbered Rebels. It is doubtful, however, that Grant would have minded; results were what he looked at, not the human cost involved. "If practicable," he characteristically ordered Sheridan, "push your success and make all you can of it."[40]

At daybreak the next morning Sheridan sent his cavalry clattering southward down the Valley Turnpike in renewed pursuit of the enemy. The rest of the army soon followed. The Rebels, marching all night, had pulled up twenty miles south of Winchester at Fisher's Hill, the steep-sided prominence from whose rocky peak Early had outfrowned Sheridan six weeks before. But circumstances now had changed, even if the two opponents had not. With more than three times as many Union guns on hand as there were Rebels confronting them, and freed at last from squeamish, interfering politicians, Sheridan would not hesitate to offer battle again, even though on its face the enemy held a formidable defensive position. At a meeting of corps commanders that night it was decided that Crook would attempt to pass undetected around the enemy left and duplicate Winchester's successful flanking maneuver.[41]

Crook was directed to delay his attack one day to allow the cavalry to circle eastward around Massanutten Mountain and throw itself across the Valley Turnpike at New Market, cutting off Early's line of retreat. Before dawn on September 22, having hidden all the previous day in a thick stand of trees behind Cedar Creek, Crook moved around the eastern base of Little North Mountain, sheltering his forces from Rebel eyes in the shadowy ravines and heavily wooded ridges west of the creek. As a further precaution, canteens and bayonets were wrapped in cloth to prevent them from clanging together and alerting enemy pickets. While Crook was skulking into position off to the right, Sheridan had Wright and Emory noisily threaten the Confederate center. This demonstration, strictly for show, had the unwanted effect of convincing Early that his seemingly impregnable position was in fact quite vulnerable to Union attack. Watching Sheridan bang away at his front and realizing that the Yankees fully intended to fight him again, Early drew up orders for a nighttime retreat. But once again the true initiative rested with the Federals. At 4:00 P.M., twelve hours after they had begun their clandestine maneuvers, Crook's veterans charged down the eastern face of Little North Mountain and rolled up the Rebel flank as easily as a North African rug merchant rolls up his wares.[42]

The subsequent stampede carried the Rebels out of their trenches and down the far side of Fisher's Hill—infantry, artillery, horses, and caissons careering wildly toward the Valley Pike. Sheridan, mounted on Rienzi, followed Wright's men up the side of the hill, reliving perhaps that other delirious autumn afternoon, ten months earlier, at Missionary Ridge. "Run, boys, run!" he shouted at his bluecoats. "Don't wait to form! Don't let 'em stop! If you can't run, then holler!"[43]

The Union pursuit continued through the night, a steady rain drenching both victor and vanquished. At Woodstock, nine miles due south, Sheridan pulled up to await news from his cavalry chief that the second part of his grand design was working and that Early was barred from escaping somewhere north of New Market. It was thus with "astonishment and chagrin" that he learned on the morning of the twenty-third that the normally dependable Torbert, with Wilson's entire division and half of Merritt's, had failed to force a passage through the Luray Valley and

around the southern end of Massanutten Mountain, and instead
had fallen back to Front Royal, at the opposite end of the range.
Immediately he ordered Torbert back into the valley, "without
regard to horseflesh," but his cherished envelopment of Early's
beaten army, for the second time in three days, had irretrievably
gone astray. "To this day," Sheridan wondered twenty years
later, "I have been unable to account satisfactorily for Torbert's
failure . . . his impotent attempt not only chagrined me very
much, but occasioned much unfavorable comment throughout the
army."[44]

Later that morning, his celebrated temper already frayed by
Torbert's inexplicable conduct, Sheridan received a second bit of
bad news from William Woods Averell, the ranking cavalryman
on the scene and thus the unwitting target of his commanding
general's self-nourishing wrath. Sheridan had assumed that Averell was somewhere south of the army, pursuing Early's "perfect
mob" of fugitives. Instead, Averell sauntered into camp from the
north, having scorned further pursuit of the enemy and blithely
bedded down for the night while Sheridan and the infantry continued harrowing the worsted Rebels. Hot words ensued between
the two, and Sheridan sent Averell away with the pointed injunction that he find some Rebels to fight—and soon. Incredibly,
Averell ignored both that direct order and a follow-up note from
Sheridan calling for "actual fighting, with necessary casualties,"
choosing instead to go into camp again before dark that afternoon.
Sheridan quickly learned of the insubordinate behavior, and by
midnight Averell was en route to Wheeling, West Virginia, out of
Sheridan's army, and sight, for good.[45]

The total breakdown of cavalry pursuit enabled the enemy to
get safely away and left Sheridan in the unusual position of being
about the only man in his army—Averell excepted—who was at
all disappointed by the twin victories at Winchester and Fisher's
Hill. At Petersburg, Grant greeted the news with another of his
patented live-ammunition salutes; other commanders across the
country followed suit. Sheridan's showing, Grant told him,

"wipes out much of the stain upon our arms by previous disasters in that locality." Keep on, he added, "and your good work will cause the fall of Richmond."[46]

Sheridan, for his part, was not so sure. "Our success," he noted, "was very great, yet I had anticipated results still more pregnant." Early's army, although twice beaten and no doubt downhearted, nevertheless remained undestroyed, sheltering in the Blue Ridge Mountains and awaiting more reinforcements from the indomitable Lee. The Union army, on the other hand, had come eighty miles south in one week of marching, stalking, fighting, and pursuing. "I am now 94 miles from Martinsburg and 104 miles from Harpers Ferry," the nearest Federal supply depots, Sheridan pointed out. To Grant's suggestion that he live off the countryside and make a concerted effort to destroy the Virginia Central Railroad at Charlottesville, Sheridan offered a less ambitious counterproposal. "I think the best policy will be to let the burning of the crops in the Valley be the end of this campaign, and let some of this army go elsewhere," he recommended. As both men knew, "elsewhere" meant back to the trenches at Petersburg; but Sheridan, convinced that Early had been suitably chastised, was willing to break up his own command and simply declare his mission a success.[47]

The alternative, a chancy pursuit over the Blue Ridge Mountains with his supply lines stretched thin and southern guerrillas nipping at his heels, did not hold much appeal for Sheridan. Convinced that Grant, under pressure from Washington, was backing a flawed plan—a matter of high-level policy-making that was not, properly speaking, Sheridan's concern—the younger general proceeded to drag his feet. At length Grant gave in. Instead of opening a second front against Lee's besieged Virginians, a move that might have shortened the war considerably, Sheridan was permitted to retrace his steps down the Shenandoah Valley. The region's undefended civilians, not Early's veteran soldiers, would become his next, unwitting targets.[48]

As September gave way to October, Sheridan sent his cavalry

galloping as far south as Waynesboro to seize or destroy livestock and provisions. Barns, mills, factories, and railroads were put to the torch as a way of "desolating the Shenandoah country so as to make it untenable for permanent occupation by the Confederates"—or anyone else, for that matter. By October 6, the day the army began withdrawing northward, four hundred square miles of prime valley farmland had been rendered uninhabitable by Union raiders. It was mean, ugly work, made more so by a series of murderous clashes between Sheridan's cavalry and Rebel guerrillas operating in the vicinity. A self-perpetuating cycle of atrocities, reprisals, and counter-reprisals soon poisoned the already sulfurous atmosphere and occasioned some of the most revolting episodes of the war.[49]

At the heart of the trouble was the refusal by Sheridan and his subordinates to recognize the 43rd Virginia Cavalry Battalion of Lieutenant Colonel John Singleton Mosby as a legally sanctioned unit of the Confederate army. In this they took their lead from Grant, who had instructed Sheridan, upon his arrival in the Shenandoah, to "hang without trial" any of Mosby's men who happened to fall into his hands. Grant's order was plainly wrong; Mosby held a direct commission from Confederate President Jefferson Davis, passed down through General Robert E. Lee and Major General J. E. B. Stuart—a more distinguished pedigree could scarcely be imagined. The confusion, not entirely accidental, arose from the fact that Mosby, although a duly sworn officer of the Confederate cavalry, conducted his operations in such a way as to blur the distinction between regular cavalry and irregular guerrillas. Hit-and-run raids on Union supply trains, midnight ambushes of foraging details, long-range sniping at unwary marchers—such were "the Gray Ghost's" favored tactics. Harassed and vengeful, Sheridan's soldiers had little patience for protocol. They simply declared all of Mosby's horsemen to be "cutthroats and robbers" and summarily executed them, justly or not.[50]

The situation came to a head in late September following a

clash between Mosby's battalion and a brigade of Union cavalry near Front Royal. At the time Mosby himself was recuperating from a severe gunshot wound, but a force of Rangers under Captain Sam Chapman brazenly attacked a Federal supply train in bright daylight. In the ensuing melee Colonel Charles Lowell's Yankee horsemen rushed to the scene and scattered the Rebels after a swirling fight. In the course of the action Lieutenant Charles McMaster of the Second U.S. Cavalry was shot and killed when his frightened horse carried him into enemy lines. Enraged rumors swept through the ranks that McMaster had been shot while trying to surrender. Subsequently, six partisan rangers were run to ground and dragged into Front Royal by their seething captors. Two were immediately taken behind a Methodist church and shot; two others, including a seventeen-year-old boy who was not even a member of Mosby's band, were similarly served. The last pair were pulled by their necks into a walnut tree and slowly strangled to death. A placard was draped over one of the victims: "Such is the fate of all Mosby's men."[51]

When Mosby learned of the Front Royal murders he bitterly vowed retribution. Meanwhile a second incident took place, this time between one of Sheridan's favorite officers and a trio of regular Confederate cavalrymen, that further darkened the liverish mood in the valley. On the afternoon of October 3, young topographical engineer John Meigs was returning to camp at Harrisonburg in the company of two orderlies. Near the village of Dayton, a mile and a half behind Union lines, the party overtook another threesome; all six were wearing waterproof ponchos against the drizzling rain. Only after it was too late to avoid trouble did Meigs and his party realize that the other group were Rebels. Each side shouted for the other to surrender, shots were fired, and Meigs thudded to the wet ground, killed instantly by bullets to the face and chest.

A dispute soon raged between the two parties over the way young Meigs had departed the world. One of the orderlies escaped capture and raced back to Sheridan's headquarters to report that the lieutenant had been shot down in cold blood "without even the chance to give himself up." Furious and heartsick over the killing, Sheridan resolved to punish the unoffending residents of Dayton, the site of the shooting, on the wrong-headed assumption that the "murderers" lived in the area and had been visiting their homes prior to the deed. Custer, who had just succeeded to command of the Third Division following the demise of Averell and the transfer of James Wilson to Sherman's army in Georgia, was directed to burn every house within a five-mile radius of the village. Cooler heads eventually prevailed, persuading Sheridan to cancel the order. Most Dayton residents were Mennonite pacifists, anyway, and the Rebels who had taken part in the shooting were not even natives of the area.[52]

Years later the southern horsemen involved in the incident told a different version of Meigs's demise. The three, George W. Martin, Benjamin F. Shavers, and F. M. Campbell, were all privates in Brigadier General Thomas Rosser's newly arrived cavalry brigade. According to them, Meigs fired first with a pistol concealed beneath his poncho, severely wounding Martin in the groin. Shavers and Campbell returned fire, dropping the young Federal from his saddle. Ironically, Martin, whose own gun had misfired, went into hiding for several years after the war, a one-thousand-dollar bounty having been placed on his head by Meigs's bereaved father, who mistakenly thought Martin had killed his son.[53]

Whichever story was true—given Meigs's previous high-handed behavior, the Rebel version certainly seems plausible—Dayton was merely one in a series of Shenandoah Valley towns fired that autumn by Federals in a deliberate campaign of looting and arson memorialized by its victims as "the Burning." While Union infantry and artillery started northward from Harrisonburg along the Valley Pike on October 6, the cavalry fanned out in a twenty-mile arc from North Mountain in the west to the Blue Ridge in the east. By the time they reached Woodstock, forty miles away, Sheridan's horsemen had burned more than two thousand barns and seventy grain mills, driven off four thousand head of cattle, and slaughtered three thousand sheep. "When this is completed," Sheridan boasted, "the Valley . . . will have but little in it for man or beast."[54]

Day after day the blue column moved northward, leaving in its wake a heavy pall of smoke clearly visible to the anguished Confederates trailing behind. The sheer remorselessness of the Yankees' deeds staggered soldier and civilian alike. To southern eyes this was not warfare but simple rapine, unredeemed by military necessity and made worse by the obvious relish many—though not all—of the destroyers took in their work. Occasionally a farmer tried fighting back, one man against many, but most did nothing except watch disconsolately as the backbreaking work of a lifetime flamed into ashes in a matter of seconds. Sheridan, who considered war a just punishment to be visited on anyone foolish enough to support it, rode in the vanguard of his devastating army, his feet propped up in a two-seater wagon, jauntily waving a cigar at his troops.

Two days out from Harrisonburg, the general's holiday mood abruptly darkened. Rebel cavalry under Rosser had been snapping away at the army's heels, an annoyance he now determined to stop. Angrily summoning Torbert to his tent on the night of October 8, Sheridan told him in no uncertain terms to attack Rosser the next morning and either "whip the Rebel cavalry or get whipped" himself. With Averell's recent disgrace as a spur, Torbert wasted little time obeying orders. At Tom's Brook, five miles south of Strasburg, the two sides met in a saber-wielding fight that quickly degenerated into a southern rout. Union cavalry swarmed over the startled enemy, turning their flanks and initiating a mad twenty-mile dash to the rear by Rosser, the self-proclaimed "Savior of the Valley," and his equally grandiose Laurel Brigade. The victorious Federals dubbed the action "the Woodstock Races," and Sheridan, watching the whole thing from a nearby mountaintop, approvingly declared it "a square cavalry fight . . . beyond my power to describe."[55]

Thus relieved of enemy obstructions, Sheridan's men went into camp around Cedar Creek. The XIX Corps held the Union right, bivouacking near the historic Belle Grove plantation of colonial army major Isaac Hite, brother-in-law of President James Madison and friendly neighbor of Thomas Jefferson, who had personally designed the limestone mansion in 1794. Crook's VIII Corps camped on high ground on the Union left, east of the Valley Turnpike, its flank resting on the Shenandoah River. The VI Corps, under Wright, continued eastward toward Front Royal on the first leg of its long journey back to Petersburg.

Far to the south at New Market, Jubal Early received word that Sheridan had detached part of his army to reinforce Grant. Hurriedly the Confederates marched northward down the valley, hailed gratefully as deliverers by ravaged survivors of "the Burning." On October 13 Early reoccupied his unlucky position at Fisher's Hill, hoping again to goad Sheridan into attacking. Ever aggressive, Sheridan might have done just that, had he not received a telegram that same day from Secretary of War Stanton requesting his presence in Washington. Stanton was about to visit Grant's headquarters at City Point; he thought a prior consultation with Sheridan would be "extremely desirable." Convinced that Early could do him no serious injury in his present condition, Sheridan nevertheless recalled Wright's corps from Front Royal, placing it in reserve on the Union right, a fateful eleventh-hour decision.[56]

Before entraining at Rectortown the next morning, Sheridan was handed a hasty message from Wright. Union signalmen at Cedar Creek had intercepted a Rebel transmission the previous afternoon: "Lieutenant-General Early: Be Ready to move as soon as my forces join you and we will crush Sheridan. (Signed) Longstreet." Sheridan rightly considered the message a ruse—Early had sent it to himself in hopes of bluffing the Yankees out of the valley by the mere mention of Lee's famous I Corps commander. Still, to be on the safe side, Sheridan canceled plans for a major cavalry raid on Charlottesville, speeding the horsemen back to camp and advising Wright to strengthen his position, "look well to your ground and be well prepared." He, Sheridan, would be back at Cedar Creek by October 18, if not sooner.[57]

Sheridan's military intuition, though hardly infallible, led him to cut short his visit to Washington. After a hurried discussion with Stanton and Halleck about future moves in the valley (he still argued against opening a second front east of the Blue Ridge), he rushed back by train and horse to Winchester, where he spent the night of October 18 at the home of local tobacco merchant Lloyd Logan. Still troubled by the situation at the front, he dispatched a courier to Cedar Creek for word of any enemy movement. All was quiet, Wright reported back; he planned to reconnoiter the Rebel position at dawn. Greatly relieved, Sheridan turned in for the night.

He was awakened just after dawn by the officer of the day, who worriedly reported artillery fire coming from the direction of Cedar Creek. Sheridan, abed, was not disturbed—merely Wright's reconnaissance, he said. Still, growing restless, he got dressed and went downstairs, ordering breakfast hurried up and Rienzi saddled and ready in the yard. By this time the duty officer had come back to report that the firing to the south was continuing. Did it sound like a battle? Sheridan asked. No, said the officer. Puzzled but not particularly alarmed, Sheridan decided to return to the front as soon as he and his staff had taken breakfast.[58]

It was nearly 9:00 A.M. before the general and his companions, Lieutenant Colonel James Forsyth, Major George "Sandy" Forsyth (no relation), Captain Joseph O'Keefe, and two Washington-based military engineers left the Logan house and rode southward out of Winchester. As they departed, Sheridan noticed that many of the townswomen "kept shaking their skirts at us and . . . were otherwise markedly insolent in their demeanor." He put it down to unregenerate Rebel sentiment. At Mill Creek, just outside town, the company picked up its prearranged escort, three hundred troopers from the 17th Pennsylvania Cavalry. By now the noise from the south was an unceasing roar, and Sheridan dismounted and put his head to the ground, Indian-style, to listen. Without doubt a battle was in progress—worse yet, the sound was moving too quickly to be accounted for by their own rate of speed. The Union army, therefore, must be falling back. The column rode on, Sheridan looking "somewhat disconcerted," in Sandy Forsyth's view, then crested a rise. Suddenly they came face to face with "the appalling spectacle of a panic-stricken army—hundreds of slightly wounded men, throngs of others unhurt but utterly demoralized, and baggage-wagons by the score, all pressing to the rear in hopeless confusion."[59]

Here Sheridan heard from a handful of frazzled officers what his eyes had already told him: the army had been surprised and routed. His first thought was to regroup outside Winchester for a last-ditch stand. But as he moved on, walking Rienzi at a measured pace while he mulled over what to do, he decided instead to go to the front. It was a momentous decision, the decision of a lifetime, and it came to Sheridan about the time his chief commissary officer arrived to tell him that the Rebels had captured his headquarters. All his life he had responded to challenge by taking immediate, aggressive action. Remaining behind in Winchester, rounding up fugitives for a defensive line, was not in keeping with Sheridan's character. Punched in the nose, the brawling little Pig Foot from back-alley Somerset instinctively gathered himself to punch back—hard.

Leaving James Forsyth and the majority of his cavalry escort to act as a glorified straggler line, Sheridan spurred Rienzi toward the sound of battle. Sandy Forsyth, O'Keefe, and twenty Pennsylvania troopers rode behind him, along with a little orderly bearing the general's distinctive swallow-tailed flag: red star on white background, white star on red. He was ten miles from Cedar Creek, but he was coming on.

Through a brilliant Indian-summer morning they rode, white dust from the turnpike powdering their dark blue uniforms. Sheridan, fifty yards in the lead, passed long files of walking wounded, as well as an equal number of soldiers who were wounded only in their pride. Occasionally taking to the fields to skirt a tangle of wagons on the roadway, he waved his little campaign cap at the knots of men huddled around improvised campfires, heating coffee. "Come on back, boys!" he shouted. "Give 'em hell, God damn 'em! We'll make coffee out of Cedar Creek tonight!" His eyes had the scary dull red glint they often showed during battle. "Come on back!" he rasped. "Face the other way. We're going to lick those fellows out of their boots!"[60]

Incredibly, the rabble did turn around—most of them, anyway. One infantry colonel, unstrung by the rout, shouted back, "The army's whipped!" and kept running. "You are," Sheridan scoffed, "but the army isn't." Still, the closer he came to the front, the more unmistakable were the signs of defeat. At Newtown the turnpike was so jammed with supply wagons, artillery caissons, and overburdened ambulances that the party again was forced to leave the roadbed and take to the fields. A young major on Crook's staff, future president William McKinley, caught sight of the general's headquarters flag and began spreading the word that Sheridan had returned.[61]

Swinging back onto the turnpike south of Newtown, Sheridan spotted the first heartening sight he had encountered since leaving Winchester. Three-quarters of a mile west of the pike an organized body of troops, which proved to be Ricketts's and Wheaton's VI Corps divisions, were standing fast in line of battle. Not everyone, it seemed, had abandoned the field. Spurring Rienzi, Sheridan crossed the road and soon caught sight of another group of soldiers, Getty's division of the VI Corps, acting as the broken army's rear guard, three miles north of Cedar Creek, where he had left it intact three days before. Alfred Torbert was the first general officer to greet him upon his arrival, and the fervor with which he gasped out, "My God, I'm glad you've come!" indicated the army's desperate straits. The cavalry leader fell in behind Sheridan, who leaped his horse over a hastily built barricade of fence rails and wheeled to face what remained of his army. "Men, by God, we'll whip them yet!" he roared. "We'll sleep in our old tents tonight!" At Sheridan's words, the soldiers shouted, cheered, and stamped their feet. Major Hazard Stevens of Getty's staff noticed an immediate change in the Union troops. "Instantly," he wrote, "a mighty revulsion of feeling took place. Hope and confidence returned at a bound. . . . Now we all burned to attack the enemy, to drive him back, to retrieve our honor and sleep in our old camps that night. And every man knew that Sheridan would do it."[62]

Behind the frontline troops a flourish of regimental flags arose, welcoming Sheridan back to the field. The color-bearers were from Crook's VIII Corps, the line itself composed mainly of officers, among whom Sheridan recognized Colonel (and future president) Rutherford B. Hayes. Riding on, he located his erstwhile corps commanders, Wright, Crook, and Emory, conversing atop a debris-strewn hill. Hurriedly dismounting, Sheridan handed Rienzi's reins to an orderly and impulsively threw his arms around the taller Crook in a comradely embrace. "What are you doing way back here?" he asked. Wright, in whose charge Sheridan had left the army, looked on silently, tired and morose. A Rebel bullet had clipped his chin; blood dribbled onto his uniform front. "Well, we've done the best we could," he said by way of greeting. "That's all right," Sheridan replied, putting the best face on things. The crusty Emory broke the fraternal mood; his troops, he said, were prepared to cover the retreat. "Retreat, hell!" Sheridan stormed. "We'll be back in our camps tonight."[63]

Now he learned what had happened in his absence. A column of Rebels, following an audacious plan worked out by Major General John B. Gordon, had circled around the base of Massanutten Mountain, forded the icy Shenandoah, and fallen on the lightly guarded left flank of the Union army just before dawn. At the same time, Kershaw's much-traveled division had struck Colonel Joseph Thoburn's exposed position half a mile south of the main Union camp, initiating a precipitate dash to the rear by Crook's entire nine-thousand-man VIII Corps, followed in short order by

Emory's smaller XIX Corps. Only the VI Corps, at the farthest end of the fight, still remained on the field two hours after the devastating attack began. It had all happened so quickly that many of the Federals had fled in their underwear.[64]

By the time Sheridan reached the battlefield, about 10:30 A.M., the enemy attack had bogged down fatally, its momentum vitiated by hunger, fatigue, and an understandable human urge on the part of the attackers to stop and plunder the well-stocked Union camp they had just overrun. After the war a recriminatory debate arose between Early and Gordon, similar to the one between Sheridan and Crook, over the failure of the Confederates to achieve total victory at Cedar Creek. Gordon, who later became governor of Georgia and an influential member of the United States Senate, charged that Early had frittered away the last chance for a major southern turnaround by disastrously halting his army, ignoring Gordon's well-taken advice to renew the assault with an airy "This is glory enough for one day." Early told a different story, citing the presence of two Union cavalry divisions off his right flank and another off his left to explain his atypical lack of resolve. Perhaps his shortest answer held the key: "The Yankees got whipped and we got scared."[65]

Whatever the reason for the Rebels' delay, its practical effect was to freeze the armies into place just as Sheridan arrived on the scene. Hastily taking stock of the situation, he brought up Wright's and Emory's other divisions, anchoring them to Getty's steadfast line, and transferred Custer's cavalry division back to the Union right. All this took time; it was nearly noon before the long blue line was contiguous. With the enemy still disdaining to renew its attacks, Sandy Forsyth suggested that Sheridan ride the length of the front to show himself to the waiting troops. As he did, swinging his hat in his right hand to give the soldiers a glimpse of his familiar bullet-shaped head, a mighty cheer swept down the line. Perhaps no other general—certainly no other northern general—could have had a comparable effect on his men at this time in the war, when virtually every soldier was a battle-scarred veteran, and not just of enemy bullets, but of his own frequently inept commanders. Phil Sheridan, unlovable though he may have been, engendered a feeling more important to an army than love: an unassailable confidence born of battles shared and won. To Major Aldace Walker of the Eighth Vermont, as to others, it seemed that "no more doubt or chance for doubt existed; we were safe, perfectly and unconditionally safe, and every man knew it."[66]

The time neared 1:00 P.M., and still the Confederates delayed their attack. Sheridan remained troubled by continued reports that Longstreet's corps was on the scene, or soon would be. After a halfhearted Rebel assault on the Union right was repulsed with comparative ease by the XIX Corps, Sheridan ordered Merritt's cavalry to ride out and capture some Southern prisoners for him to interrogate. These captives, from a nearby artillery battery, freely admitted that only Kershaw's division was on the scene; Union cavalry also reported no sign of Rebel reinforcements.[67]

The afternoon wore on, an eerie quiet blanketing the battlefield. Sheridan lounged on the grass at his hilltop headquarters, elbow propped on the ground, waiting for the rest of his army to straggle back into camp. Aides kept dashing up, urging him to retake the offensive, but Sheridan put them off with a clipped "Not yet." It was nearly 4:00 P.M. when he finally judged the time to be ripe to advance. Orders went out to the various corps commanders: Emory, on the right, was to lead the charge, swinging left as he came to drive the enemy toward the Valley Pike. Wright's VI Corps, in the center, was to move ahead more deliberately, giving Emory time to make his turning movement. Crook's corps, still disheveled from its morning beating, was to hold the Union left, blocking the turnpike and serving as a backstop to the Union pivot.[68]

Two hundred northern buglers sounded the charge, and the men of the XIX Corps moved out on the right, aiming for the Rebel left flank anchored on two small hills a half-mile away. This flank, held by Gordon's division, was perilously strung out; Gordon later estimated there was a good thirty feet between each man. Worse yet, there was a gap between his westernmost brigade and the rest of the army, which, he warned Early, ''would prove a veritable deathtrap if left open many minutes longer.'' Sheridan, his view obscured by trees and distance, had no way of knowing this; he simply sent his army forward and waited, like Napoleon, for events to unfold.[69]

Across the way his Rebel counterpart was also waiting—but for what, no man could properly say. Early had had the better part of six hours to renew his own attack, entrench his position, or withdraw from the field with his morning's hard-won booty. Whether or not he actually believed that the army had won enough glory for one day, the indisputable fact was that he had done practically nothing since his predawn attack. And the little that he had done, sending Gordon forward on a tentative, unsupported reconnaissance, had accomplished nothing except to place those men a mile closer to the Union lines and an equal distance from their own original positions. In so doing, he had shortened by two-thirds the stretch of ground the enemy would have to charge across, improving each Yankee's survival odds every step less he was under fire. At the same time he had left Sheridan free to reorganize his army, refashion his lines, and reposition his much-feared cavalry on either flank. To expect the little Irishman to remain on the defensive after such a humiliating morning was, in light of all previous evidence to the contrary, an inexplicable miscalculation on Early's part, and one for which he and his men were about to pay dearly.

A jagged orange blast of gunfire erupted along the Confederate line as Sheridan's army crossed the field. On the right Emory's men withstood a murderous Rebel volley and, fighting blindly in junglelike thickets of trees and vines, seized the hillocks of the enemy left. Sheridan, now riding his replacement mount, Breckinridge, captured at Winchester from the southern general of the same name, joined the men on the crest and directed them to wait for Custer's cavalry to lead the next wave. Custer came up and impulsively threw his arms around Sheridan's neck—a bit of grandstanding the taciturn little general did not appreciate. Disengaging himself from Custer's embrace, Sheridan galloped toward the Union left, bullets zipping through the afternoon air.[70]

The attack on the enemy center had not gone as well as the one on the left. Kershaw's and Ramseur's divisions, sheltered behind improvised stone walls, stood their ground. The rattle of rifle fire was deadly and continuous. Neither side could move forward, nor could they break off the fight; withdrawal at such close range was impossible. A state of deadlock gripped the field. Then, at four-thirty, the gray dam broke. Custer's troopers, in a reprise of Winchester, swung left behind the Rebel flank, sending panicked foot soldiers scurrying before them. One by one the Confederate regiments broke, "like hard clods of clay under a pelting rain," in Gordon's vivid phrase. For the third time in three battles, Sheridan's army had turned the enemy left, then rolled irresistibly down the shattered line.[71]

In the center of the disintegrating army, Ramseur's superb division held around a dammed millpond, then broke when its twenty-seven-year-old commander went down with a mortal wound to the chest, still wearing the white flower he had pinned to his uniform that morning in honor of his newborn daughter, whom he would never see. The remaining Confederate divisions soon followed suit, splashing back across Cedar Creek toward the sheltering shadows of Fisher's Hill. By five-thirty it was all over but for the Union cavalry pursuit, which continued well into the night. "Nothing saved us," Early reported to Robert E. Lee, "but the inability of the enemy to follow with his infantry and his expectation that we would make a stand. . . . The state of things was distressing and mortifying beyond measure."[72]

Back at Belle Grove, exultant Union officers built a bonfire in the front yard of the mansion and snake-danced around it in the growing dark. Captured or recaptured artillery and wagons rattled into the yard, while long files of stretchers shimmered white in the fireglow. Nervy and expansive, Sheridan paced back and forth in the darkness, exchanging handshakes and backslaps with his delighted subordinates. Custer, impulsive as ever, reined up to the fire, sprang from his horse, and grabbed Sheridan around the waist, whirling him around and around, shouting, "By God, Phil, we've cleaned them out of their guns and got ours back!" Old General Emory, watching the antic celebration with his aides, murmured of Sheridan, "This young man, only about thirty years old, has made a great name for himself today."[73]

So he had. Incontestably, Cedar Creek was a personal as well as a national triumph for Sheridan. From the lonely moment on the Winchester turnpike when he deliberately chose to return to the battlefield, thus wedding his fate to that of his army, he had accomplished something very like a miracle, rallying a beaten (if not necessarily routed) army, reinvigorating it with the force of his own tornadic personality, and sending it forward to an eleventh-hour victory, the likes of which had seldom if ever been seen in American military history. Back at Petersburg, Ulysses S. Grant, the presiding genius of that tradition, immediately recognized the magnitude of his bantam lieutenant's accomplishment. "Turning what bid fair to be a disaster into glorious victory stamps Sheridan, what I have always thought him, one of the ablest generals," he crowed to Stanton, who had so recently questioned his wisdom in choosing Sheridan for the post in the first place.[74]

Other encomiums were swiftly forthcoming. Lincoln had also questioned Grant's judgment about Sheridan; now he sent the young conqueror a personal note, "tender[ing] to you and your brave army the thanks of the nation, and my own personal admiration and gratitude, for the month's operations in the Shenandoah Valley; and especially for the splendid work of October 19, 1864." Thanks were not all that Lincoln tendered to Sheridan. Four days after the battle, Assistant Secretary of War Charles A. Dana—the same Dana who had so undermined William Rosecrans's position at Chattanooga exactly one year before, paving the way for Grant's ascension to power—visited Sheridan's headquarters at Belle Grove. It was well after midnight when Dana arrived, and the nation's newest hero was already in bed, but the indefatigible little bureaucrat had a special speech prepared to accompany the president's latest offering, a major generalship in the regular army. Dutifully if not enthusiastically, Sheridan trundled out of bed, heard Dana out, and went back to sleep, his peacetime career—whenever that might be—assured for as long as he cared to serve.[75]

In the usual progress of worldly fame, the sublime soon gave way to the ridiculous. A minor poet named Thomas Buchanan Read, at the urging of retired actor James E. Murdock, who had visited Sheridan's camp a year earlier at Chattanooga to claim his son's body, unburdened himself of a sixty-three-line poem, written in galloping octometer, on the subject of "Sheridan's Ride." The poem was considerably short of a masterpiece, the best lines going to the horse Rienzi, but as a piece of Republican campaign rhetoric it was unexcelled. Debuted by Murdock at Cincinnati's Pike Opera Hall on November 1, "Sheridan's Ride" took the North by storm and made its bemused subject even more of a household name. When Lincoln swamped McClellan in the presidential election a week later, many observers credited Read's poem—as much as its inspiration's achievements on the battlefield—with swelling the rout. Sheridan himself, perhaps ironically, renamed Rienzi "Winchester" in honor of the poem's famous refrain: "Winchester, twenty miles away."[76]

Generations of schoolchildren as yet unborn would stand before blackboards in northern cities reciting Read's anthropomorphic epic, as once again Rienzi completed his twenty-mile (actually twelve) ride, and announce, "I have brought you Sheridan all the way / From Winchester down, to save the day!" For now, having won three major battles, two promotions, a healthy dose of national fame, and a place in every elementary school primer for the next fifty years, all in a span of six short weeks, Sheridan the man took a respite from his labors. With Early's army now firmly and finally ruined, he sent his own army into winter quarters and turned his attention to the always rankling problem of Rebel guerrillas, particularly those under the sway of John Singleton Mosby, the dashing and charismatic "Gray Ghost of the Confederacy." It was his stomping grounds, "Mosby's Confederacy," that would be the next target of Union attention. "I will soon commence on Loudoun County," Sheridan wrote to Halleck in mid-November, "and let them know there is a God in Israel." The wording of his threat was biblical, but it was the Old Testament god of scourge and vengeance he was invoking, not the mild and loving Savior of the New.[77]

7

ENDGAMES

FOR ALL SHERIDAN'S TOUGH talk and Cromwellian posturing, the weeks immediately following Cedar Creek were barren of any meaningful results. Jubal Early, his target and victim, had retreated all the way to New Market, where he glumly halted to lick his wounds and ungenerously blame his third defeat in one month on his own famished and fought-out soldiers. "We had within our grasp a glorious victory," he wrote to Lee, "and lost it by the uncontrollable propensity of our men for plunder." The army's subsequent panic, he said, "was without sufficient cause"—five divisions of Union infantry and two of cavalry apparently not constituting to Early sufficient cause for concern. He offered to resign; Lee opted, instead, to leave him where he was, but commenced stripping him of his remaining troops.[1]

With reference to his own commanding officer, Sheridan faced a different but no less thorny problem. Instead of having to explain a loss, he had to explain a victory, or, more precisely, why he seemed unable to follow up such a signal victory with a strategically useful movement of his own. The bonfires at Belle Grove had scarcely burned out before Grant was back at the telegraph office at City Point, urging Sheridan to enlarge on his work. On October 21, two days after Cedar Creek, Grant wrote: "If it is possible to follow up your great victory until you can reach the Central road, do it, even if you have to live on half rations. . . .

If the army at Richmond could be cut off from southwest Virginia it would be of great importance to us, but I know the difficulty in supplying so far from your base."[2]

The qualified tone of Grant's message was a tribute to Sheridan's debating skills. After each of the younger man's valley triumphs—Winchester, Fisher's Hill, and Cedar Creek—Grant had suggested (though never in the shape of an order) the same course of action: moving across the Blue Ridge to Charlottesville, cutting the Virginia Central Railroad, and advancing eastward toward Richmond and the Confederate rear. It was, in fact, what he had been suggesting for six months now to a succession of valley commanders, beginning with the lamentable Franz Sigel, progressing to the slightly more competent David Hunter, and concluding with the nation's newest hero, Phil Sheridan. The names and faces had changed, but the results remained the same. The trains still ran along the Virginia Central, connecting with Lynchburg and the lower South, and Robert E. Lee still held Petersburg.

But if Sheridan was used to Grant's exhorting, like a church member who hears the same tired sermon every Sunday, he was no better pleased with its peroration. He was, in fact, heartily sick of the Virginia Central Railroad, every way station, switchplate, and tie. Almost from the day he first set foot in the state, Sheridan had been hearing its name from Grant. From his near defeat at Trevilian Station in June, to his assumption of Hunter's command of the Middle Division in August, to his ill-timed meeting with Stanton and Halleck just prior to the conflagration at Cedar Creek, the fate of the Virginia Central had been intimately yoked to his own career. Now, at the close of Sheridan's greatest triumph, the indefatigable Grant was back, singing the same well-worn hymn.

There were sound strategic reasons for Grant's continued stress on cutting the railroad, but Sheridan was neither privy to the general-in-chief's innermost hopes and fears nor prescient in his grasp of the overall situation. He was not told, for instance, that Grant lived in fear of Lee taking his army from Petersburg and linking up with Joseph Johnston's army in North Carolina, or that Grant was planning another flanking maneuver around Lee's vulnerable right with the aim of cutting the Southside, yet another of Petersburg's constellation of railroads. Had he known, it is likely that Sheridan would have taken a more helpful position on the matter than the one he now assumed. As it was, he advised Grant on October 25, two days before Grant's next unsuccessful attempt on the railroad at Petersburg, that "I have found it impossible to move on the Central railroad as you desired. . . . To move up the Valley via the routes designated would be exceedingly difficult on account of supplies and forage, and would demoralize the troops, now in magnificent trim." As for the suggestion that the Orange & Alexandria Railroad be reopened and used as a supply line for his army east of the Blue Ridge, Sheridan found such a move "impracticable" since it would require a corps of infantry to protect it adequately from the ubiquitous Rebel guerrillas operating in the area.[3]

Chief among the latter was John S. Mosby's 43rd Virginia Battalion, most recently engaged in a dual war with Sheridan's blue-coated cavalry and the nervous road gangs striving to repair the Manassas Gap Railroad to Strasburg. Mosby's raiders had been having a generally bang-up time throughout October, sniping at workers, derailing locomotives, lobbing howitzer shells into Union camps, and helping themselves to enemy paymasters' strongboxes. One such raid on the B&O in mid-October had netted Mosby and his men $173,000 in northern greenbacks and resulted in a number of innocent Federal paymasters being temporarily locked up on suspicion of having colluded in their own victimization. Nor did Mosby's men confine themselves to rifling through well-stuffed money boxes. On the same day that Sheridan was instructing Grant on the impossibility of crossing the Blue Ridge and cutting the Virginia Central, the raiders were snapping up unwary Brigadier General Alfred Duffie, almost within sight of the Union camp. "A trifling man and a poor soldier," Sheridan said of his lost brigadier. "He was captured by his own stupidity."[4]

When it came to Mosby and his rangers, Sheridan evinced something of a double mind. Depending on his audience and the impression he wished to convey, the guerrillas were either a mere annoyance that "one good regiment could clear out any time" or a looming threat to his entire army that even a corps of infantry was hard-pressed to thwart. In general, the level of difficulty presented by Mosby was directly proportional to the level of compliance Sheridan intended to give a particular order. If he was writing to Grant, then "every train, every small party, and every straggler has been bushwhacked"—Mosby was everywhere. If, on the other hand, the over-burdened garrison commander at Harpers Ferry wanted help in defending the militarily and politically sensitive railroad against repeated Rebel incursions, then the single cavalry regiment he had on hand was sufficient for the job. "If the Twelfth Pennsylvania Cavalry cannot keep that country clear of guerrillas," Sheridan thundered, "I will take the shoulder straps off of every officer belonging to [it] and dismount the regiment in disgrace."[5]

As with most things, the truth lay somewhere between the two extremes. It was easy for Sheridan to say, as he did after the war, that he considered Mosby's hardcases "substantially a benefit to me, as they prevented straggling and kept my trains well closed up"—he didn't have to ride point through Rebel-infested hills. The joke heard often around Union campfires that "Mosby is Sheridan's provost guard" took on a grim twist when contrasted to examples of similar guerrilla humor. Several members of the Fifth Michigan Cavalry, surprised that fall by Mosby's men while looting a farmhouse, were shot or hanged; hams were tied to the victims' legs, along with a card promising other foragers a similar fate. On another occasion a Union straggler was killed while skinning a sheep. A hoof was jammed into the dead man's mouth, along with the note: "I reckon you got enough sheep now." Small wonder that one Pennsylvania cavalryman considered the

Shenandoah Valley "the most dangerous place to picket I ever saw."[6]

Still, such incidents—grisly though they were—did not have much bearing on the progress of the campaign. Despite Mosby's postwar boast that his work in the valley had saved Richmond for several months, the truth was that Sheridan's defeat of Early's army, and his subsequent and equally successful campaign to thwart Grant's wishes for a second front east of the mountains, determined the course of events in the Shenandoah Valley. Mosby was a remarkably daring and resourceful ranger, but he was just a ranger, and, as such, was tangential to the larger strategic picture.

This is not to say that Sheridan ignored Mosby completely, any more than one can ignore a wasp that has gotten down one's collar. The killing of young Meigs in early October, falsely attributed to Mosby's men, and the rub-out a week later of VI Corps quartermaster Colonel Cornelius Tolles and army medical director Dr. Emil Ohlenschlager, shot dead within Union lines near Newtown, enraged Sheridan and the entire army. And it would only get worse. When Colonel William Powell's troopers caught and hanged Mosby ranger Absalom Willis on October 13 in Rappahannock County, first tying a rope to the top of a slender sapling, then bending it double, shooting Willis skyward in abrupt strangled flight, Mosby had seen enough. (Although he couldn't have seen Powell's jeering report: "I wish it distinctly understood by the rebel authorities that if two to one is not sufficient I will increase it to twenty-two to one, and leave the consequences in the hands of my Government.") As soon as he returned from his Greenback Raid, Mosby commenced evening the score.[7]

On Sunday morning, November 6, twenty-seven Union prisoners were ushered out of a brick storehouse in Rectortown and marched down to the banks of Goose Creek, half a mile away. Most, but not all, belonged to Custer's command. Mosby had concluded, on the basis of rather questionable eyewitness accounts, that Custer had directed the summary executions of the six rangers at Front Royal in September. Custer had indeed been present at Front Royal, as had Torbert and Merritt, his immediate superiors—and wherever Custer went, he stood out from the crowd. But it was Torbert who gave the orders for the killing, although some of Custer's old regiment, the Fifth Michigan, may have taken part in the act. Since that time, Mosby had begun stockpiling any of Custer's men unlucky enough to fall into his hands. As he reported to Lee on October 29: "It is my purpose to hang an equal number of Custer's men whenever I capture them." Lee, without undue gentlemanly hesitation, approved the scheme.[8]

The prisoners were lined up beside Goose Creek and made to draw slips of paper from a hat. Twenty of the slips were blank; the other seven were marked with a number. Those drawing the marked pieces were to be executed. Some of the prisoners prayed, some sobbed, some merely stared into space. One drummer boy cried, "Precious Jesus, pity me," when it came his turn to draw. When he saw that he had drawn a blank slip, he lost his seemly piety. "Damn it, ain't I lucky!" he exclaimed. When a second drummer boy, not so lucky, drew one of the marked slips, Mosby had the boy released and made the remaining nineteen soldiers draw again.[9]

The condemned, including one officer, Lieutenant Israel C. Disoway of the Fifth New York Heavy Artillery, were led down the Winchester Turnpike toward Berryville, as close to Custer's camp as possible. En route, the rangers met a second contingent of their fellows returning from a raid. Captain Richard Montjoy, in the lead, sported a Masonic pin on his lapel. Disoway, thinking quickly, flashed Montjoy the lodge's arcane distress signal. Montjoy persuaded his fellow rangers to swap Brother Disoway for a Custer trooper he had in tow, and the two prisoners exchanged places. When Mosby heard of the switch later, he angrily told Montjoy, "This is not a Masonic lodge."[10]

At four o'clock the next morning, the rangers and their prisoners stopped in Beemer's Woods, a mile west of Berryville. In the predawn darkness two of the prisoners managed to escape; two others were shot in the head and left for dead. The other three were hanged. On one of the bodies the rangers left a note: "These men have been hung in retaliation for an equal number of Colonel Mosby's men hung by order of General Custer, at Front Royal. Measure for measure." Mosby followed up his object lesson with a note to Sheridan a few days later. In it he explained the reason for his actions and promised that "hereafter any prisoners falling into my hands will be treated with the kindness due to their condition, unless some new act of barbarity shall compel me reluctantly to adopt a course of policy repulsive to humanity." Sheridan neglected to mention either the reprisal or Mosby's accompanying note in his memoirs, but the absence of any Union retaliation, then or later, strongly suggests that he took the message to heart. For all his "God in Israel" talk, Sheridan was both a professional soldier and a realist. He would not get into a killing contest with Mosby, either because he found it wrong or because he found it useless. Whatever the case, when he sent Wesley Merritt raiding into Mosby's Confederacy later that month, he was careful to specify that "no dwellings are to be burned and . . . no personal violence be offered to the citizens." There would be no more Front Royals or Beemer's Woods.[11]

Just now, Sheridan had other things to worry about. The weather had turned bad—it would be the worst winter in years in the Shenandoah Valley—and men and horses were beginning to suffer from the cold. The troopers, now experienced in the ways of camp life, stripped nearby buildings and fences of wood and stone and erected log huts for their winter quarters. Some regiments, including Custer's, built tall windscreens to protect their horses from the elements; others, less humane, left their animals out in the open, with only a blanket to shield them from the cold.[12]

On November 10, Early bestirred himself and moved north across Cedar Creek, probing Sheridan's lines. There had been reports that Sheridan was preparing to send reinforcements east to Grant. Two days later, Sheridan's cavalry routed Confederate troopers in separate engagements at Middletown and Nineveh, capturing more than two hundred Rebels and seizing artillery, caissons, and an ammunition train. Convinced that Sheridan was still at full strength, Early went back to New Market. The next day, Kershaw's weary division left to rejoin Lee at Petersburg. Early's instincts were right, but his timing was wrong. One week later, Grant directed Sheridan to send him the ten-thousand-man VI Corps. Grant being Grant, he added, "If your cavalry can cut the Virginia Central road now is the time to do it." Sheridan, without reference to the tiresome subject of the railroad, wrote back the next day, "I will comply with the request of the general-in-chief as soon as I can definitely ascertain the true condition of affairs."[13]

Sheridan was not loath to part with the infantry—he had trouble enough feeding his cavalry and horses in the picked-over, burned-out countryside—but the specter of Cedar Creek was too recent for him to let down his guard. Early still had four infantry divisions and one cavalry division with him at New Market, and Sheridan asked to retain the VI Corps for a few more days, until "the inclemency of the weather would preclude infantry campaigning." That was all right with Grant, as his intermediary Halleck replied, but Sheridan should use the extra time to break up Mosby's band of "outlaws."[14]

Sheridan knew Halleck's Dutch-uncle advice was impossible to follow, but after six weeks of relative inactivity, he could detect a certain restlessness within the Union high command. Accordingly, on November 27, he ordered Merritt to take the First Division northeastward into "the district of country bounded on the south by the line of the Manassas Gap Railroad . . . on the east by the Bull Run range, on the west by the Shenandoah River, and on the north by the Potomac"—in other words, Mosby's Confederacy. Merritt was to "consume and destroy all forage and subsistence, burn all barns and mills . . . and drive off all stock in the region." By allowing the guerrillas to live in their midst, Sheridan said, the residents of the area had forfeited their private rights, and "the responsibility of it must rest upon the authorities at Richmond, who have acknowledged the legitimacy of guerrilla bands."[15]

Merritt, by most measures Sheridan's best cavalry commander, undertook the mission with his usual quiet tenacity. At thirty, he was five years older than Custer—Sheridan's other "brave boy"—with little of Custer's flamboyant presence, but he was a solid officer in whom Sheridan placed increasing reliance. Now, with three thousand lean, rangy troopers in his wake, he proceeded to show the defenseless Virginians that there was indeed a God in Israel, though some may have wondered if He was present in Fauquier and Loudoun counties. The "Burning Raid," as it became known, resulted in over a million dollars' worth of damages in a mere four days. Barns, stables, corncribs, and smokehouses were set ablaze; cattle, sheep, hogs, and horses were carried off or consumed. Not even the fact that many of the victims were non-violent Quakers or Union sympathizers counted for anything to the blue-shirted arsonists. In this they reflected their commanding general. "Should complaints come in from the citizens of Loudoun County," Sheridan advised Brigadier General John D. Stevenson at Harpers Ferry, "tell them that they have furnished too many meals to guerrillas to expect much sympathy."[16]

While Merritt was acting as Sheridan's avenging angel, Tom Rosser's Confederate cavalry returned the favor with a raid of their own into West Virginia. Unlike the Yankees, their target was military, the Union garrison at New Creek, on the B&O Railroad. The raiders, wearing Union army overcoats, rode unmolested into the camp in broad daylight, capturing Colonel George R. Latham and his entire seven-hundred-man command, setting fire to warehouses full of supplies and tearing up rail lines before making their escape. The raid did no lasting damage, but it was nevertheless embarrassing to Sheridan, who the day before had assured Major General Darius Couch, the department commander in the area, that "there is no danger of a guerrilla raid in the Cumberland Valley." Not only that, but he had also advised Halleck that Couch's worries were merely the result of rumors "gotten up by parties interested in the branch railroad at Hagerstown . . . [who] think there will be no troops stationed at Hagerstown or its vicinity, and consequently a pecuniary loss to them."[17]

Typically, Sheridan masked his embarrassment by lashing out at the officers responsible for the fiasco. Latham, after being exchanged, was court-martialed and sentenced to be dismissed from the service. His immediate superior, Brigadier General Benjamin Kelley, felt the wonted rasp of Sheridan's tongue. "In your telegram to Major General Crook . . . you state 'that you intend to fight Rosser to the last if he attacks you.' I give you no credit for this remark, as I expect you to do so." And to politically powerful John W. Garrett, president of the B&O, Sheridan noted, "General Kelley is very cautious about that which is in little danger, and not remarkably so about that which is." Still, to mollify Garrett, Sheridan sent Crook and one division of infantry to Cumberland, Maryland, to beef up protection for the railroad, although he could not resist a parting shot at the troublesome magnate: "A sufficient force was at New Creek to have preserved that station. If the property you have at Piedmont is destroyed through this cavalry action it is your misfortune."[18]

On the last day of November, Sheridan began returning Horatio Wright's VI Corps to Petersburg. If he thought this would relieve him of further offensive responsibilities, he was quickly disabused. On December 4, Grant was back, asking, "Do you think it possible now to send cavalry through to the Virginia Central road? It is highly desirable that it be done, if it is possible. I leave the practicability of this to . . . you." It is a measure of Grant's respect and affection for Sheridan that he did not immediately relieve him of command after receiving his reply the next day. For Sheridan now went beyond assessing the practicability of the move; he questioned its usefulness, as well.

"I have contemplated a cavalry raid on the Central railroad,"

Sheridan began, "but from all the light which I have I have not estimated the breaking of the road very important. I am satisfied that no supplies go over the road toward Richmond from any point north of the road or from the Shenandoah Valley. On the contrary the rebel forces here in the Valley have drawn supplies from the direction of Richmond. To break the road at Charlottesville and up to Gordonsville would only be breaking the circuit. . . . I think that the rebels have looked at this matter about as I do, and they have not been at all fearful of my going in that direction, as the temporary destruction would only inconvenience them and would be of no great value to me. I will make the raid soon, if it is made at all, and will only go myself if all affairs here are in a healthy condition."[19]

As an example of sheer hubris, Sheridan's dispatch is almost unexcelled. Besides its questionable logic—it is unlikely that Lee, whose own troops were subsisting on a daily ration of one pint of weevil-infested cornmeal and an ounce or two of "nausea bacon," was sending any food just then to the Shenandoah Valley—the message was also remarkable for its arrogance. The fact that the general-in-chief of the Union Army wanted the railroad cut seems not to have made an impression on Sheridan, who considered the breaking of the road "of no great value to me." If Grant did not believe him, he could always ask the Rebels, who "looked at this matter about as I do."[20]

Fortunately for Sheridan, Grant ignored the message. Four days later, however, he told him that two more Confederate divisions had left Early for Petersburg. "This only leaves Rodes' and Wharton's divisions, with the cavalry, in the Valley," said Grant. "If the weather holds favorable you can make a successful offensive campaign. Try it if you can." Responded Sheridan: "We are now having . . . very bad weather; seven inches of snow and very cold." Two days later he added, for emphasis, "I have been unable to do anything toward determining absolutely these movements on account of the snowstorm and the intensely cold weather now prevailing here." Grant tried again: "If it is possible to destroy the Virginia Central road it will go far toward starving out the garrison of Richmond." "It is impossible to do anything toward the Central road until the present inclement weather is over," said Sheridan. "I will break the railroad, if possible, as soon as the weather will permit." And, he noted gratuitously, "We are a long way from Richmond."[21]

Sheridan's uncharacteristic passivity must have puzzled Grant, particularly when contrasted with the actions of Grant's other favorite, William Sherman. In less than six weeks, from mid-November to mid-December, Sherman (who was, after all, a good deal farther from Richmond than Sheridan) had cut loose from his base at Atlanta and marched audaciously to the sea, tearing up hundreds of miles of Deep South railroad and leaving a sixty-mile-wide swath of destruction, fear, and weeping in his wake. It was just the sort of hellishness Sheridan had patented in the Shenandoah Valley, and Grant must have wondered why he was now so reluctant to export it east.

Earlier, after crushing the Rebels at Winchester and Fisher's Hill, Sheridan had objected to the move on the grounds that it would have stretched him too thin, leaving him vulnerable to counterattack. Weeks of subsequent inactivity had permitted that very thing to happen at Cedar Creek, and Sheridan of all men knew how close he had come to devastating defeat. Now the situation had changed dramatically, but he was either unwilling or unable to adjust his thinking. Thrice-defeated Jubal Early, with a skeleton force of three thousand hungry and ill-clad men shivering in their huts at Staunton, was no longer a realistic threat. Even after stripping his own army of its infantry, Sheridan had more than three times as many men. But now, as he repeatedly told Grant that December, the weather was too bad to commence an advance. He had waited too long—or, perhaps, just long enough.

Finally, as a sop to the Union commander, Sheridan sent his cavalry off on December 19 to raid the Virginia Central Railroad. Torbert, commanding the First and Second Divisions, was ordered to cross the Blue Ridge at Chester Gap, strike the railroad at Gordonsville, and advance to Charlottesville and Lynchburg, tearing up track and bridges as he went. Custer, with the Third Division, was to march up the valley to Staunton and rendezvous with Torbert at Lynchburg. The weather, Sheridan took pains to advise Grant, was "so very bad" that he was "not sanguine of success." From the start, the raid was an abysmal failure. Snow, sleet, and hail pelted the miserable troopers unrelentingly; roads were atrocious, footing for horses an unhappy adventure. At Liberty Mills on the Rapidan River, enemy defenders burned the bridge, delaying Torbert's advance for a day. Falling back to Gordonsville, the Rebels threw up earthworks in the mountainous gap, and two brigades of southern infantry rushed to reinforce the position. Cold, wet, and frostbitten, Torbert quickly concluded that "it was useless to make a further attempt to break the Central railroad." He gave the doubtless welcome order to return to Winchester. Five days later he straggled back into camp with nothing to show for his misadventure but 102 casualties, 258 lost horses, and 2 captured enemy guns.[22]

Custer's part of the expedition fared no better, despite an impromptu oration by the boy general on the progress of the war, including a retelling of the ridiculous rumor that Jefferson Davis had attempted suicide. Custer airily sent word to Sheridan that he intended to spend Christmas in Lynchburg. He got only as far as Lacey Springs, nine miles north of Harrisonburg, before he was surprised and routed at reveille by hard-charging Confederate cavalry. The attack was brief, more frightening than destructive, but Custer reasoned that since he was intending to return home after the raid anyway, "the sooner my return was accomplished the better." Back at headquarters, Sheridan demanded and got—as far as it went—an explanation from Custer of how he came to be surprised in his own camp. In an impressive display of literary skill, Custer alleged that, in fact, the enemy was really "the surprised party," and "acted as if his only object was to get safely away." Without worrying too much about actual figures, he reckoned that the enemy had lost three times as many men as he had. Sheridan let it go at that, but noted for the record that the young firebrand had been forced to retreat. "Custer," he said dryly, "did not accomplish all that was expected of him."[23]

With Torbert and Custer safely back in camp, offensive operations shut down for the season. Winter settled heavily over the valley and its masters. Sheridan, in his role of military division commander, faced the usual array of administrative problems: feeding and clothing his army, replacing sick, wounded, and mustered-out soldiers, guarding his supply lines, and dealing with deserters. In early January two such offenders were executed before the entire Third Division. "I thought it best to make an example of them at once," he reported to Halleck. "We have lost a great many men by desertion, particularly in coming from Washington to join their regiments." But Sheridan was not completely hard-boiled. On Christmas Day he asked Washington for the authority to share his rations with hungry civilians living in the valley. Stanton replied, through Halleck, that "while the men of Virginia are either serving in the rebel ranks, or as bushwhackers are waylaying or murdering our soldiers, our Government must decline to support their wives and children." So much for the Christmas spirit in Washington.[24]

Sheridan had already run afoul of Stanton once that month. Ever since the Confederate raid on New Creek, gun-shy area residents had been looking over their shoulders. West Virginia Governor Andrew Boreman had wired Stanton that Rosser's troops were headed for Grafton to tear up the B&O; Stanton passed the message on to Sheridan. Saucily, Sheridan responded, "If I were to make disposition of the troops under my command in accordance with the information received from the commanders in . . . Western Virginia, whom I have found . . . always alarming in their reports and stupid in their duties . . . I certainly would have my hands full." No one talked to Stanton like that, not even the hero of Cedar Creek. Back he thundered: "No one, that I am aware of, has asked you to make disposition of your troops in accordance with the information received from the commanders in Virginia. . . . It has been supposed that such information might be useful and desired by you, as it is by other commanders who are your seniors in the service, without provoking [a] disrespectful reply. With your subordinate commanders you will take such action as you please, but such reports as come to this Department in relation to the movements of the enemy will be forwarded as heretofore, and will be expected to be received with the respect due the Department of which you are subordinate."[25]

It did not help matters any that Boreman was right—Confederate cavalry attacked the Union garrison at Beverly, West Virginia, on the night of January 11, 1865, killing and wounding twenty-nine Federal soldiers and carrying off the other 580 as prisoners. "There seems to be a total want of discipline or soldierly qualities about troops in this section of the country," Sheridan reported, in something of an understatement. Stanton, for his part, had Assistant Adjutant General E. D. Townsend sourly inform Sheridan that "the frequent disasters in your command have occasioned much regret in this Department, as indicating a want of vigilance and discipline which, if not speedily cured, may occasion greater misfortune."[26]

Worse, indeed, was yet to come. On February 21, Generals Crook and Kelley were hauled out of bed at the Revere House hotel in Cumberland by Confederate ranger Jesse McNeill and carried away on horseback to Richmond. Sheridan could scarcely be blamed for their capture, but the loss of his old West Point roommate, Crook, nevertheless was mortifying. It took the edge off the similar capture of Maryland guerrilla leader Harry Gilmor by Major H. K. Young and his scouts two weeks earlier—measure for measure, as Mosby had said.[27]

For all its echoes of triumph and fame, the Shenandoah Valley was no longer a place where Phil Sheridan cared to be. When next the call came from Grant to move east, Sheridan and his troopers were more than ready to comply. At first light on February 27 they broke camp, heading out at last for the still-unravaged countryside east of the Blue Ridge Mountains. Sheridan's orders were largely discretionary: he was to destroy the Virginia Central Railroad and James River canal, capture Lynchburg if practicable, then either join Sherman in North Carolina or return to Winchester. Grant told Meade that "the main object" of Sheridan's move was to reinforce the cavalry-poor Sherman. Sheridan, however, did not see it that way; he sensed that the war was going to end soon, in Virginia, and he intended to be there, not traipsing around North Carolina in search of Sherman, "wherever he might be found." He had gotten in the habit of interpreting Grant's orders liberally, and he was about to do so again.[28]

With Sheridan on the expedition were just under ten thousand cavalry and artillery. Hard riding was expected, and a hurried inspection was held at Kernstown to weed out all men and horses judged not to be up to the task. A small supply train was brought along, with fifteen days' rations of coffee, sugar, and salt. The countryside would furnish all other necessary foodstuffs. Conspicuous by his absence was Alfred Torbert, left behind on furlough, with orders to take over the skeleton force of cavalry remaining in the valley. Torbert's less-than-stellar performance on the pre-Christmas raid had sealed his fate with Sheridan, who also remembered the dandified Delawarean's failure to close the trap at Fisher's Hill back in September. "Torbert had disappointed me on two important occasions," wrote Sheridan, "and I mistrusted his ability to conduct any operations requiring much self-reliance." Wesley Merritt was given his place in the march, but Sheridan was personally directing things. Thomas Devin, newly promoted to brigadier general, now commanded the First Division; the irrepressible Custer held on to the Third.[29]

The column moved out in heavy rain that washed the winter snow from the ground. Crossing the north fork of the Shenandoah River at Mount Jackson on the second day out, eight troopers drowned in the swollen waters. At the middle fork the next day, Rosser's Confederates set fire to the covered bridge across the river and tried manfully to prevent the advance, but the much-larger Federal force brushed them aside like so many flies. What-ever else could be said about Jubal Early as a general, he was no quitter. Guessing Sheridan's intentions, he marched his pitifully small force northeast to Waynesboro, a hamlet guarding Rockfish Gap on the road to Charlottesville. The move left open the way to Lynchburg; Sheridan could have ridden south without further interference. Instead he turned east at Staunton, heading straight for Waynesboro. He later explained that he was reluctant to leave Early's troops—all two thousand of them—in his rear, although what possible harm they could have done in their present state was anyone's guess. Still, Early "had left word in Staunton that he would fight at Waynesboro," and Sheridan liked the five-to-one odds. Besides, each step he took to the east carried him that much closer to Grant—and that much farther away from Sher-man.[30]

Early arrayed his men along a ridge northwest of Waynes-boro, the south branch of the Shenandoah River directly to their rear. Despite his earlier professions of battle, he later said he never intended to fight at Waynesboro, but merely to delay the enemy long enough to allow him to drag his own unhorsed ar-tillery over the mountain and get away. In any case, he was too few and too late. On the afternoon of March 2, Custer's division pulled up short of Waynesboro, while Armstrong considered the field. A narrow gap lay between the Rebel left and the river. Custer dismounted three regiments and sent them charging through the gap, while the rest of the division, still on horseback, menaced the front. The attack succeeded as brilliantly as Custer's previous cavalry raid had failed. The southerners broke and ran, leaving behind sixteen hundred captured comrades, eleven pieces of artillery, two hundred ambulances, and seventeen blood-red battle flags. Federal losses amounted to a mere nine men killed or wounded. Fifteen Congressional Medals of Honor were subse-quently awarded for the battle, which, as Sheridan rightly noted, "closed hostilities in the Shenandoah Valley."[31]

The next day Custer led the way into Charlottesville, where a delegation of citizens formally surrendered the town. Sheridan, who considered the "medieval ceremony" faintly ridiculous, inherited a full set of keys to the courthouse, the jail, the University of Virginia, several churches, and a select number of taverns. The men bedded down in vacated dorm rooms at the university while work details destroyed the Virginia Central Railroad north and south of the city. In the meantime, scouting parties brought back word that the southern garrison at Lynchburg was being strengthened, but Sheridan decided to move as far south as Amherst Court House, sixteen miles north of Lynchburg, to study the situation for himself.[32]

The troopers fanned out in two wings, the First Division advancing to Howardsville with orders to burn all accessible bridges, mills, and locks on the James River Canal, the Third Division following and wrecking the railroad down to New Market. There the two wings were to reunite and cross the James for a concerted drive on Lynchburg. To Sheridan's scant disappointment, it was found that Rebel defenders had burned the only two bridges in the vicinity, at Duguidsville and Hardwicksville, making it impossible to cross the rain-swollen river and advance on Lynchburg. He quickly decided that the only thing left to do was to "join General Grant in front of Petersburg. . . . Feeling that the war was nearing its end, I desired my cavalry to be in at the death."[33]

With no organized enemy resistance, Sheridan made his way east along the north bank of the James, ravaging the countryside as he went. In twelve days' time his minions tore up fifty miles of railroad track, wrecked bridges and culverts from Staunton to the South Anna River, and destroyed millions of dollars' worth of property, including 880 hogsheads of tobacco, 600 bushels of flour, 1,000 bushels of wheat, and 500 bushels of salt. Food and forage were in such abundant supply that Sheridan's entire force, as well as three thousand black refugees following the column, was able to dine in style, giving the lie to his long-held contention that there was no reason to cut the Virginia Central Railroad, since it was no longer carrying supplies to Petersburg. If this apparent contradiction occurred to Sheridan, he let it pass without reflection.[34]

Finally, on the night of March 18, the column crossed the Pamunkey River to White House, where Grant had piles of rations and forage waiting for the new arrivals. Sheridan was given a message from the general-in-chief congratulating him on the skill and endurance displayed by his men and assuring him that "the importance of . . . your success can scarcely be estimated." Nothing was said—for the time being, at least—about reinforcing Sherman in North Carolina. Despite the dearth of enemy opposition, the grueling march to White House had taken its toll on Sheridan's cavalry. Hundreds of men were unarmed and unhorsed; others were reduced to riding captured Rebel mules. More than two thousand cases of hoof rot were reported among the horses, caused by weeks of slogging through mud. A phalanx of blacksmiths was quickly put to work reshoeing the serviceable mounts, while Sheridan personally wrote to Halleck requesting another three thousand horses. "Nothing like enough horses were at hand to replace those that had died or been disabled," Sheridan reported, "so a good many of the men were still without mounts."[35]

Grant, in his first message to Sheridan, recognized the cavalry's need for rest and refitting. "Start for this place as soon as you conveniently can," he wrote from City Point. But events were building to a climax around siege-stricken Petersburg, and Grant wrote again to hurry Sheridan along. "There is now such a possibility, if not probability, of Lee and Johnston attempting to unite," he said, "that I feel extremely desirous not only of cutting the lines of communication between them, but of having a large and properly commanded cavalry force ready to act with in case such an attempt is made." Sheridan, he explained, was to be reinforced with another six thousand cavalry, including the long-absent Second Division, which had been left behind when the rest of the cavalry moved into the Shenandoah the previous summer.

The horsemen were to destroy the Southside and Danville rail-roads, Lee's last connections to the lower South, then "either return to this army or go on to Sherman, as you may deem most practicable."[36]

The close of the message prompted a quick visit by Sheridan to Grant's headquarters at City Point. Although the order clearly gave him a choice of options, the fact that Grant was still bringing up the subject of Sherman left Sheridan with a dry taste in his mouth. Nor was he reassured when the first person he ran into at army headquarters, Grant's high-strung chief of staff, John A. Rawlins, vehemently remonstrated with him to oppose any transfer to Sherman's army. Grant may have sensed Sheridan's displeasure; the first thing he did was to assure Sheridan that he would retain the semiofficial status of army commander, thus removing him from the still-unwelcome clutches of George Gordon Meade, the Army of the Potomac's titular head. Sheridan's title would be "Commander in Chief of the Army of the Shenandoah, serving with the Army of the Potomac."[37]

That was all well and good, but Sheridan was more concerned about Sherman than he was about Meade. He was convinced, he later told longtime aide James Forsyth, that the impending campaign would end the war, and he was afraid that the Army of the Potomac would stay where it was, in the squalid trenches at Petersburg, until Sherman (with Sheridan's reluctant help) arrived on the scene to win the day. This was the line he now took with Grant, who assured him that all talk of joining Sherman was a mere "blind" to protect them both against unfavorable public opinion, should the attack on Lee's railroads somehow fail.[38]

This labored explanation, repeated in both Grant's and Sheridan's memoirs, does not bear much scrutiny. By Sheridan's own testimony, Grant's chief of staff was unaware of such chicanery, although Sheridan rightly conjectured that Rawlins "must have been acquainted of course with the program." Another presumably interested party, Sherman, was also unacquainted with Grant's plan. When he arrived at City Point for his own face-to-face meeting with the army commander a day later, Sherman took it upon himself to visit Sheridan's room, waking him early in the morning to ask him again for help. As had become his custom with Grant, Sheridan pointedly refused. He was staying in Virginia, and that was that.[39]

Whatever Grant's ultimate intentions insofar as Sheridan was concerned, the cavalry's immediate task was to cut the railroad west of Petersburg. Grant was right about Lee—the indomitable old warrior was indeed planning to abandon Petersburg and race southward to link up with Johnston in North Carolina. The day before Grant's meeting with Sheridan, Lee had attacked the Union line at Fort Stedman, hoping to threaten enemy communications and force Grant to draw reinforcements from his left flank, thereby giving the Confederates room to begin their withdrawal. The attack had failed, costing Lee another four thousand irreplaceable men and leaving him with only one remaining option: full-scale retreat.

To forestall that from happening, Grant ordered Sheridan to take his cavalry around the Rebel right in the direction of Dinwiddie Court House, a ramshackle hamlet thirteen miles south of Petersburg and five miles south of the key crossroads village of Five Forks. From there he was to wreck the Southside and Danville railroads, then either return to Grant's army or "go on into North Carolina and join General Sherman." The general tenor of the instructions again disturbed Sheridan—more proof that Grant's talk of public-opinion "blinds" was entirely after the fact. At the time, Sheridan recalled, he was afraid that Grant "had returned to his original views." Nonetheless, at five the next morning, Sheridan put his thirteen thousand troopers in motion toward Dinwiddie. Leading the way was a familiar face: long-nosed, blue-eyed George Crook, who had returned from his brief, embarrassing captivity in Richmond to assume command of the Second Division after the abrupt resignation of Brigadier General David McMurtrie Gregg a few weeks earlier. The roads were in "a frightful state"—one of the reasons Lee had delayed withdrawing

as long as he did—but the column floundered on, reaching Dinwiddie late that afternoon. The II and V Infantry Corps, commanded respectively by Major Generals Andrew A. Humphreys
and Gouverneur K. Warren, moved forward in conjunction with
the cavalry advance and camped within striking distance along the
Boydton Plank Road to the east.[40]

Sheridan and his staff were in good spirits as they settled in
for the night at the grandiloquently named Dinwiddie Hotel—
actually a falling-down tavern propped up on two sides by wooden
poles. Not even the sudden onslaught of a fierce rainstorm managed to dampen the men's elation. Lee, preoccupied by the infantry advance, had made no effort to hold Dinwiddie, "a fatal
mistake" in Sheridan's view, as it allowed the Union cavalry to
establish a toehold beyond his flank. Over a spartan supper of
cups of coffee (the supply trains had gotten stuck in the mud to
the rear), the staff gaily serenaded two young southern women
staying at the hotel. Sheridan interrupted the musicale long
enough to read a new message from Grant telling him to forget all
about the railroads and—better yet—about Sherman. "I now feel
like ending the matter, if it is possible to do so, before going
back," wrote Grant. "In the morning push around the enemy if
you can, and get on his right rear."[41]

Rain was still pouring down the next morning as Sheridan
rearranged his cavalry to carry out Grant's plan. Three brigades
were sent north to reconnoiter the way to Five Forks; a fourth was
directed to hold the vital Stony Creek crossing on the Boydton
Plank Road. Custer's Third Division, slogging through the mud,
was laboriously bringing up the supply trains. By now the men
and horses were long accustomed to rain and mud. Inclemency
alone was no excuse to dally. No sooner had the troops ridden
forth, however, than Sheridan received another message from
Grant, this one as sodden in spirit as the weather was in fact. "The
heavy rain of today will make it impossible for you to do much
until it dries up a little, or we get roads around our rear repaired,"
wrote Grant. "You may, therefore, leave what cavalry you deem

necessary to protect the left . . . and send the remainder back."
Sheridan was astonished; Grant was the last person on earth he
would have expected to flinch in the face of a little rain. Grabbing
his gray pacer, Breckinridge, Sheridan set out for Grant's new
headquarters south of Gravelly Run, determined to save him from
"a serious mistake."[42]

Dodging a volley of shots from panicky infantry pickets along
the plank road, Sheridan and his escort found Grant's headquarters tent, awash in a sea of mud in what once had been a cornfield.
A disconsolate group of staff officers huddled around a sputtering
fire. Grant was in his tent with Rawlins, arguing about the proposed suspension of activities. Sheridan stuck his head through
the flap just in time to hear Grant mutter sourly, "Well, Rawlins,
I think you had better take command," then quickly withdrew it,
making some excuse about being wet and cold. The staff officers,
including Colonel Horace Porter, were as unhappy as Sheridan
about the change in plans. He now joined them, pacing up and
down "like a hound in the leash," in Porter's picturesque phrase.
"I can drive in the whole cavalry force of the enemy with ease,"
Sheridan declared, "and if an infantry force is added to my command, I can strike out for Lee's right, and either crush it or force
him so to weaken his . . . lines that our troops . . . can break
through and march into Petersburg." He concluded his little
speech with an oath that was destined to become famous: "I tell
you, I'm ready to strike out tomorrow and go to smashing
things."[43]

Sheridan's optimism was a tonic to the soggy headquarters
staff, but Grant still had to be won over. This Sheridan accomplished soon enough, in a private conference with the general-in-
chief. He did so by pointing out that any suspension of operations
would have the very appearance of failure that Grant most wanted
to avoid. Sheridan also raised the unwelcome specter of Ambrose
Burnside and his much-ridiculed "Mud March" of early 1863, a
comedy of errors that the Army of the Potomac was still trying to
live down. Grant apparently did not need much convincing. He

heard Sheridan out, then concluded their two-man council of war with a terse but decisive, "We will go on."[44]

Having once again imposed his wishes on the more phlegmatic general-in-chief, Sheridan hurried back to camp to begin the next day's preparations. En route, he stopped at the headquarters of Gouverneur K. Warren, the V Corps commander. Warren was already asleep—a luxury the hyperkinetic Sheridan must have marveled at, a general sleeping in the afternoon—and Sheridan whiled away a few minutes talking with Colonel William Gentry, an old friend from Indian-fighting days. At length Warren appeared, and the two generals went over battle plans for the next day. Warren annoyed Sheridan by "speaking rather despondently of the outlook." Tongue firmly in cheek, Sheridan later attributed Warren's bad mood to the influence of "the depressing weather."[45]

Merritt's reconnaissance of Five Forks was equally depressing: five brigades of Rebel infantry had reinforced the cavalry corps already manning a strong line of breastworks at the crossroads. Major General George Pickett, the ill-starred hero of Gettysburg, had been detached from the Petersburg line and rushed into position by a worried Lee, with the pointed injunction, "Hold Five Forks at all hazards." Sheridan reported the enemy buildup to Grant, requesting that he be reinforced by reliable Horatio Wright and the VI Corps, but Wright was too far away. Grant offered him Warren's V Corps instead, which Sheridan declined. For the time being, he and his horsemen would have to fight alone.[46]

At first light on the thirty-first, Sheridan sent Devin's division forward in the direction of Five Forks. Despite the continuing rain, the horsemen made good progress, largely because, as Sheridan ruefully admitted, the enemy "was just then bent on other things." Pickett, using a road concealed by heavy woods, swung his force around the Union left, with an eye toward cutting off the advancing Federals. Throwing his men across Chamberlain's Creek, Pickett drove a wedge between Devin's division and the rest of the Union cavalry. Separated from each other, the two wings were in imminent danger of being overrun.[47]

Back at Dinwiddie, Sheridan took matters into his own hands. Selecting a new defensive position three-fourths of a mile northwest of the village, he ordered Crook's division to fall back slowly, while Merritt was sent to lead Devin's imperiled troopers safely around the Confederate flank. Custer, still floundering about in the rear with the mud-encrusted supply train, was told to leave the wagons where they were and hasten to the front. He arrived with a flourish, carrying the seventeen Rebel battle flags he had captured at Waynesboro, followed closely by two brass bands. Quickly moving into line, his men opened on the Confederates, who were chasing Crook's retreating brigades across the swampy ground north of Dinwiddie. The sudden appearance of Custer on his left flank caused Pickett to recoil momentarily. Sheridan seized the opportunity to ride along the Union line, shouting encouragement to the men. His official-looking entourage drew immediate fire from the enemy, emptying several saddles, among them *New York Herald* correspondent Theodore Wilson, who now got a closer look at the war than he had intended.[48]

At sundown Pickett made a final attempt to capture Dinwiddie, but was quickly repulsed. The two sides settled down for an uncomfortable night in the rain, their lines less than a hundred yards apart. Sheridan sent two messages to Grant: the first, carried by his brother Michael, indicated Sheridan's line of retreat, should he be driven from Dinwiddie; the second, somewhat more hopeful, followed the roundabout return of Devin's men. Now Sheridan proposed to "hold on to Dinwiddie Court House until I am compelled to leave." Neither message was exactly suffused with the little Irishman's customary fire, and Grant dispatched Warren's V Corps and an additional cavalry division from the Army of the James to reinforce him at Dinwiddie. Sheridan would rather have had Wright's VI Corps than Warren's unfamiliar sloggers, but Grant again explained that this was impossible. Even so, the situation at Dinwiddie was beginning to look better, the farther into the evening it became. To a visitor from Grant's headquarters who expressed concern that Sheridan was dangerously cut off from the body of the army, he declared: "This force [Pickett's] is in more danger than I am. If I am cut off from the Army of the Potomac, it is cut off from Lee's army, and not a man in it should ever be allowed to get back to Lee. We at last have drawn the enemy's infantry out of its fortifications, and this is our chance to attack it."[49]

Grant saw the same thing Sheridan did, and wasted little time communicating a sense of urgency to his truculent subordinate. "You will assume command of the whole force sent to operate with you," he wrote to Sheridan about midnight, "and use it to the best of your ability to destroy the force which your command has fought so gallantly today." Both men realized (as, belatedly, did Pickett) that the Confederate's stubborn advance, although something of a tactical victory, had left him hanging precariously beyond the reach of his fellow southerners. If Sheridan were to move quickly—more to the point, if Warren were to move quickly—the two Union wings could catch Pickett in a death grip of his own devising. Sheridan always moved quickly.[50]

Gouverneur Warren was not Phil Sheridan's favorite soldier, even in the best of times, which these clearly were not. Twice before, during Grant's Wilderness campaign, Warren had publicly criticized the "damned cavalry" for getting in his way, and had displayed noticeable ill will when asked to help Sheridan's horsemen attack the barricaded enemy on the way to Spotsylvania. Most recently, Sheridan had found him sleeping in his tent in the middle of the afternoon, "rather despondent" about the overall prospects for the army's success. Like Meade, Warren was an engineer-general, careful, methodical, and (in the eyes of such hard-nosed scrappers as Sheridan and Grant) a bit timid. In the charnel house of the Wilderness, he had suffered something like a nervous breakdown, crying out that "for thirty days it has been one funeral procession past me, and it has been too much!" Grant was concerned that Warren would fail Sheridan in the crunch, and took pains to assure him that he was in command of all forces in the vicinity, with full authority to fire Warren if and when he found him an impediment.[51]

It would be nearly twelve hours before Sheridan found Warren at all, a long night compounded of anger, anxiety, and teeth-grinding frustration. Grant had told him, unrealistically, that Warren would arrive at Dinwiddie at midnight, a logistical impossibility since Warren did not even receive his marching orders until 11:00 P.M. Wet roads, inky darkness, and swollen streams further delayed Warren, who, true to form, was not evincing much sense of haste on his own. Sheridan tried his best to speed the dilatory New Yorker along, sending him a painstakingly detailed account of the golden opportunity facing them both and urging him to attack at daylight. No answer came from Warren. "Restive as a racer," Sheridan paced in the dark.[52]

While Sheridan fumed, Pickett pulled back from his exposed position at Dinwiddie, shielding his men behind previously constructed breastworks. The works ran for about a mile along the western edge of White Oak Road, angling north at the eastern end for several hundred more yards. Cavalry patrolled the flanks, and a dozen pieces of artillery were spotted here and there along the lines. The troops holding the line had never been driven from a fortified position, and Pickett had no fear of spoiling that record. At daybreak, meanwhile, the first of Warren's divisions straggled into Dinwiddie. "Where's Warren?" Sheridan demanded of the first ranking officer he could grab, Brigadier General Romeyn Ayres. Back at the rear, said Ayres. "That's here I expected to find him," snapped Sheridan. Finally, at midday, Warren loped in, and Sheridan hurriedly gave him the plan of attack. While Merritt's dismounted cavalry menaced the Rebel front, Custer would simulate an attack on the enemy right. Meanwhile, Warren's sixteen thousand infantry would attack the angle in Pickett's line and attempt to get into his rear. Warren, who was sitting under a tree making a sketch of the area, nodded agreement, but still seemed strangely apathetic. Perhaps he was just tired. When Sheridan pointed out that Lee was less than three miles away, Warren shrugged. "Bobby Lee is always getting people into trouble," he allowed.[53]

The jumping-off point for the infantry was Gravelly Church Road, near the junction of White Oak Road, two miles away. Despite Sheridan's prodding, it took Warren three more hours to get his men into position. The cavalry had been banging away for at least that long, and Sheridan was worried they would expend their ammunition before Warren even began his attack. "This battle must be fought and won before the sun goes down," Sheridan fumed to his staff. "All conditions may be changed in the morning; we have but a few hours of daylight left." Somehow he managed to control his temper—for a little longer, anyway. Finally, at 4:00 P.M., Warren began his attack. It started badly. Ayres, commanding the lead division, dutifully sent his men crashing against the angle on the Confederate left. Unfortunately the two divisions on his right, commanded by Brigadier Generals Sam Crawford and Charles Griffin, swung too far to the north and came near to marching themselves completely out of the battle. Meanwhile, unsupported, Ayres's men were taking fire from all sides.[54]

Again Sheridan rose to the challenge. Crying "Where's my battle flag?" he spurred Rienzi toward the threatened infantry. Oblivious to the deadly zing of minié bullets whizzing about his familiar red and white guidon, he dashed from one end of the line to the other, urging Ayres's men to take the breastworks. One private, hit in the neck by a bullet, staggered to his knees, clutching his throat and crying, "I'm killed." "You're not hurt a bit," Sheridan shouted. "Pick up your gun, man, and move right on the front." The man did, taking another dozen steps, then keeled over, stone dead. Sheridan was everywhere. "Come on, men!" he urged. "Go at 'em with a will. Move on at a clean jump or you'll not catch one of them! They're all getting ready to run now, and if you don't get on to them in five minutes they'll every one get away." The omnipresent Horace Porter, of Grant's staff, rode behind Sheridan in the charge, marveling; the little general, he said, was "the very incarnation of battle."[55]

Warren, who should have drawn himself a better map of his surroundings—it was not as if he hadn't had ample time for it—was nowhere to be found. Sheridan sent word to Griffin to wheel to the left and support Ayres's attack. Brigadier General Joshua Chamberlain, like Warren a true hero at Gettysburg, smartly led his brigade into the breach caused by the misalignment. "By God, that's what I want to see: general officers at the front!" cried Sheridan, just then in the act of practicing what he preached. Thus inspired, the Union attack crested over the Rebel works. Sheridan, brandishing his twin-starred flag, leaped Rienzi over the breastworks, dropping down on a group of astonished southerners like the angel of death, or mercy. "Where do you want us all to go?" asked one of the Rebels, throwing up his hands. "Go right over there," said Sheridan. "Drop your guns; you'll never need them any more."[56]

Abruptly the Confederate stand disintegrated. Rebs by the hundreds surrendered en masse; only the cavalry managed to get away. Pickett, who had absented himself from Five Forks that morning for an ill-advised shad bake behind the lines, dashed up in time to see Ayres's infantry stave in his left and envelop his command. He tried to organize a last-ditch defense, gave it up as a bad job, and rode away from his position, his command, and much of his dearly won Gettysburg reputation. Amid the wreckage of the Confederate army, Sheridan's men rounded up more than five thousand prisoners, eighteen battle flags, ten fieldpieces, and enough muskets to corduroy the road from Dinwiddie to Five Forks. Sheridan, true to form, was trying to organize a further advance on the Southside Railroad, three miles away, when a courier rode up to him at sundown, with word from Warren that he was in the Confederate rear.[57]

"By God, sir, tell General Warren he wasn't in that fight!" roared Sheridan. The messenger, startled, asked if he could take it down in writing. "Take it down, sir!" Sheridan said. "Tell him by

God he was not at the front." Next Sheridan sought out Griffin, the senior division commander in the V Corps, and brusquely gave him command of the entire corps. A second messenger carried the unhappy news to Warren, who made somewhat better time back to Sheridan's headquarters than he had made coming to his aid or leading his infantry into battle the previous two days. White-faced and shaken, the hero of Little Round Top asked Sheridan to reconsider his order relieving Warren of command. "Reconsider, hell!" said Sheridan. "I don't reconsider my decisions. Obey the order." Like Averell and Torbert before him, Warren had failed Sheridan where it counted most, on the battlefield. Sheridan could forgive the occasional blunder by youngsters such as Custer—Armstrong fought like hell when the time came. But slowness, timidity, or caution—unwanted children of the same defeatist father—these Sheridan could not excuse. Warren rode away, his career in shambles, and Sheridan returned to the task of winning the war, which today's victory at Five Forks had brought a good deal closer.[58]

Horace Porter galloped back to Grant with the news, shouting it out from horseback even before he reined in and dismounted. Backs were slapped, hats thrown into the air, and handshakes exchanged all around. Only Grant remained seated by the campfire. "How many prisoners have been taken?" he wanted to know. Porter told him: more than five thousand. Wordlessly, Grant went into his tent, then emerged, equally taciturn, a few moments later. "I have ordered an immediate assault along the lines," he said, and sat back down. The war was in the "last ditch," as Porter correctly observed.[59]

Robert E. Lee knew it, too. The next morning, as four corps of Union infantry began their assault along his lines, Lee dictated messages to Secretary of War Breckinridge and President Davis. "I see no prospect of doing more than holding our position here till night," he warned. "I am not certain that I can do that. . . . I advise that all preparation be made for leaving Richmond tonight." With shells falling about his personal headquarters and

SHERIDAN

252

blue-coated infantry in plain sight across the way, Lee calmly rode off, remarking to an aide, "Well, Colonel, it has happened as I told them it would at Richmond. The line has been stretched until it has broken."[60]

That night Confederate troops pulled out of Richmond and Petersburg, about the same time that Davis and his cabinet ministers fled aboard the last train to leave the southern capital. Behind them they left a city in chaos; mobs of frightened refugees clogged the streets with horses, carriages, wagons, and pushcarts—whatever they could find to carry away their few remaining valuables. Meanwhile, shaven-headed convicts, newly escaped from jail, rampaged through the streets, looting and stealing. Army demolition squads, carrying torches through the night, set fire to tobacco warehouses and munitions dumps. Soon a massive conflagration engulfed the entire business district along the river. Richmond Mayor Joseph Mayo urgently appealed to the hated enemy to hurry their advance and help put out the fires.

While the Confederate capital gave way to anarchy, Sheridan hastened his cavalry toward Amelia Court House, which he correctly apprehended was to be the point of assembly for Lee's army on its march out of Virginia. "I have not yet heard from Sheridan," Grant reported to Lincoln on April 2, "but I have an abiding faith that he is in the right place and at the right time." So he was, or soon would be, pulling into Jetersville, eight miles southwest of Amelia Court House, on the afternoon of the third and throwing his force across the Richmond & Danville Railroad to block Lee's retreat. "If we press on we will no doubt get the whole army," Sheridan advised Grant. A little later, scouts brought in a prisoner who was carrying a message from Lee to his supply depots at Danville and Lynchburg, directing that 300,000 rations be sent to Burkeville for his starving army. Sheridan, whose own troops were also suffering from hunger, having outstripped their supply trains in the rush to intercept the enemy, craftily allowed the message to be transmitted, intending to pilfer the supplies for his own use. Meanwhile the Rebels squandered a full day at Amelia

Court House in a fruitless attempt to forage food from the picked-over countryside.[61]

When Lee resumed his withdrawal on April 5 he found Sheridan squarely in his way at Jetersville. By then Meade's infantry had caught up with the cavalry, and Lee decided against trying to force his way through to Burkeville, where the Richmond & Danville intersected the Southside Railroad. Instead the Confederate commander set his weary army in motion westward to Farmville, twenty-three miles away, where he hoped to secure the desperately needed rations. Sheridan's reconnaissance had alerted him to the move, and he wanted to move in turn to block the way. But Meade, who was ill with indigestion, disagreed; he still thought Lee was at Amelia Court House, and planned to attack him there the next morning. Frustrated, Sheridan wrote directly to Grant: "I wish you were here yourself. I feel confident of capturing the Army of Northern Virginia if we exert ourselves. I see no escape for Lee."[62]

Grant arrived at midnight, and he and Sheridan went to Meade's tent for a top-level strategy session. For some reason, Grant did not override Meade, even though he told him "he had no doubt Lee was moving right then." The main object, said Grant, was to get ahead of Lee and force him to fight. Sheridan, who had already gotten ahead of the enemy once, set out the next morning to do so again. "I did not permit the cavalry to participate in Meade's useless advance," he later recalled with some satisfaction, "but shifted it out toward the left to the road running from Deatonsville to Rice's Station." Marching parallel to Lee's army like an evil shadow, Sheridan's horsemen harried the exhausted Confederates, darting in and out to round up dispirited stragglers and overturn wagons, constantly probing for weak points in the spread-out enemy column.[63]

At Sayler's Creek, near Deatonsville, they found just such an opening. Custer's troopers swarmed through a gap between two Rebel corps and fell on an undefended portion of a wagon train, burning several hundred wagons and, in effect, creating a massive traffic jam that isolated Lieutenant General Richard Ewell's corps from the rest of Lee's army. Sheridan sent word to Horatio Wright, whose VI Corps was following close behind the cavalry, to fall on Ewell's rear while the Union horsemen attacked from the front. The ensuing fight, along the marshy lowlands of Sayler's Creek, was never in doubt. Although the enemy "fought like a tiger at bay," in Sheridan's rare complimentary phrase, the combined weight of his cavalry and Wright's infantry cut the dog-tired Rebels to pieces. Six southern generals, including Ewell and Robert E. Lee's son, Custis, surrendered, along with nearly ten thousand less exalted but no less gallant soldiers, for whom this war—and indeed all war—was finally over. Reporting his latest victory to Grant, Sheridan added, famously, "I am still pressing on with both cavalry and infantry. . . . If the thing is pressed I think Lee will surrender." When Lincoln received a copy of Sheridan's report, he tenaciously instructed Grant, "Let the thing be pressed."[64]

For both sides now, the end of the war was in sight. Four years of unparalleled heroism, sacrifice, hardship, and glory were ending in an unequal foot race between half-starved, wobbly-legged Confederates exhausted in both body and spirit, and exultant, emboldened Federals who made the sodden Virginia countryside ring with their thunderous cheers for Lincoln and the Union. Lee, who had watched the debacle at Sayler's Creek from a nearby hillside, exclaiming in anguish, "My God, has the army been dissolved?" had abandoned all hope of linking up with Johnston in North Carolina. Now he wished merely to make it to Farmville, feed his soldiers, and decide—or have decided for him—what to do next.

Sheridan had his troopers on horseback early the next morning, riding hard for Farmville and Prince Edward Court House, where it was feared Lee might still turn south toward Danville and the Carolina border. Crook, in the lead with the Second Division, reached Farmville first, only to be met by Confederate cavalry and driven back across the Appomattox River with severe losses, including the capture of brigade commander J. Irvin Gregg. When Sheridan got word of the engagement he realized that Lee had no intention of turning south; accordingly, he consolidated his forces that night and set out the next morning to block the enemy's westward sidle to Lynchburg. One of Major Henry Young's scouts brought word that four train cars full of rations were waiting for the Rebels at Appomattox Station, per Lee's order, which Sheridan had intercepted three days earlier. Now Sheridan drove hard for the depot, Custer's Third Division in the lead.

On the afternoon of the eighth Custer overran the station, seizing the trains and starting them back toward Farmville under the charge of gleeful troopers who had been locomotive engineers before the war. Sheridan watched with amusement, then annoyance, as the men ran the trains back and forth, screeching their whistles and generally showing off for their fellows. He was on the point of ordering the trains burned when the men "finally wearied of their fun" and took the trains east, out of harm's way. That night he made his headquarters in a little frame house at Appomattox Station. There was no sleep for anyone; excited messages flashed back and forth among Sheridan, Grant, and the infantry commanders hurrying their approach to Appomattox. Grant informed Sheridan that he had exchanged messages with Lee, calling for the Virginian's surrender. "I think," Grant said, "Lee will surrender today. . . . We will push him until terms are agreed upon." Sheridan was not so sure it would be that easy; he kept calling for infantry to support his horsemen.[65]

A few miles away Lee held his last council of war with Longstreet, John Gordon, and Lee's nephew, Fitzhugh Lee. The Confederates determined, as Sheridan expected, to try a breakout. If they could push the Union cavalry aside, they might be able to reach Lynchburg and the mountains beyond. Gordon, the architect of the near-miracle at Cedar Creek, would strike Sheridan's lines with his infantry while Fitzhugh Lee attacked with his cavalry. Sheridan, anticipating this as he had anticipated virtually every move the Rebels had made for the past week, directed that his own cavalry fall back in the face of the enemy advance and uncover the Federal infantry now massing in their rear. The forlorn Confederate attack came at dawn and ended soon after. As Sheridan's horsemen spurred away, rank after rank of Union infantry came over the hill behind them. The southern advance stopped dead in its tracks. Sheridan was in the process of organizing a counterattack when a messenger spurred up from Custer: "Lee has surrendered; do not charge; the white flag is up." "Damn them," said Sheridan. "I wish they had held out an hour longer and I would have whipped hell out of them." Clenching his gloved fist, he added, "I've got 'em like that!"[66]

But a truce was a truce. With a color sergeant in tow behind him, Sheridan set off to parley with ranking Confederates across the way. Twice he was met by a shower of bullets from enemy diehards before finally reaching Gordon's camp. A new round of firing came farther down the line, and Sheridan groused, "General, your men fired on me as I was coming over here, and undoubtedly they are treating Merritt and Custer the same way. We might as well let them fight it out." Gordon replied that it was all a mistake. "General Lee asks for a suspension of hostilities pending the negotiations he is having with General Grant," he said.

"I have been constantly informed of the process of the negotiations," snapped Sheridan, "and think it singular that while such discussions are going on, General Lee should have continued his march and attempted to break through my lines this morning. I will entertain no terms except that General Lee shall surrender to General Grant on his arrival here. If these terms are not accepted we will renew hostilities." There was no doubt as to Lee's intentions, Gordon assured him; the Rebel army was exhausted. Sheridan, somewhat mollified, sent a messenger to locate Grant and lead him to the front.[67]

Grant arrived at about 1:00 P.M. to find Sheridan and Major General Edward O. C. Ord, the senior infantry commander in the area, waiting for him on foot at the edge of Appomattox Court House, a crossroads hamlet two miles east of the railroad. "How

are you, Sheridan?'' he asked; then, ''Is General Lee up there?''
Sheridan told him Lee was waiting in a small brick house nearby.
"Come," said Grant, "let us go over." Sheridan and Ord
mounted, followed by their staffs. Inside the home of Wilmer
McLean, who had seen the war begin in his front yard at Manassas Junction, where he was then living, Lee waited with his military secretary, Lieutenant Colonel Charles Marshall, and Union
Lieutenant Colonel Orville Babcock of Grant's staff. The three
were standing when Grant, Sheridan, and the others entered the
parlor. Lee, resplendent in his best dress uniform, bowed formally
as the mud-spattered Grant presented the various members of
his party. Then Sheridan and the others went back outside as
the two commanding generals worked out the details of Lee's
surrender.[68]

A short while later, Babcock called the officers back into the
house. ''The surrender has been made; you can come in again.''
Sheridan, at least, was not greatly moved by the drama of the
moment. Still rankled by the movement of southern troops after
the cease-fire that morning, he went over to Lee and demanded
the return of two dispatches he had sent him protesting the maneuver, ostensibly so that he could make copies of them. Lee, as
always, kept his composure. ''I am sorry,'' he said. ''It is probable
that my cavalry at that point of the line did not fully understand
the agreement.'' He handed the messages back to Sheridan.[69]

After a few more minutes of strained civility, Lee left the
McLean house to break the news to his steadfast army. The
war—at least their lion's share of it—was over. Grant returned to
his camp at the same time. Meanwhile, inside the parlor where
the historic surrender had taken place, Sheridan and his fellow
officers engaged in a sudden frenzy of souvenir-hunting. Despite
the protests of homeowner McLean (who had since moved to
Appomattox from Manassas after the first great battle of the war
to escape such violence), tables, chairs, candlesticks, inkstands—
even chunks of upholstery—were carted off by the victorious
Yanks. Sheridan, who pointedly failed to mention the episode in

his memoirs, paid twenty dollars for the pine table on which Grant had signed the surrender document, using the two ten-dollar gold pieces he had carried with him for years in the event of his capture. The next day, with uncharacteristic chivalry, he presented the table to Custer as a gift for his beautiful young wife, Libbie, along with a graceful note praising her "very gallant husband" for his role in bringing about the surrender.[70]

Modesty prevented Sheridan from describing for her his own role in the melancholy demise of the Confederacy. But others saw and remembered it. "Phil Sheridan is *all right*," Lincoln had said after Cedar Creek, and the commanding general of the Union Army, the man most responsible for both the northern victory and Sheridan's own extraordinary passage from commissary clerk to cavalry chevalier, generously echoed the president's praise. Said Grant, "I believe General Sheridan has no superior as a general, either living or dead, and perhaps not an equal." Fellow Ohioan William Sherman aptly symbolized his old Perry County neighbor as "a persevering terrier dog, honest, modest, plucky and smart enough."[71]

That April of 1865, Sheridan was all those things and more. If, as he believed, Grant was "the steadfast centre about and on which everything else turned," then Sheridan was the orbiter turning most swiftly in his course. The shocking suddenness of Lee's demise was directly attributable to Sheridan and his troops. No other Union cavalry commander could—or would—have moved so swiftly and tenaciously after such wounded but still dangerous prey. For a solid week, from Dinwiddie Court House to Appomattox, Sheridan perfectly carried out the famous dictum of his closest Confederate counterpart, Nathan Bedford Forrest, to "get there first with the most men."[72]

Unfairly perhaps, Sheridan and his horsemen were not to have the privilege of witnessing the formal surrender of the Army of Northern Virginia on April 12 at the soon-to-be-famous "Surrender Triangle." Instead, on the afternoon of the ninth, orders came for them to ride east to Burkeville for resupply, preparatory to finally joining Sherman's army in North Carolina. The next morning they moved out. As a personal tribute to the troops he always held closest to his heart, Sheridan gave them their own well-deserved moment in the sun, parading them informally through Appomattox village on their way out of town. There the Army of the Potomac's proud cavalry corps glimpsed for the last time the weary, rail-thin Confederates they had harried so relentlessly for the past eleven months. Then they rode away, Lee's army already a memory, in search of other worlds to conquer.[73]

8

RECONSTRUCTING REBELS

AT NOTTOWAY COURT HOUSE, beyond Burkeville, Sheridan heard the news of Lincoln's assassination. First reports were that the president had been shot at Willard's Hotel, and Sheridan dismissed the story as a mere canard. Soon, however, official confirmation came in the form of a telegram: Lincoln was dead. Sheridan had never developed the sort of secure personal relationship with the president that Grant and Sherman had enjoyed; in all his dealings with Lincoln, there had existed a certain wry formality. Nor could Sheridan forget that he had not been the president's first choice, either as cavalry chief or as Middle Division commander. Despite an undoubted mutual respect, tempered in the storm of war, the two men do not seem particularly to have liked each other. Nevertheless, the death of Lincoln would have for Sheridan, as for the rest of the country, a profound, if in his case delayed, effect on his life.

Joseph Johnston surrendered to Sherman at Bentonville, North Carolina, before Sheridan even left Virginia. The two principal Rebel armies now had capitulated; the war, to all intents and purposes, was over. Sheridan returned to Washington, where preparations were under way for a Grand Review of the victorious army through the streets of the capital. Sheridan wanted badly to participate in the rites, but the unsentimental Grant had other plans. On May 17 he gave Sheridan command of Union forces west of the Mississippi River, with the injunction "to restore Texas, and that part of Louisiana held by the enemy, to the Union in the shortest practicable time." Edmund Kirby Smith, heading the last credible Confederate army, had yet to be run to ground.[1]

Sheridan went to see Grant about delaying his journey until after the Grand Review on May 23. The orders read "proceed without delay," but Sheridan had long been in the habit of responding to Grant's directives at his own speed. This time, however, there was no room for compromise. "The General told me that it was absolutely necessary to go at once to force the surrender of the Confederates under Kirby Smith." Whether, in fact, such haste was warranted has often been questioned. Smith surrendered before Sheridan reached New Orleans—what else was he likely to do?—and it has been suggested that Sheridan was simply hustled out of town to avoid placing him and Meade together on the same reviewing stand.[2]

Whether or not Grant was motivated by such intramural niceties, he gave Sheridan quite specific instructions for his new assignment. The first was a preview of the coming order of things in the South. Until the former Confederate states were restored to the Union, said Grant, military commanders such as Sheridan were needed to control civilian affairs. This "would not only be economical and simple, but would give the Southern people confidence, and encourage them to go to work, instead of distracting them with politics." In light of Sheridan's subsequent ensnarement in the coils of reconstruction, it is doubtful that, years later, he could quote such an unctuous homily with a straight face. As a prediction of things to come, it could not have been more wrong.[3]

The most pressing part of Sheridan's assignment, insofar as Grant was concerned, was the nettlesome presence of French troops in Mexico. In 1861, while the United States government was distracted by the first months of civil war, English, Spanish, and French forces had landed in Mexico in response to Mexican President Benito Juárez's declared two-year moratorium on foreign debt. The English and Spanish troops soon left, but forty thousand of French Emperor Napoleon III's best soldiers stayed on, propping up the puppet regime of Austrian Archduke Maximilian and, worse yet in the eyes of the Federal government, giving aid and comfort to the Confederacy. Sheridan was to monitor the Mexican-American border and, *sub rosa*, render encouragement and assistance to Juárez and his nationalists. It was a delicate task, complicated by the fact that Secretary of State William Seward adamantly opposed any overt American involvement in Mexican affairs. Having just fought one bitter and sanguinary war, Seward did not relish fighting a second, particularly one along the nation's ill-defended southern border.[4]

Sheridan left immediately for St. Louis, where he boarded a steamboat for New Orleans. Twenty years later he still regretted missing the Grand Review. (The irrepressible Custer stole the show by dashing past the reviewing stand, long hair streaming in the breeze, aboard a suspiciously "runaway" horse.) "I left Washington," lamented Sheridan, "without an opportunity of seeing again . . . the men who, while under my command, had gone through so many trials and unremittingly pursued and assailed the enemy, from the beginning of the campaign of 1864 till the white flag came into their hands at Appomattox Court House." Soon, however, he would be seeing his favorites again.[5]

Major General Edward R. S. Canby, a jug-eared, strawhaired West Point graduate and Mexican War veteran who had had great success combating Confederate incursions in the far West, was waiting in New Orleans with details of the Rebel surrender of Texas. Unsurprisingly, Sheridan was less than thrilled. Even before arriving on the scene, he was telling Grant—without factual corroboration—that "Texas has not suffered from the war and will require some intimidation." He wanted at least three corps of infantry for his rather grandly named Army of Observation to garrison the unrepentant state and worry the French along the Mexican border. "This may seem like the employment of a large force to you," Sheridan wrote to Grant's chief of staff,

John Rawlins, on June 4, "but it is always best to go in strong-handed."[6]

Grant, with an eye more toward Mexico than Texas, gave Sheridan a blank check on the subject of troop strength, and Sheridan quickly assembled an occupation force of more than fifty thousand soldiers. The XIII Corps, commanded by Sheridan's old IV Corps leader at Missionary Ridge, Major General Gordon Granger, moved quickly to occupy Galveston, Brownsville, and Shreveport, spreading inland as it came. The southernmost column, commanded by Major General Frederick Steele, began patrolling the Mexican border. To assist Steele, Sheridan dispatched the twenty-thousand-man XXV (Colored) Corps, under Major General Godfrey Weitzel, and the IV Corps, under Major General David Stanley, who had ridden across Lake Erie with Sheridan on that first, long-ago voyage to West Point in the summer of 1848.

Never content to stay behind a desk when he had troops in the field, Sheridan left New Orleans on June 20 for the first of many inspection tours of Texas. What he saw there infuriated him. Large groups of Texas Confederates, not waiting to be paroled by Canby, had spent the past three weeks roaming through the countryside, breaking into arsenals, looting stores (and in some cases, whole towns), rifling the state treasury, and generally intimidating Unionists, freed blacks, and peaceable citizens of all stripes. Nor was the misbehavior all attributable to rogue Texans. Missouri cavalryman Jo Shelby led three thousand horsemen across Texas and into Mexico, where he proffered his services to Maximilian, having first exacted tribute from several Lone Star towns along the way. The entire Confederate surrender west of the Mississippi, stormed Sheridan, was nothing more than "a swindle." He intended to make them pay for their perfidy.[7]

As he had always done when faced with a problem, Sheridan called for the cavalry. He wanted his old strikers, Merritt and Custer, at his side, to ride across Texas as they had Virginia, putting the fear of God into unregenerate Rebels and—not incidentally—moving into place for a quick thrust across the border at the "very saucy and insulting" French. Accordingly, Merritt assembled a force of 5,500 horsemen at Shreveport, while Custer took charge of another 3,500 soldiers at Alexandria. The two forces were to move in parallel columns through northeastern Texas, where Confederate sentiment was still strong, southward to San Antonio and Houston. There they would show the Union flag and be within galloping distance of the Rio Grande.[8]

Merritt, typically, completed his organizational tasks ahead of Custer and broke camp on July 9. Riding through stifling heat and dust, the column reached San Antonio thirty days later, a model march with no untoward incidents. Meanwhile, Custer was having a great deal of trouble with his division. The five Wisconsin, Indiana, and Iowa regiments were composed of veteran fighters from the western theater, and there was a decided lack of empathy between these no-nonsense midwesterners and their flamboyant new general from the East. The men, all volunteers, had expected to go home at the end of the war; instead they had been diverted to Texas. A clash of wills soon erupted, with Custer freely—and illegally—employing the lash, withholding rations, and delegating soldiers to serve as "nursemaids" for his wife, Libbie, who gaily accompanied her husband on the ride south. One Wisconsin soldier, doubtfully charged with mutiny, was led before a firing squad alongside a convicted deserter. Custer assembled the entire division for the executions and allowed the officer in charge to order "Ready" and "Aim" before pulling aside the mutinous soldier and commuting his sentence to hard labor. If such theatrics were designed to win him the respect of his men, they failed dismally. Until the day they mustered out, the troopers loathed Custer and carried out his orders grudgingly, and the cocksure general, accustomed to the idolatry of his old Michigan troops, angrily repaid them scorn for scorn.[9]

Sheridan felt he had enough men to push the French out of Mexico, should it come to that, and he was primed and ready for another Winchester or Five Forks along the banks of the Rio Grande. A "golden opportunity" soon presented itself in the form of several pieces of Confederate artillery the fleeing Rebels had turned over to General Tomás Mejia, the Imperialist *comandante* at Matamoros, just across the border from Brownsville. Sheridan instructed Steele to demand the immediate return of the artillery on the grounds that it was illegal contraband and rightfully belonged to the United States government. Mejia postured innocence, saying the guns had been purchased before the Confederate surrender, and thus were the rightful property of the emperor. Threats and protests flew back and forth, and the situation grew so ominous by mid-July that President Andrew Johnson discussed with his cabinet the possibility of war with France. The moment soon passed; Maximilian had no intention of fighting the Americans over a few pieces of disputed artillery. He ordered Mejia to return the fieldpieces—"varnished over," sneered Sheridan, "with Imperial apologies."[10]

Grant, who had joked to an aide a few days after Appomattox, "On to Mexico," now cautioned Sheridan to be a little more circumspect in his warmongering, at least in public. He added, however, that it would "be better to go to war now when but a little aid given to the Mexicans will settle the question" than to risk fighting an entrenched monarchy later. Taking the hint, Sheridan returned to Texas in late September, visiting Stanley and Merritt in San Antonio and ostentatiously reviewing the troops at hand. Then he dashed off with a cavalry regiment to Fort Duncan, where he had begun his military career twelve years earlier. There he opened indirect communications with Benito Juárez, "taking care not to do this in the dark." The transparent and somewhat juvenile sham continued with Sheridan sending a pontoon bridge to Brownsville and inquiring in a stage whisper about the best roads to take into northern Mexico.[11]

Independent of the Johnson administration, Grant had worked out an agreement with the *juarista* minister to Washington, Matías Romero, whereby Union General John Schofield would take a year's leave of absence and lead American volunteers in Mexico. The canny Seward, however, got word of the plan and sent Schofield to Paris instead, ordering him "to get your legs under Napoleon's mahogany and tell him to get out of Mexico." At the same time, a second Union general, Lew Wallace, who would later become famous as the author of *Ben-Hur*, was openly going about the country recruiting mercenaries, raising money, and passionately speechifying for the nationalist cause. Seward saw to it that Wallace's leisure time was effectively curtailed by having Johnson appoint him to head the Andersonville war crimes tribunal.[12]

The various intrigues along the Mexican border occupied much of Sheridan's time and attention during the summer of 1865. Nevertheless, he also took his first tentative steps into the quagmire of reconstruction politics, persuading Grant to curtail Canby's administrative powers in Louisiana and removing Granger from command in Texas. In both cases the changes seem to have been prompted by the offending officers' relatively lenient attitudes toward the defeated Rebels in their care. Canby, whose command was reduced from a department to a district, was loath to use all the powers that martial law gave him as Louisiana's de facto governor. Unlike his notorious predecessor, Benjamin "Beast" Butler, Canby sought to minimize army involvement in state political and economic matters. He found the ongoing confiscation of Confederate property, particularly Louisiana's lucrative cotton trade, "hopelessly complicated by . . . fraud," and recommended disassociating the army altogether from the cotton business. Similarly, he favored returning the operation of state banks and railroads to civil control.[13]

Meanwhile, in Texas, Gordon Granger had run afoul of Grant and Sheridan by becoming too friendly, too soon, with ex-Confederates there. Grant had disliked Granger ever since the Battle of Missionary Ridge in 1863, when Granger had jangled his tender nerves by repeatedly firing off a cannon at their Orchard Knob command post. While occupying Mobile at the end of the war, Granger had further alienated Grant by recommending to Johnson that the state be readmitted to the Union "with all [its] vested rights." And, while proclaiming in Galveston that "all slaves are free," he also warned the newly liberated blacks not to congregate around army bases or allow themselves to become too idle. More recently he had aggravated Sheridan by allowing Texans to organize civilian police forces and by helping white employers enforce labor contracts with blacks.[14]

Canby's and Granger's approach to reconstruction, it should be noted, was entirely in line with the views of the president. But Sheridan, whose only previous administrative experience with a conquered people consisted of placing a few rebellious Rogue River Indians in balls and chains in prewar Oregon, was not inclined to share their view. Having spent the last three years waging hard war on southern soldiers and civilians, he could not easily change overnight into a benevolent and equable administrator. Nor, as a career soldier, did he take kindly to Canby's unilateral renunciation of army prerogatives. With radical Republicans already beginning to grumble at Johnson's comparatively lenient restoration program, Sheridan the political novice took it upon himself to advise the president to "wait and trust to a little time and the working of natural causes" to bring the erring southern states back into the fold.[15]

Except for his brief midsummer foray into politics, which was more a reordering of the chain of command than a serious engagement of reconstruction complexities, Sheridan's attention remained fixed throughout 1865 and early 1866 on the military and diplomatic stalemate in Mexico. In October the French ambassador to Washington complained to Seward, not without reason, that American troops were acting "in exact opposition to the repeated assurances Your Excellency has given me concerning the desire of the Cabinet . . . to preserve the most strict neutrality in the events now taking place in Mexico." Seward forwarded the complaint to Sheridan, with a pointed reminder to refrain from "anything like active sympathy" for the nationalists. An unrepentant Sheridan fretted to Grant that the "willy-nilly" State Department was preparing to abandon Juárez and his cause.[16]

In January 1866 trouble flared again on the border, this time at Bagdad, across the river from Port Isabel. A Tennessee adventurer and ex-Confederate, R. Clay Crawford, through the intercession of Lew Wallace, had received permission from Grant to raise a company of *filibusteros* on the American side of the Rio Grande. Sheridan, who apparently was not apprised of the situation, had detained Crawford in New Orleans two months earlier, but released him after hearing from Grant that Crawford had legitimate business in Mexico. That business consisted mainly of leading an unauthorized foray across the border to Bagdad, where alert Imperialist troops quickly rounded up seventeen of Crawford's men, including a number of moonlighting black soldiers from Sheridan's army. Under the emperor's "black flag" decree, anyone caught fighting against the Empire could expect to be executed. When the American commander on the scene, General Weitzel, refused to intercede in his behalf, Crawford led his force back across the Rio Grande and took the town by surprise. Weitzel then decided that matters of "humanity" compelled him to cross over into Mexico as well. In the meantime, Crawford's soldiers of fortune began systematically looting the town.[17]

As soon as Sheridan learned of the incursion, he ordered Weitzel to hie himself back to American soil. Weitzel complied speedily, arresting Crawford and his henchmen in the process. Fortunately for the cause of world peace, the comic-opera incident was quietly forgotten by both sides, and Crawford "escaped" from his captors a few days later. Ultimately he sent Wallace a $122,000 bill for services rendered, which Wallace, surprisingly enough, did not feel obligated to pay.[18]

The Bagdad incident underscored the difficulties Sheridan was having keeping American adventurers of all stripes out of Mexico. Brownsville, in particular, was a hotbed of intrigue. Men were earning upwards of fifty dollars a month as bodyguards for parties having business across the border. The black soldiers stationed there, only recently freed from the onus of slavery themselves, were particularly sympathetic to Mexican peasants trying to throw off an oppressive monarchy. Many soldiers, white as well as black, went south to fight for Juárez as soon as they received their discharges from the army.[19]

Particularly galling to Sheridan was the presence of a large expatriate Confederate colony sixty miles west of Vera Cruz, at Córdoba. The colony, which numbered nearly five thousand at its peak, was named Carlotta in honor of Maximilian's raven-haired empress. Still banking on support from the late rebellious states, Maximilian sanctioned a plan by former Confederate naval commander Matthew Fontaine Maury to promote southern immigration to the colony. Thousands of leaflets proclaiming "Ho for Mexico!" were distributed in the South, promising free transportation, cheap land, and ready labor. Among the Confederate worthies eventually turning up at the colony were Sheridan's longtime rival Jubal Early, Edmund Kirby Smith, "Prince" John Magruder, Sterling Price, Jo Shelby, and the former Confederate governors of Tennessee and Louisiana. After trying unsuccessfully to get the "slow and poky" State Department to suppress emigration to the colony, Sheridan obtained authorization from Grant to personally review all applications for travel permits to Mexico. This, together with the worsening fortunes of Maximilian and his court, effectively discouraged further Rebel tourism.[20]

In April 1866, Napoleon III grudgingly announced that he would begin pulling French troops out of Mexico later that year. To his dying day, Sheridan believed that his elaborate pantomime had been decisive in forcing the Gallic hand. But it is more likely that French domestic pressures, the rise of a unified Prussia to the east, and, certainly not least, the subtle and brilliant diplomatic efforts of Secretary of State Seward had more impact on Napoleon's decision than did Sheridan's military theatrics. Nevertheless, American practical and moral support had added one more weight to Napoleon's carefully balanced scale of protective self-interest.[21]

As Maximilian's cardboard empire began to crumble, Sheridan turned his attention again to Louisiana, where he took steps that spring to rid himself of the troublesome Canby once and for all. Canby, though aware that Sheridan was in the midst of mustering out all volunteer forces in his command, had complained that his own troop level in Louisiana was "scarcely sufficient for the ordinary requirements of the service." Sheridan, who by the end of April had reduced his command by nearly 39,000 men, returned the favor by recommending to Grant that Canby himself be mustered out of the service. He reinforced this barbed recommendation with charges that members of his staff had uncovered evidence of fraud in the ever-troublesome cotton trade, abuses he attributed to Canby's inattention. Wearying of the fight (which, given Sheridan's close attachment with Grant, he knew he could not win), Canby at length requested a transfer, for health reasons, from Louisiana. On May 28 Sheridan replaced him with Major General Absalom Baird, a former comrade from the Chattanooga campaign currently serving as superintendent of the state Freedmen's Bureau.[22]

Preoccupied by the impending gubernatorial election in Texas, Sheridan left the inexperienced Baird on his own to deal with the explosive political situation inside the Pelican State. In time-honored Louisiana tradition, the state was riven with byzantine political combinations, ever-shifting personal alliances, bald-faced double-dealings, and simmering blood feuds. The newly reelected governor, James Madison Wells, was a case in point. A former slaveowner and cotton planter, Wells had stayed loyal to the Union during the war, even going so far as organizing a group of like-minded guerrillas to harass his former associates. Entering office as a radical, he did an abrupt flip-flop when large numbers of ex-Confederates returned to Louisiana politics under Johnson's liberal amnesty provisions. Publicly courting the anti-black vote, Wells was returned to office by a landslide in November 1865, then presided over a Democrat-controlled legislature that speedily enacted a repressive vagrancy law aimed at blacks.[23]

Louisiana politics being what they were, Wells was not long in reversing sides again, this time with deadly results. Under

Lincoln's wartime reconstruction plan, the state had held a constitutional convention in 1864 to abolish slavery and approve a new constitution. Former Confederates, who had not participated in the document-writing, understandably disavowed it; and with the election of New Orleans' wartime Democratic mayor, John T. Monroe, in the spring of 1866, the balance of power now swung to the Democrats. Fearing for his political life, Wells suddenly decided to support a call by radical Unionists to reconvene the long-discredited convention, which had not sat for nearly two years, to take up the explosive issue of black voting rights.[24]

July 30 was the date chosen for resuming the convention at Mechanics' Institute in downtown New Orleans. There were serious questions as to the legality of the reborn convention, and some radicals, including the convention's 1864 president, flatly refused to take part in the proceedings. Others, led by transplanted northern dentist A. P. Dostie, who had briefly held office during the army's wartime occupation of the state, championed the meeting and pointedly threw down the gauntlet to the city's Confederate majority. In a speech given on July 27, Dostie threatened to "exterminate" the Democrats, warning that "the streets will run with blood." He advised blacks to come to the convention armed. For their part, the Democratic lieutenant governor, state attorney general, and Mayor Monroe threatened to arrest convention delegates on sight. The tense situation was not helped by an ill-considered telegram from President Johnson to convention opponents, assuring them that the army would uphold such arrests.[25]

Clearly, passions ran high in the days preceding the convention, and there was a real need for Sheridan's strong, restraining hand. The only problem was that he was nowhere to be found. With trouble brewing in the streets of New Orleans, the Federal commander once again had galloped off to Texas, lured by the persistent siren call of military adventure. On June 24 the crucial Imperialist stronghold at Matamoros had fallen to the *juaristas*, prompting Sheridan to rush to the border in the fear (so he said) that French troops there might be surrounded, thus necessitating their reinforcement and throwing off the entire timetable for French withdrawal from Mexico. As Sheridan warned Grant, such a development would be "the diablo to pay." He wanted to monitor the situation personally.[26]

In Sheridan's absence, an increasingly befuddled Baird was bombarded on all sides by opponents of the convention, who direly warned that here, too, there would be hell to pay if the army failed to suppress the convention. But despite the seemingly clear mandate from the president to act in concert with Democratic officials, Baird continued to vacillate. Reasoning—incredibly—that the army had always held itself "strictly aloof from all interference with the political movements of the citizens of Louisiana," he refused an appeal from the mayor to forbid the meeting and warned that he would arrest anyone attempting forcibly to stop the assembly. To Monroe's not-unmerited complaints that the convention was illegal, Baird said blithely that if that were so, the meeting would merely be a "harmless pleasantry." Events would soon show it to be neither harmless nor pleasant.[27]

With Sheridan out of contact somewhere between the Mississippi and the Rio Grande, Baird sent a telegraph to Secretary of War Stanton on July 28, urgently requesting instructions. For some reason—and theories have ranged from outright conspiracy to mere bureaucratic incompetence—Stanton failed either to answer Baird directly or to forward the telegram to the White House, where it should have gone in the first place. The 860 Federal troops quartered three miles south of the city thus remained in their barracks, too far away to be of any immediate help to anyone.[28]

Monday, July 30, dawned steamy and hot. The convention opened as scheduled at noon, with no untoward incidents. A little later, however, a raucous procession of two hundred blacks suddenly appeared in the streets, heading straight for the Mechanics' Institute. Angry whites stood on the sidewalks, taunting the marchers with oaths and threats. First words, then punches, and finally pistol shots were exchanged by the two groups. The out-numbered blacks fled toward the convention site, followed closely by white civilians and members of the city police force. Once inside, the fugitives barricaded the doors, while others fired from windows into the milling crowd below. The mob, better armed if no better organized, returned fire with a vengeance.[29]

Depending on which self-serving account one chooses to be-lieve, the conventioneers inside the building either joined their black supporters in resisting the police or else attempted to sur-render by waving white handkerchiefs and holding up their hands. In any case it was now too late for such appeasement. Several convention delegates, including Dostie, were killed outright or mortally wounded by civilians or police; others, attempting to flee, were set upon by the pitiless mob. At least 38 people were killed in the fighting, 34 of them black, and another 146 injured. Nearly two hours after the fighting began, Federal troops finally arrived on the scene. Baird had decided at the last moment to keep an eye on the proceedings, but somehow thought the convention was not slated to begin until 6:00 P.M. This inexplicable mistake doomed hundreds of New Orleanians to death or injury.[30]

Sheridan, quickly getting word of the incident, hurried back from Texas the next night, but by then it was too late to do much more than clean up the blood and assess the blame. His first inclination, in keeping with his authoritarian emphasis on order and discipline, was to blame convention supporters, whom he characterized in his initial telegram to Grant as "political agitators and revolutionary men." The rump assembly, he noted with ex-emplary hindsight, had always seemed likely "to produce breaches of the public peace." Soon, however, he began changing his tune. Despite a printed proclamation by Mayor Monroe on the morning of the riot warning citizens to stay away from the convention area, Sheridan now charged that the mayor and the police had instigated the squalid incident. "The more information I obtain," he wired Grant on August 2, "the more revolting it becomes. It was no riot. It was an absolute massacre by the police, which was not excelled in murderous cruelty by that of Fort Pillow. It was a murder which the mayor and the police of the city perpetrated without the shadow of a necessity. Furthermore, I believe it was premeditated, and every indication points to this."[31]

Whether premeditated or not, the New Orleans riot could not have come at a worse time for Johnson and his presidential reconstruction program. Already increasingly at odds with Congress over his vetoes of the Freedmen's Bureau and Civil Rights Acts of 1866, the president now had the impossible task of explaining away a murderous confrontation between Louisiana political factions that opponents could sell to the northern public as a simple race riot. Johnson needlessly outraged Sheridan—and perhaps encouraged the general's sudden change of heart regarding who was to blame for the riot—by passing a garbled copy of Sheridan's first dispatch to *The New York Times*. The text, printed two days later, deleted Sheridan's criticism of the mayor and the police force, causing the author to complain loudly to Grant about a breach in military etiquette. "This emphatic protest," said Sheridan, "mark[ed] the beginning of Mr. Johnson's well-known personal hostility toward me."[32]

It did not occur to Sheridan that Johnson's ire may have been motivated, at least in part, by his own pointless absence from the city during the height of the trouble. This followed his ill-chosen campaign to depose Canby and replace him with the irresolute and inexperienced Baird, thus removing the one Federal military officer who might have been able, through his personal contacts with both sides, to prevent the senseless tragedy. By resorting to his lifelong tendency to lash out whenever he was attacked, Sheridan had heedlessly alienated his commander-in-chief and clearly set himself on the side of congressional radicals. Henceforth he and Johnson would be mortal enemies.

As a long-range employment strategy, this was perhaps not the worst position to hold, although Sheridan, removed from the partisan intrigues of Washington, could not have foreseen it at the time. Nor did he have time for leisurely reflection. Despite the continuing public clamor over the New Orleans riot, he was forced to turn his attention back to Texas, where other explosive events were making 1866 the most trying year in his memory. Less than a month after the riot, a flare-up along the Mexican border claimed the life of one of his most valued aides. Major Henry Young, chief of Sheridan's efficient band of scouts and a familiar sight at headquarters since the Shenandoah Valley campaign, was killed, along with several *filibusteros* he had recently recruited, while attempting to cross the Rio Grande into Mexico.

Sheridan, in his memoirs, maintained that Young had been hired by Mexican general José Carvajal to serve as a personal bodyguard for "the old wretch," whom Sheridan had met and found considerably less than impressive. According to Sheridan, he advised Young not to accept the job, but a tearful Young had already given his word to the *juarista* chieftain. In the interval between Young's departure from New Orleans and his arrival in Brownsville, Carvajal had been deposed by a rival general, Servando Canales, who refused Young's services. While en route to the camp of a third rebel general, Mariano Escobedo, Young and his party were attacked "by a party of ex-Confederates and renegade Mexican rancheros." Young was shot and killed and several others drowned while attempting to swim the river to safety.[33]

It may have happened the way Sheridan recalled it. But the fact that the general's chief of scouts was trafficking with Mexican nationalists near the recently fallen stronghold of Matamoros a scant few weeks after Sheridan's own hasty visit to the front justifies at least a question about Sheridan's intentions. He was sufficiently interested in the events transpiring in northern Mexico to rush away from New Orleans, even as rumors of political bloodshed were growing daily. At the same time this was going on, Lew Wallace was in the act of personally transporting five thousand Enfield rifles, one thousand pistols, six cannon, and a huge quantity of ammunition to Matamoros aboard three chartered cargo ships—one named, ironically, the *General Sheridan*. Wallace was at Carvajal's headquarters when that leader was overthrown, and then hastened to the camp of Escobedo, the same general whom Young was attempting to reach when he was killed. Nothing can be proved, but the circumstantial evidence of increased American meddling indicates that Sheridan may have been more involved in the dirty business of filibustering and arms-running than his memoirs concede. At any rate, Young's death "end[ed] pretty much all open participation of American sympathizers with the Liberal cause," although Sheridan and his generals continued to supply arms to Juárez surreptitiously.[34]

Less dramatic than the news from Louisiana and Mexico, but no less unwelcome, was the changing political situation in Texas, where a former Confederate had just been elected governor. The new chief executive was James W. Throckmorton, a transplanted Tennessean who had trounced the weak Unionist candidate for governor, Elisha Pease, in the June election. Sheridan had thought highly of the former provisional governor, A. J. Hamilton, and had cooperated with him to maintain a semblance of peace in the notoriously fractious state. Throckmorton was a different matter. Although, as former president of the state constitutional convention, he was aware that Texas had failed to abide by all the terms of Johnson's reconstruction program, he was still able through "ingenious persuasion," as Sheridan termed it, to induce the president to return control of state government to civilian hands. Then, like Madison Wells in Louisiana, Throckmorton suddenly reversed his earlier moderate position and cooperated hand-in-glove with the legislature to pass restrictive Black Codes aimed at keeping down the freedmen.[35]

Preoccupied just then by his extralegal adventuring along the Mexican border and the Machiavellian state of affairs in Louisiana, Sheridan had left the army's role in Texas to his longtime associate Major General Horatio Wright, who had replaced Gordon Granger as district commander a year earlier. Wright had worked closely with the provisional Unionist government during its stewardship, and he set out to do the same with Throckmorton's incoming regime. To Sheridan this seemed uncomfortably reminiscent of Canby's tolerant administration of Louisiana. He was particularly alarmed by Wright's endorsement of a Throckmorton plan to transfer army troops from the interior to the frontier. With the continued mustering out of volunteer regiments, Sheridan felt he had few enough men as it was to keep order in the cities; he had none to spare for Indian-fighting duty on the sparsely populated plains. Besides, he suspected that reports of Indian depredations were purposely being exaggerated to obstruct his efforts to protect blacks and Unionists from their Rebel neighbors. He continued to stymie Throckmorton's requests.[36]

As he had done with Canby, Sheridan arranged for Wright to be mustered out of the volunteer army and transferred to Washington for reassignment. He replaced him with Major General George W. Getty, another comrade from the Shenandoah Valley campaign. It was Sheridan's fervent desire to disentangle himself as much as possible from Texas politics. He complained to Grant that he was "handcuffed" to his desk in New Orleans, awash in administrative paperwork. The addition of Freedmen's Bureau duties to his workload (he had replaced Baird on the board of the Louisiana branch of the bureau) made Sheridan wonder aloud whether he might soon expect to be appointed Commissioner of Indian Affairs in Texas, as well.[37]

Unfortunately for Sheridan, Getty was still suffering from the lingering effects of a wound he had suffered in the Wilderness campaign and was in no shape physically to discharge his duties. During his scant one-month term as district commander, army abuses against the civilian population multiplied, culminating in the notorious Brenham, Texas, fire of September 1866. Brenham, a rough, brawling railroad town strategically located between Houston and Austin, supported more than its share of idlers and toughs. Union soldiers, freed blacks, and visiting northerners were frequent targets of verbal and physical abuse. The situation was immeasurably worsened by the arrival that summer of Company E, 17th Infantry Regiment. The Seventeenth had already made an unsavory name for itself in Galveston at the beginning of Federal occupation, drinking, whoring, and fighting with equal abandon. Even the pro-Union Galveston newspaper, *Flake's Daily Bulletin*, felt constrained to protest the regiment's unrestrained villainy. "We have never had a garrison that so disgraced itself, and violated the public peace," the paper groused. Army officials attempted to rein in the truculent regiment by scattering its twenty-four companies across the state.[38]

The quartering of the Seventeenth in Brenham soon produced predictable results. On the night of September 7, a group of marauding soldiers, half-drunk and typically looking for trouble, clashed with black and white townspeople at separate dances in town. Further confrontations between the sides led to a brief gun battle and the wounding of two soldiers. Major G. W. Smith, the company commander, instituted a search for the soldiers' assailants, ransacking stores and roughing up civilians. Smith and his party soon returned to camp, but sometime before dawn another unidentified group of soldiers set fire to a store and a saloon belonging to two of the suspects in the shooting. Before it could be extinguished, the fire caused $131,000 worth of damage. Townspeople immediately petitioned Throckmorton for relief.[39]

The incident, serious though it was, might have died down quickly enough had the army exhibited the same zeal for justice among its own that it demanded of occupied Texans. But a hasty and biased investigation of the fire by regimental commander Lieutenant Colonel E. C. Mason predictably exonerated the army of any wrongdoing, ridiculously imputing that the fire may have been set by civilians wearing army clothing. Several soldiers sought for questioning in the matter conveniently "deserted" before a state legislative committee could interview them. Sheridan himself entered the fray in mid-September, directing that neither Smith nor any of his men were required to surrender to local authorities. In a subsequent report to Grant, he misleadingly characterized the soldiers involved as "unarmed and inoffensive," blaming the trouble on the town's "insolent and threatening" attitude toward the army. He also downplayed the damage to the town, saying blandly that the burned buildings and their contents were not particularly valuable, anyway.[40]

After a hurried interview with Mason in New Orleans, Sheridan wearily betook himself back to Texas to look into the case more thoroughly. There was, he now told Grant, "a strong probability" that Union soldiers had, indeed, set the fire. Still, despite continued protests from Throckmorton, Sheridan did little to prosecute the matter. The two officers charged with being at the scene of the crime, Major Smith and Captain Samuel Craig, were quietly transferred to other counties, where both had subsequent brushes with the law. Craig was indicted by a Texas grand jury for illegally confiscating and destroying court records, and Smith was court-martialed for pocketing Freedmen's Bureau funds. In neither case was the miscreant punished; both were simply allowed to leave the state.[41]

The Brenham incident had the result of hardening Sheridan's already flinty attitude toward Texas and its inhabitants, starting with the former Rebel now sitting in the statehouse. It was "embarrassing in the extreme," complained Sheridan, to have to work with Throckmorton; the governor had as his standard "Pride in Rebellion; that it was a righteous but lost cause." Sheridan was particularly annoyed by Throckmorton's continued demands for more army troops along the Indian frontier, demands the skillful politician soon took over his head to Washington. Both the president and the secretary of war received details of recent Comanche depredations, and Stanton replied that the matter was under presidential consideration.[42]

As a sop to Throckmorton, Sheridan eventually transferred the Fourth Cavalry from San Antonio to Camp Verde, closer to the northwestern frontier. The governor continued his political pressure, and in October Grant advised Sheridan to look into the matter more fully. Four days later Sheridan reported that he had sent his entire twenty-one-company cavalry contingent to the west, although he remained unconvinced of the necessity. Instead he suspected that Throckmorton was building a case for raising a state militia, a force that Sheridan warned would be filled with ex-Confederates. He refused to allow the governor to hold public meetings to discuss the issue.[43]

In late October, Sheridan sent his aide, Major George A. Forsyth, to the northwestern frontier to look into reports of Comanche abuses. Like any good assistant, Forsyth anticipated what his superior wanted to hear. Even before he reached the frontier, he was authoritatively telling Sheridan that "I am convinced that many of the people who are moving in from the frontier are doing it to better their condition, and not from any fear they may have of the Indians." After a few weeks of poking around, Forsyth returned to headquarters and completed his report. In it he conceded that there had been Indian raids on settlers, but belittled the sodbusters for being "terrified beyond all comprehension." He offered the cold comfort to potential victims of Comanche depredations that the Indians' primary goal was to steal horses, not to kill whites. He recommended reopening abandoned Fort Belknap to provide a measure of protection for the settlers there.[44]

In light of his future career as the nation's preeminent Indian fighter, Sheridan was now in the ironic position of downplaying the very real danger presented by intractable Comanches to Texas homesteaders. This attitude stemmed, in part, from the characteristic reluctance of any army commander to scatter his forces over too wide an area, particularly after the vast loss of troop strength that came with mustering out the volunteer regiments. But it was also the result of a deep personal antipathy on Sheridan's part to Texans of all shapes and sizes. ("If I owned hell and Texas," he once joked to a Lone Star newspaperman, "I would rent out Texas and live in hell!") This distaste for all things Texan led Sheridan, on at least three occasions, to neglect his responsibilities as a lawgiver, in ways that were unworthy of him as an officer and a gentleman.[45]

First there was his tepid response to the Brenham incident. This was followed by two other lapses of justice that undermined

Sheridan's position as moral exemplar. In the first incident, two black soldiers were accused of hanging a white man awaiting trial for the murder of a black civilian in Victoria. This was just one of several incidents in which black troops had interfered with civil authorities by releasing fellow soldiers from the county jail. Throckmorton demanded that the troopers be turned over to local lawmen, but Freedmen's Bureau officials interceded in the soldiers' behalf. After a grand jury returned murder indictments against the pair, Sheridan reluctantly agreed to hand them over, only to find that the men had already been discharged and had melted untraceably into their hometown streets of Baltimore.[46]

Even worse, because it involved army collusion, was the fate of two Bell County Confederates named Duncan and Davis. The men were gunned down in September 1866 by a horse thief named Lindley who was afraid the two might incriminate him. Lindley cleverly got the army to arrest the men by falsely claiming that they had led a mob that hanged his pro-Union son during the war. After an army patrol arrested the two, Lindley, who was traveling with the soldiers, shot and killed the prisoners for "trying to escape," apparently with the assistance or at least acquiesence of the others. Military authorities refused to hand over either Lindley or the officer in charge of the patrol, and both were acquitted before a military court that flatly refused to allow the state attorney general to question the accused. Frontier-style justice later was served when Lindley was arrested by civil authorities in Bell County and summarily lynched by an outraged mob.[47]

Sheridan, to be sure, could not supervise every soldier in his far-flung command. But his unresponsiveness to complaints of army malfeasance was in striking contrast to his oft-stated demand that Texas civilians obey both the letter and the spirit of military rule. By repeatedly expressing doubts that Unionists, freedmen, or Federal soldiers could obtain a fair trial in civil court, he undermined state authority and helped prolong the very climate of lawlessness and vigilantism he was trying to suppress. To many Texans it appeared that he had different scales of justice for blacks and whites, Unionists and ex-Confederates. This may not have been the case, but the general's transparent cynicism and obvious dislike of Texas civilians helped create that perception. Somewhat defensively, Sheridan remarked to Grant in his year-end report, "It is strange that over a white man killed by Indians on an extensive frontier the greatest excitement will take place, but over the killing of many freedmen in the settlements, nothing is done."[48]

While Sheridan and the governor of Texas argued over the parochial issue of sending Federal troops to guard the frontier, political events on the national scene were shaping the future in larger, more comprehensive ways. In early November voters decisively rejected Andrew Johnson's course of presidential reconstruction, giving radicals in Congress a larger working majority. Without a doubt, the New Orleans riot had contributed mightily to the growing perception in the North of unregenerate southern states, bent on defying both the outcome of the war and the subsequent constitutional amendments mandating freedom and justice for newly liberated blacks. But Johnson had also been his own worst enemy, insisting on a disastrous "Swing around the Circle" prior to the election. That unparalleled political disaster (Grant, who was forced to accompany the president for part of the trip, disgustedly characterized Johnson's speeches as "a national disgrace") grievously weakened the president's hand and emboldened his congressional opponents to institute their own, much harsher, brand of reconstruction when Congress reconvened in December 1866.

The increasingly politicized Grant advised Sheridan, one week after the voters had gone to the polls, that "things have changed here somewhat since the last election." It was vintage Grant: direct, laconic, insightful, and true. Things had indeed changed; the balance of power was now with the radicals. And Sheridan, if not yet squarely in the radical camp, was sufficiently well known for his differences with Johnson to be counted upon to do Congress's bidding. In the months to come he would assiduously (and without undue reflection) take his direction from Grant, as he had done without stinting ever since the man from Galena had first become his patron and sponsor at Chattanooga in the fall of 1863.[49]

By the end of November, more by coincidence than design, Sheridan had new subordinates in place in Texas and Louisiana who mirrored the emerging consensus for radical reconstruction. In Louisiana the thoroughly discredited Absalom Baird had resigned his post as assistant commissioner of the Freedmen's Bureau and left the state. He was replaced by Brigadier General Joseph A. Mower of Vermont, who had served as chairman of the army commission looking into the New Orleans riot. Mower's commission had unsurprisingly blamed the riot on white citizens and police, despite being unable—or unwilling—to determine who had fired the first shot. Mower's icy veneer and bone-deep New England abolitionism ideally suited Sheridan's mental picture of the perfect reconstruction-era officer.

In Texas, after a long, frustrating search for a suitably strong-willed district commander, Sheridan settled on Major General Charles Griffin, the same officer he had impulsively promoted to corps command on the battlefield at Five Forks while in the process of ruining Gouverneur Warren's career. If Mower was an idealized image of Sheridan, Griffin was a virtual mirror of the man. Like Sheridan, he was a West Pointer from Ohio, a career army man, and had quarreled publicly with George Gordon Meade during the Wilderness campaign. He was also prickly and easily insulted. He had few close friends, none of them southerners. Even more than Sheridan, Griffin understood the enormous political significance of reconstruction. A dedicated Republican, he could be expected to do everything in his power to further the party's interests in Democratic Texas.[50]

The new year began satisfyingly for Sheridan with the release of a congressional committee report that blamed the New Orleans riot on city and state officials, who, it said, had interfered with a legally recalled constitutional convention. The three-man committee, consisting of two Republicans and a Democrat, predictably split along party lines, with Pennsylvania Democrat Benjamin Boyer dissenting. Boyer countered that the riot had been provoked by white agitators and their black cohorts, for the express purpose of destroying the existing civil government in Louisiana. By the time the report was released in February 1867, the question of blame was beside the point. The riot had already had the effect, intended or not, of swinging the recent election to the radicals, and it was no coincidence that the committee report was included in a bill calling for a new election in Louisiana and the sweeping disenfranchisement of thousands of former Confederate officeholders throughout the South. More to the point, insofar as Sheridan was concerned, was the absence in the report of any criticism of his own questionable handling of the riot. The now-exiled Baird conveniently took the fall for the army's failure to maintain the peace or protect the citizens.[51]

In the midst of the political turmoil surrounding the recent election and its aftermath, the French intervention in Mexico had been largely forgotten by Sheridan and his superiors. On January 10, however, a clerk at Sheridan's headquarters intercepted a coded message from Napoleon III to General Castelnau, commander of the French contingent at Mexico City. The message read, in part, "Do not compel the Emperor to abdicate, but do not delay the departure of the troops; bring back all those who will not remain there. Most of the fleet has left." The accelerated pace of French troop withdrawals—the last contingent left Mexican soil on March 12—doomed the already teetering empire and its ineffectual emperor. The military and diplomatic situation that not long before had threatened to involve the United States in another shooting war was coming to a sudden, anticlimactic end. Maximilian held out through the spring, but was captured and shot by a nationalist firing squad on June 19. A last-second appeal for mercy from Seward was too late to save the Austrian nobleman, whom Sheridan always referred to derisively as "the Imperial buccaneer"; and the general, among others, did not evince much regret at his passing.[52]

Nor were Sheridan's sympathies engaged by the transfer of Confederate General Albert Sidney Johnston's mortal remains from New Orleans to Texas in January 1867. Johnston had fought for the Texas republic in its initial revolt against Mexico and during the subsequent Mexican War, and later had commanded the famous Second Cavalry Regiment in its frontier clashes with Comanches in the 1850s. It was as a Texas freedom fighter, not as a dead Confederate general, that the people of the state wished to honor Johnston; but to Sheridan he was still a Rebel. Turning down a request by the mayor of Galveston to approve a formal funeral procession through the streets of the city, Sheridan stormed, "I have too much respect for the memory of the brave men who died to preserve our government to authorize Confederate demonstrations over the remains of anyone who attempted to destroy it." The Galveston Daily News fired back at "the malignant hatred that can thus reach down into the grave to defile the bones of a dead soldier, the craven fear that invokes authority to protect it from the tears of a mourning people." At the paper's suggestion, Galvestonians turned out anyway, silent and bareheaded, when Johnston's remains passed through the city later that month.[53]

On March 2, Congress passed the first and most sweeping of three Military Reconstruction Acts of 1867, dividing ten of the eleven former Confederate states into five military districts. (Tennessee, having already ratified the Fourteenth Amendment, was exempted.) The southern states were to be ruled over by the army until such time as they had fully complied with new congressional requirements for readmittance into the Union. Nine days after passage of the act, Johnson gave Sheridan command of the Fifth Military District, composed of Texas and Louisiana. In light of the personal differences between Sheridan and the president, it must be assumed that Grant, once again, had been the presiding agent of Sheridan's advancement.

Sheridan liked the Reconstruction Act well enough to quote it verbatim in his memoirs twenty years later. He was convinced, he said, "that the plan of reconstruction presented was, beyond

question, the policy endorsed by the people of the country"—
country meaning, in this case, the North—and "it was, therefore,
my determination to see the law's zealous execution in my district." He announced that he would be guided by the principle of
noninterference with the now-provisional state governments, but
warned that this Olympian posture was contingent upon the
proper behavior of the people themselves. When Throckmorton
wrote to Sheridan a few days later offering his full support in
reorganizing the state, he was brusquely informed that the only
way he could help was by showing "good feeling." Otherwise, he
should stand aside and let the army rule.[54]

Sheridan's nonintervention policy lasted all of eight days.
On March 27 he removed from office Mayor John Monroe of
New Orleans, Louisiana Attorney General Andrew Herron, and
District Judge Edmund Abell, all of whom he held personally
responsible for the previous summer's fatal riot. Grant, who was
steadily distancing himself from Johnson while still attending
cabinet meetings as an invited guest, immediately enthused to
Sheridan, "It is just the thing, and merits the approbation of the
loyal people at least. I have no doubt but that it will also meet
with like approval from the reconstructed." That was stretching
the point, as Grant conceded two days later. "I only wrote
this," he said, "to let you know that I at least approve what you
have done."[55]

The president was a different matter. On April 3, Johnson
ordered that no more removals be made until the United States
attorney general could rule on the legality of such steps. Grant
obediently passed along the order to Sheridan, but added a secret
message warning him that "there is a decided hostility to the
whole Congressional plan of reconstruction at the White House,
and a disposition to remove you from the command you now
have. Both the Secretary of War and myself will oppose any such
move, as will the mass of the people." He assured Sheridan that
Congress intended for the individual army commanders of the
new districts to be "their own judges of the meaning of its pro-

visions." And he bluntly told him, "Go on giving your own interpretation of the law."[56]

In light of these and subsequent instructions from Grant to Sheridan and other district commanders, it is difficult to quarrel with Johnson's later assessment that "Grant was untrue. He meant well for the first two years. . . . But Grant saw the Radical handwriting on the wall, and heeded it." To be sure, it was Grant's handwriting that Sheridan now was heeding, and he was sufficiently forewarned of presidential ire to resist the tempting suggestion by Griffin that he also remove Throckmorton from office. For the time being, said Sheridan, he intended "to make but few removals," but he allowed that he was keeping an eye on Throckmorton and Louisiana Governor Madison Wells.[57]

Throughout April and May, Sheridan busied himself with the arcane chores of voter registration in Texas and Louisiana. Under the reconstruction bill, states were required to hold new constitutional conventions to bring their constitutions into line with the laws of the land, specifically universal suffrage for all adult males (except excluded Confederates) and ratification of the Fourteenth Amendment extending the protections of full citizenship to American blacks. The Second Reconstruction Act, passed March 23, had authorized military commanders to register voters and hold elections. However, the language of the act was vague, and Sheridan and other district supervisors requested that Attorney General Henry Stanbery clarify the wording.

The crucial question concerned who was ineligible to register under the strictures of the so-called Ironclad Oath, which required prospective registrants to swear that they had never been an executive or judicial officer of a state before the war and then had engaged in insurrection or rebellion against the federal government. Everything hinged on the definition of what constituted executive or judicial duties. Griffin, for one, turned to the dictionary in his quest for clarification. "Webster distinctly says that Sheriffs and Constables [sic] duties are executive," he advised Sheridan on April 3.[58]

While Stanbery continued to ponder the legal intricacies of the question, the various commanders had to interpret the registration requirements in their own ways. Sheridan, unsurprisingly, chose to give the law the widest possible construction, disenfranchising every state official from governor to harbor pilot, auctioneer, and cemetery sexton. "The Attorney General should not hamper me too much," wrote Sheridan; "no one can conceive or estimate, at so great a distance, the precautions necessary to be taken . . . here." Grant responded with the odd reassurance that "I think your head is safe above your shoulders at least so that it can not be taken off to produce pain."[59]

Voter registration began in Louisiana on April 21, the earliest starting date for any of the ten occupied states. Sheridan, who disingenuously told Grant that his "only desire [was] to faithfully carry out the law as a military order," apparently wanted to complete the process before the attorney general rendered his opinion. Troops were dispatched to towns throughout the state's forty-seven parishes to protect the three-man registration teams, and blacks were particularly encouraged to register. To oversee the enrollment efforts, ten army officers served as supervisors at large, and Sheridan took care to appoint at least one ex-Union officer to each registration board. Whites were routinely turned away on the grounds that they had served in the Confederate army, whether or not they had ever taken the Ironclad Oath. The strictures had the desired effect: by the time registration ended on August 1, 127,639 voters were on the rolls, of whom 82,907, or sixty-five percent, were black.[60]

Besides voter registration, Sheridan confronted a number of unrelated but equally complicated problems of governance in Louisiana during the month of May. After discovering that an aide to the New Orleans police chief had intimidated prospective black voters, Sheridan dismissed the man from office and moved quickly to reorganize the entire department. He had long harbored a grudge against the police concerning their participation in the New Orleans riot ten months before, and he freely used his ex-

ecutive powers to nullify a state law requiring five years' residence for city officers. He ordered the newly appointed mayor,
Edward Heath, to see to it that, from now on, at least half of the
city's 250 policemen were Union veterans.[61]

Next, Sheridan was drawn into a political battle between the
Louisiana legislature and the governor over the makeup of the
state Board of Levee Commissioners. The legislature had approved
a four-million-dollar bond issue to repair flood-ravaged levees and
appointed a slate of commissioners to oversee the juicy patronage
plum. But Wells, angry at being bypassed by the lawmakers,
abolished the board and selected his own set of commissioners.
Each side appealed to Sheridan to dismiss the other's board. But
Sheridan, in a bit of Solomonic wisdom, simply removed both
boards and appointed his own.[62]

A few days later racial trouble threatened over the use of
segregated streetcars in New Orleans. The so-called "star car"
system of public transport required blacks to ride only horse-
drawn streetcars marked with painted stars, but increasing numbers of blacks—including armed members of the 39th Infantry
Regiment—began forcing their way onto unmarked cars. Officials
of the affected transport companies asked Sheridan to help enforce
the segregation order, but he refused, warning instead that he
would ban the streetcars altogether if the discriminatory practice
continued. Soon the races were riding alongside each other,
though not without mutual bitterness and suspicion.[63]

In the midst of the trouble-fraught month, Attorney General
Stanbery finally delivered his opinion on the question of voter
qualifications in the South. His finding, released May 24, inter-
preted the Reconstruction Act much more liberally than Sheridan
and his registrars had been doing. Stanbery ruled that statewide
officeholders such as governors, lieutenant governors, treasurers,
auditors, and attorneys general could be excluded from voting,
but not municipal officers of cities and towns. Also released from
disenfranchisement were state-appointed road commissioners,
bank examiners, poorhouse overseers, and superintendents of lu-

natic asylums. Given the kind of month he had been having, Sheridan might have been forgiven for wondering whether the last category applied particularly to him.[64]

Unlike other military commanders in the South, Sheridan did not issue new guidelines to registrars following Stanbery's ruling. Stringent loyalty tests continued to be applied to prospective white voters, while hundreds of black voters in Texas were permitted to register, even after listing their place of birth as Africa, which should have disqualified them from voting under the terms of that litmus test of American citizenship, the Fourteenth Amendment. Nor was Sheridan cooperative on the matter of extending the cutoff date for registration. The other four military districts had set August 1 as the last date on which to register, and Johnson likewise wanted the books kept open in Louisiana and Texas until then. After much persuading by Grant, Sheridan complied with the president's wishes, but not before complaining in writing that such a move would create "a broad macadamized road for perjury and fraud to travel on." He maintained, erroneously, that "the number of persons who, under the law, were qualified for registry was about exhausted," a charge given the lie by the fact that nearly forty thousand Louisiana voters came forward to register between July 1 and August 1.[65]

In his open defiance of presidential orders, Sheridan was supported—if not, in fact, encouraged—by his commanding general in Washington. More and more, Grant was sidling away from Johnson's control and encouraging his subordinates to do the same. When copies of Stanbery's legal opinion were transmitted to the five military district commanders in mid-June, with a cover letter signed "By order of the President" stating that Johnson had accepted the finding as "a practical interpretation" of the law, Grant wrote to Sheridan: "Enforce your own construction of the military bill unless ordered to do otherwise. The opinion of the Attorney General has not been distributed . . . in language or manner entitling it to the force of an order. Nor can I suppose that the President intended it to have such force." This was remarkable advice, whether military or legal, particularly when coming from a non-lawyer like Grant. Still, Sheridan willingly followed it, convinced that "to adopt Mr. Stanbery's interpretation of the law . . . would defeat the purpose of Congress, as well as add to my perplexities."[66]

Sheridan's uncooperative stance had not gone unnoticed by the White House, and there was renewed talk of dismissing him from command. On June 24, Grant reassured Sheridan: "Removal cannot hurt you if it does take place, and I do not believe it will. You have carried out the acts of Congress, and it will be difficult to get a general officer who will not." That may have been Grant's opinion; it was definitely not Johnson's. Sheridan had infuriated the president by removing Wells from the governor's chair in Louisiana earlier that month, following the abrupt dismissal with a tartly worded telegram accusing Wells (not without justice) of being "a political trickster and a dishonest man," whose "conduct has been as sinuous as the mark left in the dust by the movement of a snake." Again, it was Sheridan's language, as much as his actions, that gave offense. Few Louisianans were sorry to see Wells go. The *New Orleans Times* spoke for many when it punned, "All's well that ends Wells."[67]

A few days after Wells's removal, Sheridan turned his wrath on Galveston Mayor J. E. Haviland, who had had the nerve to reject several unqualified Republican police appointees in his city. In approving Griffin's dismissal of Haviland, Sheridan pointedly denounced the mayor's "contumacious conduct," which included, in his view, Haviland's sponsorship of Albert Sidney Johnston's funeral parade in Galveston earlier in the year.[68]

In mid-July Congress passed a Third Reconstruction Act, in effect rebutting Stanbery's findings. Registrars now were given a free hand to rule on all questions of voter eligibility, including the power to disenfranchise persons who previously had qualified under the old guidelines. The act redefined "executive and judicial offices" as being "all civil offices created by law for the administration of . . . a State," and gave military commanders the power to remove from office any official considered a detriment to the reconstruction process. For good measure, the act advised district commanders that neither they nor their appointees needed to obey "any opinion of any civil officer of the United States"—meaning Stanbery—thus vindicating Sheridan's de facto policy of noncompliance.[69]

Alarmed by the draconian potentialities of the new act, particularly when wielded by so loose a cannon as Sheridan had become, Johnson sent Brigadier General Lovell Rousseau to New Orleans in late July to keep watch over the president's unruly subordinate. Rousseau had reentered the army after a brief and turbulent stint in Congress, during which time he had been forced to resign his seat in the House of Representatives after—shades of Preston Brooks and Charles Sumner—taking a cane to fellow congressman Joseph Grinnell of Iowa in a less-than-collegial disagreement over reconstruction policies. (He was later reelected by voters in his home state of Kentucky.) Despite having served together at Perryville and Stones River, there was no love lost between Sheridan and Rousseau, whom Sheridan knew to be a loyal supporter of Johnsonian-style democracy.[70]

If Rousseau's presence was intended to constrain Sheridan from using his newfound removal powers, it had the predictable opposite effect. Always, when faced with a direct challenge to his authority, whether personal, civil, or military, Sheridan lashed out quickly and instinctively. There was certainly no lack of targets, and Sheridan characteristically chose the largest. On July 30, after months of importuning by Griffin, he removed Throckmorton as governor of Texas, replacing him with the very man Throckmorton had defeated a year earlier, Republican standard-bearer Elisha Pease. Throckmorton's removal, Sheridan told Grant, was necessary to remove "an impediment to the reconstruction of the State."[71]

In four months' time, Sheridan had removed the governors of Louisiana and Texas, the mayors of New Orleans and Galveston, the Louisiana attorney general, and a district judge. Nor was he finished. Two days after sacking Throckmorton, he removed twenty-two New Orleans city councilmen; he then dismissed the city treasurer, surveyor, comptroller, and attorney. Next came the removal of the mayors of Lake Charles and Shreveport, their councilmen and aldermen, a justice of the peace and the sheriff of Rapides Parish, and three district judges in Texas. "General Sheridan has done so much for the Union men with his sword," exulted one Texas supporter; "he now completes the job with his pen."[72]

Back in Washington, Andrew Johnson had begun the chief drama of his presidency, the firing of Secretary of War Edwin Stanton, which ultimately would lead to his impeachment and trial by Congress. A very reluctant Grant was pressed into service as interim war secretary, and immediately began warning Sheridan of his own impending dismissal. "In case the President insists upon your removal," Grant told Sheridan through his aide, James Forsyth, "whoever may be assigned to your command can be directed . . . to carry out the Military Reconstruction Acts as interpeted by you, and . . . will have to carry out the Law as you have viewed it; and without the opportunity to change your programme." Two days later Grant repeated his warning, but instructed Sheridan to "go on your course exactly as if this communication had not been sent to you, and without fear of consequences. That so long as you pursue the same line of duty that you have followed thus far in the service you will receive the entire support of these Headquarters."[73]

After days of indecision and cabinet-level discussions, Johnson finally acted on August 17, relieving Sheridan of command of the Fifth Military District and transferring him to the Department of the Missouri, with headquarters at Fort Leavenworth. He would be changing places with Major General Winfield Scott Hancock, the hero of Gettysburg, a rock-ribbed Democrat who had recently made a less-than-heroic showing against rebellious Indians in the West. Grant angrily tried to dissuade Johnson from making the move, urging him "in the name of a patriotic people, who have sacrificed hundreds of thousands of loyal lives and thousands of millions of treasure to preserve the intregrity and union of this country—that this order be not insisted on. It is unmistakably the expressed wish of the country that General Sheridan should not be removed from his present command." Johnson responded sourly that he was not aware Sheridan's popularity had ever been put to a vote. "His rule has, in fact, been one of absolute tyranny," said the president, "without references to the principles of our government or the nature of our free institutions." Patriotic considerations demanded that Sheridan "should be superseded by an officer, who, while he will faithfully execute the law, will at the same time give more general satisfaction to the whole people, white and black, North and South."[74]

Perhaps because he had seen it coming, Sheridan received the news of his transfer with uncharacteristic equability. He turned over temporary command of the Fifth Military District to Griffin (who, shockingly, would die of yellow fever ten days later), and departed New Orleans on September 5. Curiously, in his memoirs Sheridan attributed his removal to an order he issued on August 24 limiting jury duty in Louisiana to registered voters. This labored construction pointedly ignores Grant's letter to Johnson a week earlier protesting his removal, which Sheridan himself quotes a page later. Nor does he mention his firing of Throckmorton, preferring instead to see his own dismissal merely as evidence of the president's "personal enmity toward me." At any rate, "I heartily welcomed the order that lifted from me my unsought burden."[75]

Like much relating to the unhappy era of reconstruction, Sheridan's twenty-six-month reign in the trans-Mississippi South remains a matter of continuing controversy. While only a lifelong friend like Henry Greiner would describe the congenitally combative Sheridan as "a diplomat and strategist," it is equally inaccurate to consider him simply a despot—"Prince Philip of Orleans," as one local newspaper styled him. His final orgy of removals disguised the fact that, for much of his time as district commander, Sheridan attempted to work with—or at least around—elected officials. At the same time, his peremptory style of governance and his unconcealed dislike for southerners in general, and Texans in particular, made any close working relationship with former Confederates difficult, if not impossible. As a general he was accustomed to having his word obeyed swiftly and unquestioningly. The army, after all, is not the best school for cooperative democracy.[76]

To a great extent, the tempestuous nature of Sheridan's reign was determined by the peculiar character of the states themselves. Louisiana has long been notorious for its explosive political atmosphere, and the history of Texas is redolent with violence, separatism, and revolt. Neither state, located on the southwestern periphery of the war, had endured anything like the horrific level of devastation visited upon other southern states, and the resultant lack of war-weariness had a strong negative effect on the willingness of its citizens to cooperate with Sheridan or other Union officers. Nevertheless, the general's prickly personality and inflexible preconceptions undoubtedly exacerbated the situation, and his too-hasty sacking of Canby and Wright—two officers who might have served as effective intermediaries between army and civilians—needlessly complicated the inevitable friction.

In the end, however, it was not Sheridan's strained relations with southern civilians that caused his ouster, but his insubordinate attitude toward his commander-in-chief. His scornful disregard for Johnson reflected that of the more politically subtle Grant, and mirrored the growing congressional opposition to Johnson and his administration. The increasingly powerful hand that Congress took in reconstruction greatly strengthened, in turn, the role of the military, and frequently placed it at odds with the president. Sheridan and his fellow district commanders thus were caught in the middle of a brutal power struggle between the two elective branches of government. Given the mind-numbing complexities of reconstruction, it was, as Sheridan wrote, "a most unenviable" position in which to be. Even so, his unconvincing protestation that he "tried to guard the rights of everybody in accordance with the law" is, upon reflection, a bit much to swallow.[77]

A more accurate measure of his attitude toward his duties may be found in a letter to former aide F. C. Newhall. "If I am disliked," wrote Sheridan, "it is because I cannot and will not cater to rebel sentiment. . . . I did not care whether the Southern States were readmitted tomorrow or kept out for twenty years. . . . The more I see of this people the less I see to admire." Given that posture, it is no wonder his presence among them was a mutually unhappy experience for himself and his charges.[78]

9

"AT BEST AN INGLORIOUS WAR"

AFTER NEARLY TWO AND a half years of arduous, controversial, and, to his mind, unappreciated service in the Deep South, Sheridan was in no particular hurry to take up his new command out west. Leaving New Orleans to the ill-fated Griffin, he proceeded upriver to St. Louis, where he was feted at a massive torchlight parade of Union war veterans orchestrated by former comrade-in-arms Major General Carl Schurz, local commander of the Grand Army of the Republic. Typically, the guest of honor saw the turnout as a sign of popular support for "the course I had pursued in the Fifth Military District," and relished the vigorous denunciations of Andrew Johnson and the unregenerate Confederacy. With a chorus of cheers ringing in his ears, Sheridan happily left the South and its truculent, unreconstructed inhabitants behind.[1]

The next day he arrived at Fort Leavenworth, headquarters of the Department of the Missouri, to exchange commands formally with Hancock. A little ironically, perhaps, Sheridan said his "technical compliance" with the president's orders had been done to allow his brother general to hasten to New Orleans "if he so desired." Given the yellow fever epidemic then raging through the city, Hancock had enough sense not to desire it for another three months. Feeling a little run-down himself, Sheridan tarried only briefly at Leavenworth before leaving the post in the hands of Colonel A. J. Smith and heading east on extended leave.[2]

A brief side trip to Somerset, his first in three and a half years, fulfilled Sheridan's filial responsibilities. Then he was off to New York with friend and aide Colonel John Schuyler Crosby for a round of high-society parties, late-night dinners, and gala theater-going. George Templeton Strong, inveterate diarist and bon vivant, hosted one such party for Sheridan and Crosby that season. Crosby, he gushed, was "among the handsomest young men I ever saw"; he could not say as much for Sheridan. "The general," wrote Strong, "is a stumpy, quadrangular little man, with a forehead of no promise and hair so short that it looks like a coat of black paint." Appearances aside, rank has its privileges, and Sheridan and Crosby left Strong's party that night with a pair of attractive young ladies on their arms.[3]

The new year found Sheridan in Washington, serving on an army review board alongside his friend and commander William Sherman. The good life apparently agreed with him, much to the annoyance of his austere superior. "I am pushing Sheridan as hard as I can to work," Sherman wrote to his wife, Ellen, who had attended school across the meadow from Sheridan's boyhood home, "but he don't want to hurry through. He rather enjoys the parties." It was Leap Day, 1868, before Sheridan finally returned to Leavenworth, displacing his houseguests, Lieutenant Colonel and Mrs. George Armstrong Custer, who had occupied the general's residence in his absence while Custer unsuccessfully defended himself at court-martial proceedings stemming from charges of unprofessional conduct during the previous summer's Indian campaign.[4]

Custer's problems, which Sheridan now inherited in spades, had their genesis in the army's failure to control or accommodate the Indians on the central plains, across whose land great rivulets of settlers ceaselessly streamed. In the decade between 1860 and 1870, a million white faces were added to the West, and by the end of the next decade there would be nearly 5 million new citizens on the rolls. Hancock's ill-considered burning of a Sioux and Cheyenne village on Pawnee Fork, near Fort Larned, ten months earlier had needlessly inflamed the Indians, who retaliated by riding the warpath for several months, raping and killing their way as far north as the Platte River of southern Nebraska. Custer and his cavalry had trailed impotently behind, failing to bring the Indians to bay, while the bright Civil War reputations of the erstwhile boy general and Hancock the Superb tarnished daily in the western sun. Tiring of the fruitless chase, Custer eventually took off on an unauthorized side trip to Fort Riley, Kansas, to succor his pining young wife, and quickly found himself brought up on charges.

As a result of Hancock's mishandled campaign, Congress empaneled a special Peace Commission in July 1867 to address the burgeoning aboriginal problem. An uneasy assortment of generals, congressmen, Indian Bureau commissioners, and eastern reformers were named to the board, including a most reluctant Sherman. The subsequent Medicine Lodge Treaty of October 1867 initially promised a workable solution to Indian and white grievances. In return for perpetual hunting rights south of the Arkansas River and thirty years' worth of government annuities in the form of food, clothing, weapons, tools, and farm supplies, the southern Plains Indians—Cheyenne, Kiowa, Kiowa-Apache, Comanche, and Arapaho—agreed to sign over title to all ancestral lands and resettle their tribes on giant new reservations in Indian Territory.[5]

As with most of the treaties between Indians and whites, what sounded good around the council fire did not sound as sweet in the marbled halls of Congress or on the windswept western prairies. The chiefs may have signed the treaty, but that did not mean the wild young braves in their camps felt any obligation to honor its terms. Nor did Congress, preoccupied just then with the looming impeachment of Andrew Johnson, worry unduly about appropriating funds to fulfill the government's promises. For all its encouraging signs, the Medicine Lodge Treaty proved to be as worthless, in practice, as the cheapjack trinkets dispensed as lagniappe at the formal signing.

Consequently, the Department of the Missouri was quiet when Sheridan returned to Fort Leavenworth to take command in late February 1868, but it was a decidedly uneasy quiet. Rumors of renewed bloodshed swept daily through the dreary post. Not content to rely on the unsupported apprehensions of nervous sodbusters or the spurious professions of peace from dubiously loyal squaw men, Sheridan quickly organized a personal inspection tour of the district. What he found was scarcely reassuring. Among the Cheyenne, Kiowa, and Arapaho camped along the Arkansas River near Fort Larned the overriding mood was one of surly discontent. "The young men were chafing and turbulent," he later recorded; neither they nor their elders seemed to understand the terms of the new treaty they were supposed to observe. But when a delegation of chiefs attempted to meet with Sheridan at Fort Dodge to air their grievances he cavalierly refused to receive them, reasoning that "Congress had delegated to the Peace Commission the whole matter of treating with them, and a council might lead only to additional complications." It was reminiscent of his high-handed treatment of southern officials in Texas and Louisiana—with one important difference: the governor of Texas did not lead a band of "reckless and defiant" warriors who could hit a moving target from horseback with a bow and arrow or lift an unlucky farmer's scalp in less time than it took him to hoe a weed.[6]

Sheridan returned to headquarters with an uneasy presentiment that trouble was just over the horizon with the returning buffalo and the greening prairie grass. Worse yet, to a general who believed in concentration of force and superiority of numbers, the 2,600-man contingent now on hand in the District of the Upper Arkansas, where trouble was most likely to break out, was less than half the combined might of the Indians in the region. And even that force was scattered among eight forts, two major wagon trails, and the ever-westering Kansas Pacific Railroad. The quality, as well as the quantity, of Sheridan's soldiers was also a concern. The citizen-soldier of the Civil War, highly motivated and, by war's end, battle-hardened and touched by fire, was now a distant memory. In his place in the stripped-down regular army was the thirteen-dollar-a-month recruit, drawn increasingly from the immigrant urban poor, ill-clothed, ill-housed, ill-fed, and ill-trained. The *New York Sun* voiced the sentiments of many when it charged that "the Regular Army is composed of bummers, loafers, and foreign paupers."[7]

Not all western soldiers were that bad, of course, and at any rate they were usually led by experienced, West Point–trained career officers. But the combination of poor living conditions, harsh discipline, bad food, tainted water, and brutal weather worked against military cohesion and esprit de corps. The three D's—death, desertion, and discharge—produced a staggering annual turnover rate of between twenty-five and forty percent, and those who stayed on were in constant jeopardy from such catastrophic diseases as cholera, malaria, pneumonia, and dysentery, to say nothing of such familiar occupational hazards as alcoholism and venereal disease. The western soldier, in fact, was five times more likely to contract a disease than he was to suffer a battle wound, though that was cold comfort, at best, to troopers who had seen the butchered victims of an Indian raid.[8]

By contrast, the Plains warriors they faced were the products of an age-old culture that glorified combat and the skills it required: courage, endurance, strength, cunning, horsemanship, and weaponry. What was more, they were fighting on homeland they knew as well as a white easterner knew the street where he lived. The Cheyenne braves who later told Sheridan to his face that they could drive away his soldiers with sticks may have been somewhat overstating the case, but there is little doubt that, man for man, the Plains Indians were more than a match for their blue-coated counterparts. It was Sheridan's task to see that the army's traditional advantages of firepower, discipline, organization, and leadership were brought to bear at the right time and place, should the need arise, as now seemed increasingly likely.

In keeping with his habitual emphasis on intelligence-gathering, Sheridan organized a three-man network of spies to go among the Indians and send back assessments of their changing mood. The spies, whom he preferred to call "mediators," included William "Medicine Bill" Comstock, Abner "Sharp" Grover, and Richard Parr. Each had lived on the plains for several years, trapping and hunting with the Indians, and were well acquainted with all the principal chiefs. They were to report to Lieutenant Frederick W. Beecher, nephew of the abolitionist preacher Henry Ward Beecher and Harriet Beecher Stowe, author of *Uncle Tom's Cabin*. Sheridan considered Beecher "a very intelligent man"; but the young lieutenant, partly crippled by a Rebel shell at Gettysburg, would prove to have no better luck than Sheridan's first chief of scouts, Henry Young, who had died facedown in the Rio Grande two years earlier.[9]

Still, as summer heightened over the plains, Sheridan began to hope that renewed bloodshed could be averted. He fed the Indians "pretty freely" from his stores, and the scouts reported no untoward aggression on the part of their charges. Peace might truly have flowered, had the Cheyenne not misconstrued the terms of their implicit captivity. But in late June 1868 a Cheyenne war party made a nocturnal visit to the camp of some unoffending Kaw Indians, making off with some of their livestock. To the Cheyenne way of thinking this was business as usual—one raided and was raided in return. Furthermore, since no whites had been involved, no treaty terms had been violated. Unfortunately, Indian Affairs Superintendent Thomas Murphy did not see things that way. He directed the agent in charge of Cheyenne relations, Edward Wynkoop, to withhold a long-promised consignment of arms and ammunition.[10]

Furious at the white man's inexplicable change of heart, a bad-intentioned band of Cheyenne and Arapaho, augmented by a few visiting Sioux, left their camps along Pawnee Creek in early August and fell like the fiends of Pandemonium on unsuspecting white settlers along the Saline and Solomon rivers in north central Kansas. The method of attack was unvarying: the Indians would show up on a homesteader's doorstep, asking for food, and then, after gaining admittance, throw hot food and coffee into their victims' faces. The men would be killed, the women raped repeatedly and otherwise sexually abused (in some cases, sharp sticks were forced into the women's vaginas). Between August 10 and 12, fifteen men and women were killed, five houses were burned, and two little girls named Bell were carried off, never to be heard from again.[11]

The day before the murderous attacks began, Lieutenant Colonel Alfred Sully, commanding the District of the Upper Arkansas, persuaded the Indian Affairs office to reverse its decision on issuing firearms to the Cheyenne. Sully, an old hand at fighting Indians, apparently believed that turning over a few dozen obsolete rifles and pistols to the Indians, as promised in writing by the federal government, did not constitute a grievous threat to peace. He may have been right, but he was a day too late to test his theory—the genie was already out of the bottle. Sheridan, who held Sully partly responsible for the trouble to come, caustically said of his subordinate, "Indian diplomacy had overreached Sully's experience."[12]

Anticipating trouble, Beecher sent two of his mediators into the Cheyenne village of Chief Turkey Leg on the headwaters of Solomon Creek. Comstock and Grover knew the chief as a special friend, having lived with the tribe during hunting season, and they were confident of receiving a cordial welcome. Instead they were brusquely informed that the Cheyenne were on the warpath and their presence in camp was an intolerable affront. They quickly took the hint and left, accompanied by an escort of self-appointed guardians. They didn't get far. The Indians, professing friendship and concern, suddenly dropped back and blasted the scouts with a volley of rifle fire. Comstock was killed instantly, but Grover, though seriously wounded, somehow managed to hold off the attackers until dark, then crawled away and hid in a nearby ravine until the assassins at length lost interest in his scalp.[13]

Back at Leavenworth, Sheridan was already fuming over "the devilish work" of "red fiends" in the Saline valley when he received word of the scouts' ambush. Immediately he began making plans to retaliate, convinced, he said, that "there was not the slightest provocation offered by the soldiers or citizens for the commencement of this war by the Indians." There was little, at first, that he could do. With Hancock's and Custer's disgrace still fresh in his mind, he had no intention of mounting another massive expedition against the fast-moving, will-o'-the-wisp Indians—not yet, anyway. Instead he concentrated on garrisoning the forts along the Smoky Hill Road and the Santa Fe Trail, the two chief immigrant thoroughfares through western Kansas, and making sure that the work crews busily laying track for the Kansas Pacific Railroad around Fort Hays were well protected.[14]

This last precaution was paramount: for two years now, it had been one of the army's primary missions to safeguard construction of the transcontinental railroad. Sherman, whose brother, Senator John Sherman, had sponsored the Pacific Railroad Act of 1864 that doubled federal land grants to the fledgling roadbuilders, had gone on record in his 1866 Annual Report as pledging that "it is our duty to make the progress of construction of the great Pacific railways . . . as safe as possible." And Grant had said that same year that "completion of these roads will . . . go far towards a permanent settlement of our Indian difficulties." From the standpoint of army-railroad relations, it did not hurt that the president and superintendent of the Kansas Pacific were both veterans of Sherman's March to the Sea, or that the chief engineer of the rival Union Pacific Railroad was Grenville Dodge, longtime friend of Sherman, Grant, and Sheridan.[15]

Despite the drain on available manpower—he had fewer than eight hundred troopers left after making his various defensive arrangements—it was against Sheridan's nature to remain totally passive in the face of enemy aggression. Consequently, in late August he ordered Major George A. Forsyth to organize a fifty-man ranger contingent to carry the fight to the Indians. Sandy Forsyth had ridden with Sheridan that famous morning at Win-

Chief Black Kettle, seated behind officer in hat, died at Washita.
COLORADO HISTORICAL SOCIETY

Custer's attack on the Cheyenne village at Washita River, December, 1868.
CUSTER BATTLEFIELD NATIONAL MONUMENT

Cheyenne chief Roman Nose, right, died fighting at Beecher's Island.
COLORADO HISTORICAL SOCIETY

Irrepressible Kiowa chief Satanta, long a thorn in Sheridan's side.
CUSTER BATTLEFIELD NATIONAL MONUMENT

A bearded Custer, as he looked at Washita.
CUSTER BATTLEFIELD NATIONAL MONUMENT

Sheridan and staff, 1872. Left to right: George A. Custer, George A. Forsyth, Sheridan, M. V. Asche, Nelson B. Sweitzer, Michael Sheridan, and James W. Forsyth.
CUSTER BATTLEFIELD NATIONAL MONUMENT

Custer and Russian Grand
Duke Alexis.
CUSTER BATTLEFIELD
NATIONAL MONUMENT

Sheridan and Grand Duke
Alexis with members of
their gala hunting party.
DENVER PUBLIC LIBRARY

Sheridan's old friend and scout, Buffalo Bill.

Chief Dull Knife led his people on a desperate race home.

Sheridan, now commanding gene[...]
of the army, shows his ag[...]

Nez Percé spokesman, Chief Joseph,
died of a broken heart.

President Chester A. Arthur, center, with Sheridan and party at
Yellowstone National Park, 1883. Michael Sheridan is standing, far left.
Seated at Arthur's left is Secretary of War Robert Lincoln.

Irene Rucker Sheridan in 1879.

Sheridan, newly promoted to
lieutenant general, in 1869.

A weary Sheridan with his family at Nonquitt, Massachusetts, in the summer of 1887. From left: Irene, Mrs. Michael Sheridan, Michael Sheridan, Philip Jr., Irene Rucker Sheridan, Louise, Mary, and Sheridan.
NATIONAL ARCHIVES

Sheridan's remains are brought ashore at Nonquitt, August 6, 1888.
NATIONAL ARCHIVES

chester four years earlier, and had come out of the Civil War with a colonel's brevet and four Rebel wounds to show for his trouble. Now, given the opportunity to command in the field, he quickly recruited fifty scouts—dubbed "Solomon's Avengers" in memory of the slaughtered settlers on the Solomon River—and rode out of Fort Hays on August 29, bound for Fort Wallace on the Kansas-Colorado border.[16]

Accompanying Forsyth and his Avengers were Lieutenant Beecher, a still-recuperating Sharp Grover, Sergeant (former Brigadier General) W. H. McCall, and army surgeon John H. Mooers. (The Pennsylvania-born McCall, who had come out of the Civil War with a general's brevet, had reverted to his prewar rank of sergeant in the massive reshuffling after the war.) The scouts made Fort Wallace without any trouble, but word soon came that a war party had attacked a supply train near the new (and no doubt judiciously named) town of Sheridan, at the western terminus of the Kansas Pacific. Forsyth and his scouts tracked the perpetrators northwestwardly along the Beaver Creek fork of the Republican River. Three days later they found another, more heavily traveled, trail following the north fork of the river, Arickaree Creek. It was obvious to the group's experienced trackers that this was no small band of Indians they were chasing. Some even suggested breaking off the hunt. Forsyth, having learned his soldiering under Sheridan, snorted derisively, "Didn't you sign on with me to fight Indians?" and pressed ahead.[17]

Unknown to the soldiers, three large villages of Sioux, Cheyenne, and Arapaho were less than a dozen miles away. Worse yet, they were the bands of Sioux chief Pawnee Killer and Cheyenne warriors Tall Bull and Roman Nose, leaders of the virulently hostile Dog Soldiers, a tribe-within-a-tribe of elite fighters who had sworn unrelenting resistance to the whites. While the party camped for the night along Arickaree Creek, near a small island in the middle of the stream, the Indians got up a welcoming committee ten times as large as their visitors' force. At dawn the hostiles fell on the unsuspecting camp.[18]

Cut off from escape by a thicket of Indians who seemed, said

Forsyth, to have sprung from the very earth itself, the troopers splashed across the shallow stream to the island. Frantically they dug rifle pits in the shallow sand as the Indians kept up a withering fire from the rocks beyond. The promising young Beecher was among the first to fall, his spine fatally shattered by a Cheyenne bullet. Forsyth took two quick wounds to the leg, then was creased in the forehead by a third bullet. Surgeon Mooers, going to his aid, fell mortally wounded with a head wound of his own. On the Indian side, the remarkable leader Roman Nose was killed, together with his compatriots Dry Throat, White Weasel Bear, Killed by a Bull, White Thunder, Prairie Bear, and Little Man. Two unnamed Sioux also fell in the fight.[19]

The Indians maintained a loose siege of the island for a week, but two of Forsyth's best scouts sneaked through enemy lines and made it back to Fort Wallace for help. Sheridan, apprised of the situation by the fort's commander, Captain H. C. Bankhead, ordered him to spare no effort in relieving the force. A relief column of black "Buffalo Soldiers" from the Tenth Cavalry rushed to the site, forever afterward to be known as Beecher's Island, and brought out the nearly delirious Forsyth and the other forty-two survivors of the fight, nineteen of whom were also wounded. It would take Forsyth nearly two years to recover from his injuries, and he would remain partially crippled for the rest of his life. In compensation, Sheridan saw to it that he was promoted to brigadier general.[20]

While Forsyth was fighting for his life at Beecher's Island, the already discredited Sully was doing further violence to his military reputation—though not, suffice it to say, to the Indians—by leading a fruitless expedition against Cheyenne and Arapaho villages farther south, in Indian Territory. Sheridan, who had been prevented by command responsibilities from accompanying the eight-regiment column into the field as he had wished, settled for giving the troops a personal sendoff. By menacing the Indians in their own backyard, he hoped to provide terrified Kansas settlers with a little breathing space. But Sully, leading the campaign from ambulance rather than horseback, never managed to reach the hostile camps along the North Canadian River. Beset by Cheyenne skirmishers, sand fleas, and chiggers, the expedition bogged down in the scrub brush south of the Cimarron River. After only a week in the field, Sully ordered a general retreat, exclaiming to the disgusted cavalry officers riding alongside him, "Oh, these sand hills are interminable."[21]

The twin failures of Forsyth and Sully convinced Sheridan, if indeed he needed convincing, that such half-measures would never defeat the Indians. As an old cavalryman himself, he understood the tremendous tactical advantages the Plains warriors enjoyed over their less mobile opponents. Striking when and where they wanted, then melting away into the vast, inhospitable wilderness at the first sign of danger, the Indians were uncomfortably reminiscent of John Singleton Mosby's Confederate rangers in the Shenandoah Valley, the sole exception being that Mosby's men had not scalped their victims after killing them. Sheridan had learned the hard way that a few determined riders, properly led and motivated, could tie up an army many times their size, to say nothing of making life a particular hell for incautious stragglers and unprotected railroad workers.

What he now proposed to do—with Sherman's enthusiastic blessing—was to extend the similarity between Cheyenne and Confederate by introducing to the plains the same sort of total warfare the two had pioneered in Georgia and Virginia four years earlier. Properly adapted to the changing conditions of the western frontier—for one thing, the Indians did not own anything worth burning, except, presumably, their horses and tepees—it could have the same discouraging effect on the red men that it had had on southern whites. Best of all, it would allow the army to reclaim the strategic initiative, instead of conceding supinely, in Sherman's words, "that forty millions of whites are cowed by a few thousand savages."[22]

Taking the war to the Indians meant mounting and waging a winter campaign, when the tribes were more or less stationary in their camps. Till now, the hostiles had generally confined their rampages to the summer months, when there was abundant grass for their ponies and buffalo and other game for themselves. When the weather turned cold the warriors returned to their lodges, secure in their belief that the fort-hugging soldiers would not follow them home through the howling winds and snow of a brutal prairie winter. Sheridan, however, did not believe in allowing an opponent the luxury of rest, and he set to work immediately stockpiling supplies for the upcoming campaign. Sherman gave the go-ahead on October 9, promising Sheridan that "I will back you with my whole authority." And, he added ominously, "If it results in the utter annihilation of these Indians, it is but the result of what they have been warned again and again. . . . I will say nothing and do nothing to restrain our troops from doing what they deem proper on the spot, and will allow no more vague general charges of cruelty and inhumanity to tie their hands, but will use all the powers confided in me to the end that these Indians, the enemies of our race and our civilization, shall not again be able to begin and carry out their barbarous warfare."[23]

The day before that ringing endorsement of racial warfare, Sherman and the other peace commissioners had concluded another sulfurous meeting in Chicago. With the crimson example of Beecher's Island and the Solomon River valley fresh in their minds, and with the Republican Party's newly nominated presidential candidate, Ulysses S. Grant, seated alongside them at the conference table, the commissioners set out to undo in a day what had taken them months to accomplish. Sherman and the other generals on the commission pushed through resolutions calling for the use of military force to drive the Indians onto their reservations, the transfer of the Indian Bureau to the War Department, and an end to negotiating with individual tribes as sovereign domestic nations. Previously guaranteed hunting rights were also withdrawn, meaning in essence that any Indians caught outside the reservations could be treated as hostiles and shot on sight.

Explaining the commission's abrupt reversal of policy, Sherman grumpily told a *New York Times* reporter after the meeting, "Too many scalps have disappeared from the heads of their legitimate owners to make it safe to prolong this policy."[24]

When fellow commission member Samuel F. Tappan accused Sherman and his lieutenants of preparing for a war of extermination against the Indians, Sherman thundered back: "As to 'extermination,' it is for the Indians themselves to determine. We don't want to exterminate or even to fight them. At best it is an inglorious war, not apt to add much to our fame or personal comfort; and for our soldiers . . . it is all danger and extreme labor, without a single compensating advantage. To accuse us of inaugurating or wishing such a war, is to accuse us of a want of common sense, and of that regard for order and peace which has ever characterized our regular army."[25]

While Sherman was making his case for the army's supposed pacifism, Sheridan was out west, busily preparing for the winter campaign. In the wake of Sully's ridiculous showing, Sheridan had importuned Sherman for reinforcements. These came in the form of six companies of infantry and two of cavalry from the Department of the Platte, a regiment of volunteer cavalry raised and led by Kansas Governor Samuel Crawford, and seven companies of the Fifth Cavalry, recalled from reconstruction duty in the South. There was one other soldier, in particular, whom Sheridan wanted for his command: George Armstrong Custer, currently cooling his heels back home in Monroe, Michigan, and writing the highly colored sketches of the last campaign that later would become his somewhat precocious memoir, *My Life on the Plains*, which some who had been there would quickly dub *My Lie on the Plains*. Again Sherman was agreeable, and Sheridan telegraphed Custer with the good news. "Generals Sherman, Sully and myself, and nearly all the officers of your regiment, have asked for you," he said. "Can you come at once? Eleven companies of your regiment will move about the 1st of October against the hostile Indians." Custer came, arriving at Fort Hays in time to have breakfast with Sheridan three days later. "Now I can smoke a cigar in peace," Sheridan greeted his wayward young charge.[26]

In late October word came from an unlikely source on the whereabouts of the Indians' winter camps. Colonel William B. Hazen, Sheridan's old nemesis from Missionary Ridge, reported from Fort Larned that large numbers of Cheyenne were moving south to winter in the vicinity of the Antelope Hills in western Indian Territory, near the Texas Panhandle. Hazen, an ally and confidant of Sherman, had been sent by the general to administer the southern Indian reservation at Fort Cobb. En route he had picked up news of the Cheyennes' departure, which he passed along to Sheridan through the person of a hard-riding young scout and buffalo hunter named William F. Cody. Sheridan was grateful for the information and sufficiently impressed by Cody's daring and resourcefulness to retain him as chief of scouts for the Fifth Cavalry Regiment. It was the beginning of a lifelong friendship between Sheridan and the soon-to-be-famous "Buffalo Bill."[27]

Sheridan's plan of attack called for three separate assault columns, moving variously from Fort Dodge, Kansas, Fort Bascom, New Mexico, and Fort Lyon, Colorado, to converge on the Indian camps from the north and west. The two western columns were to act as "beaters," in the way that natives preceded hunters in Africa, driving the game toward the mouth of their guns. Major A. W. Evans would lead the Bascom column, Major Eugene A. Carr the Lyon contingent, and Sully and Custer the central force moving due south from Fort Dodge. As an added precautionary measure, Sheridan intended to accompany the problematical Sully and, if necessary, steel his soldierly resolve.

On November 12 the main column moved out, with orders to establish a forward supply depot on the banks of the North Canadian River in Indian Territory. The careful marshaling of supplies, which Sheridan had excelled at from the time he was fourteen, was critical to the ultimate success of the mission. Experienced frontiersmen descended on headquarters with dire warnings of sudden blizzards, starving animals, and foundering men adrift on a pitiless prairie. Even old Jim Bridger, the famous mountain man, hurried west from St. Louis to add his voice to the chorus of doom. But Sheridan, calling on his years of quartermastering, reasoned that properly fed and clothed soldiers, moving quickly and with purpose, could strike the enemy where they were most vulnerable, in the bosom of home and family.[28]

Accompanied by a cavalry escort, Sheridan moved south a few days later to join the lead elements of the column at newly established Camp Supply. The first night out the general had good reason to remember Bridger's warning. A sudden blizzard struck the party, carrying away tents and drenching riders to the skin. Sheridan himself took shelter beneath a wagon, wet and shivering, and waited out the miserable night. The next night's lodgings were altogether more pleasant, a convivial stay with his brother Michael at Fort Dodge, where the younger Sheridan was now post commandant.[29]

Sheridan's lifelong love of hunting almost got him killed two days later. After making camp on an island in the middle of a creek, he and newspaper correspondent DeBenneville Keim strolled out to a hill a mile from camp to watch a party of hunters tracking game. Studying the twilit valley through army binoculars, Sheridan noticed movement on a distant hillside. Deciding not to risk running into Indians, the two men hurried back to camp, only to find the tracks of a large war party in the dry creekbed. Had they left a few minutes sooner, Sheridan and Keim would literally have bumped into the hostiles, and the history of the West would have been changed in an instant. After his narrow brush with mortality Sheridan stayed close to camp for the rest of the trip.[30]

Arriving at Camp Supply on November 21, Sheridan was met in person by a fuming Custer. Predictably, he and Sully had already quarreled over battlefield tactics and brevet commands. The brevet rank, an honorary designation, had been around since Revolutionary War days; in the Civil War it had been so liberally distributed that the Union numbered more than 1,700 brevet generals at war's end. Custer, for example, was a brevet major general, although his regular army rank was lieutenant colonel. Sully was also a lieutenant colonel, but as district commander, he was a brevet brigadier general and thus, through the army's arcane system of privilege, outranked Custer within his district. It would have been a mere technicality, except for the fact that Custer's Osage Indian scouts had come across a fresh trail of warriors heading north toward Kansas on another raid. Custer wanted to trace the trail to the Indians' camp and attack. Sully refused to take offensive action until Governor Crawford's cavalry arrived. Custer argued that since they had left Sully's district, he now outranked Sully by virtue of his brevet major generalcy and could do as he pleased.[31]

The two were still arguing over rank and precedence when Sheridan arrived. His own scouts had come across the same trail, and Sheridan agreed with Custer that it represented a perfect opportunity to uncover the Indians' winter camp and strike them a devastating blow. Sully was sent back to Fort Harker to reassume command of his district, while John Schuyler Crosby drew up a copy of Sheridan's latest set of orders for Custer: "To proceed south in the direction of the Antelope Hills, thence toward the Washita River, the supposed winter seat of the hostile tribes; to destroy their villages and ponies; to kill or hang all warriors, and bring back all women and children." That night Custer and his staff, accompanied by the regimental band, serenaded Sheridan outside his tent.[32]

The next day was spent preparing for the march. The troopers were told to travel light, no tents or excess clothing, although extra grain was loaded for the horses. Custer, being Custer, devoted special attention to outward appearance; some companies were ordered to switch mounts in order to present a uniform color. Armstrong himself sported a new fur cap given to him by Sheridan. He would need it—over a foot of snow fell that day, cloaking the camp in near-zero visibility. Sheridan was concerned that the blizzard conditions would inhibit the cavalry's mobility, but Custer assured him that the weather worked to their advantage by keeping the Indians holed up in their tents. A week of snow, he said, would be fine with him.[33]

In the predawn gloom on November 23 Custer's troopers ate a quick, tasteless breakfast, then mounted up and road out of camp, Custer and his Osage scouts in the lead. The band played the jaunty tune "The Girl I Left Behind Me" as the eleven companies disappeared into the swirling snow. Three days later they struck a new Indian trail heading back from the north. The snow had ceased and the plummeting temperatures made it easy to follow the frozen tracks. Like a road map, they led the soldiers straight to the village of the Cheyenne chief Black Kettle. The village, nestled in a stand of timber on the south side of the Washita River, forty miles east of the Antelope Hills, was pretty much where Hazen had said it would be.[34]

Black Kettle was one of the unluckiest—or at least unwariest—Indians who ever lived. Four years earlier, at Sand Creek, Colorado, his band had been set upon by Colonel John Chivington and a regiment of volunteer cavalry as they camped near Fort Lyon. Black Kettle had been under the naive impression that the huge American flag he was flying over his lodge, which white officials had given him for signing the Fort Wise Treaty in 1861, would protect him from attack. He was wrong. Chivington, a murderous, crazed ex-preacher who styled himself "the fighting parson," led a pitiless assault on the unoffending village. Old men, women, and children were shot down indiscriminately (most of their warriors were away on a buffalo hunt). A total of 105 Indians were killed, and horrific mutilations were committed on their corpses. Black Kettle himself miraculously escaped. Now he was camped along the Washita, waiting for another group of hunters to return—this time from hunting *wasichus* (white men) in the north.[35]

Less than a week earlier, Black Kettle had paid a visit to Hazen at Fort Cobb, seeking sanctuary for his people on the new reservation. "I have always done my best to keep my young men quiet," he told Hazen, "but some will not listen, and since the fighting began I have not been able to keep them at home. But we all want peace." That pacific sentiment no doubt would have been news to the Kansas farmers whose scalps his obstreperous tribesmen were even then in the process of lifting. At any rate, Hazen's hands were tied. He knew that Sheridan was in the field looking for hostile Cheyenne and Arapaho, and by Black Kettle's own admission some of his people fit that description. Unhelpfully, if not unsympathetically, he advised the chief to find Sheridan and make peace—the sooner, the better. Instead, Black Kettle settled his people in winter camp, and another band of young men went off on a raid. It was their trail that Custer's scouts had found in the snow.[36]

Word came from a passing Kiowa war party that soldiers were approaching Black Kettle's camp; but the old chief, perhaps refusing to believe that such a thing could happen twice in four years to anyone, discounted the warning. The Cheyenne might still have been saved: the morning star rose on the twenty-seventh with such brilliance that Custer and his men were sure they had been spotted. But the Cheyenne brave on sentry duty that night, Double Wolf, had ill-advisedly gone back inside his lodge to sleep. By the time the ever-present regimental band blared out the first few notes of the Seventh Cavalry's theme song, "Garry Owen," abruptly lifting Double Wolf, Black Kettle, and the rest of the village out of their buffalo robes, it was too late. Custer was among them.[37]

The foot of soft, wet snow blanketing the ground had effectively muffled the hoofbeats of the horses, and Custer had taken the added precaution of having the hunting dogs that routinely accompanied the regiment killed beforehand to prevent any inconvenient barking. The force was divided into four separate assault columns to fall on the camp from south, west, and north at the sound of a single bugle blast. Despite the careful preparations, an Indian woman somehow discovered the approaching soldiers and dashed back to camp shouting an alarm. Black Kettle hurried out of his tent and fired his rifle into the air to awaken the others. At the same instant, the bugler sounded the charge and eight hundred shouting troopers tore into the camp.[38]

Custer personally led the attack across the river and into the fifty Cheyenne lodges scattered in an arc on the south side of the water. He snapped off a pistol round at one Indian and bowled over another with his horse before riding out of the camp and taking up position on a nearby hill. Half-clothed Indians, struggling to throw off their robes and arm themselves against the howling soldiers, dodged frantically among the tepees. The troopers, firing seven-shot Spencer carbines and Colt revolvers and swinging heavy cavalry sabers, strong-armed their horses after them. Some of the tribe made it to the frigid river and leaped into the chest-deep water, others sought refuge in ravines and among scraggly cottonwood trees. Black Kettle, having done this before, climbed onto a horse, scooped up his wife, and rode for his life. This time he was too slow. A hail of bullets dumped the elderly couple into the Washita, dead before they sank beneath the crimsoned stream.[39]

Within ten minutes of the first rifle shot Custer's men controlled the camp. One hundred three Indians were dead, including a disputed number of women and children. Regimental losses were light, two dead and fourteen wounded. One of the former was the well-liked Captain Louis Hamilton, Alexander Hamilton's twenty-four-year-old grandson, the youngest captain in the regular army, who fell in the first seconds of fighting with a bullet in the heart, compliments of the aptly named Cheyenne warrior Cranky Man. Among the wounded was Captain Albert Barnitz, shot through the stomach with what was first thought to be a mortal wound. The bullet, after bouncing off a trio of ribs, missed the captain's spine by inches and exited through his back. Thirty-four years later, aged seventy-seven, Barnitz did indeed die from the effects of his wound, and a subsequent autopsy disclosed that he had carried a piece of army overcoat lodged inside his body all that time.[40]

Barnitz's fellow officer, Major Joel Elliott, was not so long-lived. While the rest of the regiment was busying itself at Black Kettle's camp, Elliott led a platoon of nineteen volunteers into the tall grass east of the village, chasing a covey of fugitives. "Here goes for a brevet or a coffin!" he shouted back to a friend. About the same time Elliott left, Lieutenant Edward S. Godfrey crossed the north bank of the river and poked his head over the next ridge. What he saw made his hair stand on end: mile after mile of Indian tepees, as far as the eye could see, and an angry swarm of warriors leaping onto their horses and heading due west, straight in his direction. Godfrey hurried back to Custer with the news, but it seems to have made little impression on him. "What's that?" Custer asked, and went back to his business. Meanwhile, Elliott's force, finding itself rapidly surrounded by furious Cheyenne and Arapaho warriors, dismounted and lay down in the grass below Sergeant Major Creek. This was a mistake. The Indians had the high ground and, almost at their leisure, picked off all twenty in about an hour. It was a harbinger of what would happen to a much larger group of soldiers eight years later at Little Bighorn, although of course no one—white or Indian—could have known it at the time.[41]

Custer's men rounded up fifty-three surviving women and children and set fire to Black Kettle's camp. Tepees, saddles, clothes, weapons, tobacco, ammunition, cooking pots, lariats, and dried food all went up in smoke. In addition, nearly nine hundred Indian ponies were herded together and shot down by a squad of riflemen. A forlorn cache of photograph albums, household utensils, and unmailed letters—loot from the most recent Kansas raid—was saved as proof of the hostile inclinations of the camp. Then, without bothering to look for Elliott, Custer gave the order to pull back. The band played an ironic ditty, "Ain't I Glad to Get Out of the Wilderness," as the troopers rode off. Hundreds of anguished Indian warriors watched them leave from the ridges nearby, but were either too shocked or too saddened by the day's events to mount an effective counterattack. "We have cleaned

Black Kettle and his band out so thoroughly that they can neither fight, dress, sleep, eat or ride without sponging upon their friends," Custer wrote to Sheridan. "It was a regular Indian 'Sailor's Creek.' "[42]

By harking back to Sayler's Creek, Custer was attempting in his usual unsubtle way to engage his commander's old loyalties. For a time it worked. Custer's chief scout, "California Joe" Milner, a longtime associate of Sheridan's from his Oregon days, dashed into Camp Supply two days later with the electrifying news from the front. The general and the scout sometimes conversed in Chinook, much to the amusement of the uninitiated, but this time the talk was in English. Sheridan read the report aloud to his staff, then dictated a quick reply: "The Battle of the Washita River is the most complete & successful of all our private battles, and was fought in such unfavorable weather & circumstances as to reflect the highest credit on Yourself & Regt."[43]

Three days later Custer and his entourage rode into camp, their prisoners chained behind them like so many latter-day Gauls. First in line were the regiment's Osage scouts, their spears and ponies festooned with still-moist Cheyenne scalps (one, purported to be Black Kettle's, was not; the old warrior at least had escaped the scalping knife). Shrill war cries rent the air as Sheridan and his staff formally reviewed the returning troops. Next came the civilian scouts, including California Joe, and the gaily tootling regimental band. Custer, bearded like the proverbial pard, followed in all his isolate glory, his familiar sharp features obscured by his new facial growth. Then came the prisoners, women and children terrified into speechlessness by the expectation that they were being paraded to their deaths. Finally, in the rear, marched the enlisted men, last as always in Custer's reckoning. Conspicuous by his absence was Elliott.[44]

That night, while the Osages held a "hideous scalp dance," Sheridan had Custer recount the battle. What had become of Elliott and his party? Custer was forced to admit that he did not know. Rather lamely he suggested that the major had gotten himself lost during the battle and might still turn up—"a very unsatisfactory view of the matter," Sheridan observed tartly. From that day on, Custer never fully enjoyed the confidence of either Sheridan or the men in his regiment, although, to be fair, Cheyenne warriors who were at Washita that day later defended Custer's decision to withdraw, claiming with some plausibility that he would surely have been killed had he delayed his departure to search for the straying—and by then already dead—Elliott.[45]

In any event, Sheridan was more concerned with following up Custer's victory than with "uselessly speculating" about Elliott's fate. After a few days of rest and refitting, Sheridan personally led a new expedition south toward the Washita and the Wichita Mountains beyond. The second day out from camp the party ran into a howling norther, with temperatures plunging well below zero. Horses froze to death where they stood, and men were forced to march in place all night to avoid having the same thing happen to them. Still Sheridan pressed on, and on December 10 the group made camp a few miles north of the battle site. With Custer providing a running commentary, Sheridan envisioned the predawn encounter. It did not take long to find Elliott and the others. They were lying, frozen stiff, where their fates had left them, a couple of miles east of Black Kettle's village. All had been horribly mutilated. For some reason, Sheridan claimed falsely in his memoirs that none had been scalped, but a confidential report by the regimental doctor who examined the bodies contradicts this perhaps well-intentioned evasion. The fate of Private Carson Myers of M Troop provides a fair approximation of the devastation visited upon the soldiers' corpses: "Several bullet holes in head, scalped, nineteen bullet holes in body, penis cut off, and throat cut."[46]

A few miles farther downstream the soldiers made another disheartening discovery. Among the detritus of abandoned Indian camps they found the murdered bodies of a beautiful young white woman and her two-year-old son. The victims, Mrs. Clara Blinn and her son, Willie, had been abducted by Arapahos near Fort Lyon, Colorado, on October 9, while en route by wagon train from their Kansas home to the Pacific Coast. They had not gotten very far. An open letter from the frantic woman had been delivered to Hazen a few weeks later, urging someone—anyone—to ransom her and her little boy before their captors sold them into slavery in Mexico, or worse. In a poignant postscript she added, "I am as well as can be expected, but my baby, my darling, darling little Willie, is very weak. O, God, help him! Save him, kind friend, even if you cannot save me."[47]

The victims had been killed at the beginning of Custer's attack, an act of sheer spitefulness that eastern philanthrophists would have been hard put to explain. Mrs. Blinn had been shot in the forehead at close range with a rifle, the gunpowder disfiguring her face, and then scalped; Willie had been picked up by the ankles and swung headfirst into a tree. A pitiful scrap of cornbread was found concealed in the slain woman's bodice. A captured Cheyenne woman now traveling with Sheridan's party, Mahwisa, told the general that Mrs. Blinn had been the personal captive of Kiowa chief Satanta—"reserved to gratify the brutal lust of the chief," was how Sheridan put it—and that Satanta himself had murdered the prisoners. Apparently this was a lie; seeking to shelter her Arapaho friends, Mahwisa had simply fingered the most prominent suspect from another tribe. It was Satanta's misfortune that he fit the part. Big, burly, bluff, and loud, the Kiowa Hotspur had made a habit of insolent behavior. A year earlier, dressed in the general's uniform that Hancock had given him, he had singlehandedly run off the mule herd at Fort Dodge, doffing his plumed hat in mock chivalry as he fled.[48]

Whether Mahwisa was unusually convincing, or whether, in fact, the Kiowas' geographic and symbolic position as the next target on Sheridan's battle map simply made them a convenient bogeyman, the army moved south toward Fort Cobb in hot pursuit of Satanta and his gang. They were painstakingly in the process of closing the gap when, on the morning of December 17, an army courier rode up with a message from Colonel Hazen: "I send this to say that all the camps this side of the point reported to have been reached [by the army] are friendly, and have not been on the war path this season." Hazen also suggested, in all good faith, that the troopers personally contact Satanta and ask him where the Cheyenne and Arapaho could be found. Hazen's letter, which in effect granted Satanta and his kinsmen immunity from attack, amazed and infuriated Sheridan. It was, he said mirthlessly, "a pretty good joke." Still, mindful of Hazen's appointed role as supervisor of the Indian reservation around Fort Cobb (and, not incidentally, of Hazen's close friendship with Sherman), he could do no more than accede to a parley with the exasperating Kiowa chief.[49]

Accordingly, he sent Custer, Crosby, and a company of officers and scouts galloping ahead of the main column toward the Indian camp on Rainy Mountain Creek. Satanta and Lone Wolf, the main chief of the tribe, waited for them on the valley floor. Theatrical as always, Satanta wore bright red paint and carried a long lance bedecked with matching red streamers. He tried to shake hands with Custer and Crosby, but his stab at cross-cultural communications was coolly rebuffed. Undeterred, he summoned one of his warriors, Walking Bird, who had picked up a smattering of the white man's lingo while hanging around Fort Cobb. Going up to Custer, he stroked the general's arm in the way he had seen soldiers stroking their horses' flanks. "Heap big nice sonabitch," he said amiably.[50]

The dialogue declined from there. Not without cause, Satanta decided that he had been snubbed by the officers. Thumping his chest, he roared, "Me Kiowa!" Custer and his party began casting troubled glances at the surrounding hills, where hundreds of Satanta's kinsmen paced back and forth on their ponies, occasionally coming out with a chorus of war whoops. The chief seemed on the verge of inviting them down to finish the conversation when Sheridan and the rest of the army hove into view. That gentled Satanta, to the point that he readily agreed to

Custer's demand that the Kiowas come with him to Fort Cobb to prove their peacefulness. Sheridan, although greatly regretting that Hazen's message prevented him from pitching into Satanta's tribe at once and ending the discussion, consoled himself with the thought that once the Kiowas were brought onto the reservation he could continue his pursuit of the Cheyenne and Arapaho. Still, suspecting that the chiefs were stalling for time while their village escaped, he had them placed under arrest and held hostage to the continued good faith of their people.[51]

Arriving at Fort Cobb, Sheridan was met by Hazen, who assured him that Satanta and Lone Wolf had been having breakfast with him on the morning of the Washita fight. But even this eyewitness testimony carried little weight with Sheridan; he was convinced that Kiowas had fought against Custer that day, and, besides, the two chiefs were undoubtedly "guilty of untold murders and outrages." He decided to "put on the screws" by giving the order to hang the prisoners unless the rest of the tribe came into the fort as promised. This had the desired effect; Satanta's son, Tsa'lante, came galloping back at the last moment with the others. But Sheridan viewed his arrival as something of a mixed blessing. "I will always regret," he later wrote, "that I did not hang these Indians; they had deserved it many times." Evincing a newfound concern for Lone Star Confederates, he added, "Their devilish propensities led them into Texas, where both engaged in the most horrible butcheries."[52]

For the time being, however, the bulk of the Indian-fighting was over. Sheridan and the others settled in for the holidays at mud-encrusted Fort Cobb, while Indian emissaries were sent out to bring in their recalcitrant brothers. Christmas Day was celebrated with a cocktail party in Hazen's tent, followed by a banquet in Sheridan's quarters. Besides the satisfying progress of the winter campaign, Sheridan and his fellow officers gave thanks for another recent blessing—the election of U. S. Grant as president. The reconstruction controversy, in which Sheridan had been a leading player, had so weakened Andrew Johnson that he could not even win his party's nomination in 1868. The subsequent electoral landslide for Grant, the avatar of Appomattox, had been a foregone conclusion. Still, it could only mean good news for Sheridan and the rest of the loyal brotherhood of old Union men.

Sheridan hoped to tie up the loose ends of the Indian campaign in time to attend Grant's inauguration in early March. Accordingly, he pressed his officers in the field to round up stray hostiles and herd them onto the reservation. On Christmas Day, Major A. W. Evans struck a band of Nakoni Comanches camped along the north fork of the Red River, sixty miles west of Fort Cobb, killing a score of Indians and, Custer-like, burning down their lodges. News of the latest army success reached the camps of neighboring Cheyenne and Arapaho, whose principal chiefs, Little Robe and Yellow Bear, straggled into Fort Cobb on New Year's Eve to sue for peace. Sheridan was agreeable, although he warned the chiefs that they could not expect to make peace during the winter and then go back on the warpath in the spring. Little Robe, who had succeeded the luckless Black Kettle, could muster little resistance. "It is for you to say what we have to do," he shrugged.[53]

But if Sheridan and the army were winning the campaign in the West, they seemed in danger of losing it back East. In angry church sermons and impassioned newspaper editorials, well-meaning humanitarians decried the Washita incident as another Sand Creek massacre, conveniently overlooking the fact that white belongings had been found in Black Kettle's camp. Edward Wynkoop, the Cheyenne agent who had unwittingly played a role in the Cheyenne uprising by withholding the promised consignment of arms and ammunition to the Indians in June, now charged that the chief had "met his death at the hands of white men in whom he had too often fatally trusted and who triumphantly report the fact of his scalp in their possession." There was a certain amount of truth to this, at least insofar as Black Kettle himself was concerned, but Sheridan thundered back ungenerously that the chief was merely "a worn-out and worthless old cypher" who had foolishly refused the opportunity to surrender. Wynkoop and other "good and pious ecclesiastics," he charged in his annual report, were nothing more than "aiders and abettors of savages who murdered, without mercy, men, women and children . . . ravishing the women sometimes as often as forty and fifty times in succession." For added effect he threw in a few hair-raising details about the Indians' preferred raping techniques.[54]

The chorus of liberal disapproval notwithstanding, Sheridan's winter campaign against the southern Cheyenne and their allies had proven to be a great success. Although not nearly so revolutionary a concept as he and his staff apparently believed (William Henry Harrison, for instance, had gotten himself elected president on the strength of his predawn attack on a wintering Shawnee village at Tippecanoe Creek, Indiana, nearly sixty years earlier), the current campaign nevertheless had been a risky, if ultimately rewarding, venture. Never again would the Indians of the Great Plains be able to rest easy in their camps, secure in their belief that bad weather and great distance would keep them safe from the enemy's reach. Custer's victory on the Washita, whatever its moral and tactical deficiencies, had been an enormous psychological blow to the Indians, comparable in effect to the demoralization of southern civilians in the Shenandoah Valley four years earlier. It had also elevated Custer, in the popular mind at least, to the status of the nation's preeminent Indian fighter, a transformation that would have unimaginable consequences for both him and his opponents a few years later.

As winter ebbed, Sheridan oversaw the establishment of a new fort near Medicine Bluff, at the foot of the Wichita Mountains in Indian Territory. This post he named Fort Sill in honor of his friend and classmate Joshua Sill, killed almost exactly six years earlier fighting Confederates at Stones River. On March 2, back at Camp Supply, he received a peremptory order from President-elect Grant to report to Washington immediately. Accompanied by Crosby, Quartermaster A. J. McGonigle, Surgeon Nathan Asch, and the peripatetic newspaper correspondent DeBenneville

Keim, Sheridan started east. Four days later, just south of the Smoky Hill River near Fort Hays, the party was overtaken by a courier from the post. With a fine sense of occasion the trooper reined to a halt, saluted Sheridan with a flourish, and announced, "I have the honor to deliver a dispatch to the Lieutenant General." With Sherman succeeding Grant as army commander, Sheridan in turn had moved up the ladder, leapfrogging such disappointed office-seekers as Henry Halleck and George Gordon Meade, both of whom outranked him on paper but not where it counted most, in the president's heart. The news was particularly welcome on this, of all days—Sheridan's thirty-eighth birthday.[55]

When Sheridan arrived in Washington, Grant stunned him by suggesting that he return to New Orleans and resume command of the Fifth Military District. "This was not at all to my liking," Sheridan said, "so I begged off." Nor did he wish to return to the Pacific Northwest, "for many reasons some of which are personal." His old Indian girlfriend, Frances, had visited him in Washington after the Civil War, and despite the fact that she had since married a Canadian fur trapper, Sheridan had no desire to risk reopening a bygone relationship. He preferred to stay where he was, in the West, and Grant (as usual) accommodated him.[56]

Behind the president's evident eagerness to remove Sheridan from the western frontier was a planned change in Indian policy, a change that Grant would not have expected his intense, combative subordinate to approve. In the months prior to his inauguration, the basically nonreligious Grant had fallen under the sway of eastern humanitarians, particularly members of the Society of Friends, or Quakers. The Quakers urged the incoming president to abandon the use of coercive force on hostile Indians in favor of a light-handed, Christianized approach, a "conquest by kindness." No one was more surprised than the Friends when Grant unhesitatingly accepted their suggestion. "Gentlemen, your advice is good," he reportedly told them. "Now give me the names of some Friends for Indian agents and I will appoint them. If you can make Quakers out of the Indians it will take the fight out of them. Let us have peace."[57]

The Quakers eventually furnished Grant with eighteen such nominees from among their pacific brethren. Another sixty-eight agents were chosen from the ranks of the army. In addition, a ten-man Board of Indian Commissioners was appointed to oversee governmental policy, with great care taken to include representatives of all major Protestant denominations. Each church group made its own recommendations for Indian agents, and each tribe was to be the special charge of a particular sect: Episcopalian vied with Presbyterian, Dutch Reformed with Quaker, to see who could bring the blessings of civilization most quickly to the heathens. In practice this ecumenical approach to Indian administration would lead to some decidedly non-Christian infighting. The Catholic Church, for instance, of which Phil Sheridan was at least a nominal member, would even go so far as to establish a Washington bureau to lobby for its fair share of Indian souls.[58]

In the long run the so-called Quaker Policy—like much else in the Grant administration—would fall victim to corruption, confusion, misprision, and mismanagement. For the time being, however, Sheridan and the generals serving under him as department heads were caught between the president's surprising new policy and the day-to-day reality of the Indian frontier. "The whole Indian question is in such a snarl, that I am utterly powerless to help you by order or advice," Sherman wrote to Major General John Schofield, Sheridan's successor as commander of the Department of the Missouri. "Do the best you can." Sheridan, charged with administering a one-million-square-mile division stretching from Canada to the Rio Grande and from Chicago to New Mexico, faced an admittedly daunting task. Within his sprawling department resided a clear majority of all the Indians then living in the United States, something in the neighborhood of 175,000 Sioux, Cheyenne, Arapaho, Kiowa, Apache, Comanche, Ute, Shoshoni, Blackfoot, Pawnee, Pueblo, and Navajo. Not all were hostile, and never at the same time, but all were problematical. It was not long before Sheridan faced his first crisis.[59]

Throughout the fall of 1869 complaints flooded into Sheridan's new division headquarters at Chicago concerning the sporadic depredations of a small branch of the Blackfeet tribe, the Piegans, in northern Montana. The chief complainant was the all-too-familiar Alfred Sully, now serving as Indian affairs superintendent in the Big Sky State. Sully charged that the Piegans were stealing horses and other goods and trading them across the Canadian border for whiskey and guns. With rather more aggressiveness than he had exhibited the previous autumn in Indian Territory, Sully threatened to raise a volunteer company of civilians and chastise the Piegans himself. Sheridan, although he disliked and distrusted Sully, at length agreed to a punitive expedition. He recommended that Major E. M. Baker of the Second Cavalry, who had served under him in the Shenandoah Valley, be given the job. "If the lives and property of the citizens of Montana can best be protected by striking Mountain Chief's band [of Piegans]," advised Sheridan, "I want them struck. Tell Baker to strike them hard."[60]

Baker's subsequent attack on January 23, 1870, was an absolute debacle—and not just for the Indians who suffered its fury. The reputations of Baker, Sully, and Sheridan himself were variously blackened in the aftermath. Against the advice of his scouts Baker ordered an attack on an unoffending Piegan village along the banks of the Marias River. This band, under Chief Heavy Runner, had been given a safe-conduct pass by the Indian Bureau and had not engaged in any hostile activities that fall—it could scarcely have done so, being ravaged just then by a raging smallpox epidemic. Despite the pass, which Heavy Runner hastened to show the attacking soldiers, receiving a fatal wound for his troubles, Baker's men blazed away for over an hour. When they had finished, 173 Piegans lay dead, at least 53 of whom, by Baker's own count, were women and children. (Later studies raised the figure of estimated noncombatant deaths to as many as 140.)

Meanwhile, the actual miscreants, Mountain Chief's band, melted back across the border without suffering a single casualty.[61]

Predictably, the massacre on the Marias provoked an immediate firestorm of protest back east. Vincent Colyer, a member of the Board of Indian Commissioners and a longtime Christian activist, charged in a letter to the House of Representatives that all but fifteen of the Piegan victims had been noncombatants, of whom at least fifty were children under the age of twelve, shot down in their parents' arms. Influential newspapers such as *The New York Times* trumpeted Colyer's criticism of the army, and Boston abolitionist turned Indian reformer Wendell Phillips told a public gathering that the only savages he knew by name were Baker, Custer, and Sheridan. As always, Sheridan lashed out quickly and instinctively at his critics. In an angry letter to Sherman a month after the incident he charged that Colyer was the tool of a shadowy "Indian Ring" bent on controlling Indian affairs "so that the treasury can be more successfully plundered." With equally wobbly logic, he recycled frontier atrocity stories, noting that "since 1862 at least 800 men, women and children have been murdered within the limits of my present command, in the most fiendish manner; the men usually scalped and mutilated, their ———— cut off and placed in their mouths; women ravished sometimes fifty and sixty times in succession, then killed and scalped, sticks stuck up their persons, before and after death." He himself had spoken with one woman, he said, who, while pregnant, had been "ravished over thirty times successively by different Indians." The assaults in question had been committed by Cheyennes, not Piegans, but Sheridan conveniently ignored that salient point.[62]

Coming hard on the heels of Custer's equally controversial, if more justified, attack on Black Kettle's village on the Washita, the Piegan massacre had the effect politically of destroying any chance the army had of gaining control of Indian affairs from the Department of the Interior. A transfer bill giving the War Department administrative and financial control of the Indian Bureau was rejected that summer by angry lawmakers, who also put an end to the practice of appointing army officers as Indian agents. Henceforth, Sheridan and his subordinates would face an increasingly skeptical public and a parsimonious Congress. It was a high price to pay for such a sordid "victory."

The controversy also had the effect, if Sheridan's brother Michael is to be believed, of tarring the general with a famously dark brush. "Some fool friend in Montana," he later wrote, "attributed to General Sheridan the expression that 'A dead Indian is the only good Indian,' and though he immediately disavowed the inhuman epigram, his assailants continued to ring the change on it for months." Michael Sheridan notwithstanding, a second witness, Captain Charles Nordstrom of the Tenth Cavalry, had already attributed a similar witticism to the general. In January 1869, back at Fort Cobb, Nordstrom said Comanche Chief Tosawi had boasted to Sheridan, "Me, Tosawi; me good Injun." To which Sheridan had replied with a trace of a smile, "The only good Indians I ever saw were dead." What, if anything, Sheridan may actually have said regarding the Indian and his self-professed behavior, the quote has survived, with his name behind it, as "the only good Indian is a dead Indian." From a strictly grammatical perspective, there is a subtle but important difference between "The only good Indians I ever saw were dead" and "The only good Indian is a dead Indian." The first expression seems to suggest that only dead Indians are good, in the sense of good behavior. The second implies that dead Indians are preferable to live ones, and that therefore they should be killed. The sardonic little jest to Tosawi sounds like something Sheridan would have said; the more familiar phrase does not. Nevertheless, that is what history credits Sheridan with saying, and it has been used by friends and enemies ever since to characterize and castigate his Indian-fighting career.[63]

Back home in Chicago, where he had established his new divisional headquarters, Sheridan gratefully transferred his attention from the western frontier to the European continent. War clouds were gathering over France and Germany, and Sheridan had a professional soldier's natural curiosity about other countries' arms. Ten days after France's Napoleon III declared war on the allied German states Sheridan visited Grant at the president's summer home in Long Branch, New Jersey, and secured permission to represent the United States at the front. He set sail with James Forsyth a few days later, armed with a glowing letter of introduction from Grant to the crowned heads of Europe praising the holder as "one of the most skillful, brave and deserving soldiers developed by the great struggle through which the United States Government has just passed."[64]

After brief stopovers in London, Brussels, and Berlin, Sheridan caught up with the German army at Pont-a-Mousson in eastern France, where he was graciously received by Chancellor Otto von Bismarck and Prussian King Wilhelm I. Still nursing a grudge against Napoleon III over the failed empire-building of the pretender Maximilian in Mexico, Sheridan had opted to travel with the Germans, who he correctly assumed would win the war. The day after his arrival he accompanied the Prussian high command to the front for the impending Battle of Gravelotte. There, on a hillside littered with two-day-old dead, the American general watched German troops storm French positions on a far ridgeline, not unlike his own fateful day at Missionary Ridge seven years earlier. It was, he wrote in his memoirs, a spectacle "of unsurpassed magnificence and sublimity."[65]

Sheridan made his own contribution to the war effort a short time later when he noticed that French troops were moving toward the German flank. With his quick, experienced eye, Sheridan predicted that French artillery would soon open up to support the advance; he suggested that the king and his party retire to a less exposed position. Wilhelm was reluctant to comply, but two hundred exploding enemy cannon quickly changed his mind. Bismarck and the other Prussian officers were duly impressed with their visitor's military acumen.[66]

Sheridan got along well with the Prussians. Their punctilious professionalism and attention to detail mirrored his own, as did their authoritarian view of the world. If he had ever heard Chief of Staff Helmuth von Moltke's famously dismissive judgment of the American Civil War as a mere disorganized melee between armed mobs, he gave no indication of it. Nevertheless, he was far from awed by the Germans' performance on the field of battle. The Prussians, he wrote to Grant a few weeks later, were "very good brave fellows" who "had gone into each battle with the determination to win." But aside from that, "there is nothing to be learned here professionally." In particular, he thought their cavalry poorly handled, in the same way that Meade had made poor use of his own cavalry prior to Sheridan's explosion during the Wilderness campaign. The infantry "was as fine as I ever saw," but it had the advantage of marching and fighting in the rich farmlands of France, and "I think that under the same circumstances our troops would have done as well." He left to conjecture how well the Germans might have fared in the much rougher conditions of northern Virginia, eastern Tennessee, and central Georgia.[67]

Sheridan stayed with the Prussians for six weeks, during which time they effortlessly stormed across France, capturing Napoleon III and 83,000 troops at Sedan and besieging Paris itself. Sheridan and Forsyth happened to be on hand when Napoleon, smoking a cigarette and affecting a nonchalant air, rode out of Sedan in a carriage to surrender personally to Wilhelm I. It was a particularly satisfying sight to Sheridan, who had spent many steamy months along the Mexican-American border doing what he could to frustrate Napoleon's transatlantic provocations and losing a valued aide in the still-lamented Henry Young. From the start, he said, the French had made "stupendous errors" in the war, and, as Sheridan disgustedly told Grant, "All my boyhood fancies of the soldiers of the great Napoleon have been dissipated."[68]

Sheridan and Forsyth left the Prussians camped outside Paris and embarked on a side trip to eastern Europe, visiting Vienna,

Budapest, Constantinople, and Athens, before doubling back to Sicily and Italy. They dined with kings and queens, prime ministers and grand viziers, toured the ruins of Pompeii and the galleries of Rome, and shot deer on the private hunting estate of Italian King Victor Emmanuel. After hurrying back to Paris to observe the Germans' triumphal march through the French capital, they said good-bye to Bismarck and the others and concluded their grand tour with a sentimental visit to England, Scotland, and the old sod of Ireland. It had been a pleasant year for Sheridan—perhaps, from a purely personal standpoint, the most peaceful of his adult life. He set sail for America with a renewed respect for himself and the army, having seen nothing on the battlefields of Europe to make him question his deeply held notions of innate American superiority. The Europeans, he told Grant, had much to learn from them about how to fight wars, while "I saw no new military principles developed, whether of strategy or grand tactics." It was heady stuff indeed for a man who little more than a decade before had been stockading Indians on an out-of-the-way army post and hoping against hope to win his captain's bars.[69]

10
GENERAL OF THE WEST

WHEN SHERIDAN STEPPED OFF the gangplank in New York harbor in mid-September 1871, the familiar aquiline visage of George Armstrong Custer was waiting for him. Custer was off on another of his extended leaves—this time with pay—prowling the canyons of Wall Street and the salons of Park Avenue, seeking investors for a Colorado silver mine. Resplendent in his new Brooks Brothers clothes, he had come down to the docks to meet the general, although once again he was entertaining serious notions of leaving the army and becoming a stockbroker. Sheridan, who cared little about money and everything about war, immediately regaled the younger man with stories of French and Prussian ineptitude, and flatly declared that Custer himself, with only his old Civil War division, could have captured King Wilhelm a dozen times over.[1]

After their brief reunion, Custer went off to rejoin elements of his regiment on detached duty near Louisville, Kentucky, and Sheridan went home to Chicago. All told, he had been away for thirteen months, during which time the Indians on the Great Plains, with the exception of his old nemesis Satanta and a small group of Texas-raiding Kiowas and Comanches, had remained peaceable, if not exactly happy. As if to underline the newfound safety of the plains, Sheridan hosted a gala buffalo hunt in late September and early October for a carefully selected party of businessmen, newspaper editors, and former comrades-in-arms. Included on the trip were James Gordon Bennett of the *New York Herald*; Charles L. Wilson of the *Chicago Evening Journal*; Anson Stager of Western Union; Leonard W. Jerome, New York millionaire and future grandfather of Winston Churchill; retired Union general Henry Davies, who had commanded a cavalry division under Sheridan in the Shenandoah and one day would write an adoring biography of the general; old friend John Schuyler Crosby, who had left the army ten months earlier to pursue a career in business and politics; and other assorted bigwigs from New York and Chicago.[2]

The party traveled by train to Fort McPherson, in southern Nebraska, where they were met with a formal dress parade by Major Eugene Carr and the Fifth Cavalry. Also on hand to greet them was Buffalo Bill Cody, resplendent in white buckskin, crimson shirt, and black sombrero. Cody, with the help of dime novelist Ned Buntline, was already well on his way to becoming famous. Grateful to Sheridan for his start in the business, he had offered his services as chief scout for the expedition. Sheridan and the others left the railroad at Fort McPherson and headed south toward Fort Hays in a gala convoy of sixteen wagons (including two specifically reserved for iced-down wine) and three army ambulances for the gentleman hunters. A one-hundred-man cavalry escort went along on the off-chance the party ran into trouble—the public-relations aspect of the trip would be severely strained if one of the honored guests returned home with a Cheyenne arrow in his back for a souvenir. But despite venturing through the Solomon River valley where hostile raiders had butchered homesteaders three years earlier, the hunters encountered no such difficulties. In ten days' time they covered two hundred miles, bagged six hundred buffalo and hundreds of antelope, elk, and wild turkey, and formally greeted each new buffalo kill with a fresh round of champagne toasts for the sharp-eyed sportsmen.[3]

The hunt went so well that Sheridan was enlisted by Sherman to lead an even larger one for Grand Duke Alexis, son of the reigning Czar of Russia, when the twenty-one-year-old blueblood arrived in Chicago at the end of his ducal swing through major American cities that fall. Planning was already well under way when Mrs. O'Leary's cow—or some other bovine or human culprit—touched off the calamitous Great Chicago Fire on the night of October 8 and threatened for a time to remove the Windy City altogether from the grand duke's ambitious travel itinerary.

There is no disagreement over where the fire started, in the barn at the rear of the Patrick O'Leary residence at 137 DeKoven Street, on the west side of the city. Nor is the time of the flash-point disputed; a one-legged drayman named Daniel Sullivan, called Peg Leg for obvious reasons, saw the first arrows of flame burst through the O'Learys' barn at about eight-thirty that evening. As for suspects, however, there has never been a dearth of candidates, beginning with Mrs. O'Leary herself, who, the *Chicago Times* later charged, had started the fire in revenge for having been taken off the Cook County welfare rolls. Some credence was given to this theory, despite the fact that the newspaper listed the unfortunate woman as twice her actual age—thirty-five—and could produce no tangible proof that she had ever been on the public dole to begin with. Other suspects included the infamous cow (although which of the O'Learys' five now-deceased animals could not be ascertained); some roistering Irishmen in the house behind the O'Learys who were said to have snuck into their neighbors' barn to steal some milk; an unnamed trio supposedly trying out their new terrier on the O'Learys' barn rats; an anonymous group of cardplayers out for some of the O'Learys' delicious milk; and assorted other crackpots, revolutionaries, and self-confessed arsonists. It has even been suggested that the barn may have combusted spontaneously, which, given the enormous volume of pedestrian traffic alleged to have passed through it on the night in question, seems no less likely than the other explanations.[4]

However the fire started, it spread rapidly through the largely wood-framed city, which had already been sweltering through an unusually dry autumn. By the time word of the conflagration reached Sheridan at his Michigan Avenue residence, shortly before midnight, whole sections of the city's South Side, including the notorious Irish slum known as Conley's Patch, had been destroyed. Carried aloft on gale-like gusts of sixty-mile-per-hour winds, flaming bits of debris fell onto the city's shoulders like hot red snow, defeating all efforts by weary firefighters to keep ahead of the blaze. Sheets of fire, sounding like the flapping of enormous sails, raced from building to building. One frantic furniture store owner offered firemen a thousand dollars to save his building. You might as well offer a million, he was told—nothing could save it now.[5]

Sheridan quickly dressed and headed on foot toward division headquarters, located at the corner of LaSalle and Washington streets, across from the courthouse and city hall. By now the streets were jammed with terror-stricken citizens, some pushing cartloads of precious belongings, others bringing away nothing but the singed clothes on their backs. Lost dogs circled aimlessly about, whining for masters they would never find. Abandoned horses tore dangerously through the crowds, and desperate house cats leaped fences and raced along rooftops, sometimes vanishing in a ball of flame. Thick brown rats, driven from hiding by the fire, scurried hideously underfoot. Cows, goats, and pigs wandered aimlessly back and forth.[6]

Accustomed to the chaos and fog of battle, Sheridan kept going until, a few blocks from the center of town, intense heat and flames drove him back. Setting up a temporary command post near the lakefront, he attempted to establish order on the Dantesque scene around him. He summoned staff members to his makeshift headquarters; the LaSalle Street building was already in ruins. The fire was pushing steadily northeast, gobbling courthouse and pigsty, elegant hotel and corncrib brothel with egalitarian indifference. A firebreak was formed by blowing up every building on Harrison Street, from State Street on the west to the

Wabash Avenue Methodist Church on the east. Other explosions followed. At one point a workman keeping watch over the city's gunpowder supply failed to recognize Sheridan and pulled a revolver on him. Beating a strategic retreat, the general resumed his demolition work by hand, chopping away with an ax on a Southside mansion.[7]

By the time the blaze guttered to an end the next evening, helped by a providential if tardy rainfall, nearly 100,000 people were homeless and between two and three hundred others were dead. Seventy-three miles of streets and 17,500 buildings within a four-mile radius lay in ruins. Property damage was a staggering $200 million. At its height the heat from the fire was so intense it was felt as far away as Holland, Michigan, one hundred miles to the north. All of Sheridan's personal and professional papers were destroyed, along with the files of the Military Division of the Missouri. His home, lying south of the fire, had been spared; but his favorite gray pacer, Breckinridge, captured from that eponymous Confederate officer at Winchester in 1864 and ridden often during the remainder of the war, was a much-regretted victim of the flames.[8]

With amazing resilience and civic goodwill, Chicagoans began digging out of the rubble the next morning. Sheridan, always handy in an emergency, did what he could to help. As many as thirty thousand homeless people had taken refuge in Lincoln Park, and the general called in tens of thousands of rations, tents, and blankets from army stores in St. Louis and Jeffersonville, Indiana, to ease their suffering. Sherman, in Washington, wholeheartedly supported his actions. "Use your power of relief to the maximum, giving away field blankets, overcoats, shoes & socks without stint," he advised Sheridan. "The U.S. Govt. can better afford this means of relief than any other body." President Grant chipped in with a one-thousand-dollar personal contribution.[9]

Cities across the Midwest—St. Louis, Milwaukee, and Cincinnati, in particular—rushed trainloads of food and clothing to the stricken area, and the governors of Wisconsin, Michigan,

Iowa, and Ohio formally issued proclamations urging citizens to give all they could. Illinois Governor John Palmer, from whom much would soon be heard, called a special session of the legislature to appropriate money for the city's relief. On a more humble level, donors as varied as the hack drivers of Washington, the newsboys of Cincinnati, and the thespians of something called the Jane Coombs Comedy Company pledged their earnings and gate receipts for the needy. One unreconstructed southerner, remembering Sherman's march to the sea, took a different tack; he offered to buy one hundred bales of hay for Mrs. O'Leary's cow.[10]

Rumors of widespread looting and gangs of out-of-town toughs and safecrackers set to descend on the prostrate city darkened the mood in the aftermath of the fire. A delegation of leading citizens, including city prosecutor Thomas W. Grosvenor, called on Sheridan on October 9 and asked him to put the city under martial law. This was not, strictly speaking, his decision to make, but lame-duck mayor R. W. Mason went along with it. "The preservation of the good order and peace of the city is hereby entrusted to Lieutenant General P. H. Sheridan, U.S. Army," Mason proclaimed two days later. "The Police will act in conjunction with the Lieut. General in the preservation of the peace and quiet of the city, and the Superintendent of Police will consult with him to that end." Sheridan himself dictated a closing paragraph, or, at any rate, an incomplete sentence: "The intent hereof being to preserve the peace of the city, without interfering with the functions of the City Government."[11]

With this quasi-legal authority in hand, Sheridan called in six companies of regular infantry from Nebraska and Kansas. After further consultation with worried officials, he also created a one-thousand-man volunteer regiment, inevitably dubbed the Sheridan Guards, and selected former general Francis T. Sherman of Chicago, who had served under him at Perryville and Chattanooga and tumbled down the mountainside with him at Sewanee, to head the unit. Two days later Sheridan reported to Mason, "I am happy to state that no case of outbreak or disorder has been reported. No authenticated case of incendiarism has reached me, and the people of the city are calm, quiet and well-disposed."[12]

Unfortunately, the same could not be said for the governor of Illinois. John McAuley Palmer was something of a congenital gadfly: abolitionist Kentuckian, southern-born Unionist, Democrat-turned-Republican-turned-Democrat politician (twice he would manage, at different times in his career, to oppose his own party's presidential nominee; once he even shared a splinter ticket with former Confederate general Simon Bolivar Buckner, against whom he had fought at Chickamauga), and unsparing critic of the professional army. When Sheridan's recent buffalo-hunting companion Anson Stager wired Palmer that "roughs and thieves" were roaming the streets at will, the governor dispatched a company of state militia to meet the threat. After getting word from his militia commander that Sheridan already had seven hundred regulars of his own in the city, Palmer traveled to Chicago to meet with the general and the mayor. They told him that things were quiet, but somehow forgot to tell him that the city was currently under martial law. Five days later, when Palmer finally learned the full extent of Sheridan's policing power, he exploded. In a savage letter to Mason he accused the mayor of abdicating his responsibilities by allowing regular army troops to illegally patrol the city.[13]

The situation worsened a day later when a trigger-happy college boy named Theodore Treat, a member of the Sheridan Guards, shot and killed city prosecutor Grosvenor while that incautious worthy was walking home from a late-night party for a local judge. Nine days earlier Grosvenor had headed the delegation that asked Sheridan to take command of the city. Treat, who had never loaded or fired a gun before, said by way of exculpation that he was unaware Grosvenor was an influential man. Besides, he said, it was dark.[14]

Palmer reacted to the mishap by attempting to have Sheridan, Mason, Sherman, and Treat indicted for murder, but a Cook County grand jury refused to hear the case. Trying again, Palmer took the issue before the Illinois Supreme Court, which upheld his position but did nothing about it. Three days after the shooting the volunteers disbanded and Sheridan sent the army troops back to the frontier. Most Chicagoans defended his quick, decisive actions during the emergency and agreed with Sherman, who said that Sheridan had "by means of a very few soldiers . . . kept substantive good order amidst the chaos of ruin, and probably saved the city."[15]

As the year 1872 got under way, Sheridan exchanged his Chicago peacekeeping duties for another stint as Wild West hunting impresario. Grand Duke Alexis and his party of Russians arrived in Omaha on January 12, and Sheridan and his staff were on hand to greet them. Elaborate plans were already in place for the duke's visit; half the army, at one time or another, seems to have been involved in the pre-hunt preparations. Supplies had been stockpiled, buffalo herds scouted, escort companies detailed—Sheridan had even arranged for a complaisant band of Sioux warriors to join the hunt and entertain the duke with an authentic Indian war dance and powwow. Also chosen to give Alexis a taste of the real West were Buffalo Bill Cody and George A. Custer, recalled from his semi-exile in Kentucky especially for the hunt.[16]

The international affair was the brainchild of the landscape painter Albert Bierstadt, who had met Alexis a few months earlier during an art-promoting tour of Europe (and who later would paint a massive canvas titled, fittingly enough, *The Last of the Buffalo*). The duke had mentioned his desire to witness a real buffalo hunt, and Bierstadt passed along his imperial wishes to Sherman. The matter went all the way to the White House, where President Grant was more than willing to see the son of Czar Alexander II royally treated to American hospitality. The czar had won a lasting place in Grant's heart by steadfastly supporting the Union during the Civil War, and the president was eager to show his gratitude by playing tour guide for the Romanov heir.[17]

The hunting party traveled by special train from Omaha to Grand Platte, where it was met by four companies of cavalry and infantry under the command of Colonel Innis Palmer. From there the hunters pitched their tents along Red Willow Creek, a branch of the Republican River, and engaged in a jolly night of toast-making, yarn-spinning, and pipe-smoking, all beneath the flickering lights of Chinese lanterns hung from a clump of cottonwood trees. Sheridan gave a brief opening speech, followed by the Sioux chief Spotted Tail, who was an old hand at such things, having visited Washington two years earlier along with Chief Red Cloud and other tribal emissaries and dined at the White House on such delicacies as strawberries and ice cream. Duke Alexis, for his part, handed out silver half-dollar pieces, blankets, and ivory-handled hunting knives to the Indians.[18]

For the next two days the sportsmen banged away at the buffalo herd. Alexis killed two of the great beasts with Buffalo Bill's favorite rifle, "Lucretia," Sheridan dropped two more, and the rest of the party slaughtered another thirty or forty. "The Grand Duke killed his first buffalo today," Sheridan reported to Secretary of War William Belknap, "in a manner which elicited the admiration of the party." The duke's own admiration was elicited later that evening when a Sioux warrior, Two Lance, herded a buffalo into camp and demonstrated the killing power of the bow and arrow by firing a missile completely through the animal. The duke, who earlier had belittled the humble bow, kept the arrow as a souvenir.[19]

The hunters moved on to Kit Carson, Colorado, to try their luck with another herd. Fresh mounts, brought in from Fort Wallace, enlivened the festivities—a little too much, it soon developed. The new horses, intended for the cavalry, were untrained as hunters, and the smell of buffalo blood readily spooked them. A nest of prairie dog holes helped send riders sprawling; Sheridan, who took a couple of bad falls, decided to sit out the rest of the hunt. He and a companion, the improbably named Denver musician Chalkley Beeson, spied a pair of wounded buffalo on a nearby hillside and set out on foot to finish them off. At the same time, Alexis, Custer, and a gang of fellow hunters roared up from the opposite direction, blazing away at the wounded beasts. Beeson, with admirable reactions for a tenderfoot, reversed direction and took off down the hill, bullets zinging around his ears. But Sheridan, with a lifetime of experience under fire—and vivid memories of what a high-caliber bullet could do to a person's skull—dove face-first into the nearest clump of prairie grass.[20]

The embarrassed shooters, with no hunting license for lieutenant generals, abruptly stopped firing, and Sheridan—"the maddest man I ever saw," said Beeson—jumped to his feet and gave them a royal cussing. "I don't know what kind of language Pa Romanoff used to Alexis when he got mad," said Beeson, "but that slip of royalty got a cussing from Phil Sheridan that day I bet he'll never forget." The general "didn't spare anybody in the bunch . . . and he included all their kinsfolk, direct and collateral. It was a liberal education in profanity to hear him."[21]

No harm had been done, except to his dignity, and Sheridan recovered that article soon enough. An international incident was thus avoided, and the duke left for New Orleans shortly afterward with his new friend Custer and Custer's ubiquitous wife, Libbie, in tow. Sheridan, meanwhile, returned to Chicago, where he later received a medal from the czar for his western hospitality. The hunt had been a great success, but the brown-black humps of slaughtered buffalo scattered obscenely across the plains presaged a new outbreak of unrest and violence among the Indians living there. As usual, one of the chief instigators was the incorrigible Satanta, now behind bars in a Texas penitentiary. The trouble had begun while Sheridan was still in Europe. Sherman, making a rare inspection tour of the West, had visited Fort Sill to look into complaints of Indian raids in Texas. Satanta, living up to his largely ironic title of Orator of the Plains, had bragged about leading one such raid on a party of Lone Star teamsters. Sherman immediately had him arrested, along with his chief henchmen, Satank and Big Tree.

Locking up their principal chiefs, however, had not had the desired quieting effect on the Kiowas and Comanches around Fort Sill. Part of the problem was the president's much-derided Peace Policy, which inadvertently had created a soldier-free sanctuary on the reservation from which the Indians could stage raids into Texas and Mexico with virtual impunity. Enjoined against entering the reservation, Sheridan's cavalry could only stand by and watch as Quaker Indian agents attempted to reason with the hostiles on the basis of religion. "If a white man in this country commits a murder we hang him, if he steals a horse we put him in the penitentiary," thundered Sheridan. "If an Indian commits these crimes we give him better food & more blankets. I think I may with reason say under this policy the civilization of the Wild Red Man will progress slowly."[22]

The raids continued throughout 1872 and into 1873, motivated in part by the government's failure to supply the reservation Indians with enough food and clothing to compensate for their loss of hunting privileges. At the same time that they were going hungry, the Indians watched with impotent disgust as growing numbers of white buffalo hunters set up their forked rifle sticks on ancestral hunting grounds and slew the animals in staggering numbers with their .50-caliber Sharps buffalo guns. In 1872–73 alone, 1,250,000 hides were shipped east to fashionable furriers. By the end of 1874, an estimated 4,373,730 buffalo had been slain, of which a grand total of 150,000 had been taken by the Indians. In their stead professional hunters with such names as Shoot-em-up Mike, Light-fingered Jack, Shotgun Collins, Prairie Dog Dave, Dirty-face Jones, and Dutch Henry Born played their own unheralded parts in the winning of the West.[23]

The hunters' intrusion on tribal lands was patently illegal, but the army did little to stop it. Quaker Indian agent John D. Miles, on the Cheyenne-Arapaho reservation at Darlington, did have eleven hunters arrested in early 1874 for trespassing on Indian land, but soon let them go, noting with exquisite Christian charity that "they are all very poor, and they say that the cries of their children for bread is what induced them to engage in the chase." Perhaps that was true in this particular case, but it was also true that most buffalo hunters were young, single drifters, motivated not by hungry mouths to feed, but by the going rate of $3.50 per buffalo hide. In fact, one of the most successful of the hunters, New England Yankee Josiah W. Mooar, who killed nearly 21,000 buffalo in three years, had no children, hungry or otherwise, waiting back home in Vermont.[24]

Despite the Medicine Lodge Treaty, which had outlawed white intrusion on Indian land, the unofficial attitude of the government toward the hunters was one of de facto cooperation. Interior Secretary Columbus Delano, whose department was charged with looking out for the Indians' welfare, stated bluntly in his annual report, "I would not seriously regret the total disappearance of the buffalo from our western prairies, in its effect upon the Indians, regarding it rather as a means of hastening their sense of dependence upon the products of the soil." Sheridan, who had rather less confidence in the farming capabilities of the Indians, nevertheless looked upon the slaughter of the buffalo as an effective means of subjugating the tribes and breaking their wills. When the Texas legislature briefly considered passing a bill outlawing buffalo poaching on native lands, Sheridan made a personal appearance before the lawmakers in Austin. Rather than penalize the hunters, he said, the legislature ought to give them each a medal, engraved with a dead buffalo on one side and a discouraged-looking Indian on the other.[25]

Given that attitude, it is not surprising that the Indians on the reservations increasingly felt the need to strike back at the hunters. Raids continued throughout 1873, despite (or perhaps because of) the early release of Satanta and Big Tree from prison in October. Freed from the constraint of having to act as guarantors of their leaders' safekeeping, the Kiowas and their Comanche allies, together with a number of disgruntled Cheyenne from the Darlington agency, rode the warpath in Kansas and Texas. On June 27, 1874, a force of several hundred Cheyennes and Comanches attacked the buffalo hunters' main camp at Adobe Walls in the Texas Panhandle. Alerted by a mixed-breed scout that an attack was imminent, the twenty-eight hunters at the camp, including the young Bat Masterson, not yet a famous lawman and gunfighter, barricaded themselves inside their dwellings and picked off the circling Indians with well-aimed blasts. Attacking a bunch of Deadeye Dicks in broad daylight was not a particularly well-thought-out tactic on the Indians' part. As many as seventy of the hostiles fell during the daylong fight, compared to only three of the defenders—four, if you count the camp's Labrador retriever, which put up a deathly struggle of its own against the Indians, and had the rare honor—for a dog—of being scalped for its trouble.[26]

The Battle of Adobe Walls, as it became known, was the opening salvo of the Red River War. Three weeks later Sheridan received orders from Sherman to "act with vindictive earnestness" against the hostile tribes and to "make every Kiowa & Comanche knuckle down." Immediately he set to work planning strategy for the upcoming campaign. It was to be modeled on the 1868 campaign, except that this time it would take place in high summer instead of winter. "I am not at all sanguine that much can be done at this season of the year," he told Brigadier General John Pope, commander of the Department of the Missouri, "but if we let the Indians run unrestrained, nearly all those who are for peace may have to join them." As it was, special provisions were made to enroll friendly Indians on the reservations and ensure their safety so long as they stayed within agency boundaries.[27]

Pope and fellow department commander Christopher Augur were charged with coordinating the day-to-day prosecution of the war. Five converging columns would descend on the desolate Texas Panhandle section, where the hostiles had taken refuge after the Adobe Walls fight. From the north, Colonel Nelson Miles would move into Indian Territory from Fort Dodge. From the west, Major William R. Price would head eastward from Fort Bascom. Moving up from the south were Colonel Ranald Mackenzie and Lieutenant Colonel George P. Buell. Finally, Lieutenant Colonel John W. Davidson would strike westward from Fort Sill.

The beginning of the war was accompanied by a severe, scorching drought. Temperatures on the plains soared to as high as 110 degrees, and precious water holes dried up or turned alkaline in the dust. A plague of locusts the previous year had eaten most of the sparse vegetation in the region, making the landscape even more purgatorial than usual. At one point some of the hard-driving Miles's men were reduced to cutting open their arms and drinking their own blood. Unlike the 1868 campaign, there was no overwhelming moral or military defeat such as Custer had inflicted upon the Cheyenne at Washita. The closest to it was Mackenzie's rout of Kiowa, Comanche, and Cheyenne forces at Palo Duro Canyon in late September. Only three Indians were killed in the fight, but several hundred lodges were burned, along with food stores, weapons, and camp accouterments. Worst of all, from the hostiles' perspective, was the loss of more than one thousand ponies, slaughtered by the soldiers at the rim of the canyon, where the escaping Indians could hear their screams and see them fall.[28]

Much of the Red River campaign was characterized by exhausting marches and countermarches, midnight raids, and long-range sniping. Bad weather tortured both Indian and soldier. After the summer heat wave, heavy rains fell throughout September, followed by an early winter filled with northers, blizzards, and subzero temperatures. By early 1875 nearly all of the hostiles, including Satanta, Lone Wolf, Mow-way, and the extraordinary young Comanche leader, Quanah Parker, had turned themselves in to agency authorities.

Sheridan, who had come west from Chicago to Fort Sill in mid-October to follow the campaign more closely, typically favored hard and swift military justice for the ringleaders in the Red River debacle. Harking back to his defeat and hanging of rebellious Cascade Indians in the Pacific Northwest in 1857, Sheridan recommended that Pope and Augur make an example of the worst offenders, noting that "if a few of the murderers can be hanged, the effect will be salutary." There was a more recent precedent for this approach; the year before, Modoc Indians had assassinated Sheridan's troublesome ex-subordinate Edward R. S. Canby in California, and Canby's killers had been condemned and executed by military tribunal. To Sheridan's subsequent disappointment, U.S. Attorney General George H. Williams ruled that, in this case, the Indians could not be subjected to such a body, since the Peace Commission in 1867 had mandated that Indians were no longer members of independent nations, but wards of the United States government, and hence could not be tried by soldiers. Sherman, who had served on that commission, regretted that the army had not "managed to kill more bucks," but consoled himself with the thought that the soldiers had prosecuted the campaign "with the relish that used to make our hearts *glad* in 1864–5."[29]

Although frustrated by the attorney general's ruling, Sheridan did manage to gain a measure of personal revenge by seeing to it that Satanta, his rebel spirit finally broken by defeat, was hastily returned to the Texas penitentiary at Huntsville to serve out a life sentence. (Even then, Satanta managed to frustrate Sheridan; he gave himself the ultimate parole by jumping out of a top-story window four years later.) Other tribal leaders were shipped off to the old Spanish fort known as the Castillo de San Marcos, in St. Augustine, Florida, along with an arbitrarily chosen group of lesser warriors, village malcontents, and juvenile delinquents. Kiowa chief Kicking Bird, forced to select members of his own tribe for deportation, was poisoned by his people a few days later for his reluctant role in the process. Sheridan then had the Kiowas' and Comanches' horses sold at auction to raise money to buy them sheep to raise, reasoning elementarily that there were no longer any buffalo for them to hunt, anyway.[30]

The Red River campaign may not have been, as Sheridan boasted, "the most successful of any Indian campaign in this country since its settlement by the whites," but it did serve to break for all time the Indians' hold over the southern plains. It also had the effect—entirely welcome, from the army point of view—of destroying the last vestiges of Grant's Peace Policy. Abuses within the agencies, both white and Indian, had undermined the authority of the Quaker agents and strengthened the army's hand in pursuing and punishing wrongdoers. Henceforth the Indians would be dealt with from a position of strength, not forbearance.[31]

Nowhere was the need for stricter agency control more evident than on the northern plains, where the obstreperous Sioux, long the most warlike of all the western Indians, had reduced their agencies to a state of near anarchy. Under the provisions of a separate 1868 treaty between the government and the tribe, the Sioux had been granted a giant reservation west of the Missouri River in present-day South Dakota. Included in the grant were the legendary *Paha Sapa*, the Black Hills, sacred to them as the center of the world. Here warriors underwent spiritual purification and vision quests. (One young warrior, called Curly by his peers, had a vision of his horse dancing wildly in the snow; henceforth he named himself Crazy Horse.) The intent of the treaty was for the Sioux to draw their rations at agencies established along the Missouri River. But Red Cloud and Spotted Tail, the two most powerful Sioux chiefs, balked at this plan. They wanted to receive their government largesse at agencies nearer to their traditional hunting sites in northern Nebraska.

The government at length acquiesced to their wishes, but the Sioux did not respond with gratitude. At the Red Cloud and Spotted Tail agencies on the White River, seventy-five miles from the nearest soldiers, rebellious warriors killed an army lieutenant, an agency clerk, and a number of peaceable Indians. They also butchered cattle, stampeded horses, and chopped down an agency flagpole that offended them by flying the American flag. Nor did they confine their abuses to the reservation. Traditional enemies such as the Crow, the Pawnee, and the Shoshoni periodically felt their practiced wrath, as did white settlers well north of their hunting grounds in Wyoming and Montana. Army patrols and railroad surveying parties also came under frequent attack. Unlike their counterparts on the southern plains, the Sioux had never felt the sting of military defeat. Consequently they had no particular fear of the white man.[32]

Faced with a deteriorating situation in the West, Sheridan complained loudly, if largely unsuccessfully, throughout 1873–74. A provision in the annual congressional appropriations bill of 1874 reduced the army to a bone-thin 27,000 men, exactly half the number serving under arms when Sheridan took over as division commander in 1869. The consequent loss of manpower was compounded by the Sioux' adamant refusal to stay on the agencies any longer than it took them to claim their regular food supplies and sell the hides of their slaughtered cattle back to the agency for $2.50 apiece. Sheridan was convinced the Indians were using their financial windfall to buy arms and ammunition, with the deleterious effect of further stiffening their already strong resolve.[33]

In an attempt to keep closer watch on the wide-ranging Sioux, Sheridan received permission from Grant in late 1873 to mount an expedition into the Black Hills to scout locations for a new fort in the area. Custer and the Seventh Cavalry spent the better part of eight weeks the next summer exploring the sacred territory. As usual, Custer turned the expedition into a combination picnic, big-game hunt, and public-relations extravaganza, sending back glowing reports of the region's vast animal and mineral resources. Injudiciously, he also fanned the flames of public greed by claiming, with some exaggeration, that pieces of gold could be plucked from the very ground that one walked on. At the first mention of gold, hundreds, then thousands, of ears pricked up. It was, after all, the Gilded Age, and fortune-making was the national sport.[34]

News of the gold strike led to a rapid—and illegal—influx of would-be millionaires into the Black Hills that fall. The president strictly forbade white intrusions onto set-aside Indian lands, and Sheridan issued standing orders to burn wagon trains, destroy equipment, and arrest ringleaders of any such expeditions. The treaty of 1868, he pointed out, "virtually deeds this portion of the Black Hills to the Sioux." He suggested instead that miners and homesteaders try their luck farther west in the unceded lands of Wyoming and Montana. The Sioux had hunting rights there, too, but Sheridan hoped to nullify these rights by encouraging the further depopulation of buffalo and other game. When there was no longer anything left to hunt, he reasoned, the Indians would have no more hunting rights to lose. Needless to say, the Sioux were unamused by this line of reasoning.[35]

In the midst of the fluid and potentially explosive situation out west, Sheridan was abruptly ordered back to New Orleans, the scene of his unhappiest hours, in December 1874. For two years now the Grant administration had found itself trapped in the familiar morass of Louisiana politics. In 1872 the state gubernatorial election had ended in deadlock, with both candidates, Republican carpetbagger William Kellogg and Democrat John McEnery, claiming victory. Grant, for personal as well as political reasons (his brother-in-law, James F. Casey, was collector of customs for the port of New Orleans and a power in local Republican circles), had propped up the corrupt Kellogg regime with federal bayonets. When McEnery supporters, alarmed by a new law giving the governor the right to appoint all election registrars, staged an attempted coup in September 1874, Grant dispatched five thousand troops and three gunboats to the state to restore Kellogg to power. The legislative election six weeks later bore out Democratic fears: the Republican-controlled returning board juggled enough ballots to reduce the Democrats' total of seats in the state house of representatives from eighty to fifty-three—by improbable coincidence the exact number of seats the Republicans now held. The five remaining races were too close to call.[36]

Anticipating trouble when the new legislature convened in January, Grant directed Secretary of War Belknap to send Sheridan back to New Orleans to monitor the situation and, if need be, reassume command of the forces there. A cloak of secrecy shrouded the mission, suggesting the unsavory elements implicit in the undertaking. Sheridan was told to communicate only with the secretary of war, and to do so in cipher; no formal orders were to be entered on the record books unless subsequent, unspecified actions had to be taken. Neither Sherman, Sheridan's direct superior, nor Irvin McDowell, commander of the division in which Louisiana was located, was informed of the mission ahead of time. Belknap told Sheridan that it was "best that the trip should appear to be one as much of pleasure as of business," so Sheridan obligingly brought with him his brother Michael, aide George A. Forsyth, and a number of other ladies and gentlemen, including the dark-haired twenty-one-year-old daughter of Quartermaster General Daniel Rucker, Irene Rucker, whom he had met at a wedding a few months earlier. The traveling party let it be known they were on their way to Havana for the holidays.[37]

The ruse fooled no one, particularly not after Sheridan met publicly with Colonel William Emory, commander of the Department of the Gulf, to discuss the extramilitary ramifications of his mission. Emory, who had commanded the XIX Corps under Sheridan during the Shenandoah Valley campaign, showed him a copy of his own set of orders from Washington: "The President directs that you make arrangements to be in readiness to suppress violence, and have it understood that you will do it." Sheridan regarded the orders as "explicit and unambiguous"; he approved of Emory's placing an infantry regiment within striking distance of the state capital. To Belknap, Sheridan reported that, although the city was "feverish," he did not expect any serious trouble when the legislature convened on January 4.[38]

In making his prediction Sheridan failed to take into account the brazen resourcefulness of Louisiana Democrats. As soon as the legislative session began, the Democrats set into motion a well-crafted plan to seize parliamentary control of the house. A temporary speaker was quickly named, former New Orleans mayor Louis Wiltz, and Wiltz in turn appointed a cadre of pistol-packing sergeants-at-arms to back his play. Republican lawmakers, caught off guard, attempted to leave the room to prevent a quorum, but opposition doorkeepers collared enough of them to make the proceedings—roughly speaking—legal. The five disputed house seats were forthwith awarded to deserving Democrats.[39]

Reveling in their apparent victory, the Democratic solons added insult to injury by calling on Colonel Phillipe de Trobriand, commander of the federal troops at the statehouse, to remove Republican "idlers" from the hallways. De Trobriand, a naturalized citizen who had immigrated to America from France in time to serve in the Union army during the Civil War, surprisingly complied. Clad in civilian clothes to present a suitably low profile, the Frenchman gently but firmly persuaded the Republicans to leave the building. As he left the hall the Democrats gave him a round of applause. Two hours later, however, de Trobriand returned, this time in uniform, at the head of a bayonet-wielding force of federal soldiers. Governor Kellogg, hearing of the Democrats' latest coup, had formally asked him to remove "all persons not returned as legal members of the house of representatives by the returning-board of the State." Now it was the Republicans who applauded as de Trobriand and his troopers went onto the floor of the house and forcibly ejected the five newly seated Democratic legislators. For the second time in two months federal troops had intervened in Louisiana's domestic politics. Many northerners, as well as southerners, had severe reservations about such a naked use of force. A firestorm of criticism raged across the country.[40]

Sheridan, who had read Kellogg's note and strongly recommended immediate compliance with it, reacted in character to the outrage that followed. In sharp contrast to his letter two days earlier, Sheridan now warned Belknap that "a spirit of defiance to all lawful authority" had swept across the state. He urged that the government simply declare all opponents of Kellogg's regime "banditti" and permit the army to arrest and try them as criminals, in the same way that he had sought unsuccessfully to have the ringleaders of the Red River War hauled before a military tribunal. Presumably he did not expect to ship large numbers of Louisiana Democrats to the Castillo de San Marcos, but that is far from assured. As it was, he told a visiting Massachusetts congressman that the thing to do was to "suspend the what-do-you-call-it," meaning the right of habeas corpus. Then the army could do what it wanted to restore law and order.[41]

Most of Sheridan's fellow citizens, northern as well as southern, did not share his unique approach to the constitution. In public meetings throughout the nation, speaker after speaker rose to denounce the general and the Grant administration. No less a personage than New England poet-pamphleteer William Cullen Bryant thundered that Sheridan should "tear off his epaulets and break his sword and fling the fragments into the Potomac." Democratic Senator Thomas F. Bayard, a future secretary of state, said on the floor of Congress—with undoubted passion but a poor choice of words—that Sheridan was unfit "to breathe the air of a Republican government." Newspaper columnists were even more savage. The *New Orleans Daily Picayune* noted that "for the first time in the history of the United States, armed soldiers have invaded a legislative hall, and bayonets have been used to expel the representatives of the people from their seats." It was, said the newspaper, "the most violent, the most illegal, the most shameless act yet permitted by an administration whose history is one of violence, illegality and shamelessness unparalleled in the history of any free government." The *New York World* headlined: "Tyranny! A Sovereign State Murdered!" Even the good gray *New York Times*, ordinarily a Republican mouthpiece, worried fastidiously "that a very able graduate of West Point, and a soldier who has so gallantly and faithfully fought for the supremacy of the Constitution, should know so little of its requirements."[42]

The able graduate was completely unworried by all the criticism. He served at the pleasure—or perhaps now the sufferance—of the president, and Secretary of War Belknap had already assured him that "the President and all of us have full confidence and thoroughly approve your course." As for the rest, including those New Orleans diners who groaned and hissed whenever he entered his hotel dining room and sent over waiters with carefully underlined newspaper articles suggesting, as did one Atlanta paper, that he should be called before "Judge Lynch" and dangled from a lamppost, Sheridan professed indifference. "Some of the Banditti made idle threats last night that they would assassinate me because I dared to tell the truth," he telegraphed Belknap. "I am not afraid and will not be stopped . . . the very air has been impregnated with assassination for some years." Nevertheless, his faithful aide Forsyth took to carrying a loaded revolver in his pocket whenever he and the general went out in public.[43]

Despite Belknap's hasty words of encouragement, Grant and his cabinet were having second thoughts about Sheridan's Louisiana adventure. On January 13, Grant sent a special message to the Senate maintaining—a little weakly, given the circumstances —that he had "no desire to have United States troops interfere in the domestic concerns of Louisiana or any other State." He went to some pains to stress that the army had merely responded to a lawful request from the governor to remove "a body of unauthorized persons" from the statehouse. Any errors the soldiers may have made, said Grant, had been on the side of preserving law and order. As for Sheridan's notorious "banditti" message, it was simply a suggestion of "summary modes of procedure . . . which, though they cannot be adopted, would, if legal, soon put an end to the troubles and disorders in that State." Somewhat plaintively, Grant concluded by asking Congress to send a committee of its own down to New Orleans to investigate matters.[44]

A delegation headed by Massachusetts congressman George F. Hoar subsequently spent three weeks in the Crescent City hearing testimony and gathering evidence. Sheridan, seeking to put his actions into some sort of local context, told the committee that as many as 3,500 political murders had taken place in Louisiana since 1866. This suspiciously round figure was immediately seized upon by opponents of the general, whom the *Daily*

Picayune now took pleasure in calling the "eminent author and statistician." Undeniably there had been hundreds, if not thousands, of acts of politically motivated violence in the state during reconstruction, but Sheridan undercut his position by wildly revising his figures, first downward, then upward, before arriving at a still-suspect estimate of 2,141 murders. Nevertheless, the Republican-dominated committee concluded its visit by defending the army's intervention and working out a compromise whereby Louisiana Democrats were regiven control of the house in return for a promise not to overthrow the Kellogg regime for a third, possibly charmed, time.[45]

With the conclusion of the committee's work, Sheridan began making plans to leave New Orleans. Despite his public show of indifference, he well may have shared the opinion (though not the terminology) of a young army lieutenant, Lorenzo Cook, who told the visiting congressmen that he "would rather be among the Comanches than among these ignorant . . . priest ridden people." Before he could leave, however, Sheridan felt it was necessary to change department commanders. To his mind, Emory was altogether too vacillating and conciliatory "to keep things steady and inspire confidence." He was, said Sheridan, "a very weak old man [Emory was sixty-three], entirely unfitted for this place." As a replacement, Sheridan suggested the mercurial young Colonel Ranald Mackenzie, whose recent experience fighting Kiowas and Comanches might possibly have prepared him for Louisiana Democrats. But Mackenzie was judged too high-strung for such a sensitive position (he would end his life in a New York City insane asylum), so Sheridan turned instead to Brigadier General Christopher Augur, former commandant of cadets at West Point, who had served in Louisiana during the Civil War and held a number of administrative posts under Sheridan in the West.[46]

With Augur safely in place in New Orleans, Sheridan returned to his headquarters in Chicago. Waiting on his desk was a letter from Brigadier General Alfred Terry, commander of the troubled Department of Dakota, where the Black Hills were located. Terry, one of Sheridan's most urbane, civilized, and gentlemanly officers, was concerned that "the whole of the hill country will be over-run by miners as soon as the season will permit." He wanted more troops to patrol the region. Sheridan, however, downplayed the problem, telling Sherman a few days later that he was confident the army, as currently constituted, could stem the tide of rapacious treasure-seekers flooding into the Dakotas. But by early summer, more than one thousand miners were working the Black Hills, tearing out chunks of the sacred land, and Indian patience, never a particular virtue of the Sioux in the best of times, was rapidly wearing thin.[47]

The Department of the Interior added to the turmoil by sending a trained geologist into the Black Hills to determine the putative asking price of the land on the open market—not that the Sioux had any intention of selling it. Professor Walter P. Jenney of the New York School of Mines headed the new expedition, accompanied by four hundred U.S. cavalrymen and an uninvited but undiscouraged horde of prospectors who obligingly pointed out the best sites for mining gold. Jenney subsequently reported that gold was indeed present in the Black Hills, but that it would take a well-funded and well-organized effort to extract it. Far from discouraging further incursions onto the Indians' land, the Jenney report merely stimulated more-moneyed capitalists to enter the game. Sheridan looked askance at the whole affair. "To expect me to keep miners out of the Black Hills," he said, "while the Indian Bureau, by this examination, is affording an opportunity for skilful and practical miners to ascertain the minerals in it, and newspaper correspondents to publish it to the world, is putting on me a duty which my best skill and most conscientious desire to perform . . . will make a failure of."[48]

Part of Sheridan's frustration may have stemmed from the fact that he had other things on his mind just now than Indians and geologists. He was getting married. His friendship with Irene Rucker had blossomed, quite unexpectedly, into love. At forty-four he was exactly twice her age, but neither considered the difference an unconquerable handicap. Irene, a true army brat, had been around soldiers all her life, and Sheridan, while graying visibly and putting on weight, still seemed—outwardly, at least—as vital and energetic as much younger men. Longtime friends such as Sherman, who had known the Rucker family for years, were delighted with the match, which immediately began having a softening effect on the bark-rough old cavalryman.

The marriage ceremony was held at the Rucker home in Chicago on June 3, 1875, followed by an ice-cream reception in the backyard. In deference to Sheridan, whose father had recently passed away from blood poisoning after being kicked in the wrist by a horse, the guest list was kept simple. Besides the immediate family, brother generals Sherman, Terry, Crook, Pope, and Augur attended the brief ceremony, which the *Chicago Inter-Ocean* reported under the headline, "Great Cavalry Leader Vanquished by a Blonde." *Harper's Weekly* artist Thomas Nast contributed a fanciful sketch of the humbled general, bound with cupid's garlands and led to the altar by little "banditti." Sheridan roared with laughter when he saw the drawing.[49]

The couple embarked on a delayed three-month honeymoon trip to the Pacific Northwest that fall, but the trip was cut short by mounting concerns over the ugly impasse with the Sioux. A special commission, headed by Iowa Senator William B. Allison, had met with Red Cloud and other tribal leaders in late September in an attempt to persuade them to sell, or at least lease, the Black Hills to the government. The terms, $6 million to buy the land outright or $400,000 per year to rent it, were laughed at by the Sioux. Non-agency Indians, led by the glowering and intractable Hunkpapa chieftain Sitting Bull, refused even to entertain thoughts of selling their land. Sitting Bull and Crazy Horse did not bother to attend the council, but sent a personal representative, Little Big Man, to make their position clear to their fellow Indians—he offered to shoot any chief who so much as broached the subject. The commissioners, threatened, scolded, and scorned at every turn, returned to Washington and recommended that the government simply set its own price for the Black Hills and present it to the Indians as a *fait accompli.*[50]

Armed with the commission report, Grant summoned Sheridan to the White House on November 3, 1875, for a confidential meeting on the Sioux problem. Also in attendance were Belknap, Commissioner of Indian Affairs E. P. Smith, Brigadier General George Crook, and newly installed Interior Secretary Zachariah Chandler, who had replaced the scandal-ridden Columbus Delano a few weeks earlier. William Sherman, who had recently moved his headquarters to St. Louis to escape Washington political intrigue, was conspicuous by his absence. Still entertaining thoughts of a third term in office, Grant was reluctant to buck the tide of widespread public support for a military solution to the Black Hills dilemma. He left standing the order prohibiting miners from the area, but implied that the army should be none too punctilious in enforcing the law. At the same time the president decided to compel Sitting Bull and his non-reservation faction to resettle on agency land, where they could be better monitored and, so it was hoped, controlled. The bands in question were given until January 31, 1876, to report to the agencies.[51]

No one seriously expected Sitting Bull or the other "belligerents" to comply meekly with the government decree. Sheridan, for his part, told the secretary of the interior that the Indians would consider such demands "a good joke." And he warned, "Unless they are caught before early spring, they cannot be caught at all." But by locking themselves into a specific deadline, the bureaucrats in Washington had effectively foreclosed any move by the army until actual offense had been given. True to form, Sitting Bull and Crazy Horse declined the white man's proffered hospitality. The deadline passed without compliance, and on February 1, Secretary Chandler officially notified Secretary Belknap that "said Indians are hereby turned over to the War Department for such action on the part of the Army as you may deem proper under the circumstances." In turn, Belknap notified Sheridan.

The wheels had been put into furious motion for the bloodiest confrontation on the western plains.[52]

Sheridan envisioned a winter campaign similar to the one in 1868, but severe weather and concomitant supply problems delayed the start of hostilities until mid-March, when a force of three hundred soldiers under Colonel Joseph Reynolds attacked a large village of Sioux and Cheyenne near the Powder River in southeastern Montana. The Indians, although initially surprised, mounted a strong counterattack and drove the troopers from their camp. Reynolds fell back to the main column, commanded by Crook, and the entire body limped back to Fort Fetterman. Sheridan, being generous, blamed the severity of the weather for the humiliating setback, which ultimately resulted in Reynolds's court-martial. Grant, a classmate of Reynolds at West Point, quietly rescinded the conviction, and Reynolds hastily and ingloriously retired.[53]

Further campaigning was suspended until spring. As before, Sheridan planned a multi-pronged assault on the Indians. Crook, despite his Powder River failure, was directed to move north again from Fort Fetterman. Terry would move west from Fort Lincoln, North Dakota, while Colonel John A. Gibbon would lead a column east from Fort Ellis, Montana. Somewhere between the three forces, presumably, the Sioux would obediently allow themselves to be trapped and punished. While preparations continued apace at the various forts, Sheridan's most famous Indian-fighter languished in a purdah of his own making. George Custer, with more courage (or political calculation) than tact, had enraged and embarrassed Grant by testifying against Belknap at congressional hearings investigating the alleged selling of post traderships. Belknap, a friend of Sheridan, as well as of Grant, had resigned in disgrace before the hearings began, but House Democrats, eager to damage the president, continued their investigation. Custer appeared twice before the committee, repeating largely hearsay allegations against Belknap and Grant's own brother, Orvil. The president was understandably furious. He ordered

Custer stripped of command of the Fort Lincoln column, and kept him cooling his heels in Washington. Meanwhile, the Custer-less column was completing preparations to take the field against the Sioux.[54]

Swallowing his pride, Custer telegraphed Grant, appealing to him as a soldier "to spare me the humiliation of seeing my regiment march to meet the enemy and I not to share its dangers." As he had done previously in 1868 when Custer had been suspended prior to the campaign against the southern Cheyenne, Sheridan interceded in his behalf with the president. "I am sorry Lieutenant Colonel Custer did not manifest as much interest by staying at his post to organize and get ready his regiment and the expedition as he does now to accompany it," he wrote. "On a previous occasion, in eighteen sixty-eight, I asked executive clemency for Colonel Custer to enable him to accompany his regiment against the Indians and I sincerely hope if granted this time it will have sufficient effect to prevent him from again attempting to throw discredit on his profession and his brother officers." In his testimony, Custer had not discredited fellow officers, unless one counted U. S. Grant among that number, but Sheridan's point was well taken by the one for whom it was intended, and Grant—at least partially—relented. Custer could accompany Terry's column as commander of his regiment, but Terry would retain overall leadership of the force.[55]

Sheridan, at Sherman's urging, left the actual conduct of the campaign to his two department commanders, Crook and Terry. This proved to be a disastrous mistake, and one that might have been foreseen. Crook had served on the northern plains for only a year, and despite the high regard Sheridan had for his old West Point roommate, the fact was that Crook knew comparatively little about his new opponents, the Sioux. His dreadful showing in March, attributed conveniently to the scapegoat Reynolds, should have alerted Sheridan to Crook's deficiencies, but it did not. Nor did Sheridan take into account the similar inexperience of his other department commander, Terry, who had never before faced

the trials and dangers of an Indian campaign. Most damaging of
all, Sheridan refused to credit continuing reports of a massive
buildup of Indian strength in the Powder River area. All these
factors, combined with the eleventh-hour return of a chastened
and somewhat demoralized Custer to field command, contributed
in turn to the fatally compromised campaign that followed.

From the outset things went badly. Evil omens dogged the
Terry-Custer column as it departed Fort Lincoln on May 17. A
thick ground fog blanketed the post, and the sun reflecting over-
head made it appear that the soldiers were riding away across the
sky. Libbie Custer, for one, thought it a bad sign. Next, the
column came upon an Indian burial ground. Well-preserved
corpses of men, women, and children, swaddled in buffalo skins
and pitiful bits of calico, lay on scaffolds or in the forks of trees.
A warrior's scaffold, painted red and black to denote the occu-
pant's earthly bravery, was pulled down on Custer's orders. Soldiers helped themselves to the dead man's belongings, and the
body was thrown into a nearby river and used as bait for scav-
enging fish. Farther out, the troopers discovered the charred remains of a fellow cavalryman, beaten and burned to death by the
Indians. This sight, at least, seemed to unsettle Custer; for once,
he was speechless.[56]

While the gloomy column rode west from Fort Lincoln,
Crook's thousand-man force moved north from Fort Fetterman.
Once again Crook ran into a hornet's nest. On the banks of the
Rosebud River in southern Montana, a large band of Sioux and
Cheyenne, led by Crazy Horse, attacked the column at daylight
on June 17. In a swirling six-hour fight over broken, heavily
ravined terrain, the bluecoats managed to hold off their attackers,
but were so badly bloodied in the process that Crook abruptly
broke off his campaign and limped back to base camp. Meanwhile,
unaware of Crook's repulse or the atypically large and united
force of Indians that had confronted him, Terry and Custer continued moving west. Because telegraph lines were down in the
region, Sheridan did not expect to hear from Terry for some time.

He went ahead with plans to attend the gala Centennial celebration in Philadelphia on July 4.

Sheridan was staying at the Continental Hotel in Philadelphia when the first reports reached the East of George Armstrong Custer's death and apotheosis on the banks of the Little Bighorn River on Sunday, June 25, 1876. Sheridan had just received a forwarded message from Terry, dated June 21, stating that they had found fresh traces of a large Indian camp on the Rosebud and expressing the now mordantly ironic hope that one of his columns would soon locate the Indians. Four days later, Custer did. Surprisingly, at a time when the national press was not particularly noted for its speed or accuracy, the newspapers had the story before either Sheridan or Sherman knew what had happened, or why. On the record, both denied reports that Custer and his command had been wiped out. Nothing of the sort had yet been reported to headquarters.[57]

But, as both men secretly feared, it was true. A confidential report from Terry arrived the next day in Chicago and was forwarded to Sheridan in Philadelphia. Custer and the 215 men who had followed him down a sloping hillside in southern Montana toward what they supposed was a badly surprised Indian camp were dead. Another 47 troopers, in a separate attack force led by Major Marcus Reno, had also been killed by the swarming hordes. The Indians—Sioux mostly, with a smattering of Cheyenne, Arapaho, Blackfeet, and lesser tribes—had ridden away from their shocking triumph without even knowing, at first, whom they had killed. Few of the northern Plains Indians had ever fought Custer before; he was merely another *wasichu* attacking another unoffending village. But in Custer's hometown of Monroe, Michigan, it was a different story. Every bell in town tolled incessantly for the general, his brother Tom, their younger brother Boston, eighteen-year-old nephew Autie Reed, brother-in-law James Calhoun, and the other 211 officers and men of the Seventh Cavalry left strewn like so many chewed-up rag dolls across the rolling hillsides above the Little Bighorn River. Back at Fort Lincoln,

Libbie Custer stoically pulled a black shawl about her shoulders and went to inform the other widows of their loss.[58]

News of Custer's massacre, coinciding as it did with the nation's one-hundredth birthday celebration, electrified his countrymen. Sheridan, after the initial shock, was more sickened than stunned. He knew Custer for what he was, and for what he was not. As far back as Custer's inglorious 1864 campaign against winter-wracked Rebel cavalry in the Shenandoah, Sheridan had seen him fail at independent command. This failing had been reinforced by Custer's lackadaisical showing and subsequent court-martial during Hancock's War in 1867. And even his startling triumph over the Cheyenne on the Washita River had very nearly resulted in the exact sort of tragedy that fate ultimately had reserved for him eight years later. But always Custer could attack, and for this reason, more than simple friendship, Sheridan had interceded with the president in his behalf, trusting Terry and Crook to formulate a winning battle plan and—not incidentally—keep Custer on a short leash.

Predictably, the public cried out for revenge. From Bismarck to Boston, editorial writers thundered against the Indians and called on the army to avenge their fallen brothers. Offers of volunteers, like those who had gaily marched off to be slaughtered fifteen years earlier in the fatal summer of 1861, poured in from all quarters. In Custer's New Rumley, Ohio, birthplace, schoolboys solemnly swore on McGuffey's First Reader to kill Sitting Bull on sight. Even in the South, where the rubbing out of a couple hundred Yankee soldiers would not ordinarily have elicited much mourning, such former foemen as Joseph E. Johnston, John McCausland, and Jo Shelby lamented Custer's passing and defended his actions. Thomas Rosser, Custer's old West Point classmate and frequent Civil War opponent, flatly attributed his friend's death to the unpopular Major Reno, who, said Rosser, had cravenly taken to the hills and left the general to fight alone.[59]

But Sheridan, sifting through reports at his Chicago office, was not so quick to absolve Custer of all the blame for his own death. To Sherman he wrote, "I deeply deplore the loss of Custer and his men. I feel it was an unnecessary sacrifice, due to misapprehension and a superabundance of courage—the latter extraordinarily developed in Custer." More pointedly, he observed that "Terry's column was sufficiently strong to have handled the Indians, if Custer had waited for the junction." Grant, whose disciplining of Custer had contributed in part to his fatal impetuosity, had even less doubt—and less charity—about where to put the blame for the sorry catastrophe. "I regard Custer's Massacre," he said, "as a sacrifice of troops brought on by Custer himself, that was wholly unnecessary—wholly unnecessary."[60]

Sheridan, unavoidably feeling some of the responsibility for Custer's demise, did not have time for the luxury of grief. Noting angrily that the ill-starred campaign had been occasioned, to a great degree, by Congress's failure to approve his standing request for more military forts on the northern frontier, he successfully obtained authorization to build two new posts in the Yellowstone region of Montana. He also demanded and got the right to police the Indian agencies. Finally, and most important, he brought a much-needed infusion of fresh blood into the campaign in the persons of Nelson Miles and Ranald Mackenzie. While Crook and Terry remained in nominal control of the war effort, their younger, more vigorous subordinates increasingly took responsibility for pressing the action to a successful conclusion.

Throughout the autumn and winter of 1876–77 Miles and Mackenzie harried the hungry, scattered, and increasingly demoralized Indians across Montana and northern Wyoming. The great convocation of forces that ultimately had misled Custer into attacking a superior enemy at the wrong place and time—and had equally misled Sheridan about the Indians' ability to sustain and use a large force in the field—had proven to be a once-in-a-lifetime occurrence. In this, at least, Sheridan had been right, although that in itself was no doubt small consolation to Custer and his men. Sitting Bull, still undefeated but now weary of the war that now bore his name, led his people into Canada to find sanctuary. A few months later Crazy Horse rode into the Red Cloud Agency with what remained of his followers, threw his rifles to the ground, and quit the fight. Four months later he was dead, slain in a scuffle with agency guards. In the meantime a new congressional commission had paid yet another visit to the Indians and obtained their marks on another scrap of paper, this one ceding permanent control of the Black Hills to the government and putting an end to Sioux hunting privileges along the Yellowstone and Powder rivers. The chairman of the commission, appropriately enough, was named Manypenny.[61]

While the war with the Sioux dragged on to its inevitable conclusion, Sheridan made his third and last official visit to New Orleans in mid-November 1876. The just-concluded presidential election, like the Louisiana legislative contest two years earlier, had ended in a morass of fraud, corruption, and voter intimidation. What was worse, it had produced no clear winner. The Democratic candidate, New York Governor Samuel J. Tilden, had won a clear majority of the popular vote—4,284,265 to 4,033,295 for the Republican standard-bearer, Ohio Governor Rutherford B. Hayes. But the issue in the all-important electoral college was not so clear-cut. On the morning after the election Tilden controlled an undisputed 184 electoral votes, to 166 for Hayes. A total of 185 was needed to win election. But fast-thinking Republican campaign operatives had seized upon the returns in three contested southern states—Florida, South Carolina, and Louisiana—whose votes were too close to call. With an almost literary aptness the states' nineteen electoral votes were exactly enough, if handled properly, to give Hayes a one-vote triumph. And all three states were in the hands of Republicans.[62]

In Louisiana, which was used to this sort of thing, department commander Augur rapidly assembled a twenty-five-company force of soldiers to patrol the streets. Sheridan had confidence that Augur could handle the assignment without his help, but an increasingly nervous Grant was not so sure. On

November 10 he ordered Sheridan back to New Orleans "to keep the peace and to protect the legal canvassing board in the performance of its duties." Sheridan protested that "there is no military necessity for my presence here," but, good soldier that he was, returned again to his least favorite city.[63]

Events soon proved Sheridan correct. Meeting in early December, the state Returning Board (dubbed "the Overturning Board" by the always irreverent *Daily Picayune*) threw out just enough Democratic votes to certify Hayes the winner. The other two southern states did the same. Outraged Democrats in the affected states promptly certified minority returns giving Tilden the edge. For a time it seemed as if a Third Battle of Bull Run might be fought over the contested election, this time between Democrats and Republicans. In the nation's capital, rumors ran rampant that mysterious forces with such ominous-sounding names as the Knights of the Golden Circle and the Sons of Liberty were planning to march on Washington and put Tilden in the White House by force. Tilden Minutemen organizations sprang up in several states. "Tilden or blood," some Democrats cried.[64]

Grant, who had believed from the start that Tilden had been legally elected, now worried that real disorders could come to the streets of the capital. Accordingly he directed Sheridan to hurry troops to Washington from the West. As it transpired, such drastic measures proved unnecessary. A complex and controversial compromise was worked out between Republican supporters of Hayes and southern Democrats, who agreed to abandon their ineffectual party standard-bearer in return for an understanding that President Hayes would remove federal troops from the three southern states still under army occupation. Sheridan, for the past eleven years the most stalwart and unyielding upholder of such occupation, now gladly left New Orleans and its endemic electoral shenanigans behind him. With another Republican president safely in place in the White House, albeit at the cost of some of the same party regulars he and the army had been keeping in power in the South for the better part of a decade, Sheridan left the political arena for good. Turning his eyes westward, he scanned the horizon for new worlds to conquer. But, like Tennyson's aging Ulysses, he was rapidly running out of enemies to fight. Perhaps it was just as well. At the comparatively youthful age of forty-six, Phil Sheridan was getting old.

11

TAPS

IN LATE JULY 1877, thirteen months after Custer's death at the Little Bighorn, Sheridan paid a one-day visit to the battlefield. A month before, his brother Michael, British-born Captain Henry Nowlan, and a delegation of Seventh Cavalry horsemen had journeyed to the site to reclaim the remains of Custer and ten other regimental officers who had died alongside him that scarlet afternoon. (An eleventh, Lieutenant John J. Crittenden, the son of Sheridan's old Army of the Cumberland compatriot, Major General Thomas Crittenden, had been buried, at his family's request, "where he fell.") Custer's remains, in accordance with Libbie's wishes, were shipped to West Point for reburial—an ironic choice, given Custer's less-than-stellar performance there. The enlisted men were buried in a common grave near the crest of the ridge; a pile of rocks, topped by a buffalo skull, marked their final resting place.[1]

Saddle-high grass now grew over the battleground, and the smell of wildflowers had replaced the stench of dead bodies, which the summer before had been so overpowering that even the ordinarily unsqueamish Indians had stayed away. Riding over the field, Sheridan refought the battle in his mind. More than ever he was convinced that Custer could have survived his initial misjudgment, his hasty and "usual hurrahs," as Reno had termed them, if only he had not divided his command. But then Custer was nothing if not rash. Sheridan consoled himself with the knowledge that now, only a year after buffalo and Indian had freely roamed the countryside, there were "no signs of either . . . but in their places we found prospectors, emigrants and tramps." It was indicative of his state of mind that he preferred the sight of hobos, saddle tramps, and sodbusters swarming over the virgin territory to the native ecology of its original inhabitants.[2]

Back home in Chicago life was considerably more domesticated. Under the fond but firm tutelage of his wife, Irene, Sheridan had exchanged the rowdy bachelor pleasures of racetrack and social club for the parlor pleasantries of an officers' brunch. Mrs. Sheridan, though still quite young, had proven uncommonly adept as a hostess. Early on she had learned the virtue, shared by her husband, of keeping her own counsel. She had decided, said family friend Frank G. Carpenter, "that she would think before she spoke, and if she had nothing to say she would remain silent." To this newfound domesticity was added in 1876 a first child, a daughter, named Mary after Sheridan's mother. The next year, twin girls, Irene and Louise, arrived, and on July 28, 1880, a son was born, given the honor—and burden—of bearing the name Phil Sheridan, Jr. The general, for his part, doted on the children, particularly "Little Phil," and made liberal use of the military telegraph during his frequent forced absences.[3]

The last three years of the decade saw the final subjugation of the northern Plains Indians. In the summer of 1877 construction was completed on the two permanent forts Sheridan had demanded for the Yellowstone River valley. Fort Custer was opened on the bluffs overlooking the Bighorn and Little Bighorn rivers, fifteen miles north of the battlefield. Fort Keough, named for one of Custer's fallen company commanders, Captain Myles Keough, was constructed on the Tongue River, one hundred miles farther northeast. Contemporaneously, the last resisting bands of rebellious Sioux and Cheyenne surrendered to the army, quietly bringing to a close the costliest and, from a military standpoint, most embarrassing campaign in frontier history.[4]

Sheridan's ardent and industrious young subordinate, Nelson Miles, who had overseen construction of the two forts and the subsequent surrender of Sioux hostiles following his victory over them at the Battle of Muddy Creek in early May 1877, also figured prominently in the sorry spectacle of the army's 1,700-mile chase of Chief Joseph's Nez Percé Indians in October of that year. The Nez Percés, who had been at peace with the white man for nearly three-quarters of a century, had finally made the mistake of living on land that settlers and gold-diggers coveted. Given thirty days to leave their homeland in the Wallowa Valley of northeastern Oregon, the tribe embarked instead on an epic flight for freedom across four states, outmarching and outfighting army forces several times their size. Bible-thumping Brigadier General Oliver O. Howard (dubbed "Uh-Oh" Howard for his various Civil War misadventures) led the increasingly fruitless pursuit. When, after four months of chasing the Indians, it appeared that they would make good their escape into Canada, Howard called on Miles to block their path.[5]

An extraordinarily ambitious young officer, Miles had married the niece of commanding general William Sherman, whom the young couple bombarded with incessant pleas for advancement and preferral. After one such demand on family loyalty, a frustrated Sherman complained to Sheridan, "I know no way to satisfy [Miles's] ambitions but to surrender to him absolute power over the whole Army, with President & Congress thrown in." Still, Miles had demonstrated his worth as an Indian-fighter on numerous occasions, and he quickly moved to stop the Nez Percés' escape. After a five-day siege of the fugitives' position in the Bear Paw Mountains of Montana, Miles induced Chief Joseph to surrender, promising him in good faith that Joseph and his people could return to the Lapwai Reservation in Idaho. Unfortunately, Sheridan had not been consulted on the matter, and he adhered to his unshakable belief that rebellious Indians should be punished for their misbehavior. Instead of being returned to the reservation nearest their ancestral home, the Nez Percés were shipped off to

Fort Leavenworth, Kansas, where dozens rapidly sickened and died, and then were moved to another location in Indian Territory. Chief Joseph, best remembered for his heartbreaking surrender speech, concluding, "From where the sun now stands I will fight no more forever," never did make it home. He died in 1904; the attending physician attributed his death to a broken heart.[6]

Even less creditable to the army, collectively, and Sheridan, personally, was the plight of Cheyenne Chief Dull Knife and his bedraggled followers the next September. The Cheyenne, who had surrendered along with Crazy Horse the previous spring, had expected to live with the Sioux on the Red Cloud (later Pine Ridge) Agency. Instead, at Sheridan's behest, they had been marched to the southern Cheyenne agency in Indian Territory. Like the Nez Percés, the northern plains Cheyenne died in droves among the dusty, mosquito-ridden sand hills of Indian Territory. They had been told, or at any rate believed they had been told, that they could return north if they found their new government accommodations unsuitable. Accordingly, in mid-September 1878 they started home.

Enraged by their action, Sheridan warned that the entire reservation system was in imminent danger of collapsing. All across Kansas forts emptied in pursuit of the ragged fugitives. After six weeks of gallant if pitiable resistance, Dull Knife and his 148 followers surrendered to the army at Fort Robinson, Nebraska, on October 23, 1878. Once again, Sheridan demanded that tribal leaders be exiled to Florida; the rest should be returned to Oklahoma. The post commander at Fort Robinson, Captain Henry W. Wessells, Jr., sympathized with the Indians' plight, but no one bucked a Sheridan order. In an attempt to force the Cheyenne to comply, Wessells cut off all food, water, and fuel supplies. The Indians, barricaded inside a camp barracks, replied that they would rather die than return to the south. On the night of January 9, 1879, after a week of freezing starvation, the prisoners suddenly opened fire on their captors with a handful of rifles they had hidden away. Eleven guards were killed in the breakout. The Indians, mostly women and children, leaped from the barracks windows into the snowy darkness. The soldiers, after the initial shock, gave chase. Sixty-four Cheyenne were killed, among them Dull Knife's only daughter. The rest, including the chief himself, were soon recaptured.[7]

The ensuing public revulsion over the treatment of the little band stirred Sheridan, as always, to bitter defensiveness. "I am quite convinced," he wrote Sherman, "there was no unnecessary cruelty at Fort Robinson, on the contrary, the officers were governed by the highest sentiments of humanity throughout." That was bad enough, but Sheridan did not stop there. He accused the warriors of using their women and children as human shields while making their escape, a charge that no one familiar with the Indian reverence for their own people took seriously. Ultimately, despite Sheridan's huffing and puffing, the exhausted remnants of Dull Knife's band were allowed to stay with their friends the Sioux at Pine Ridge Agency.[8]

On one matter, at least, Sheridan did find himself in agreement with both agency Indians and right-thinking junior officers. That concerned the near-criminal ineptitude of the Indian Bureau, in general, and Secretary of the Interior Carl Schurz, in particular. The old question of army versus civilian control of Indian affairs, an issue that went back as far as 1849, when the newly created Department of the Interior was given charge of the Indian Bureau, flared again in late 1878, about the time Dull Knife and his people were preparing to make their last despairing break for freedom. Officers investigating unrest at the southern agency reported that the Cheyenne were not receiving, either in quantity or quality, enough food to support them. Colonel Ranald Mackenzie, scarcely a soft touch when it came to handling Indians, complained to Sheridan, "I am expected to see that Indians behave properly whom the government is starving—and not only that, but starving in flagrant violation of agreement." He flatly told the post commander at Fort Reno not to track down any Indians who had fled the reservation in search of buffalo, since it would place the army "in the position of assisting in a great wrong."[9]

Sheridan, in his annual report to the secretary of war, complained that the Cheyenne had been treated "in a bungling and impolitic manner" prior to their flight north from Oklahoma. The Indian Bureau, he said, had made a mess of things on the reservation, failing to provide their charges with adequate supplies to keep them from starving, and "almost any race of men will fight rather than starve." Schurz, who had seen the same reports as Sheridan, admitted that bureau appropriations had failed to supply all the Indians' needs; he only hoped that careful management and economizing would improve conditions in the future. But, in a bit of tortured logic comparable to Sheridan at his worst, Schurz blamed the Cheyenne breakout on the chiefs themselves, who, he charged, wanted "to keep up the old traditions and to keep the other Indians from work."[10]

Sheridan had despised Schurz ever since the German-born general-turned-politician had publicly criticized his role in the Louisiana "banditti" controversy of 1875. Furthermore, as a member of the reformist wing of the Republican Party, Schurz had figured prominently in frustrating U. S. Grant's hopes of winning a third term as president. As early as 1872, Schurz had headed a national convention in Cincinnati demanding honest government and an end to "notoriously corrupt and unworthy men in places of power." He had kept up a steady drumbeat of criticism of Grant from his position as junior senator from Missouri, and had also helped prosecute investigations into the so-called Whiskey Ring and Belknap scandals of the mid-1870s that had effectively blocked Grant's reelection bid. This, in turn, had induced simon-pure Rutherford B. Hayes to select Schurz to head the Department of the Interior and implement the new president's cherished goal of civil-service reform. Given the fact that the corrupt Republican administration in Louisiana had helped deliver the extremely questionable electoral votes necessary to put Hayes into office in the first place, Sheridan had ample reason to consider Schurz something of a hypocrite when it came to the question of good government.[11]

When Sheridan repeated the familiar army accusations about

a shadowy "Indian Ring" of corrupt politicians, bumbling bureaucrats, and thieving government contractors colluding to deprive the Indians of basic human necessities, Schurz demanded to see his evidence. Sheridan responded with a twenty-page list of "rascalities and irregularities at a great majority of the agencies in the Military Division of the Missouri." At the same time he bridled at Schurz's sanctimonious reminder that the military was subservient to civil authority. "It is not necessary to remind me of the superiority of the civil to the military in this country," Sheridan wrote. "I drank that in my milk from the time I was born. I did not have to learn it." *Harper's Weekly* cartoonist Thomas Nast, a longtime friend of the general's, chimed in with a vitriolic sketch showing a harried Schurz cobbling together a shoddy cabinet under the sign, "The Indian Bureau is in perfect order now. It was rather rotten once."[12]

Sheridan and Schurz crossed swords again in 1879, following a bloody outbreak of fighting on the Ute Indian reservation in western Colorado. The Utes had been at peace with the whites since 1855, and had scouted for Kit Carson in his crushing 1862 campaign against the Navajos in the southwest. But, like the Nez Percés, they suffered the misfortune of living on mineral-rich real estate. The Colorado silver strike of the early 1870s had forced them to cede 4 million acres, or one-fourth of their reservation, to silver miners, but even that was not enough. Colorado had won its statehood in 1876, just in time to cast three crucial electoral votes for Hayes, and now, as their reward, Colorado voters wanted the Utes completely out of the state. "The Utes must go!" became a sure-fire applause line at local political gatherings. The tribe was blamed for all manner of crimes—even accused of starting forest fires. Their situation was not helped by the appointment of an eccentric old agronomist named Nathan C. Meeker as Indian agent in 1878. A visionary utopian and friend of the late Horace Greeley, Meeker wanted the Utes to call him "Father"; instead, with perhaps unintended demonism, they called him Nick.[13]

Meeker set out to make the Utes instant farmers and Christians, in pretty much that order. He disapproved of their favorite sport of horse racing, so he tore up the racetrack and built a school in its place. (When he insisted that the Utes send their children to the new school that September, they replied that it was "too hot" for them to be in school.) The disagreements might have stayed at that innocuous level, had Meeker not overreacted to being pushed down by a grumpy young warrior and ill-advisedly called in the army. Rumors spread through the Indians' ranks that the soldiers were going to take them to Indian Territory. On September 29, 1879, a planned parley between the two sides escalated into a firefight on the banks of Milk Creek, just inside the reservation. The commanding officer, Major Thomas Thornburgh, and ten of his men were killed, along with twenty-three Utes. Other Indians, enraged at their agent, whom they rightly blamed for the needless violence, massacred Meeker and nine of his employees. Mrs. Meeker, her daughter, and another woman were carried off and repeatedly raped.[14]

The Utes besieged the outnumbered soldiers for several days until Colonel Wesley Merritt arrived with reinforcements from Rawlins, Wyoming, where they had rushed by train. Sheridan hurried still more reinforcements to the front. As always, he and Sherman favored swift punishment of guilty Indians, but Schurz wanted to hold off any offensive action until the female hostages had been released. Sheridan, who, in a similar situation a few years earlier involving a white woman held captive by hostile Cheyenne, had declared it "mock humanity" to ransom her from a fate he clearly considered worse than death, was less concerned with rescuing the hostages than with avenging the dead. But Schurz outranked him, and the soldiers stayed where they were. Negotiations, not force, eventually extricated the women from their captors. Meanwhile Merritt, stuck for the winter with 1,500 hungry men at the ruined White River agency, complained about "being equipped for a campaign by one arm of the government and halted in its execution by another arm of the same government." Sheridan chimed in: "We went to the agency at the solicitation of the Indian Bureau, whose agent was murdered and our men killed and wounded, and now we are left in the heart of the mountains with our hands tied and the danger of being snowed in staring us in the face. I am not easily discouraged, but it looks as though we had been pretty badly sold out in this business."[15]

Sold or not, Sheridan and Merritt were not permitted to punish the Utes for the Milk Creek massacre. Instead, Schurz named another government peace commission to look into the matter. The commission later determined, with admirable hindsight, that the Indians had not intended to fight Thornburgh in the first place and thus were not accountable for their actions. Twelve other Utes, positively identified as those responsible for killing Meeker and the others, were never brought to justice. Only sixty-year-old Chief Douglas, whom the unfortunate Mrs. Meeker had discreetly identified as one of her attackers, was locked up for a time at Fort Leavenworth on politely unspecified charges. He was later quietly released to avoid embarrassing the Widow Meeker.[16]

The frustrating end of the Ute uprising marked the final chapter in the army's long struggle to pacify the plains. Sporadic fighting occasionally broke out in the years to come, but no major campaign was undertaken in the north following Merritt's truncated effort in 1879. In the eleven and a half years since Sheridan had taken command in the West, there had been no smashing, romantic victories such as he had won at Winchester, Cedar Creek, or Five Forks. The most famous battle had been a loss, the slaughter of Custer and his men at the Little Bighorn, and even Custer's singular triumph at the Washita River in 1868 had been—somewhat inaccurately—portrayed as a mere massacre of unarmed women and children. At the same time, the heroism of Sandy Forsyth and his command at Beecher's Island had been offset, in the public mind at least, by the vicious destruction of Heavy Runner's unoffending Piegan village two years later. Still, given the changing conditions on the post–Civil War frontier and the lack of a firm national consensus on the question of the Indians and their place in white-dominated society, the army regulars under Sheridan had performed about as well as could have been expected in such a thankless and perilous job. More than 1,200 of them had been killed or wounded—263 on a single afternoon in southern Montana—and many more Indians and settlers had become casualties in the clash of two radically different cultures. The winning of the West had come at last, but not without great cost to both victor and vanquished.

With the passing of the Indian as a major threat to civilization, Sheridan could now afford to be magnanimous. In a rare moment of sympathetic introspection, he looked beneath the mask of savagery and inhumanity he had placed over the Indian's face and found, with a mixture of guilt and regret, the proud, combative, spiritually minded individualist he had been fighting relentlessly all these years. "We took away their country and their means of support," he wrote in 1878, "broke up their mode of living, their habits of life, introduced disease and decay among them and it was for this and against this they made war. Could any one expect less?" In keeping with his newfound interest in Native American ethnology, he encouraged two young officers on his staff, Captain William Philo Clark and Lieutenant John G. Bourke, to study, respectively, the northern and southern Plains Indians. Clark produced a ground-breaking work, *The Indian Sign Language*, before his unexpected death from peritonitis in 1884, and Bourke published a number of scholarly articles and a well-received study of tribal rituals, *Scatologic Rites of All Nations*, that featured in its German edition a foreword by no less an expert than Sigmund Freud. Ironically, like Clark, Bourke also died young, suffering a fatal heart attack at the age of forty-nine.[17]

But if Sheridan was willing, on occasion, to look at the Indian with a more generous eye, he proved considerably less charitable toward former Civil War comrades who somehow had displeased or disappointed him. In 1879, after years of trying, Gouverneur K. Warren persuaded President Hayes to reopen hearings into his dismissal by Sheridan at the Battle of Five Forks in April 1865. (Grant, during his eight years in office, had consistently blocked Warren's request.) Sheridan's loyal subordinate Brigadier General Christopher Augur and Brigadier General John Newton made up the panel, which began hearing testimony in December 1879. Angered beyond words by the new tribunal, Sheridan retained the services of distinguished trial lawyer Asa Bird Gardner to represent him, and later appeared before the closed-door hearings in person to defend his long-ago actions. He came away from the proceedings with a deep sense of injury. "The court ignored the plainest statements of facts, and every military principle, in its endeavors to justify General Warren," he complained. Warren, although ultimately vindicated of the most serious charges placed against him, received even less satisfaction. Embittered and exhausted by his long stay in the professional wilderness, he died three months before the court's findings were published in late 1882. On his instructions, he was buried in civilian clothes, without military ceremony, the last casualty, in a way, of the Battle of Five Forks and, indeed, of the Civil War.[18]

That same year Sheridan showed rather more generosity toward his wife's father, Colonel Daniel H. Rucker, the army's assistant quartermaster general. The serving quartermaster general, Montgomery C. Meigs, had held the post since almost the beginning of the Civil War, managing a wartime budget of $1.5 billion and consistently working miracles with an undersized, overtaxed department. His son, twenty-two-year-old Lieutenant John R. Meigs, had been killed in a skirmish with Confederate cavalry while serving on Sheridan's staff in the Shenandoah Valley. Despite Sheridan's residual affection for young Meigs, he nevertheless exerted pressure on President Chester A. Arthur to remove the elder Meigs from office and replace him with Sheridan's father-in-law. At sixty-five, Meigs was five years younger than Rucker, but the president retained the right to relieve any officer who had served for more than forty-two years or had reached the age of sixty-two. With Sheridan's enthusiastic backing, Rucker succeeded Meigs in February 1882, then retired abruptly ten days later, having achieved his long-desired, if briefly held, sinecure.[19]

The next summer Sheridan returned the favor to the president, personally escorting Arthur on a twenty-five-day journey through Yellowstone National Park in northwestern Wyoming. For Sheridan the trip was a way of combining business with pleasure. He had long taken an active interest in the Yellowstone Valley region, sponsoring a number of military expeditions into the area, which had led in turn to the establishment of the country's first national park in 1872. Ten years later Sheridan revisited the park, only to find that poachers were systematically stripping the land of its animals, while a privately owned monopoly, the rather inappropriately named Yellowstone Park Improvement Company, was just as assiduously stripping the land of its minerals. Hastily organizing a powerful band of supporters, including Buffalo Bill Cody, naturalist George Bird Grinnell, and Montana territorial governor John Schuyler Crosby, his old friend and aide, Sheridan lobbied Congress with partial success to expand the size of the park, set aside a game preserve, and empower the army to act as guards.[20]

There the matter rested in 1883, when the general devised the notion of a presidential visit to the park, similar to the gala buffalo hunts he had conducted on the plains in the early 1870s. Arthur, although hardly a well man—he would die of complications from Bright's disease within two years of leaving office—gladly agreed to the trip, and Sheridan and his staff swung into action, planning the visit with all the precision of a military campaign. A handpicked troop of the Fifth Cavalry would act as armed escorts, though no Indian trouble was anticipated. Accompanying the presidential party were Secretary of War Robert Lincoln; Missouri Senator George G. Vest, who had led the fight for the park in Congress; Governor Crosby; Anson Stager of Western Union, an old hand at Sheridan-sponsored excursions; Captain William Philo Clark; New York Judge Daniel G. Rollins; and

Lieutenant Colonel Michael Sheridan, who, judging from photographs made during the trip, now looked more like Phil Sheridan than Phil Sheridan did.[21]

The party covered 350 miles in twenty-five days, following the Snake River into the Teton Basin, visiting Old Faithful and other geysers—including one nicknamed "Editor's Hole" since it was always bubbling and throwing mud—and enjoying a mock battle and war dance put on for their benefit by friendly Shoshoni and Arapaho Indians. (The authenticity of the event was somewhat compromised when the ferociously warpainted Indians began twirling gaily colored umbrellas. "I suppose the Secretary of the Interior furnished those parasols," Sheridan grumbled.) The president, an avid fisherman, later joined Senator Vest in hooking 105 pounds of fish in one day's time, although Sheridan scrupulously forbade hunting within park boundaries. The trip, though devoid of any concrete results, was generally accorded a great success, in part because Sheridan had carefully managed the news aspect of it by prohibiting reporters from coming along and arranging, instead, to have his brother send back glowing press releases concerning the park and its natural wonders.[22]

Sheridan had scarcely returned from the West when he received word that Sherman was planning to step down as general of the army. It was a move the irascible, incorruptible Sherman had long been contemplating. Disgusted by the political aspects of the position, he had temporarily moved his headquarters to St. Louis in 1874 after losing a power struggle with then–Secretary of War Belknap over the day-to-day control of army affairs. As old General Winfield Scott had discovered two decades earlier, the role of commanding general was, in peacetime, largely ornamental. The real power in Washington resided with the president and the secretary of war, who in turn controlled the army through the auspices of the War Department staff and its many bureaus. Sherman had warned Grant about becoming ensnared in politics, not understanding that his seemingly phlegmatic friend was, in reality, a consummate politician. In turn, Sheridan had criticized Sherman harshly for moving to St. Louis and conceding—as the Constitution clearly intended but Sheridan himself never fully accepted—civilian control of the military. Now, with Sherman stepping down, Sheridan was set to inherit both the position of commanding general and the myriad frustrations attendant upon it.[23]

Sherman's retirement would not become final until February 1884, but he turned over the reins to Sheridan in November 1883 to allow his successor time to prepare his budgetary and personnel requests to Congress. As befitted two old comrades who had worked together closely for many years, the formal transfer of power was carried out with as little ceremony, Sherman observed, as a lieutenant colonel taking over a regiment. Said Sheridan in a brief speech, "There is no one who will feel his loss more than I will."[24]

From his long years of experience as a department and division commander, Sheridan knew firsthand the dominance staff officers had achieved over their counterparts in the field. Politically savvy and close to the seats of power, members of the various bureaus enjoyed all the comforts and amenities of the capital, while line officers faced the rigors and dangers of frontier campaigning. Promotions came more easily; nearly half the army's brigadiers, colonels, lieutenant colonels, and majors held staff positions. One Washington correspondent joked that enough high-ranking officers could be found at any one time in the billiard parlor across the street from the War Department to fill the entire Turkish army.[25]

Despite his stated intention to reclaim the initiative lost by Sherman, Sheridan proved no better able to rein in the staff officers and their bureaus than his predecessor had been. An early attempt to do so by issuing orders directly to the staff, rather than going through the secretary of war, drew a pointed rebuke from Sheridan's recent Yellowstone companion, Robert Lincoln, who forcefully reminded the new commanding general of his proper place in the Washington hierarchy. Thenceforth, Sheridan left the bureaus pretty much alone.[26]

One order he did give, soon after assuming office, concerned the melancholy fate of one of his most promising young officers, Ranald Mackenzie, now serving as commander of the Department of Texas. A year earlier, at the age of forty-two, Mackenzie had become the youngest brigadier general in the army. Sheridan, who years before had tried to have Mackenzie installed as commander of the Department of the Gulf following the Louisiana "banditti" crisis, considered him the finest field officer in the service. But the moody and emotional Mackenzie, personally difficult in the best of times, had suddenly and irrevocably gone insane. Twenty years of constant campaigning, from First Bull Run to the Arizona Apache wars of 1881–82, had physically and mentally drained him (there is also the possibility, owing to a subsequent medical diagnosis of "general paresis," that he was suffering from tertiary syphilis). After only a month at his Texas post, Mackenzie had been found, drunk and disheveled, lashed to a cartwheel behind a seamy San Antonio saloon.[27]

The young officer's sister Harriet contacted Sheridan with the distressing news, and the general immediately offered his sympathetic assistance. Told that Mackenzie had taken to raving about the need for a complete reorganization of the army, from top to bottom, Sheridan sent him a bogus telegram requesting that he come to Washington at once to help put the army back into shape. Accompanied by his sister, Mackenzie left by train for the capital, but phony new orders redirected him to New York. Disembarking there, he was met by doctors from Bloomingdale Asylum, who examined the befuddled young officer and notified Sheridan that he was "totally unfit for military service." Three months later a retiring board voted him a full pension, on the grounds of "mental illness due to wounds received and exposure in the line of duty as an officer in the Army." Five years after that, Ranald Mackenzie died in confinement, still two years shy of his fiftieth birthday.[28]

In the summer of 1884 the nation prepared to elect another president. Chester A. Arthur, the Republican incumbent by virtue of James A. Garfield's assassination in 1881, declined to run for reelection. Briefly there was a boomlet for retired General Sherman, but Sherman effectively deflated the movement by issuing a famous one-sentence refusal: "If nominated, I will not accept; if elected, I will not serve." Sheridan, who had himself been mentioned as a candidate four years earlier, even receiving one delegate's vote at the 1880 convention (he promptly threw his minuscule support to Grant), remained on the sidelines this time around. Ironically, given his Catholic religion, the election between GOP nominee James G. Blaine and Democratic standard-bearer Grover Cleveland turned on the issue of Catholicism. Blaine, whose own mother was Catholic, had been fatally tarred by a campaign supporter's taunt at a New York City rally that the Democratic Party was the party of "Rum, Romanism, and Rebellion." Blaine subsequently lost New York by a razor-thin 1,149 votes out of over a million cast, and with New York, the election. Cleveland became the first Democrat elected president since James Buchanan in 1856.[29]

Surprisingly, the now-overweight Republican, Sheridan, got along well with the equally corpulent Democrat, Cleveland. Regulars at the White House quickly became used to the sight of the badly winded general trudging laboriously into the president's outer office, wheezing and mopping his brow, only to be ushered in to see the president ahead of other appointment holders. During his first months in office, Cleveland gladly drew upon Sheridan's assistance to help right a wrong being done to Cheyenne and Arapaho tribesmen by a consortium of western cattlemen in Indian Territory. The cattlemen, under a private agreement with the tribes, had leased millions of acres of reservation land at two cents an acre on which to graze their herds. Many of the Indians opposed the practice and refused to accept lease payments for their land. Cleveland, alarmed by the prospect of a new outbreak of western fighting, sent Sheridan to the reservation to meet with tribal chieftains and hear their side of the story. After listening to both Indians and cattlemen, Sheridan recommended that the president put a stop to the exploitative practice and summarily order the business interests off the reservation. Cleveland wired back that the cattlemen wanted a year to comply with such an order. Forty days was time enough, said Sheridan. That winter, in a grisly epilogue to an honorable act, eighty-five percent of the cattle died after being moved onto overcrowded ranges in Texas, Kansas, and Colorado.[30]

On another celebrated occasion during Cleveland's first term of office Sheridan broke ranks with the administration over a proposed plan by the government to return Confederate battle flags to the individual southern states. The seemingly innocuous plan was first suggested to the president by Secretary of War William C. Endicott, with whom Sheridan had clashed on a number of occasions. Endicott, in turn, had merely been following the recommendation of Adjutant General Richard C. Drum, who reported that the captured Rebel standards were taking up room and collecting dust in the basement of the War Department. Storming home one afternoon, Sheridan paced back and forth in front of his wife, sputtering about the "outrageous idea" of giving back the flags. The day was coming, he said, when their own children would have to listen to the federal government apologizing to the South for their father's misdeeds.[31]

As the first Democratic president since the start of the Civil War, Cleveland was already vulnerable to charges of pro-southern bias. No sooner had he signed on to Endicott's plan than the northern press, Republican politicians, and various Union veterans' groups ganged up to denounce the well-meaning gesture as a vile act of betrayal. "The Old Slave Whip Cracking Again," groused the *New York Tribune*, "Slapping the Veterans in the Face." Lucius Fairchild, national commander of the Grand Army of the Republic, then nearing its peak of 409,489 members, thundered, "May God palsy the hand that wrote that order . . . the brain that conceived it, and . . . the tongue that dictated it." Sheridan did not go that far, but his publicly expressed opposition helped persuade Cleveland to rescind the order. It would be well into the next century before the southern states got back their flags.[32]

For the most part, however, Sheridan stayed resolutely out

of the limelight, preferring to pass the time quietly with his wife and children in their handsome $44,000 home at the corner of Rhode Island Avenue and Seventeenth Street in northwest Washington, D.C. The structure had been purchased for Sheridan as a going-away present by a group of Chicago admirers when he left for Washington to take command of the army. His benefactors included longtime friend and traveling companion Anson Stager; meatpacking tycoon Philip D. Armour; sleeping-car wizard George M. Pullman; *Chicago Tribune* editor Joseph Medill; and department store maven Marshall Field. A few years earlier the same group had presented newborn infant Phil Sheridan, Jr., with a generous trust fund of telephone stock. It was their way of saying thank-you to Sheridan for his firm but calm actions during Chicago's Great Fire a decade earlier.[33]

Sheridan did attend one public event in early August 1885, in both a personal and professional capacity: the New York City funeral of his dear friend and patron, Ulysses S. Grant. The former president had died of throat cancer on July 23 after a gallant and successful effort to complete his two-volume military memoirs, which were soon to be published by Mark Twain's own publishing firm, Charles L. Webster & Company. Like the rest of the country, Sheridan had known for months that the general was dying, but he could not bring himself to visit Grant at his deathwatch in Mount McGregor, New York. Instead, he told friends, he wanted to remember Grant as he had been before the onset of his wasting illness. Now, together with Sherman and two former Confederate generals, Joseph Johnston and Simon Buckner, Sheridan rode in the five-hour funeral procession from New York's city hall, up Fifth Avenue, to Grant's temporary resting place in Riverside Park.[34]

With the passing of Grant, Sheridan lost the person who had been, in many ways, the most important figure in his life. The two Ohioans, so different in basic temperament, shared one crucial, defining characteristic: an absolute refusal to quit, coupled with an equally stubborn belief in their own essential rectitude.

Grant, in all his military career, admitted to second-guessing himself only once, for the suicidal attack at Cold Harbor. Sheridan, as he told the unfortunate Gouverneur Warren at Five Forks, never reconsidered his own orders. From the moment that he organized a hasty pursuit of retreating Confederates at Missionary Ridge, Sheridan had won Grant's heart, and nothing he did afterward—not even the virtually insubordinate position he took on the matter of opening a second front behind Lee's army in the fall of 1864—ever lost him that favor. To Grant he owed his promotion to cavalry commander, his free hand in the use of that command, and his subsequent advancement to head of the Army of the Shenandoah. There he had won his greatest fame, and there, too, burning farms and destroying crops, he had acquired his somewhat exaggerated reputation for cruelty. It was not a reputation that troubled Sheridan, but, as with Sherman's image after his notorious march to the sea, it had been acquired, for good or ill, in the commission of acts planned and ordered by Grant himself. Sheridan may have been, as Grant conceded, the more magnetic personality, but he was no more ruthless in waging war.

For his part, Sheridan had seldom disappointed Grant. Whether turning Lee's flank at Five Forks, smashing a fourth of his army at Sayler's Creek, or harrying him toward surrender at Appomattox, menacing the imperialist Maximilian in Mexico, or cracking down on civilians in the postwar South, Sheridan had willingly followed Grant's lead, even if—as in Louisiana—it sometimes had meant disobeying the president of the United States. For this he was rewarded with more promotions, more fame, and more responsibilities, until at last he reached the pinnacle of his soldierly profession and found, like Sherman, that it was powerless. Without Grant, Sheridan would have been merely a good Union divisional commander—all things considered, not a bad legacy—but it is doubtful he would have progressed beyond, at best, command of a corps. For one thing, Sherman was in his way. Grant changed that equation by bringing Sheridan east with him in 1864. And, unlike many who had benefited from Grant's self-destructive penchant for rewarding and advancing his personal friends, Sheridan had never forgotten him for it. Now Grant was dead.

A year later Sheridan lost another old friend—not to death this time, but to mutual bitterness and misunderstanding. Since the fall of 1882 George Crook had been commander of the Department of Arizona, charged with enforcing some semblance of peace on the often-intractable Apaches living there. Relying largely on Indian auxiliaries, Crook had managed by mid-1885 to coerce most of the Apache leaders, including the fearsome Geronimo, into settling on the San Carlos Reservation. But a renewed outbreak of raiding later that year, occasioned in part by unpopular agency prohibitions against Indians drinking, embarrassed Crook with the Cleveland administration and brought Sheridan west to confer with him. As always, Sheridan felt the solution to the problem lay in exiling the uncooperative Indians to Florida. Crook, who had spent years living among them and winning—as much as a white man could—their trust, disagreed with his friend. Sheridan grudgingly let Crook have his way, but after Geronimo and some of his supporters, hopped-up on mescal, escaped from camp while supposedly in the process of surrendering, Sheridan lost his celebrated temper and lectured Crook by telegraph, not without reason, on the need for taking better precautions.[35]

With twenty years' worth of resentment already inside him for Sheridan's supposedly unjust arrogation of battle honors at Winchester and Fisher's Hill (conveniently forgetting Sheridan's role in getting him promoted to major general and his atypically lenient reaction to Crook's long string of failures, from Cedar Creek to the Battle of the Rosebud), Crook abruptly offered to resign. Just as swiftly, Sheridan accepted. The nearly forty-year-long friendship, which in recent years had been decidedly one-sided in Sheridan's favor, disappeared overnight. After Geronimo was captured and shipped east by Crook's replacement, Brigadier General Nelson Miles, the erstwhile Indian-fighter joined the Indian Rights Association and campaigned tirelessly for Geronimo's return. Two years after Sheridan's death, and not long before his own, Crook was still speaking ill of his former friend.[36]

The campaign against Geronimo was about the only excitement, vicarious though it was, of Sheridan's brief stint as army commander. Increasingly now, it was the old battles of his youth he was refighting, imaginatively, on paper; he had undertaken to write his own memoirs for Grant's old publisher, Charles Webster & Company. The Twain-owned company had pretty much cornered the market on war memoirs, publishing, besides Grant's great volumes, reminiscences by George B. McClellan, Winfield Scott Hancock, and George Armstrong Custer's widow, Libbie, as well as a reprint of Sherman's memoirs. For a year and a half Sheridan worked diligently, if unenjoyably, at the task, closeting himself daily in his private study at the rear of the Rhode Island Avenue house.[37]

There, amid the relics of his eventful career—swords, pistols, medals, commissions, Indian war bonnets, Mexican sombreros, foreign coins of all denominations—the commanding general of the United States Army remembered his ungloried days as a dry-goods clerk, West Point cadet, and shavetail second lieutenant. He revisited in his mind the squalid army camps of prewar Texas and Oregon, the hilariously inept campaign against the Yakimas, his first brush with death at the Battle of the Cascades. And then, at great length, with great pride, he turned to recalling his Civil War: Missouri and Mississippi; his borrowed colonel's eagles; Booneville and Perryville; murderous Stones River; the terrible day at Chickamauga and the wonderful day at Missionary Ridge; Yellow Tavern, Haw's Shop, the Rapidan, the Wilderness. There was the Shenandoah Valley campaign—Winchester and Fisher's Hill and Cedar Creek (he underplayed his famous ride; others had already told it for him), Merritt and Custer, Early and Mosby, and Crook. Then east to join Grant, and Five Forks and Sayler's Creek and the breathless dash to Appomattox, John B. Gordon, James Longstreet, and Lee. The surrender scene in Wilmer McLean's parlor. And always the honor roll of the dead: David

Russell, Joshua Sill, Frederick Schaefer, George Roberts, William
Terrill, William Lytle, John Meigs, Henry Young. Good men,
young men, Union men, dead now—most of them—for a quarter
of a century.

Soon Sheridan would join them. He had been slipping for
several years, overweight, breathless, "a miserable dyspeptic,"
always flushed and often tired. In November 1887 army physician
Robert O'Reilly diagnosed his trouble as heart disease, specifically
a deterioration of the mitral and aortic valves. If there is a trace of
Grant's laconic style in Sheridan's own writings, perhaps it is
because, like Grant, he was racing against time and could not
afford to waste any of it on flowery descriptions or philosophical
asides. Or perhaps, again like Grant, he was merely plainspoken
and quick to the point. In any event, he completed the rough draft
of his manuscript with a lengthy description of the Franco-
Prussian War and sent it off to his publishers in New York in
March 1888. Two months later, after returning home from a tour
of the proposed site of Fort Sheridan, north of Chicago, he suffered a massive heart attack.[38]

Other attacks followed four days later, leading a priest to
administer last rites. But Sheridan, ever the fighter, rallied. "I
nearly got away from you that time, doctor," he joked at one
point. He had already dictated his will, leaving everything—such
as it was—to Irene and the children. Besides the houses in Washington and Chicago, the estate consisted of less than twenty thousand dollars in cash, stocks, and personal belongings. For a leading
figure of the Gilded Age, it was eloquent testimony to his personal
integrity.[39]

News of Sheridan's illness stunned the capital. He was, after
all, only fifty-seven. But hard living and hard campaigning, coupled with a lifelong love of good food and drink, had taken its toll
on Sheridan. His once-black hair had long since turned gray, and
his strange little figure, whippet-thin in his prime, had ballooned
to over two hundred pounds. A *New York World* reporter, professionally observant if typically unkind, wrote an unflattering

portrait of the general not long before his illness: "He wore upon the back of his round, bullet head an oldfashioned silk hat about two sizes too small; a short, light, yellow-gray overcoat which had only two buttons and they were ready to fly off from the undue strain of Sheridan's round figure. The trousers were a gray plaid and fitted very snugly to the General's fat legs." The stern soldier had become a variety-show comic.[40]

Acting quickly, Congress voted to revive the rank of four-star general, which Grant and Sherman had held before him. President Cleveland promptly signed the bill into law. A congressional delegation hand-delivered the commission to Sheridan's bedroom, where the general, though in pain, delighted in the news. His first and last order as general of the army was to promote brother Michael and Captains Sanford Kellogg and Stanhope Blunt to colonels on the general staff. Meanwhile, letters and telegrams poured in by the hundreds from old friends, comrades, and simple well-wishers.[41]

Thinking to ease Sheridan's discomfort and improve his spirits through a change of scene, the family decided—against doctors' wishes—to move the general from sweltering Washington to Nonquitt, Massachusetts, where he had recently built a vacation cottage. On June 30 Sheridan was carried downstairs from his home and driven by ambulance to the navy shipyard, where the steamship *Swatara* was waiting to transport him north. A *New York Times* reporter caught a glimpse of Sheridan, swaddled in blankets, a heavy dressing gown, and skullcap, as orderlies were inching him up the gangplank on a stretcher. "General Sheridan," he wrote, "was very pale and his face appeared to be almost as white as the pillow upon which his head rested. He was much emaciated." Two sisters from the Baltimore convent of the Order of Le Bon Secour, a nursing order, accompanied the patient on board the ship. Michael Sheridan and Irene also went with him.[42]

Throughout the nine-day ocean voyage—lengthened by a wait of several days at Fort Monroe for calmer seas—the press kept the nation breathlessly informed of Sheridan's condition.

Headlines were hopeful: "Said To Be Convalescent," "The Prospect Favorable," "Resting Comfortably." At one point, ship commander John McGowan, annoyed by the smaller vessels constantly heaving up alongside with shouting reporters, threatened personally to toss overboard any representative of the news media that he caught on his ship. This, too, was duly noted in the press.[43]

While waiting for Sheridan to arrive at Nonquitt, an exclusive if rather isolated resort on Buzzard's Bay, below New Bedford, *New York Times* reporters gave their readers a somewhat qualified description of the place. "It is really a very healthy place," the account began. "Before a week passes new arrivals lose their distinguishing marks, a healthy hue appears on faces that were white and tired looking, and in a few weeks you can hardly believe these same people ever could have a pain or ache. It is a great place for sleep." But even aside from the fact that Sheridan was unlikely to be doing any serious sunbathing at Nonquitt, the article presented a less than glowing recommendation of the town itself: "Just 50 or 60 very common looking summer cottages straggling in a crazy, irregular fashion. . . . It doesn't look like a village even, for there's only one road. . . . There have always been more or less artists and people with tendencies in that direction here."[44]

In truth, Nonquitt was an unlikely place for Sheridan to end his days, but the family had visited there the year before and liked it so well that they had constructed a new two-and-a-half-story redwood cottage a few hundred yards from the bay. On July 9 the *Swatara* finally reached Nonquitt, and a *Times* correspondent managed to walk alongside Sheridan's stretcher as he was being carried from the ship. "With his left hand, which is still plump and freckled," noted the reporter, "he held up the edge of the blanket to protect his eyes from the bright rays of the sun. His face is far from emaciated, but it is white, and the old-time ruddy look has disappeared. His cheeks had an unhealthy flush—in fact, they were almost purple—but his eyes were seemingly as bright as ever."[45]

Sheridan was carried inside his new vacation home, seeing it for the first time from his stretcher, and installed in a shuttered bedroom at the rear of the cottage. For another month he lay there, attended by his doctors, his wife, his brother, and the two nuns, Sister Justinia and Sister Urban. Colonel Kellogg and his wife brought up the children by train. And still the newspaper headlines were hopeful: "General Sheridan Improving," "His Appetite Improving," "Encouraging For Sheridan," "Sheridan Hopeful of Better Health." At one point the general (who had been on a strict milk diet) managed to eat some chicken and pork chops, but the *Times* scrupulously pointed out that "his increased appetite does not indicate that his condition is any the less critical, but merely that the fresh ocean breezes are having their natural effect upon his appetite." Only once was Sheridan allowed visitors, Mrs. Kellogg and his next-door neighbor at Nonquitt, C. F. Berend, who had kindly sent over some fresh-caught trout. It was too much for him. The man whose harsh, clipped voice had sent untold thousands charging into battle, from the Cascades in Washington state to Five Forks, Virginia, could not speak; tears streamed freely down his cheeks. After that, no other visitors were permitted to see him.[46]

On Sunday, August 5, Irene and Mike went to dinner at the Nonquitt Hotel, then looked in on Sheridan. He was resting comfortably. Ten minutes later, after his brother had taken his leave for the night, at 9:30 P.M., Sheridan suffered another massive heart attack. Doctors Robert O'Reilly and Washington Mathews worked frantically to save him, injecting Sheridan with digitalis and jolting him with electrical shocks, but it was no use. At 10:20 P.M., with his wife looking on and Sister Justinia praying beside him, Phil Sheridan died. A day earlier he had completed reading the proofs of his memoirs, remarking as he sent them off, "I hope that some of my old boys will find the book worth the purchase."[47]

Telegrams went out that night to the president and secretary of war, but in each case it was decided to wait until morning to wake them. The next day Sheridan lay in state in the front parlor of his never-to-be-enjoyed vacation cottage, while Colonel

Kellogg hurried to Washington to bring back the general's dress uniform and personal sword. At Mrs. Sheridan's wishes, a formal military funeral was planned, but pomp and ceremony were to be kept to a minimum. No veterans' groups or political organizations would be allowed to participate. Major General John Schofield, one of Sheridan's old classmates at West Point, now acting head of the army, was given charge of the services.[48]

The funeral mass was held at St. Matthew's Church, on the corner of Fifteenth and H streets, Northwest, in Washington on the morning of August 11, 1888. President and Mrs. Cleveland led the 1,500 invited mourners. William Sherman and Wesley Merritt were among the pallbearers. Former members of Sheridan's personal staff, including James Forsyth, Sandy Forsyth, John Schuyler Crosby, and Fred Grant, General Grant's son, were specially requested to attend, as was Michigan Governor Russell Alger, who had hand-delivered Sheridan's colonel's commission to him in Mississippi twenty-six years earlier. At the head of the coffin stood the red-and-white swallow-tailed flag Sheridan had carried along the front ranks at Cedar Creek. Behind the coffin were the blue cavalry guidon borne by his horsemen at Yellow Tavern and his old divisional flag from Perryville, Stones River, Chickamauga, and Missionary Ridge.[49]

The funeral oration was given by Cardinal Gibbons, who took as his text First Maccabees 9:19–21: "How is the mighty fallen that saved the people of Israel." Then the funeral procession moved out along Pennsylvania Avenue to Arlington National Cemetery, led by a battalion of cavalry from the Fourth and Sixth regiments. The general's horse, Guy, carried a riderless saddle with boots reversed in the stirrups (Rienzi had long since passed to his own reward). At the gravesite, a hundred paces from the front door of Robert E. Lee's old home at Arlington, Sheridan's coffin was laid to rest, while a bugler played taps and the military escort fired—a little raggedly, thought *The New York Times*—the traditional seventeen-gun salute for a general of the army. William Sherman wept.[50]

Phil Sheridan, Jr., eventually followed his father to West Point, where he graduated near the bottom of his class in 1902. He served as a lieutenant in the Fifth and Ninth cavalry regiments, and for two years was a military aide to President Theodore Roosevelt. When the United States entered World War I, the ever-combative Roosevelt sought permission from President Woodrow Wilson to raise a combat division for the front, to be led by himself and the sons or grandsons of such famous Civil War figures as Sheridan, Stonewall Jackson, James A. Garfield, Nathan Bedford Forrest, and Fitzhugh Lee. But Wilson respectfully declined, and Phil Sheridan, Jr., now a major, stayed in Washington with the general staff. Unhappily, he followed his father's lead in another way, dying of heart trouble on February 17, 1918, at the early age of thirty-seven.[51]

Following the unveiling of Sheridan's statue in November 1908, Mrs. Sheridan and the three girls moved from their Rhode Island Avenue home to a house at 2551 Massachusetts Avenue, Northwest, in order to be near the general's monument. From time to time, the still-young widow was rumored to be planning another marriage, but she effectively quashed such speculation with the unambiguous declaration, "I would rather be the widow of Phil Sheridan than the wife of any man living." She never did remarry, dying in 1938 after an even fifty years of widowhood. None of the three girls ever married, either, though all lived well into their eighties. Each morning, so the story goes, they would lean out their bedroom window and call to their father's statue, "Good morning, Papa!" But Phil Sheridan never heard them. He was busy rallying his army at Cedar Creek.[52]

NOTES

Chapter 1

1. *New York Times*, 26 November 1908. *Chicago Daily Tribune*, 26 November 1908. *Washington Post*, 26 November 1908.

2. *Washington Post*, 26 November 1908. *New York Times*, 26 November 1908.

3. *Washington Post*, 26 November 1908. Myrtle M. Murdock, *Your Memorials in Washington* (Washington, D.C.: Monumental Press, 1952), 25. Robert J. Casey and Mary Borglum, *Give the Man Room* (Indianapolis: Bobbs-Merrill, 1952), 99–100.

4. U.S. War Department, *The War of the Rebellion: A Compilation of the Official Records of the Union and Confederate Armies*, vol. 43, pt. 1 (Washington, D.C.: U.S. Government Printing Office, 1880–1901), 53; hereafter cited as *OR*. Casey and Borglum, *Give the Man Room*, 100. Stephen Z. Starr, *The Union Cavalry in the Civil War*, vol. 2 (Baton Rouge: Louisiana State University Press, 1981), 312.

5. Richard J. O'Connor, *Sheridan the Inevitable* (Indianapolis: Bobbs-Merrill, 1953), 18–19, 361. Boyd B. Stutler, ed., "Notes & Queries," *Civil War History* (June 1960), 192–93. Shelby Foote, *The Civil War: A Narrative*, vol. 1 (New York: Random House, 1958–74), 732.

6.   Philip H. Sheridan, *Personal Memoirs of P. H. Sheridan*, vol. 1
        (New York: Charles L. Webster & Co., 1888), 1. O'Connor,
        Sheridan, 18–19.

7.   O'Connor, *Sheridan*, 20–21.

8.   Henry C. Greiner, *General Phil Sheridan As I Knew Him* (Chi-
        cago: J. S. Hyland, 1908), 350. O'Connor, *Sheridan*, 22. Frank
        A. Burr and Richard J. Hinton, *The Life of General Philip H.
        Sheridan: Its Romance and Reality* (Providence, R.I.: J. A. and
        R. A. Reid Publishers, 1888), 24.

9.   Burr and Hinton, *Life of Sheridan*, 34.

10.   O'Connor, *Sheridan*, 29. Lloyd Lewis, *Sherman: Fighting
        Prophet* (New York: Harcourt, Brace, 1932), 47. Greiner, *Phil
        Sheridan*, 19.

11.   Greiner, *Phil Sheridan*, 353. O'Connor, *Sheridan*, 23–24. Sheri-
        dan, *Memoirs*, 1:1, 3–5

12.   O'Connor, *Sheridan*, 27. Greiner, *Phil Sheridan*, 14–15.

13.   Sheridan, *Memoirs*, 1:5–7.

14.   Ibid., 7, 19. Lawrence Frost, *The Phil Sheridan Album: A Pic-
        torial Biography of Philip Henry Sheridan* (Seattle: Superior
        Publishing Co., 1968), 13.

15.   Sheridan, *Memoirs*, 1:7–8. D. S. Stanley, *Personal Memoirs of
        Major-General D. S. Stanley, U.S.A.* (Cambridge: Harvard
        University Press, 1917), 17–18.

16.   Ibid., 8–9. James L. Morrison, Jr., *The Best School in the
        World: West Point, the Pre-Civil War Years, 1833–1866* (Kent,
        Ohio: Kent State University Press, 1986), 65–66. *Official Reg-
        ister of the Officers and Cadets of the U.S. Military Academy*,
        West Point, New York, June 1853, 7.

17.   Stephen E. Ambrose, *Duty, Honor, Country: A History of
        West Point* (Baltimore: Johns Hopkins University Press, 1966),
        152. Morrison, *Best School*, 65–71.

18.   Morrison, *Best School*, 66–68. Sheridan, *Memoirs*, 1:9.

19.   Morrison, *Best School*, 106. Sheridan, *Memoirs*, 1:10–11.

20. Ambrose, *Duty, Honor, Country*, 149–54. Morrison, *Best School*, 81.

21. Morrison, *Best School*, 81–82. Francis F. McKinney, *Education in Violence: The Life of George H. Thomas and the History of the Army of the Cumberland* (Detroit: Wayne State University Press, 1961), 12.

22. Ambrose, *Duty, Honor, Country*, 153. Quoted in William S. McFeely, *Grant: A Biography* (New York and London: W. W. Norton, 1982), 16.

23. John W. Masland and Laurence I. Radway, *Soldiers and Scholars: Military Education and National Policy* (Princeton: Princeton University Press, 1957), 76–78. McKinney, *Education in Violence*, 14. Morrison, *Best School*, 131–32, 174–82. Edward M. Coffman, *The Old Army: A Portrait of the American Army in Peacetime, 1784–1898* (New York and Oxford: Oxford University Press, 1986), 46–47.

24. McFeely, *Grant*, 15. Morrison, *Best School*, 152. Coffman, *Old Army*, 231. U. S. Grant, *Personal Memoirs of U. S. Grant*, vol. 1 (New York: Charles L. Webster, 1885–86), 44.

25. Morrison, *Best School*, 94–96. McKinney, *Education in Violence*, 19. Ambrose, *Duty, Honor, Country*, 99–102. See also Russell F. Weigley, *Towards an American Army: Military Thought from Washington to Marshall* (New York: Columbia University Press, 1962), 38–53.

26. McFeely, *Grant*, 16. Morrison, *Best School*, 76–77. O'Connor, *Sheridan*, 34.

27. Sheridan, *Memoirs*, 1:11–12. William R. Terrill to Bradford R. Alden, 9 September 1851, "Report of the Arrest of Cadet Sheridan to Chief Engineer," Old Army Branch, Record Group 94, National Archives, Washington, D.C.

28. Terrill to Alden, 10 September 1851. Sheridan to Alden, 9 September, 1851, "Report of the Arrest of Cadet Sheridan." Sheridan, *Memoirs*, 1:12.

29. *Official Register of the Officers and Cadets of the U.S. Military Academy, First Class, 1853*, 7–8. O'Connor, *Sheridan*, 37–38.

Robert E. Lee, Roll of 1st Class, 30 June 1853, Old Army Branch, Record Group 94, National Archives.

30. Sheridan, *Memoirs*, 1:31. Robert M. Utley, *Frontiersmen in Blue: The United States Army and the Indian, 1848–1865* (New York: Macmillan, 1967), 11–12, 18.

31. Utley, *Frontiersmen in Blue*, 13, 18.

32. Ibid., 31–34. Coffman, *Old Army*, 59.

33. Utley, *Frontiersmen in Blue*, 38–41. Coffman, *Old Army*, 137–41.

34. Sheridan, *Memoirs*, 1:15–19.

35. Ibid., 20–24.

36. Ibid., 25–27. Richard W. Johnson, *A Soldier's Reminiscences in Peace and War* (Philadelphia: J. P. Lippincott, 1886), 85.

37. Sheridan, *Memoirs*, 1:28–34.

38. Ibid., 29–30.

39. Ibid., 35. Edward S. Curtis, *The North American Indian*, vol. 7 (New York: Johnson Reprint Corp., 1970), 14.

40. Curtis, *North American Indian*, 14–18. Utley, *Frontiersmen in Blue*, 179.

41. Curtis, *North American Indian*, 20–21. Utley, *Frontiersmen in Blue*, 180.

42. Curtis, *North American Indian*, 21–23. Utley, *Frontiersmen in Blue*, 181.

43. Sheridan, *Memoirs*, 1:36, 44–45. For the elite Second Cavalry Regiment, see Roy Morris, Jr., "Cavalry Blooded," *Wild West* (December 1990), 34–40.

44. O'Connor, *Sheridan*, 46. Sheridan, *Memoirs*, 1:53–54. Utley, *Frontiersmen in Blue*, 189.

45. Sheridan, *Memoirs*, 1:54–56.

46. Ibid., 57–62.

47. Ibid., 62–64.

48.   Ibid., 66–69.

49.   Ibid., 69–72. Utley, *Frontiersmen in Blue*, 191–93. J. P. Dunn, Jr., *Massacres of the Mountains: A History of the Indian Wars of the Far West, 1815–1875* (New York: Archer House, 1886), 182–83.

50.   Sheridan, *Memoirs*, 1:72–74. Dunn, *Massacres of the Mountains*, 185–86.

51.   Sheridan, *Memoirs*, 1:74–76.

52.   Ibid., 76–84.

53.   Ibid., 83–84, 89.

54.   Ibid., 85–90. Dunn, *Massacres of the Mountains*, 186.

55.   O'Connor, *Sheridan*, 51.

56.   Sheridan, *Memoirs*, 1:90–98.

57.   Ibid., 99–104.

58.   This exchange is in *Letters Received by the Office of the Adjutant General, Main Series, 1822–1870*, April 1857, National Archives.

59.   Grace E. Cooper, "Benton County Pioneer-Historical Society," *Oregon Historical Quarterly* 57 (March 1956), 83–84. Sheridan to U. S. Grant, 19 January 1869, Philip H. Sheridan Papers, Manuscript Division, Library of Congress, Washington, D.C. Sheridan, *Memoirs*, 1:106–8.

60.   Sheridan, *Memoirs*, 1:108–10.

61.   Ibid., 110–11.

62.   Ibid., 111–20.

Chapter 2

1.   Whitelaw Reid, *Ohio in the War*, vol. 1 (Cincinnati: Moore, Wilstach & Baldwin, 1868), 500.

2.   Sheridan, *Memoirs*, 1:123.

3. Ibid., 120.

4. Ibid., 121. Patricia L. Faust, ed., *Historical Times Illustrated Encyclopedia of the Civil War* (New York: Harper & Row, 1986), 21–22.

5. Sheridan, *Memoirs*, 1:122–25. Greiner, *Phil Sheridan*, 77.

6. Sheridan, *Memoirs*, 1:125–26. William E. Parrish, "Fremont in Missouri," *Civil War Times Illustrated* (April 1978), 9. Roy P. Basler, ed., *Collected Works of Abraham Lincoln*, vol. 4 (New Brunswick: Rutgers University Press, 1953–55), 506.

7. Parrish, "Fremont in Missouri," 44.

8. Edward G. Longacre, "A Profile of General Justus McKinstry," *Civil War Times Illustrated* (July 1978), 18–19.

9. Sheridan, *Memoirs*, 1:126–27. Longacre, "Profile of McKinstry," 15.

10. Sheridan, *Memoirs*, 1:127.

11. Ibid., 129. Grenville Dodge, *The Battle of Atlanta and Other Campaigns* (Council Bluffs, Iowa: Monarch Printing Co., 1911), 139.

12. Dodge, *Battle of Atlanta*, 16. Sheridan, *Memoirs*, 1:129–30.

13. Sheridan, *Memoirs*, 1:131. Thomas W. Knox, *Camp-Fire and Cotton-Field: Southern Adventure in Time of War* (New York: Blelock, 1865), 123.

14. Faust, *Illustrated Encyclopedia*, 585. See also Randy Krehbiel, "Indians Blue and Gray," *America's Civil War* (January 1991), 30–36.

15. For Battle of Pea Ridge, see George T. Wilson, "Battle for Missouri," *America's Civil War* (January 1990), 27–32. Richard O'Connor, *Wild Bill Hickok* (New York: Doubleday, 1959), 55–61.

16. Wilson, "Battle for Missouri," 30–31. Foote, *The Civil War*, 1:285–88.

17. Foote, *The Civil War*, 1:291.

18.   Sheridan, *Memoirs*, 1:133. Sheridan to Curtis, 10 March 1862, *Letters Received, Southwest District of Missouri*, National Archives.

19.   Sheridan, *Memoirs*, 1:133–34. Sheridan to F. J. McKinney, 5 March 1862, Philip H. Sheridan, *Synopsis of Military Service*. Curtis to Thomas Allen, 11 March 1862, *Register of Letters Received, Southwest District of Missouri*, National Archives.

20.   Sheridan, *Memoirs*, 1:133.

21.   Curtis to Nathaniel H. McLean, 17 March 1862, *Register of Letters Received, Southwest District of Missouri*, National Archives.

22.   Dodge, *Battle of Atlanta*, 29–30. Sheridan, *Memoirs*, 1:135.

23.   Sheridan, *Memoirs*, 1:135–36.

24.   Foote, *The Civil War*, 1:334.

25.   Ibid., 351. Grant, *Memoirs*, 1:368–69.

26.   Sheridan, *Memoirs*, 1:136–37.

27.   Dodge, *Battle of Atlanta*, 29. Sheridan, *Memoirs*, 1:137.

28.   Sheridan, *Memoirs*, 1:137. McFeely, *Grant*, 119.

29.   Foote, *The Civil War*, 1:376. Stephen Z. Starr, "The Second Michigan Cavalry: Another View," *Michigan History* 60 (1976), 170.

30.   Sheridan, *Memoirs*, 1:137–39.

31.   Ibid., 139. O'Connor, *Sheridan*, 61.

32.   Sheridan, *Memoirs*, 1:140. Starr, "Second Michigan," 163.

33.   Sheridan, *Memoirs*, 1:140–41. O'Connor, *Sheridan*, 62.

34.   Sheridan, *Memoirs*, 1:141.

35.   Ibid., 141–43.

36.   Ibid., 144–45. Mark M. Boatner III, *The Civil War Dictionary* (New York: David McKay Co., 1959), 263. Stephen Z. Starr, "Hawkeyes on Horseback: The Second Iowa Cavalry," *Civil War History* 23 (1977), 212.

37.   Sheridan, *Memoirs*, 1:145. *OR*, 10, pt. 1, 861–62.

38.   Sheridan, *Memoirs*, 1:145–57. *OR*, 10, pt. 1, 861–62.

39.   Sheridan, *Memoirs*, 1:148. Foote, *The Civil War*, 1:381–84.

40.   *OR*, 10, pt. 1, 863–67. Beauregard to *Mobile Evening News*, 17 June 1862, Beauregard Papers, Library of Congress. Sheridan, *Memoirs*, 1:149–50.

41.   *Cincinnati Commercial*, 9 June 1862. Dodge comment in Sheridan Papers, reel 101, Library of Congress. *OR*, 10, pt. 1, 863–65. Sheridan, *Memoirs*, 1:149.

42.   Sheridan, *Memoirs*, 1:150.

43.   Ibid., 150–52.

44.   *OR*, 10, pt. 1, 733. Sheridan Papers, reel 1, Library of Congress.

45.   Sheridan, *Memoirs*, 1:153–54. Foote, *The Civil War*, 1:385–86.

46.   Foote, *The Civil War*, 1:542. Starr, *Union Cavalry*, 3:64.

47.   Sheridan, *Memoirs*, 1:153–54.

48.   Ibid., 155. For Rosecrans, see William M. Lamers, *The Edge of Glory: A Biography of William S. Rosecrans, U.S.A.* (New York: Harcourt, Brace & World, 1961).

49.   Sheridan, *Memoirs*, 1:156. Faust, *Illustrated Encyclopedia*, 124.

50.   Sheridan, *Memoirs*, 1:156–58. *OR*, 17, pt. 2, 62.

51.   Sheridan, *Memoirs*, 1:156. Starr, *Union Cavalry*, 3:65–66.

52.   Sheridan, *Memoirs*, 1:158–60. *OR*, 17, pt. 1, 19–20.

53.   Sheridan, *Memoirs*, 1:160–61.

54.   Ibid., 162–63. An account of Alger's role is in Sheridan Papers, reel 101, Library of Congress.

55.   Sheridan, *Memoirs*, 1:163–64. *OR*, 17, pt. 2, 63.

56.   *OR*, 17, pt. 1, 20. For Alger's postwar career, see Sidney Glazer, *Detroit: A Study in Urban Development* (New York: Bookman Associates, Inc., 1965), 59; and G. J. A. O'Toole, *The Spanish War* (New York: W. W. Norton, 1984), 376.

57.   Faust, *Illustrated Encyclopedia*, 71. *OR*, 17, pt. 1, 18, 66, 76.

58.   Sheridan, *Memoirs*, 1:167–71.

59.   *OR*, 17, pt. 2, 231.

60.   Ibid., 139.

61.   Edward L. Volpe, *A Reader's Guide to William Faulkner* (New York: Noonday Press, 1964), 7. Sheridan, *Memoirs*, 1:175–77. *OR*, 17, pt. 1, 41.

62.   Volpe, *Reader's Guide*, 8. See also Victor Hoar, "Colonel William C. Falkner in the Civil War," *Journal of Mississippi History* 27 (February 1965), 42–62.

63.   *OR*, 17, pt. 1, 40–42.

64.   Ibid., 42. Sheridan, *Memoirs*, 1:177–80.

65.   Foote, *The Civil War*, 1:582.

66.   *OR*, 16, pt. 2, 497. *OR*, 17, pt. 2, 200.

Chapter 3

1.   Sheridan, *Memoirs*, 1:181–82.

2.   McFeeley, *Grant*, 18, 52–54. Grant, *Memoirs*, 1:122.

3.   Sheridan, *Memoirs*, 1:181. Grant, *Memoirs*, 1:402–3.

4.   Sheridan, *Memoirs*, 1:182–83.

5.   Foote, *The Civil War*, 1:652–54. See also Roy Morris, Jr., "Battle in the Blue Grass," *Civil War Times Illustrated* (December 1988), 15–23.

6.   Sheridan, *Memoirs*, 1:184. *OR*, 16, pt. 2, 510.

7.   Sheridan, *Memoirs*, 1:184–86.

8.   *Louisville Journal*, 1 September 1862. Robert Emmett McDowell, *City in Conflict: Louisville in the Civil War, 1861–1865* (Louisville: Louisville Civil War Round Table Publishers, 1962), 81. *OR*, 16, pt. 2, 469. Sheridan, *Memoirs*, 1:188–89.

9.   *OR*, 16, pt. 2, 822–23.

10. Kenneth A. Hafendorfer, *Perryville: Battle for Kentucky* (Utica, Ky.: McDowell Publications, 1981), 58. *OR*, 23, pt. 2, 471. For Turchin, see Roy Morris, Jr., "The Sack of Athens," *Civil War Times Illustrated* (February 1986), 26–32.

11. Sheridan, *Memoirs*, 1:190–92.

12. McDowell, *City in Conflict*, 86. *Louisville Journal*, 24 September 1862.

13. James B. Fry, *Killed by a Brother Soldier* (New York: G. P. Putnam's Sons, 1885), 486. See also James P. Jones, Jr., " 'Bull' and the 'Damned Puppy,' " *American History Illustrated* (November 1972), 12–21.

14. *OR*, 16, pt. 2, 539, 555.

15. Sheridan, *Memoirs*, 1:189–90. *OR*, 16, pt. 1, 662–65. Faust, *Illustrated Encyclopedia*, 310.

16. Sheridan, *Memoirs*, 1:191–92. Hafendorfer, *Perryville*, 77. *OR*, 16, pt. 1, 1019–20. Faust, *Illustrated Encyclopedia*, 818.

17. Hafendorfer, *Perryville*, 83. McDowell, *City in Conflict*, 108.

18. General Order No. 4, Headquarters 11th Divison, 2 October 1862, Sheridan Papers, Library of Congress.

19. L. G. Bennett and W. M. Haigh, *History of the 36th Regiment Illinois Volunteers* (Aurora, Ill.: Knickerbocker & Hodder, 1876), 240–41.

20. Ibid., 244–45.

21. Hafendorfer, *Perryville*, 80–81.

22. Sheridan, *Memoirs*, 1:193–94. *OR*, 16, pt. 1, 238, 1081–83.

23. *OR*, 16, pt. 1, 238–39, 1158.

24. Ibid., 239, 1081–83. Sheridan, *Memoirs*, 1:194–95.

25. *OR*, 16, pt. 1, 239, 1037. Sheridan, *Memoirs*, 1:194.

26. *OR*, 16, pt. 1, 1158. Sheridan, *Memoirs*, 1:195.

27. Clarence C. Buel and Robert U. Johnson, eds., *Battles and Leaders of the Civil War*, vol. 3 (New York: Castle Books, 1956), 53.

28. Sheridan, *Memoirs*, 1:195–96. *OR*, 16, pt. 1, 667. *Louisville Journal*, 13 October 1862.

29. *OR*, 16, pt. 1, 90. Sheridan, *Memoirs*, 1:12–13. Buel and Johnson, *Battles and Leaders*, 3:57.

30. Hafendorfer, *Perryville*, 234. *OR*, 16, pt. 1, 1060. For Terrill, see James M. Hillard, "You Are Strangely Deluded," *Civil War Times Illustrated* (February 1975), 12–18.

31. Bennett and Haigh, *Thirty-Sixth Illinois*, 259. W. T. Blakemore, "Portrait of Lytle," *Confederate Veteran*, 5:249.

32. Buel and Johnson, *Battles and Leaders*, 3:57.

33. *OR*, 16, pt. 1, 557, 1072, 1076.

34. Bennett and Haigh, *Thirty-Sixth Illinois*, 264–68.

35. Ibid., 270–72. Sheridan, *Memoirs*, 1:197. *OR*, 16, pt. 1, 283.

36. Sheridan, *Memoirs*, 1:198–99.

37. Ibid., 199.

38. *OR*, 16, pt. 1, 1036. Sheridan, *Memoirs*, 1:201. Sam R. Watkins, "*Co. Aytch*" (New York: Collier Books, 1962), 61.

39. Sheridan, *Memoirs*, 1:200–203.

40. Ibid., 203.

41. Lamers, *Edge of Glory*, 182. James Lee McDonough, *Stones River: Bloody Winter in Tennessee* (Knoxville: University of Tennessee Press, 1980), 41.

42. Lamers, *Edge of Glory*, 444. Reid, *Ohio in the War*, 1:323.

43. Sheridan, *Memoirs*, 1:203–4.

44. Ibid., 206. Lamers, *Edge of Glory*, 190. McDonough, *Stones River*, 60. Bruce Catton, *This Hallowed Ground* (New York: Doubleday, 1956), 251.

45. Sheridan, *Memoirs*, 1:206.

46. Ibid., 206–9.

47. Ibid., 209.

48. Edwin B. Parsons, "Sheridan," *War Papers: Commandery of the State of Wisconsin, Military Order of the Loyal Legion of the United States* (1891), 176. Quoted in O'Connor, *Sheridan*, 85–86.

49. McDonough, *Stones River*, 56. *OR*, 20, pt. 2, 117–18.

50. Lamers, *Edge of Glory*, 195–96.

51. Ibid., 200–201.

52. McDonough, *Stones River*, 69. *OR*, 20, pt. 2, 248. Roger Thomas Zeimet, "Philip H. Sheridan and the Civil War in the West" (Ph.D. dissertation, Marquette University, 1981), 219.

53. Lamers, *Edge of Glory*, 214. Sheridan, *Memoirs*, 1:220–22.

54. Sheridan, *Memoirs*, 1:222.

55. Quoted in Foote, *The Civil War*, 2:87.

56. Ibid. Lamers, *Edge of Glory*, 220.

57. McDonough, *Stones River*, 99. Sheridan, *Memoirs*, 1:222–23. Lamers, *Edge of Glory*, 220.

58. Sheridan, *Memoirs*, 1:225.

59. Ibid., 227–28. Lamers, *Edge of Glory*, 220.

60. *OR*, 20, pt. 1, 351.

61. Sheridan, *Memoirs*, 1:227. Reid, *Ohio in the War*, 1:505–6.

62. Sheridan, *Memoirs*, 1:210. McDonough, *Stones River*, 157.

63. Sheridan, *Memoirs*, 1:231.

64. Lamers, *Edge of Glory*, 227.

65. Ibid., 225. Sheridan, *Memoirs*, 1:235.

66. *OR*, 20, pt. 1, 545.

67. Lamers, *Edge of Glory*, 237. Sheridan, *Memoirs*, 1:237–38.

68. Sheridan, *Memoirs*, 1:242–43. Quoted in O'Connor, *Sheridan*, 99.

69. *OR*, 20, pt. 1, 198, 257.

Chapter 4

1. Lamers, *Edge of Glory*, 245, 247. Sheridan, *Memoirs*, 1:246. Basler, *Collected Works of Lincoln*, 6:424.

2. Sheridan, *Memoirs*, 1:240–41.

3. Lamers, *Edge of Glory*, 253.

4. Sheridan, *Memoirs*, 1:252–55.

5. Ibid., 247–52.

6. Lamers, *Edge of Glory*, 254. O'Connor, *Sheridan*, 102. Sheridan, *Memoirs*, 1:256.

7. Sheridan, *Memoirs*, 1:258. Faust, *Illustrated Encyclopedia*, 778.

8. *OR*, 23, pt. 2, 83. Sheridan, *Memoirs*, 1:247. Parsons, "Sheridan," 276–77.

9. Sheridan, *Memoirs*, 1:256. For Lytle, see Roy Morris, Jr., "I Am Dying, Egypt, Dying," *Civil War Times Illustrated* (October 1986), 24–31.

10. Lamers, *Edge of Glory*, 251. John Beatty, *Memoirs of a Volunteer* (New York: Norton, 1946), 239. Glenn Tucker, *Chickamauga: Bloody Battle in the West* (Indianapolis: Bobbs Merrill, 1961), 46–51.

11. *OR*, 30, pt. 1, 601–3.

12. Sheridan, *Memoirs*, 1:259–60. Lamers, *Edge of Glory*, 270.

13. *OR*, 23, pt. 1, 8. Lamers, *Edge of Glory*, 272.

14. Sheridan, *Memoirs*, 1:267–70.

15. *OR*, 23, pt. 2, 518. Lamers, *Edge of Glory*, 291.

16. *OR*, 23 pt. 2, 552, 592, 601–2. Lamers, *Edge of Glory*, 297.

17. O'Connor, *Sheridan*, 105–6. The exchange between Sheridan and Rosecrans is quoted in Zeimet, "Philip H. Sheridan," 322–23.

18. Sheridan, *Memoirs*, 1:272–73. Lamers, *Edge of Glory*, 303.

19. Sheridan, *Memoirs*, 1:273–76.

20.   Charles A. Dana, *Recollections of the Civil War* (New York: Appleton, 1898), 107. For Dana and Rosecrans, see Roy Morris, Jr., "A Bird of Evil Omen: The War Department's Charles Dana," *Civil War Times Illustrated* (January 1987), 20–29.

21.   Greiner, *Phil Sheridan*, 232–33.

22.   Tucker, *Chickamauga*, 130.

23.   Sheridan, *Memoirs*, 1:276–78.

24.   John W. Rowell, *Yankee Artilleryman: Through the Civil War with Eli Lilly's Indiana Battery* (Knoxville: University of Tennessee Press, 1975), 117–18. Tucker, *Chickamauga*, 174.

25.   Sheridan, *Memoirs*, 1:279. *OR*, 30, pt. 1, 191.

26.   Lamers, *Edge of Glory*, 334–35. Tucker, *Chickamauga*, 195–98. Dana, *Recollections*, 113–15. Lester L. Swift, "The Preacher Regiment at Chickamauga and Missionary Ridge," *Lincoln Herald* (Summer 1970), 55.

27.   Tucker, *Chickamauga*, 203. Dana, *Recollections*, 114–15.

28.   Tucker, *Chickamauga*, 253–54. Lamers, *Edge of Glory*, 342–43.

29.   Tucker, *Chickamauga*, 254.

30.   Lamers, *Edge of Glory*, 348–49. Tucker, *Chickamauga*, 267–69.

31.   Tucker, *Chickamauga*, 293. Morris, "I Am Dying, Egypt, Dying," 30.

32.   Charles Eugene Belknap, *History of the Michigan Organizations at Chickamauga, Chattanooga, and Missionary Ridge* (Lansing, Mich.: R. Smith Publishing, 1897), 54. Tucker, *Chickamauga*, 295. Robert S. Walker, "Pyramids at Chickamauga," *Chattanooga Times*, 13 September 1936.

33.   Sheridan, *Memoirs*, 1:282–83. *OR*, 30, pt. 1, 580. Tucker, *Chickamauga*, 307.

34.   Sheridan, *Memoirs*, 1:283.

35.   Lamers, *Edge of Glory*, 353–55. Tucker, *Chickamauga*, 311–14. For Garfield's role at Chickamauga, see John Taylor, "With

More Sorrow Than I Can Tell," *Civil War Times Illustrated* (April 1981), 20–29.

36.   *OR*, 30, pt. 1, 142–43.

37.   Ibid., 580–81. Sheridan, *Memoirs*, 1:283–84. Tucker, *Chickamauga*, 304.

38.   John B. Turchin, *Chickamauga* (Chicago: Fergus Printing Co., 1888), 29–30.

39.   Tucker, *Chickamauga*, 315–19; Samuel C. Williams, *General John T. Wilder, Commander of the Lightning Brigade* (Bloomington: Indiana University Press, 1936), 34.

40.   Buel and Johnson, *Battles and Leaders*, 3:663–65.

41.   Thomas B. Van Horne, *History of the Army of the Cumberland* (Cincinnati: Robert Clarke & Co., 1875), 375. *OR*, 30, pt. 1, 581. Sheridan, *Memoirs*, 1:283–84.

42.   Donn Piatt, *General George H. Thomas: A Critical Biography* (Cincinnati: Robert Clarke & Co., 1893), 431. Archibald Gracie, Jr., *The Truth About Chickamauga* (Boston: Houghton Mifflin, 1911), 116–31.

43.   *OR*, 30, pt. 1, 38.

44.   Sheridan, *Memoirs*, 1:286–88.

45.   Tucker, *Chickamauga*, 392.

46.   Lamers, *Edge of Glory*, 443. Dana, *Recollections*, 122–23. Morris, "Bird of Evil Omen," 27–29.

47.   Basler, *Collected Works of Lincoln*, 6:498, 510.

48.   Foote, *The Civil War*, 2:804. John Wilson, *Chattanooga's Story* (Chattanooga: Chattanooga Publishing Co., 1980), 99. Sheridan, *Memoirs*, 1:295.

49.   Lamers, *Edge of Glory*, 386. Grant, *Memoirs*, 2:24–26.

50.   McKinney, *Education in Violence*, 273–74. *OR*, 30, pt. 4, 479.

51.   Henry Halleck to Grant, 20 October 1863, William T. Sherman Papers, Library of Congress. Sheridan, *Memoirs*, 1:301.

52.   Sheridan, *Memoirs*, 1:301–2.

53. Foote, *The Civil War*, 2:836. James L. McDonough, *Chattanooga—A Death Grip on the Confederacy* (Knoxville: University of Tennessee Press, 1984), 106–8. *OR*, 31, pt. 2, 216.

54. McDonough, *Chattanooga*, 63–64. Thomas F. Connelly, *Autumn of Glory: The Army of Tennessee, 1862–1865* (Baton Rouge: Louisiana State University Press, 1967), 247–50.

55. *OR*, 31, pt. 2, 24, 136. Sheridan, *Memoirs*, 1:303–6.

56. Lewis, *Sherman*, 320. McDonough, *Chattanooga*, 153–54.

57. *OR*, 31, pt. 2, 44. Foote, *The Civil War*, 2:850.

58. McKinney, *Education in Violence*, 294.

59. *OR*, 31, pt. 2, 131. Foote, *The Civil War*, 2:853. Zeimet, "Philip H. Sheridan," 433.

60. Sheridan, *Memoirs*, 1:310. Adam Badeau, "Lieut.-General Sheridan," *Century Magazine* 27 (February 1884), 500. Glenn Tucker, "The Battles for Chattanooga," *Civil War Times Illustrated* (September 1971), 39.

61. *OR*, 31, pt. 2, 190. Buel and Johnson, *Battles and Leaders*, 3:725.

62. Buel and Johnson, *Battles and Leaders*, 3:725.

63. Sheridan, *Memoirs*, 1:312–13. McDonough, *Chattanooga*, 202. Foote, *The Civil War*, 2:856–57. Buel and Johnson, *Battles and Leaders*, 3:726.

64. *OR*, 31, pt. 2, 68. Foote, *The Civil War*, 2:859.

65. *OR*, 31, pt. 2, 191–92. Sheridan, *Memoirs*, 1:313–15.

66. Buel and Johnson, *Battles and Leaders*, 3:707. *OR*, 31, pt. 2, 81, 192–93.

67. *OR*, 31, pt. 2, 192. Sheridan, *Memoirs*, 1:320. O'Connor, *Sheridan*, 140.

Chapter 5

1. Horace Porter, *Campaigning with Grant* (New York: The Century Co., 1897), 18–19.

2. Sheridan, *Memoirs*, 1:335.

3. Ibid., 328–30.

4. Ibid., 336. O'Connor, *Sheridan*, 144.

5. *OR*, 32, pt. 3, 122. Adam Badeau, *Grant in Peace* (Hartford: S. S. Scranton & Co., 1887), 531–32.

6. Sheridan, *Memoirs*, 1:341.

7. Ibid., 342. Starr, *Union Cavalry*, 2:245. Grant, *Memoirs*, 2:133.

8. Sheridan, *Memoirs*, 1:344–46.

9. Ibid., 346–47.

10. Ibid., 339. Henry E. Davies, *General Sheridan* (New York: D. Appleton & Co., 1909), 92–93. Grant, *Memoirs*, 2:133.

11. Starr, *Union Cavalry*, 2:13–14, 58–65. For Dahlgren-Kilpatrick Raid, see James O. Hall, "Fact or Fabrication? The Dahlgren Papers. A Yankee Plot to Kill President Davis," *Civil War Times Illustrated* (November 1983), 30–39.

12. Davies, *General Sheridan*, 93–95.

13. Starr, *Union Cavalry*, 2:75. O'Connor, *Sheridan*, 165. Benjamin W. Crowninshield, "Sheridan at Winchester," *Atlantic Monthly* 42 (1878), 690.

14. O'Connor, *Sheridan*, 151. *OR*, 32, pt. 3, 246.

15. *OR*, 33, pt. 2, 891–92.

16. Sheridan, *Memoirs*, 1:354–56. *OR*, 33, pt. 2, 909.

17. Sheridan, *Memoirs*, 1:356.

18. Starr, *Union Cavalry*, 2:76. *OR*, 33, pt. 2, 862.

19. *OR*, 33, pt. 2, 941. Starr, *Union Cavalry*, 2:86–87.

20. *OR*, 33, pt. 2, 428, 513, 515.

21. Foote, *The Civil War*, 3:148.

22. Starr, *Union Cavalry*, 2:92.

23. *OR*, 36, pt. 2, 466, 515.

24. Sheridan, *Memoirs*, 1:365. *OR*, 36, pt. 2, 553.

25. Starr, *Union Cavalry*, 2:94–95.

26. *OR*, 36, pt. 2, 551, 553.

27. Porter, *Campaigning with Grant*, 83–84. Sheridan, *Memoirs*, 1:368–69.

28. Foote, *The Civil War*, 3:160–61. Porter, *Campaigning with Grant*, 84.

29. *OR*, 36, pt. 2, 552.

30. Sheridan, *Memoirs*, 1:370–71.

31. Starr, *Union Cavalry*, 2:97. Foote, *The Civil War*, 3:225.

32. Starr, *Union Cavalry*. 2:101.

33. Sheridan, *Memoirs*, 1:374–75.

34. Ibid., 376–78. Starr, *Union Cavalry*, 2:103.

35. *OR*, 51, pt. 2, 912.

36. Emory Thomas, *Bold Dragoon: The Life of J. E. B. Stuart* (New York: Harper & Row, 1986), 291.

37. Sheridan, *Memoirs*, 1:377–78.

38. Thomas, *Bold Dragoon*, 291–92. Starr, *Union Cavalry*, 2:107.

39. Thomas, *Bold Dragoon*, 293–96. O'Connor, *Sheridan*, 169–70. Sheridan, *Memoirs*, 1:379–80.

40. Sheridan, *Memoirs*, 1:380–81. Starr, *Union Cavalry*, 2:110–11.

41. Buel and Johnson, *Battles and Leaders*, 4:191.

42. Sheridan, *Memoirs*, 1:381–82. Buel and Johnson, *Battles and Leaders*, 4:191.

43. O'Connor, *Sheridan*, 171. Sheridan, *Memoirs*, 1:382–83. *OR*, 36, pt. 1, 791.

44. Sheridan, *Memoirs*, 1:384–85. O'Connor, *Sheridan*, 171.

45. *OR*, 36, pt. 2, 765.

46. Porter, *Campaigning with Grant*, 144.

47. Sheridan, *Memoirs*, 1:398. Robert A. Williams, "Haw's Shop: A 'Storm of Shot and Shell,' " *Civil War Times Illustrated* (January 1971), 13.

48. Starr, *Union Cavalry*. 2:117–18. *OR*, 36, pt. 1, 854. Sheridan, *Memoirs*, 1:398–402.

49. Sheridan, *Memoirs*, 1:402–6. *OR*, 36, pt. 1, 784, 805.

50. Sheridan, *Memoirs*, 1:406. *OR*, 36, pt. 1, 783; pt. 3, 411. Buel and Johnson, *Battles and Leaders*, 4:193.

51. Sheridan, *Memoirs*, 1:409–10. Buel and Johnson, *Battles and Leaders*, 4:193. Porter, *Campaigning with Grant*, 179.

52. Sheridan, *Memoirs*, 1:413–15. *OR*, 36, pt. 3, 599, 628.

53. Sheridan, *Memoirs*, 1:417. Starr, *Union Cavalry*, 2:134.

54. Sheridan, *Memoirs*, 1:417–20. Starr, *Union Cavalry*, 2:134–35.

55. Sheridan, *Memoirs*, 1:420–21. *OR*, 36, pt. 1, 823, 831. Starr, *Union Cavalry*, 2:138–39.

56. Sheridan, *Memoirs*, 1:421–22. O'Connor, *Sheridan*, 181. See also Jay Monaghan, "Custer's 'Last Stand'—Trevilian Station, 1864," *Civil War History* 8 (September 1962), 245–58.

57. *OR*, 36, pt. 3, 903. Sheridan, *Memoirs*, 1:422.

58. Sheridan, *Memoirs*, 1:423–24. Starr, *Union Cavalry*, 2:145–46.

59. *OR*, 36, pt. 3, 784, 794. Sheridan, *Memoirs*, 1:434.

60. Starr, *Union Cavalry*, 2:204. *OR*, 40, pt. 1, 169. Sheridan, *Memoirs*, 1:444. James H. Wilson, *Under the Old Flag* (New York: D. Appleton, 1911), 397–98.

61. Wilson, *Under the Old Flag*, 528–29. *OR*, 40, pt. 3, 15–16.

62. *OR*, 36, pt. 1, 801.

63. Sheridan, *Memoirs*, 1:447.

64. Foote, *The Civil War*, 3:460. For Early's Raid, see Millard K. Bushong, *Old Jube: A Biography of General Jubal A. Early* (Shippensburg, Pa.: White Mane, 1955), 192–209.

65. *OR*, 47, pt. 2, 433–34, 558. Starr, *Union Cavalry*, 2:245.

Chapter 6

1. Sheridan, *Memoirs*, 1:462–63.

2. Basler, *Collected Works of Lincoln*, 7:476.

3. Sheridan, *Memoirs*, 1:463–64. Grant, *Memoirs*, 2:319.

4. Sheridan, *Memoirs*, 1:500.

5. *OR*, 43, pt. 1, 628.

6. Ibid., pt. 2, 366.

7. Jeffry D. Wert, *From Winchester to Cedar Creek: The Shenandoah Campaign of 1864* (Carlisle, Pa.: South Mountain Press, 1987), 18–19.

8. Wert, *From Winchester*, 20. Faust, *Illustrated Encyclopedia*, 243.

9. Sheridan, *Memoirs*, 1:501.

10. Wert, *From Winchester*, 21–22. *OR*, 37, pt. 2, 582.

11. Sheridan, *Memoirs*, 1:503. For Meigs, see George F. Skoch, "In the Shadow of the Valley: Lieutenant Meigs Dies," *Civil War Times Illustrated* (September 1984), 35–39.

12. *OR*, 43, pt. 1, 54, 720, 739.

13. Ibid., 18–19.

14. Ibid., 43. Buel and Johnson, *Battles and Leaders*, 4:522.

15. Wert, *From Winchester*, 35. *OR*, 43, pt. 1, 917.

16. Jubal A. Early, *Autobiographical Sketch and Narrative of the War Between the States* (Philadelphia: J. B. Lippincott, 1912), 415. *OR*, 43, pt. 1, 911–12.

17.   Basler, *Collected Works of Lincoln*, 7:514. Edward McPherson, *The Political History of the United States During the Great Rebellion* (Washington, D.C.: Philp and Solomons, 1865), 419–20.

18.   Foote, *The Civil War*, 3:552.

19.   *OR*, 43, pt. 2, 202; pt. 1, 45.

20.   Sheridan, *Memoirs*, 2:1–2. For Young, see Richard P. Weinert, "The South Had Mosby; The Union: Maj. Henry Young," *Civil War Times Illustrated* (April 1964), 38–42.

21.   Sheridan, *Memoirs*, 2:2–6.

22.   Ibid., 4. For Wright, see Sylvia G. Dannett, "Rebecca Wright—Traitor or Patriot?" *Lincoln Herald* (Fall 1963), 103–12.

23.   Dannett, "Rebecca Wright," 105. Sheridan, *Memoirs*, 2:6.

24.   Sheridan, *Memoirs*, 2:9. *OR*, 43, pt. 2, 83–84.

25.   Grant, *Memoirs*, 2:327–28.

26.   Ibid., 329. Sheridan, *Memoirs*, 2:9.

27.   *OR*, 43, pt. 2, 105–6. Sheridan, *Memoirs*, 2:10. Wert, *From Winchester*, 44–45.

28.   Sheridan, *Memoirs*, 2:10–14.

29.   Ibid., 14–16. Starr, *Union Cavalry*, 2:260, 272. Wert, *From Winchester*, 49.

30.   Sheridan, *Memoirs*, 2:18. Starr, *Union Cavalry*, 2:270. Wert, *From Winchester*, 50.

31.   *OR*, 43, pt. 1, 554–55.

32.   Sheridan, *Memoirs*, 2:21–23. *OR*, 43, pt. 1, 456–57. Wert, *From Winchester*, 55–56.

33.   O'Connor, *Sheridan*, 202. Sheridan, *Memoirs*, 2:23. Wert, *From Winchester*, 67.

34.   Sheridan, *Memoirs*, 2:23–24. Wert, *From Winchester*, 68–70.

35.   Sheridan, *Memoirs*, 2:24. *OR*, 43, pt. 1, 47, 361.

36.   *OR*, 43, pt. 1, 361–62. Wert, *From Winchester*, 94–95.

37.   Sheridan, *Memoirs*, 2:26–27. Early, *Autobiographical Sketch*, 425–26. Bushong, *Old Jube*, 236.

38.   Sheridan, *Memoirs*, 2:28. Dannett, "Rebbeca Wright," 109.

39.   *OR*, 43, pt. 1, 25. Foote, *The Civil War*, 3:554.

40.   *OR*, 43, pt. 1, 61; pt. 2, 118, 131. Sheridan, *Memoirs*, 2:29–30. Foote, *The Civil War*, 3:555.

41.   Sheridan, *Memoirs*, 2:33–35. *OR*, 43, pt. 1, 48.

42.   Martin F. Schmitt, ed., *General George Crook: His Autobiography* (Norman, Okla.: Oklahoma University Press, 1946), 130–31. *OR*, 43, pt. 1, 556.

43.   Quoted in Wert, *From Winchester*, 129.

44.   Sheridan, *Memoirs*, 2:41–42. *OR*, 43, pt. 2, 156.

45.   Sheridan, *Memoirs*, 2:43–44. *OR*, 43, pt. 1, 499–500.

46.   *OR*, 43, pt. 1, 61–62; pt. 2, 152.

47.   Sheridan, *Memoirs*, 2:40. *OR*, 43, pt. 2, 177, 249.

48.   Sheridan, *Memoirs*, 2:53–55.

49.   Ibid., 54–55.

50.   *OR*, 43, pt. 1, 509, 811. Jeffry D. Wert, *Mosby's Rangers* (New York: Simon and Schuster, 1990), 69–71.

51.   Wert, *Mosby*, 213–18. For Mosby's account of the incident, see "Retaliation: The Execution of Seven Prisoners by Col. John S. Mosby—A Self-Protective Necessity," *Southern Historical Society Papers* 27 (1899), 314–22.

52.   Sheridan, *Memoirs*, 2:50–52. Wert, *From Winchester*, 145.

53.   Skoch, "In the Shadow of the Valley," 39.

54.   *OR*, 43, pt. 1, 30–31.

55.   Sheridan, *Memoirs*, 2:56–59. *OR*, 43, pt. 2, 339.

56.   Sheridan, *Memoirs*, 2:59–60. *OR*, 43, pt. 1, 51.

57.   Sheridan, *Memoirs*, 2:62–64.

58.   Ibid., 68–71.

59.   Ibid., 71–76. George A. Forsyth, *Thrilling Days in Army Life* (New York and London: Harper & Brothers, 1900), 136.

60.   Sheridan, *Memoirs*, 2:80. Edward J. Stackpole, *Sheridan in the Shenandoah: Jubal Early's Nemesis* (Harrisburg, Pa.: Stackpole, 1960), 325. John W. DeForest, *A Volunteer's Adventures* (New Haven: Yale University Press, 1946), 221.

61.   O'Connor, *Sheridan*, 227. Sheridan, *Memoirs*, 2:81–82.

62.   Sheridan, *Memoirs*, 2:82. Hazard Stevens, "The Battle of Cedar Creek," *Papers of the Military Historical Society of Massachusetts*, vol. 6, 1907, 125.

63.   Sheridan, *Memoirs*, 2:83–84. Wert, *From Winchester*, 223.

64.   Joseph P. Cullen, "Cedar Creek," *Civil War Times Illustrated* (December 1969), 44.

65.   John B. Gordon, *Reminiscences of the Civil War* (New York: Charles Scribner's Sons, 1904), 341–42. Early, *Autobiographical Sketch*, 446. Henry Kyd Douglas, *I Rode with Stonewall* (Chapel Hill: University of North Carolina Press, 1940), 305.

66.   Sheridan, *Memoirs*, 2:85–86. Aldace F. Walker, *The Vermont Brigade in the Shenandoah Valley* (Burlington, Vt.: The Free Press Association, 1869), 148.

67.   Sheridan, *Memoirs*, 2:87.

68.   Forsyth, *Thrilling Days*, 154, 158.

69.   Wert, *From Winchester*, 230. Gordon, *Reminiscences*, 347.

70.   Wert, *From Winchester*, 231. Sheridan, *Memoirs*, 2:88–89.

71.   Gordon, *Reminiscences*, 348.

72.   Gary W. Gallagher, *Stephen Dodson Ramseur: Lee's Gallant General* (Chapel Hill: University of North Carolina Press, 1985), 158. *OR*, 43, pt. 1, 562–63.

73.   Forsyth, *Thrilling Days*, 167; quoted in Thomas A. Lewis, *The Guns of Cedar Creek* (New York: Harper & Row, 1988), 288. DeForest, *Volunteer's Adventures*, 228.

74.   *OR*, 43, pt. 2, 423.

75. Sheridan, *Memoirs*, 2:91. Dana, *Recollections*, 248–49.

76. Foote, *The Civil War*, 3:574. Wert, *From Winchester*, 248.

77. *OR*, 43, pt. 2, 671–72.

Chapter 7

1. *OR*, 43, pt. 1, 563. Lewis, *Guns of Cedar Creek*, 296.

2. *OR*, 43, pt. 1, 436.

3. Ibid., 465.

4. Wert, *From Winchester*, 225–43. *OR*, 43, pt. 1, 35.

5. *OR*, 43, pt. 1, 30, 35; pt. 2, 273.

6. *OR*, 43, pt. 1, 55. Wert, *From Winchester*, 195–96; quoted in Wert, *Mosby*, 201.

7. Sheridan, *Memoirs*, 2:99. Kevin H. Siepel, *Rebel: The Life and Times of John Singleton Mosby* (New York: St. Martin's Press, 1983), 128. *OR*, 43, pt. 1, 508–10.

8. Wert, *Mosby*, 245. Wert, *From Winchester*, 152. *OR*, 43, pt. 2, 910.

9. Wert, *Mosby*, 246. Mosby, "Retaliation," 314–22.

10. Wert, *Mosby*, 247.

11. Ibid., 248–50. *OR*, 43, pt. 1, 55–56.

12. Starr, *Union Cavalry*, 2:350–53.

13. Sheridan, *Memoirs*, 2:97–98. *OR*, 43, pt. 1, 36; pt. 2, 645, 649.

14. *OR*, 43, pt. 2, 653, 671.

15. Ibid., 679.

16. Wert, *Mosby*, 261–63. *OR*, 43, pt. 1, 687.

17. Starr, *Union Cavalry*, 2:358–59. *OR*, 43, pt. 2, 671, 682.

18. *OR*, 43, pt. 2, 684, 692.

19. Ibid., 740, 743–44.

20.   Foote, *The Civil War*, 3:629. *OR*, 43, pt. 2, 744.

21.   *OR*, 43, pt. 2, 765, 772, 778, 780.

22.   Sheridan, *Memoirs*, 2:102. *OR*, 43, pt. 1, 677–79; pt. 2, 804.

23.   Starr, *Union Cavalry*, 2:338–40. *OR*, 43, pt. 1, 677–79; pt. 2, 816. Sheridan, *Memoirs*, 2:102.

24.   *OR*, 46, pt. 2, 56. *OR*, 43, pt. 1, 831.

25.   Starr, *Union Cavalry*, 2:360. *OR*, 43, pt. 2, 822–24.

26.   Starr, *Union Cavalry*, 2:361. *OR*, 46, pt. 2, 108, 449.

27.   *OR*, 46, pt. 2, 620–25. Sheridan, *Memoirs*, 2:107–8.

28.   *OR*, 46, pt. 2, 605–6, 609. Sheridan, *Memoirs*, 2:112–13.

29.   Starr, *Union Cavalry*, 2:367–68. Sheridan, *Memoirs*, 2:112.

30.   *OR*, 46, pt. 1, 504–5. Sheridan, *Memoirs*, 2:114. Starr, *Union Cavalry*, 2:370–71.

31.   Bushong, *Old Jube*, 278. *OR*, 46, pt. 1, 476. Sheridan, *Memoirs*, 2:116.

32.   Sheridan, *Memoirs*, 2:118. Davies, *General Sheridan*, 210.

33.   *OR*, 46, pt. 1, 478; pt. 2, 848. Sheridan, *Memoirs*, 2:119.

34.   *OR*, 46, pt. 1, 481–82.

35.   Ibid., pt. 3, 24. Sheridan, *Memoirs*, 2:124–25.

36.   *OR*, 46, pt. 3, 41, 46.

37.   Sheridan, *Memoirs*, 2:128.

38.   Sheridan, *Memoirs*, 2:128–29. Starr, *Union Cavalry*, 2:425. Grant, *Memoirs*, 2:437–38.

39.   Sheridan, *Memoirs*, 2:129, 133.

40.   *OR*, 46, pt. 1, 52. Sheridan, *Memoirs*, 2:134–38.

41.   Sheridan, *Memoirs*, 2:139–40. *OR*, 46, pt. 3, 266.

42.   Sheridan, *Memoirs*, 2:142–44. *OR*, 46, pt. 3, 325.

43.   Sheridan, *Memoirs*, 2:144. Porter, *Campaigning with Grant*, 428–29.

44. Sheridan, *Memoirs*, 2:145.

45. Ibid., 145–46.

46. Ibid., 146–47.

47. Ibid., 149–50.

48. Ibid., 150–53. Starr, *Union Cavalry*, 2:439–40.

49. Sheridan, *Memoirs*, 2:153–54. *OR*, 46, pt. 3, 381. Buel and Johnson, *Battles and Leaders*, 4:711.

50. *OR*, 46, pt. 3, 381.

51. Sheridan, *Memoirs*, 2:146, 160. Bruce Catton, "Sheridan at Five Forks," *Journal of Southern History*, 21 (1955), 309.

52. Starr, *Union Cavalry*, 2:444. Sheridan, *Memoirs*, 2:156. Buel and Johnson, *Battles and Leaders*, 4:711.

53. Foote, *The Civil War*, 3:869. Sheridan, *Memoirs*, 2:160–61.

54. Buel and Johnson, *Battles and Leaders*, 4:713. Sheridan, *Memoirs*, 2:162–63.

55. Porter, *Campaigning with Grant*, 438–39. Foote, *The Civil War*, 3:872. Buel and Johnson, *Battles and Leaders*, 4:713–14.

56. Foote, *The Civil War*, 3:872. O'Connor, *Sheridan*, 253.

57. Sheridan, *Memoirs*, 2:165.

58. Foote, *The Civil War*, 3:873–74.

59. Porter, *Campaigning with Grant*, 442. Foote, *The Civil War*, 3:875.

60. Foote, *The Civil War*, 3:880–81.

61. *OR*, 46, pt. 3, 449, 556. Sheridan, *Memoirs*, 2:175–76.

62. Sheridan, *Memoirs*, 2:177. Douglas S. Freeman, *R. E. Lee: A Biography*, vol. 4 (New York: Charles Scribner's Sons, 1934–35), 74–76. *OR*, 46, pt. 3, 582.

63. Sheridan, *Memoirs*, 2:178–79.

64. Ibid., 180–87. *OR*, 46, pt. 3, 609–10.

65. Sheridan, *Memoirs*, 2:189–91. *OR*, 46, pt. 3, 652–53.

66.   Foote, *The Civil War*, 3:934–35. Sheridan, *Memoirs*, 2:192–94.
        Bruce Catton, *Grant Takes Command* (Boston: Little, Brown,
        1969), 462.

67.   Sheridan, *Memoirs*, 2:194–98.

68.   Ibid., 200–201.

69.   Ibid., 201.

70.   Foote, *The Civil War*, 3:950. O'Connor, *Sheridan*, 272.

71.   O'Connor, *Sheridan*, 233. George F. Hoar, *Autobiography of
        Seventy Years*, vol. 1 (New York: Charles Scribner's Sons,
        1906), 209. M. A. DeWolfe Howe, *Home Letters of General
        Sherman* (New York: Charles Scribner's Sons, 1909), 314.

72.   Sheridan, *Memoirs*, 2:204.

73.   Starr, *Union Cavalry*, 2:489–90. Sheridan, *Memoirs*, 2:206.

Chapter 8

1.   Sheridan, *Memoirs*, 2:208.

2.   Ibid., 108–9. Starr, *Union Cavalry*, 2:501.

3.   Sheridan, *Memoirs*, 2:209.

4.   Ibid., 210. Glyndon G. Van Deusen, *William Henry Seward*
        (New York: Oxford University Press, 1967), 487–95.

5.   Sheridan, *Memoirs*, 2:210.

6.   Ibid., 211. Sheridan to Grant, 29 May 1865, Grant Papers,
        Library of Congress. *OR*, 48, pt. 2, 767.

7.   William L. Richter, "The Army in Texas During Reconstruc-
        tion, 1865–1870," (Ph.D. dissertation, Louisiana State Univer-
        sity, 1970), 27. Sheridan to Grant, 28 June 1865, Grant Papers,
        Library of Congress.

8.   Sheridan to Grant, 16 December 1865, Grant Papers, Library of
        Congress. William L. Richter, *The Army in Texas During Re-
        construction, 1865–1870* (College Station, Texas: Texas A&M
        University Press, 1987), 18–19.

9.   Richter, "Army in Texas," 44–47. Robert M. Utley, *Cavalier in Buckskin: George Armstrong Custer and the Western Military Frontier* (Norman, Okla.: University of Oklahoma Press, 1988), 36–37.

10.   Sheridan, *Memoirs*, 2:214. Edward K. Beale, ed., *Diary of Gideon Welles*, vol. 2 (New York: W. W. Norton, 1960), 332–33.

11.   Porter, *Campaigning with Grant*, 493. Richter, *Army in Texas*, 23. Sheridan, *Memoirs*, 2:215.

12..   Van Deusen, *Seward*, 483, 489. Robert E. and Katharine M. Morsberger, *Lew Wallace: Militant Romantic* (New York: McGraw-Hill, 1980), 197.

13.   Joseph G. Dawson III, *Army Generals and Reconstruction: Louisiana, 1862–1877* (Baton Rouge: Louisiana State University Press, 1982), 26–28. Canby to Stanton, 12 August 1865, Department of the Gulf, Record Group 393, National Archives.

14.   Richter, *Army in Texas*, 20. General Order 3, 19 June 1865, Department of Texas, Record Group 94, National Archives.

15.   Sheridan to Johnson, 26 November 1865, Sheridan Papers, Library of Congress.

16.   Sheridan, *Memoirs*, 2:217. Richter, "Army in Texas," 73.

17.   Morsberger and Morsberger, *Lew Wallace*, 199–200. Grant to Sheridan, 28 November 1865, Sheridan Papers, Library of Congress. For Bagdad incident, see microfilm 619, roll 452, National Archives.

18.   Morsberger and Morsberger, *Lew Wallace*, 200.

19.   Richter, *Army in Texas*, 24.

20.   Gene Smith, *Maximilian and Carlotta* (New York: William Morrow, 1973), 201–2. Sheridan, *Memoirs*, 2:217–19.

21.   Sheridan, *Memoirs*, 2:228.

22.   Dawson, *Army Generals*, 34–35.

23.   George C. Rable, *But There Was No Peace: The Role of Violence in the Politics of Reconstruction* (Athens: University of Georgia Press, 1984), 43–46. Eric Foner, *Reconstruction:*

America's Unfinished Revolution, 1863–1877 (New York: Harper & Row, 1988), 182. Dawson, *Army Generals*, 30–32.

24. Dawson, *Army Generals*, 36. Rable, *But There Was No Peace*, 46–48. Foner, *Reconstruction*, 263.

25. Patrick W. Riddleberger, *1866: The Critical Year Revisited* (Carbondale and Edwards, Ill.: Southern Illinois University Press, 1979), 189–92. Joe G. Taylor, *Louisiana Reconstructed, 1863–1877* (Baton Rouge: Louisiana State University Press, 1974), 106–8. Rable, *But There Was No Peace*, 48–50.

26. Sheridan to Rawlins, 21 July 1877; Sheridan to Grant, 3 July 1866, Grant Papers, Library of Congress.

27. Rable, *But There Was No Peace*, 49.

28. Riddleberger, *1866: The Critical Year*, 192–95. Rable, *But There Was No Peace*, 50.

29. Dawson, *Army Generals*, 39–40. Rable, *But There Was No Peace*, 51–52. Riddleberger, *1866: The Critical Year*, 196. Taylor, *Louisiana Reconstructed*, 109–10.

30. Riddleberger, *1866: The Critical Year*, 197.

31. Sheridan, *Memoirs*, 2:235. Riddleberger, *1866: The Critical Year*, 199.

32. Sheridan, *Memoirs*, 2:236–37. Rable, *But There Was No Peace*, 55.

33. Sheridan, *Memoirs*, 2:221–22. Weinert, "Henry Young," 42.

34. Morsberger and Morsberger, *Lew Wallace*, 203–4. Sheridan, *Memoirs*, 2:223.

35. Richter, *Army in Texas*, 50, 59–62. Sheridan, *Memoirs*, 2:232–33.

36. Richter, "Army in Texas," 111–12. Richter, *Army in Texas*, 69.

37. Sheridan to Grant, 22 August 1866, Sheridan Papers, Library of Congress.

38. Richter, *Army in Texas*, 29.

39. William L. Richter, "The Brenham Fire of 1866: A Texas Reconstruction Tragedy," *Louisiana Studies* (Fall 1975), 305–9.

40. Ibid., 302, 308. Sheridan to Grant, 20 September 1866; Sheridan to Rawlins, 1 October 1866, Grant Papers, Library of Congress.

41. Sheridan to Grant, 21 September 1866, Grant Papers, Library of Congress. Richter, "Brenham Fire," 311–12.

42. *OR*, 48, pt. 1, 301. Richter, *Army in Texas*, 66.

43. Richter, *Army in Texas*, 66–69.

44. Ibid., 70–71, 223.

45. Quoted in Paul Andrew Hutton, *Phil Sheridan and His Army* (Lincoln and London: University of Nebraska Press, 1985), 22.

46. Charles W. Ramsdell, *Reconstruction in Texas* (New York: Columbia University Press, 1910), 130–31. Richter, *Army in Texas*, 63–64.

47. Richter, *Army in Texas*, 64.

48. *OR*, 48, pt. 1, 301.

49. Grant to Sheridan, 15 November 1866, Sheridan Papers, Library of Congress. For Andrew Johnson's presidency, see Hans L. Trefousse, *Andrew Johnson: A Biography* (New York and London: W. W. Norton, 1989).

50. Richter, *Army in Texas*, 73–74.

51. Foner, *Reconstruction*, 274. Riddleberger, *1866: The Critical Year*, 199–200. Sheridan, *Memoirs*, 2:240.

52. Sheridan, *Memoirs*, 2:226–27.

53. Richter, *Army in Texas*, 85. *Galveston Daily News*, 29 January 1867.

54. Sheridan, *Memoirs*, 2:243–49, 253. Richter, "Army in Texas," 115–116.

55. Sheridan, *Memoirs*, 2:254–55. Grant to Sheridan, 27 March and 29 March 1866, Sheridan Papers, Library of Congress.

56.   Grant to Sheridan, 3 April and 7 April 1867, Sheridan Papers, Library of Congress.

57.   "Anecdotes of Andrew Johnson," *Century Magazine* 85 (January 1913), 440. Sheridan to Grant, 2 April 1867, Andrew Johnson Papers, Library of Congress.

58.   James E. Sefton, *The United States Army and Reconstruction, 1865–1877* (Baton Rouge: Louisiana State University Press, 1967), 128.

59.   Ibid., 130. Sheridan to Grant, 21 April 1867; Grant to Sheridan, 21 April 1867, Sheridan Papers, Library of Congress.

60.   Joseph G. Dawson III, "General Phil Sheridan and Military Reconstruction in Louisiana," *Civil War History* 24 (January 1978), 137. Sheridan to Grant, 5 August 1867, Grant Papers, Library of Congress.

61.   Sheridan, *Memoirs*, 2:264.

62.   Ibid., 265–67.

63.   Dawson, "General Phil Sheridan," 139.

64.   Sefton, *United States Army and Reconstruction*, 131–32.

65.   Richter, *Army in Texas*, 106. Sheridan, *Memoirs*, 2:269–70. Dawson, "General Phil Sheridan," 143.

66.   Sefton, *United States Army and Reconstruction*, 134. Sheridan, *Memoirs*, 2:270.

67.   Grant to Sheridan, 24 June 1867, Sheridan Papers, Library of Congress. Dawson, "General Phil Sheridan," 141. Taylor, *Louisiana Reconstructed*, 140.

68.   Richter, *Army in Texas*, 110–11.

69.   Sefton, *United States Army and Reconstruction*, 135.

70.   Sheridan, *Memoirs*, 2:279. Dawson, "General Phil Sheridan," 144. Faust, *Illustrated Encyclopedia*, 645.

71.   Richter, *Army in Texas*, 113.

72.   Sheridan, *Memoirs*, 2:272–74. Richter, *Army in Texas*, 112.

73. Grant to Sheridan, 12 August and 14 August 1867, Sheridan Papers, Library of Congress.

74. Grant to Johnson, 17 August 1867; Johnson to Grant, 19 August 1867, Grant Papers, Library of Congress.

75. Richter, *Army in Texas*, 115. Sheridan, *Memoirs*, 2:274–80.

76. Greiner, *Phil Sheridan*, 70.

77. Sheridan, *Memoirs*, 2:279.

78. Sheridan to Newhall, 20 November 1866, Sheridan Papers, Library of Congress.

Chapter 9

1. Hutton, *Phil Sheridan*, 1. Sheridan, *Memoirs*, 2:281.

2. Sheridan, *Memoirs*, 2:281–83.

3. O'Connor, Sheridan, 296–97. Allan Nevins and Malton H. Thomas, eds., *The Diary of George Templeton Strong*, vol. 4 (New York: Macmillan, 1952), 165.

4. Hutton, *Phil Sheridan*, 28. Utley, *Cavalier in Buckskin*, 57.

5. Robert M. Utley, *The Indian Frontier of the American West, 1846–1890* (Albuquerque: University of New Mexico Press, 1984), 108–16. Utley, *Cavalier in Buckskin*, 47–53.

6. Sheridan, *Memoirs*, 2:285–86.

7. Utley, *Indian Frontier*, 22–23.

8. Ibid., 23, 86.

9. Sheridan, *Memoirs*, 2:284–85.

10. Ibid., 284. Hutton, *Phil Sheridan*, 37–38. Utley, *Indian Frontier*, 122.

11. Utley, *Indian Frontier*, 122–23. Sheridan, *Memoirs*, 2:290–91.

12. Sheridan, *Memoirs*, 2:289–90.

13. Ibid., 292–93.

14. Ibid., 290. Sheridan, "Report, In the field, Fort Hays, Sept. 26, 1868," Sheridan Papers, Library of Congress.

15. *Annual Report of the Secretary of War [1866]*, 21–22. John Hoyt Williams, *A Great and Shining Road: The Epic Story of the Transcontinental Railroad* (New York: Times Books, 1988), 121.

16. Jerry Keenan, "Cheyenne Island Siege," *Wild West* (June 1988), 37.

17. Sheridan, *Memoirs*, 2:302. G. A. Forsyth, "A Frontier Fight," *Harpers New Monthly Magazine* 91 (June 1895), 45. Hutton, *Phil Sheridan*, 46.

18. Keenan, "Cheyenne Island Siege," 38.

19. Sheridan, *Memoirs*, 2:305. For the Indians' side, see George Bird Grinnell, *The Fighting Cheyennes* (Norman, Okla.: University of Oklahoma Press, 1956), 278–92.

20. Hutton, *Phil Sheridan*, 48.

21. Ibid., 48–49. Utley, *Cavalier in Buckskin*, 60.

22. Carl Coke Rister, *Border Command: General Phil Sheridan in the West* (Norman, Okla.: University of Oklahoma Press, 1944), 48.

23. Hutton, *Phil Sheridan*, 54.

24. Utley, *Indian Frontier*, 124–25. *New York Times*, 16 October 1868.

25. Rister, *Border Command*, 66–67.

26. Hutton, *Phil Sheridan*, 49–50. Utley, *Cavalier in Buckskin*, 54, 57, 61.

27. Sheridan, *Memoirs*, 2:301.

28. Ibid., 307.

29. Ibid., 310–11. Hutton, *Phil Sheridan*, 60.

30. Hutton, *Phil Sheridan*, 60–61.

31. Ibid., 61–62. Faust, *Illustrated Encyclopedia*, 79. Utley, *Cavalier in Buckskin*, 63.

32. Hutton, *Phil Sheridan*, 62–63.

33. Ibid., 63. Utley, *Cavalier in Buckskin*, 63.

34. Hutton, *Phil Sheridan*, 63. Utley, *Cavalier in Buckskin*, 64.

35. Utley, *Indian Frontier*, 92–93.

36. Hutton, *Phil Sheridan*, 57–58. Utley, *Cavalier in Buckskin*, 64.

37. Evan S. Connell, *Son of the Morning Star: Custer and the Little Bighorn* (San Francisco: North Point Press, 1984), 182–83. Utley, *Cavalier in Buckskin*, 67.

38. Connell, *Son of the Morning Star*, 182. Dee Brown, *Bury My Heart at Wounded Knee: An Indian History of the American West* (Toronto, New York, London: Bantam Books, 1972), 163.

39. Utley, *Cavalier in Buckskin*, 67. Brown, *Bury My Heart*, 164.

40. Connell, *Son of the Morning Star*, 184–86.

41. Utley, *Cavalier in Buckskin*, 68–69.

42. Ibid., 69–70.

43. Ibid., 70. Sheridan, *Memoirs*, 2:319. Connell, *Son of the Morning Star*, 191–92.

44. Sheridan, *Memoirs*, 2:320. Hutton, *Phil Sheridan*, 70–73. Connell, *Son of the Morning Star*, 191–92.

45. Sheridan, *Memoirs*, 2:320. Grinnell, *Fighting Cheyennes*, 305.

46. Sheridan, *Memoirs*, 2:322–28. Connell, *Son of the Morning Star*, 194.

47. Sheridan, *Memoirs*, 2:330–31. Connell, *Son of the Morning Star*, 182, 198–99.

48. Connell, *Son of the Morning Star*, 199. Sheridan, *Memoirs*, 2:331. Hutton, *Phil Sheridan*, 82. Robert M. Utley, *Frontier Regulars: The United States Army and the Indian, 1866–1891* (New York: Macmillan, 1973), 118–19.

49. Hutton, *Phil Sheridan*, 83–84.

50. Brown, *Bury My Heart*, 237–38.

51. Hutton, *Phil Sheridan*, 85. Sheridan, *Memoirs*, 2:334–35.

52. Sheridan, *Memoirs*, 2:334–36. Hutton, *Phil Sheridan*, 88–89.

53. Sheridan, *Memoirs*, 2:336–38. Rister, *Border Command*, 137–38.

54. Brown, *Bury My Heart*, 165. *Annual Report of the Secretary of War [1869]*, 1:47.

55. Sheridan, *Memoirs*, 2:346–47. Hutton, *Phil Sheridan*, 113.

56. Sheridan, *Memoirs*, 2:347. Sheridan to Grant, 19 January 1869, Sheridan Papers, Library of Congress. Hutton, *Phil Sheridan*, 376.

57. Utley, *Indian Frontier*, 129.

58. Ibid., 132–33. McFeely, *Grant*, 308.

59. Sherman to Schofield, 9 June 1869, Letters Sent by the Adjutant General's Office, National Archives. Hutton, *Phil Sheridan*, 117.

60. Hutton, *Phil Sheridan*, 186. "Report of General James A. Hardie," 29 January 1870, Sheridan Papers, Library of Congress. See also Dunn, *Massacres of the Mountains*, 443–455.

61. Hutton, *Phil Sheridan*, 191–92. Utley, *Indian Frontier*, 133.

62. Hutton, *Phil Sheridan*, 192, 196. Sheridan to Sherman, 28 February 1870, Sheridan Papers, Library of Congress.

63. Sheridan, *Memoirs*, 2:463–64. Hutton, *Phil Sheridan*, 180.

64. Sheridan, *Memoirs*, 2:349, 359. O'Connor, *Sheridan*, 308–9.

65. Sheridan, *Memoirs*, 2:360–63, 370.

66. Ibid., 374. Hutton, *Phil Sheridan*, 203.

67. O'Connor, *Sheridan*, 310. Sheridan to Grant, 13 September 1870, Sheridan Papers, Library of Congress. Sheridan, *Memoirs*, 2:450–51.

68. Sheridan, *Memoirs*, 2:407, 448. Sheridan to Grant, 13 September 1870, Sheridan Papers, Library of Congress.

69. Sheridan, *Memoirs*, 2:453. Sheridan to Grant, 13 September 1870, Sheridan Papers, Library of Congress.

Chapter 10

1. Utley, *Cavalier in Buckskin*, 109–10. Hutton, *Phil Sheridan*, 206.

2. Hutton, *Phil Sheridan*, 207.

3. Ibid., 207–08. O'Connor, *Sheridan*, 321.

4. Robert Cromie, *The Great Chicago Fire* (New York, Toronto, London: McGraw-Hill, 1958), 26, 29–30, 278–79.

5. Ibid., 55, 70.

6. Ibid., 121–22. Sheridan, *Memoirs*, 2:471–72.

7. Cromie, *Chicago Fire*, 218–22. Hutton, *Phil Sheridan*, 209.

8. O'Connor, *Sheridan*, 313. Hutton, *Phil Sheridan*, 209–10.

9. Cromie, *Chicago Fire*, 262. Sherman to Sheridan, 16 October 1871, Sheridan Papers, Library of Congress.

10. Cromie, *Chicago Fire*, 278.

11. Ibid., 271. Sheridan, *Memoirs*, 2:475–76.

12. Hutton, *Phil Sheridan*, 210. Herman Kogan and Robert Cromie, *The Great Fire: Chicago, 1871* (New York: G. P. Putnam's Sons, 1971), 69.

13. Faust, *Illustrated Encyclopedia*, 554–55. Cromie, *Chicago Fire*, 273. Palmer to Mason, 21 October 1871, Sheridan Papers, Library of Congress.

14. Cromie, *Chicago Fire*, 274–75.

15. Ibid., 275. Hutton, *Phil Sheridan*, 212. Sherman to Sheridan, 16 October 1871, Sheridan Papers, Library of Congress.

16. Hutton, *Phil Sheridan*, 212–13. O'Connor, *Sheridan*, 322.

17. David M. Delo, "Melee on the Plains," *Wild West* (December 1988), 44.

18. Ibid., 44–45. Brown, *Bury My Heart*, 179.

19. Delo, "Melee on the Plains," 43, 46. O'Connor, *Sheridan*, 323.

20. Delo, "Melee on the Plains," 46. Hutton, *Phil Sheridan*, 215–16.

21. Delo, "Melee on the Plains," 46.

22. Utley, *Frontier Regulars*, 207–12. Hutton, *Phil Sheridan*, 243.

23. Utley, *Frontier Regulars*, 213. Brown, *Bury My Heart*, 254. James L. Haley, *The Buffalo War: The History of the Red River Indian Uprising of 1874* (Norman, Okla.: University of Oklahoma Press, 1976), 22, 32.

24. Haley, *Buffalo War*, 22, 29, 37–38.

25. Ibid., 38. O'Connor, *Sheridan*, 325.

26. Haley, *Buffalo War*, 67–78.

27. Sherman to Sheridan, 23 July 1874, Sheridan Papers, Library of Congress. Hutton, *Phil Sheridan*, 248–51.

28. Utley, *Frontier Regulars*, 223–26.

29. Hutton, *Phil Sheridan*, 255–58. Sherman to Sheridan, 30 October 1874, Sheridan Papers, Library of Congress.

30. Brown, *Bury My Heart*, 259–60. Hutton, *Phil Sheridan*, 258–60.

31. Sheridan to Whipple, 23 November 1875, Sheridan Papers, Library of Congress. Utley, *Frontier Regulars*, 214.

32. Brown, *Bury My Heart*, 265–66. Utley, *Frontier Regulars*, 240–41.

33. Hutton, *Phil Sheridan*, 137, 289.

34. Utley, *Cavalier in Buckskin*, 135–41.

35. Utley, *Frontier Regulars*, 244. Hutton, *Phil Sheridan*, 291–92.

36. McFeely, *Grant*, 417. William Gillette, *Retreat from Reconstruction 1869–1879* (Baton Rouge: Louisiana State University Press, 1979), 119–20. Dawson, *Army Generals*, 196–97.

37. O'Connor, *Sheridan*, 328–29. Dawson, *Army Generals*, 198–99.

38. Dawson, *Army Generals*, 201–2. Sheridan to Belknap, 2 January 1875, Sheridan Papers, Library of Congress.

39. Dawson, *Army Generals*, 203–4. Gillette, *Retreat from Reconstruction*, 123. Taylor, *Louisiana Reconstructed*, 305.

40. Dawson, *Army Generals*, 204–6. Gillette, *Retreat from Reconstruction*, 123. Taylor, *Louisiana Reconstructed*, 305.

41. Dawson, *Army Generals*, 207. Gillette, *Retreat from Reconstruction*, 124. Taylor, *Louisiana Reconstructed*, 306. O'Connor, *Sheridan*, 330.

42. O'Connor, *Sheridan*, 330. Hutton, *Phil Sheridan*, 268. Dawson, *Army Generals*, 206, 209. Gillette, *Retreat from Reconstruction*, 126.

43. Dawson, *Army Generals*, 209. O'Connor, *Sheridan*, 331. Sheridan to Belknap, 6 January 1875, Sheridan Papers, Library of Congress. Hutton, *Phil Sheridan*, 269.

44. Hutton, *Phil Sheridan*, 270–71. Gillette, *Retreat from Reconstruction*, 128–31.

45. Hutton, *Phil Sheridan*, 271–72. Dawson, *Army Generals*, 210. Gillette, *Retreat from Reconstruction*, 132.

46. Dawson, *Army Generals*, 212–13. Sheridan to Belknap, 9 February 1875, Sheridan Papers, Library of Congress.

47. Hutton, *Phil Sheridan*, 293.

48. Ibid., 293–94. Utley, *Cavalier in Buckskin*, 141–43.

49. O'Connor, *Sheridan*, 333–34. Hutton, *Phil Sheridan*, 273–75. Burr and Hinton, *Life of Sheridan*, 371–72.

50. Utley, *Frontier Regulars*, 245. Brown, *Bury My Heart*, 270–71.

51. Utley, *Frontier Regulars*, 246–47. Hutton, *Phil Sheridan*, 298–99.

52. Hutton, *Phil Sheridan*, 301. Utley, *Frontier Regulars*, 248.

53. Utley, *Frontier Regulars*, 249–51, 264.

54. Hutton, *Phil Sheridan*, 305–10. Utley, *Cavalier in Buckskin*, 158–61.

55.   Utley, *Cavalier in Buckskin*, 162–63. O'Connor, *Sheridan*, 339.

56.   Utley, *Cavalier in Buckskin*, 165–67. Connell, *Son of the Morning Star*, 253–55.

57.   Hutton, *Phil Sheridan*, 315.

58.   Ibid., 315–16. Connell, *Son of the Morning Star*, 324–25.

59.   Connell, *Son of the Morning Star*, 331–32. Utley, *Cavalier in Buckskin*, 6.

60.   Sheridan to Sherman, 7 July 1876, Sheridan Papers, Library of Congress. Utley, *Cavalier in Buckskin*, 6.

61.   Utley, *Frontier Regulars*, 272–79.

62.   For the election of 1876, see Roy Morris, Jr., " 'Master Fraud of the Century': The Disputed Election of 1876," *American History Illustrated* (November 1988), 28–33, 48.

63.   Dawson, *Army Generals*, 236–40.

64.   Ibid., 240. Morris, "Master Fraud," 48.

Chapter 11

1.   Connell, *Son of the Morning Star*, 343. Hutton, *Phil Sheridan*, 329. O'Connor, *Sheridan*, 343.

2.   O'Connor, *Sheridan*, 342–44.

3.   Ibid., 334–35. Rister, *Border Command*, 198–200.

4.   Utley, *Frontier Regulars*, 281.

5.   Ibid., 296–319. Brown, *Bury My Heart*, 300–14.

6.   Hutton, *Phil Sheridan*, 140. Sherman to Sheridan, 8 March 1879, Sheridan Papers, Library of Congress. Utley, *Frontier Regulars*, 314–15.

7.   Hutton, *Phil Sheridan*, 334–36. Utley, *Frontier Regulars*, 283–84. Brown, *Bury My Heart*, 321–31.

8.   Hutton, *Phil Sheridan*, 336–37. Brown, *Bury My Heart*, 331.

9.   Hutton, *Phil Sheridan*, 337. Brown, *Bury My Heart*, 320.

10.   Hutton, *Phil Sheridan*, 337. Brown, *Bury My Heart*, 321.

11.   Paul F. Boller, Jr., *Presidential Campaigns* (New York: Oxford University Press, 1984), 128. McFeely, *Grant*, 380–83. William A. DeGregorio, *The Complete Book of U.S. Presidents* (New York: Dembner Books, 1984), 287.

12.   Hutton, *Phil Sheridan*, 339. Sheridan to Sherman, 12 November 1878, Sheridan Papers, Library of Congress. *Harper's Weekly*, 25 January 1879.

13.   Brown, *Bury My Heart*, 355–57. DeGregorio, *U.S. Presidents*, 285.

14.   Brown, *Bury My Heart*, 353, 359–65. Utley, *Frontier Regulars*, 333–37.

15.   Utley, *Frontier Regulars*, 337–39. Sheridan to Sherman, 30 November 1872, Sheridan Papers, Library of Congress.

16.   Utley, *Frontier Regulars*, 339. Brown, *Bury My Heart*, 366–67.

17.   *Annual Report of the Secretary of War [1878]*, 1, 36. Hutton, *Phil Sheridan*, 341–42. Coffman, *Old Army*, 258–59.

18.   O'Connor, *Sheridan*, 346–48. Sheridan to ———, 30 July 1880. Sheridan Papers, Library of Congress. Foote, *The Civil War*, 3:874.

19.   Hutton, *Phil Sheridan*, 141.

20.   Paul A. Hutton, "Phil Sheridan's Crusade for Yellowstone," *American History Illustrated* (February 1985), 7, 10–15. Hutton, *Phil Sheridan*, 163–65.

21.   Hutton, *Phil Sheridan*, 356–58.

22.   Ibid., 358–59. O'Connor, *Sheridan*, 353.

23.   Utley, *Frontier Regulars*, 30–33. Sheridan to Sherman, 26 May 1874, Sheridan Papers, Library of Congress.

24.   Hutton, *Phil Sheridan*, 346–49.

25.   Utley, *Frontier Regulars*, 31.

26.   Hutton, *Phil Sheridan*, 349–50. *Army and Navy Register*, 5 September 1885.

27. Peter Edwards, "Warrior Without Rest," *Military History* (October 1987), 65.

28. Ibid., 66.

29. Boller, *Presidential Campaigns*, 149–50. O'Connor, *Sheridan*, 348. DeGregorio, *U.S. Presidents*, 326.

30. Hutton, *Phil Sheridan*, 360–64. Allan Nevins, *Grover Cleveland: A Study in Courage* (New York: Dodd, Mead & Co., 1932), 229–30.

31. Nevins, *Grover Cleveland*, 332–36.

32. Ibid., 336. Gaines M. Foster, *Ghosts of the Confederacy: Defeat, the Lost Cause, and the Emergence of the New South* (New York: Oxford University Press, 1987), 154–55.

33. Hutton, *Phil Sheridan*, 347. Burr and Hinton, *Life of Sheridan*, 357.

34. John Lauber, *The Inventions of Mark Twain* (New York: Hill and Wang, 1990), 233.

35. Brown, *Bury My Heart*, 384–85. Utley, *Frontier Regulars*, 386.

36. Hutton, *Phil Sheridan*, 367–68. Utley, *Frontier Regulars*, 390. Crook, *Autobiography*, 134.

37. Lauber, *Inventions of Mark Twain*, 254–55. Hutton, *Phil Sheridan*, 371. Burr and Hinton, *Life of Sheridan*, 362–64.

38. Hutton, *Phil Sheridan*, 370–71.

39. Ibid., 371.

40. O'Connor, *Sheridan*, 349.

41. Ibid., 354. Hutton, *Phil Sheridan*, 371–72.

42. Hutton, *Phil Sheridan*, 372. *New York Times*, 1 July 1888.

43. *New York Times*, 7, 8, 9 July 1888. See also Burr and Hinton, *Life of Sheridan*, 376–84.

44. *New York Times*, 8 July 1888.

45. O'Connor, *Sheridan*, 354. *New York Times*, 9 July 1888.

46. *New York Times*, 11, 12 July, 2, 5, 6 August 1888.

47.   Ibid., 6 August 1888. O'Connor, *Sheridan*, 356. Burr and Hinton, *Life of Sheridan*, 380–81.

48.   *New York Times*, 6 August 1888. Burr and Hinton, *Life of Sheridan*, 386–87.

49.   Burr and Hinton, *Life of Sheridan*, 402, 407–8.

50.   Ibid., 409–10, 414–17. *New York Times*, 12 August 1888.

51.   Elting E. Morrison, ed., *The Letters of Theodore Roosevelt*, vol. 8 (Cambridge: Harvard University Press, 1954), 1088–89, 1189–97. *New York Times*, 8 February 1917. *Washington Post*, 8 February 1917.

52.   O'Connor, *Sheridan*, 356–57.

BIBLIOGRAPHY

Manuscripts

Beauregard, Pierre G. T., Papers. Manuscript Division, Library of Congress, Washington, D.C.

Grant, Ulysses S., Papers. Manuscript Division, Library of Congress, Washington, D.C.

Johnson, Andrew, Papers. Manuscript Division, Library of Congress, Washington, D.C.

Letters Received by the Office of the Adjutant General, 1822–1860. Record Group 393, National Archives, Washington, D.C.

Letters Received by the Office of the Adjutant General, 1861–1970. Record Group 393, National Archives, Washington, D.C.

Letters Received, Southwestern District of Missouri. Record Group 393, National Archives, Washington, D.C.

Letters Sent by the Adjutant General's Office. Record Group 393, National Archives, Washington, D.C.

Letters Sent, Department of the Gulf. Record Group 393, National Archives, Washington, D.C.

Letters Sent, Division of the Missouri. Record Group 393, National Archives, Washington, D.C.

Official Register of the Officers and Cadets of the U.S. Military Academy, West Point, N.Y., June 1853.

Papers Relating to the Examination of Cadets, 1816–1865. Record Group 94, National Archives, Washington, D.C.

Printed Orders, Department of Texas. Record Group 94, National Archives, Washington, D.C.

Register of Letters Received, Southwestern District of Missouri. Record Group 393, National Archives, Washington, D.C.

"Report of the Arrest of Cadet Sheridan to Chief Engineer." Record Group 94, National Archives, Washington, D.C.

Sheridan, Philip H., Papers. Manuscript Division, Library of Congress, Washington, D.C.

Sheridan, Philip H., File No. 1612. United States Military Academy Archives, West Point, N.Y.

Sheridan, Philip H., Synopsis of Military Service. Record Group 94, National Archives, Washington, D.C.

Sheridan, Philip H., Personal File. Record Group 94, National Archives, Washington, D.C.

Sherman, William Tecumseh, Papers. Manuscript Division, Library of Congress, Washington, D.C.

Government Documents

Annual Reports of the Secretary of War, 1866–1888.
U.S. War Department. *The War of the Rebellion: A Compilation of the Official Records of the Union and Confederate Armies.* 128 vols. Washington, D.C.: U.S. Government Printing Office, 1880–1901.

Books, Articles, and Dissertations

Ambrose, Stephen E. *Duty, Honor, Country: A History of West Point.* Baltimore: Johns Hopkins University Press, 1966.

———.*Halleck: Lincoln's Chief of Staff.* Baton Rouge: Louisiana State University Press, 1962.

Anderson, David D. "The Second Michigan Cavalry Under Philip H. Sheridan." *Michigan History* (September 1961), 210–18.

Badeau, Adam. *Grant in Peace.* Hartford: S. S. Scranton, 1887.

———."Lieut.-General Sheridan." *Century Magazine* 27 (February 1884), 496–511.

Basler, Roy P., ed. *The Collected Works of Abraham Lincoln.* 9 vols. New Brunswick: Rutgers University Press, 1953–55.

Beatty, John. *Memoirs of a Volunteer.* New York: W. W. Norton, 1946.

Belknap, Charles E. *History of the Michigan Organizations at Chicka-mauga, Chattanooga, and Missionary Ridge.* Lansing: R. Smith Publishing, 1897.

Bennett, L. G., and W. M. Haigh. *History of the 36th Regiment Illinois Volunteers*. Aurora, Ill.: Knickerbocker & Hodder, 1876.

Bischoff, William N. "The Yakima Campaign of 1856." *Mid-America* 31 (April 1949), 163–208.

Blakemore, W. T. "Portrait of Lytle." *Confederate Veteran* 5, 249–54.

Boatner, Mark M. *The Civil War Dictionary*. New York: David McKay, 1959.

Boller, Paul F., Jr. *Presidential Campaigns*. New York: Oxford University Press, 1984.

Brown, Dee. *Bury My Heart at Wounded Knee: An Indian History of the American West*. Toronto, New York, London: Bantam Books, 1972.

Buel, Clarence C., and Robert U. Johnson. *Battles and Leaders of the Civil War*. 4 vols. New York: Castle Books, 1956.

Burr, Frank A., and Richard J. Hinton. *The Life of Gen. Philip H. Sheridan: Its Romance and Reality*. Providence: J. A. and R. A. Reid Publishers, 1888.

Bushong, Millard K. *Old Jube: A Biography of General Jubal A. Early*. Shippensburg, Pa.: White Mane, 1955.

Byers, S. H. M. *Iowa in War Times*. Des Moines: W. D. Condit, 1888.

Casey, Robert J., and Mary Borglum. *Give the Man Room*. Indianapolis: Bobbs-Merrill, 1952.

Castel, Albert. *General Sterling Price and the Civil War in the West*. Baton Rouge: Louisiana State University Press, 1968.

Catton, Bruce. *Grant Takes Command*. Boston: Little, Brown, 1969.

———. *This Hallowed Ground*. New York: Doubleday, 1956.

———. "Sheridan at Five Forks." *Journal of Southern History* 21 (1955), 305–15.

Cist, Henry M. *The Army of the Cumberland*. New York: Charles Scribner's Sons, 1882.

Coffman, Edward M. *The Old Army: A Portrait of the American Army in Peacetime, 1784–1898*. New York and Oxford: Oxford University Press, 1986.

Connell, Evan S. *Son of the Morning Star: Custer and the Little Bighorn*. San Francisco: North Point Press, 1984.

Connelly, Thomas F. *Army of the Heartland: The Army of Tennessee, 1861–1862*. Baton Rouge: Louisiana State University Press, 1967.

———. *Autumn of Glory: The Army of Tennessee, 1862–1865*. Baton Rouge: Louisiana State University Press, 1971.

Cooper, Grace E. "Benton County Pioneer-Historical Society." *Oregon Historical Quarterly* 57 (March 1956), 83–84.

Cromie, Robert. *The Great Chicago Fire*. New York, Toronto, London: McGraw-Hill, 1958.

Crowninshield, Benjamin W. "Sheridan at Winchester." *Atlantic Monthly* 42 (1878), 684–90.

Cullen, Joseph P. "Cedar Creek." *Civil War Times Illustrated* (December 1969), 5–9, 42–48.

Cummings, Charles M. *Yankee Quaker, Confederate General: The Curious Career of Bushrod Rust Johnson*. Rutherford, N.J.: Fairleigh Dickinson University Press, 1971.

Curtis, Edward S. *The North American Indian*. Vol. 7. New York: Johnson Reprint Co., 1970.

Dana, Charles A. *Recollections of the Civil War*. New York: D. Appleton, 1898.

Dannett, Sylvia G. "Rebecca Wright—Traitor or Patriot?" *Lincoln Herald* (Fall 1963), 103–12.

Davies, Henry E. *General Sheridan*. New York: D. Appleton, 1909.

Dawson, Joseph G. III *Army Generals and Reconstruction: Louisiana, 1862–1877*. Baton Rouge: Louisiana State University Press, 1982.

———."General Phil Sheridan and Military Reconstruction in Louisiana." *Civil War History* 24 (January 1978), 133–51.

DeForest, John W. *A Volunteer's Adventures*. New Haven: Yale University Press, 1946.

DeGregorio, William A. *The Complete Book of U.S. Presidents*. New York: Dembner Books, 1984.

Delo, David M. "Melee on the Plains." *Wild West* (December 1988) 43–49.

Dodge, Grenville. *The Battle of Atlanta and Other Campaigns*. Council Bluffs, Iowa: Monarch Printing Co., 1911.

Douglas, Henry Kyd. *I Rode with Stonewall*. Chapel Hill: University of North Carolina Press, 1940.

Dunn, J. P. Jr. *Massacres of the Mountains: A History of the Indian Wars of the Far West, 1815–1875*. New York: Archer House, 1886.

Dupuy, R. Ernest. *Men of West Point: The First 150 Years of the United States Military Academy*. New York: Sloane, 1951.

Durham, Walter T. *Nashville: The Occupied City*. Nashville: Tennessee Historical Society, 1985.

Early, Jubal A. *Autobiographical Sketch and Narrative of the War Between the States*. Philadelphia: J. B. Lippincott, 1912.

Edwards, Peter. "Warrior Without Rest." *Military History* (October 1987), 8, 63–65.

Egan, Ferol. *Fremont: Explorer for a Restless Nation*. New York: Doubleday, 1977.

Faust, Patricia L., ed. *Historical Times Illustrated Encyclopedia of the Civil War*. New York: Harper & Row, 1986.

Fitch, John. *Annals of the Army of the Cumberland*. Philadelphia: J. B. Lippincott, 1864.

Fleming, Thomas J. *West Point: The Men and Times of the United States Military Academy*. New York: William Morrow, 1969.

Foner, Eric. *Reconstruction: America's Unfinished Revolution, 1863–1877*. New York: Harper & Row, 1988.

Foote, Shelby. *The Civil War: A Narrative*. 3 vols. New York: Random House, 1958–74.

Forsyth, George A. "A Frontier Fight." *Harper's New Monthly Magazine* 91 (June 1895), 42–62.

———. *Thrilling Days in Army Life*. New York: Harper & Brothers, 1900.

Foster, Gaines M. *Ghosts of the Confederacy: Defeat, the Lost Cause, and the Emergence of the New South*. New York: Oxford University Press, 1987.

Freeman, Douglas S. *R. E. Lee: A Biography*. Vol. 4. New York: Charles Scribner's Sons, 1934–35.

Frost, Lawrence. *The Phil Sheridan Album: A Pictorial Biography of Philip Henry Sheridan*. Seattle: Superior Publishing Co., 1968.

Fry, James B. *Killed by a Brother Soldier*. New York: G. P. Putnam's Sons, 1885.

Gallagher, Gary W. *Stephen Dodson Ramseur: Lee's Gallant General*. Chapel Hill: University of North Carolina Press, 1985.

Gillette, William. *Retreat from Reconstruction 1869–1879*. Baton Rouge: Louisiana State University Press, 1979.

Glazer, Sidney. *Detroit: A Study in Urban Development*. New York: Bookman Associates, Inc., 1965.

Gordon, John B. *Reminiscences of the Civil War*. New York: Charles Scribner's Sons, 1904.

Gracie, Archibald Jr. *The Truth About Chickamauga*. Boston: Houghton Mifflin, 1911.

Grant, Ulysses S. *Personal Memoirs of U. S. Grant*. 2 vols. New York: Charles L. Webster & Co., 1885.

Greiner, Henry C. *General Phil Sheridan as I Knew Him*. Chicago: J. S. Hyland Co., 1908.

Grinnell, George Bird. *The Fighting Cheyennes*. Norman, Okla.: University of Oklahoma Press, 1956.

Hafendorfer, Kenneth A. *Perryville: Battle for Kentucky*. Utica, Ky.: McDowell Publications, 1981.

Haley, James L. *The Buffalo War: The History of the Red River Indian Uprising of 1874*. Norman, Okla.: University of Oklahoma Press, 1976.

Hall, James O. "Fact or Fabrication? The Dahlgren Papers. A Yankee Plot to Kill President Davis." *Civil War Times Illustrated* (November 1983), 93–95.

Hammond, Paul F. "Campaigns of General E. Kirby Smith for Kentucky, in 1862." *Southern Historical Society Papers* 9 (1881), 229–254.

Harrison, Lowell. "Death on a Dry River." *Civil War Times Illustrated* (May 1979), 6–9, 44–47.

Hassler, William W. "Yellow Tavern." *Civil War Times Illustrated* (November 1966), 4–11, 46–48.

Hathaway, John L. "Recollections of Sheridan as a Cadet." *War Papers: Commandery of the State of Wisconsin, Military Order of the Loyal Legion of the United States* (1891), 270–74.

Hergesheimer, Joseph. *Sheridan: A Military Biography*. Boston and New York: Houghton Mifflin, 1931.

Hillard, James M. "You Are Strangely Deluded." *Civil War Times Illustrated* (February 1975), 12–18.

Hoar, George F. *Autobiography of Seventy Years*. 2 vols. New York: Charles Scribner's Sons, 1906.

Hoar, Victor. "Colonel William C. Falkner in the Civil War." *Journal of Mississippi History* 27 (February 1965), 42–62.

Horn, Stanley F. *The Battle of Stones River*. Gettysburg, Pa.: Historical Times, Inc., 1972.

Howe, M. A. DeWolfe, ed. *Home Letters of General Sherman*. New York: Charles Scribner's Sons, 1909.

Hutton, Paul Andrew. *Phil Sheridan and His Army*. Lincoln and London: University of Nebraska Press, 1985.

———."Phil Sheridan's Crusade for Yellowstone." *American History Illustrated* (February 1985), 7, 10–15.

Johnson, Richard W. *A Soldier's Reminiscences in Peace and War*. Philadelphia: J. B. Lippincott, 1886.

Jones, James P. Jr. " 'Bull' and the 'Damned Puppy': A Civil War Tragedy." *American History Illustrated* (November 1972), 12–21.

Jones, Virgil C. *Ranger Mosby*. Chapel Hill: University of North Carolina Press, 1944.

Kaser, David. "Nashville's Women of Pleasure in 1860." *Tennessee Historical Quarterly* (December 1964), 380–82.

Kennan, Jerry. "Cheyenne Island Siege." *Wild West* (June 1988), 35–41.

Knox, Thomas W. *Camp-Fire and Cotton-Field: Southern Adventure in Time of War.* New York: Blelock & Co., 1865.

Kogan, Herman, and Robert Cromie. *The Great Fire: Chicago, 1871.* New York: G. P. Putnam's Sons, 1971.

Lamers, William M. *The Edge of Glory: A Biography of General William S. Rosecrans, U.S.A.* New York: Harcourt, Brace & World, 1961.

Laubers, John. *The Inventions of Mark Twain.* New York: Hill and Wang, 1990.

Leech, Margaret. *Reveille in Washington, 1860–1865.* New York: Harper and Brothers, 1941.

Lewis, Lloyd. *Sherman: Fighting Prophet.* New York: Harcourt, Brace, 1932.

Lewis, Thomas A. *The Guns of Cedar Creek.* New York: Harper & Row, 1988.

Longacre, Edward G. "Cavalry Clash at Todd's Tavern." *Civil War Times Illustrated* (October 1977), 12–22.

———. "A Profile of General Justus McKinstry." *Civil War Times Illustrated* (July 1978), 15–21.

Lonn, Ella. *Foreigners in the Union Army and Navy.* Baton Rouge: Louisiana State University Press, 1951.

Masland, John W., and Laurence I. Radway. *Soldiers and Scholars: Military Education and National Policy.* Princeton: Princeton University Press, 1957.

McDonough, James Lee. "The Battle of Stones River, Tennessee." *Civil War Times Illustrated* (June 1986), 13–51.

———. *Chattanooga—A Death Grip on the Confederacy.* Knoxville: University of Tennessee Press, 1984.

———. *Stones River: Bloody Winter in Tennessee.* Knoxville: University of Tennessee Press, 1980.

McDowell, Robert E. *City of Conflict: Louisville in the Civil War, 1861–1865.* Louisville: Louisville Civil War Roundtable, 1962.

McFeely, William S. *Grant: A Biography.* New York: W. W. Norton, 1981.

McKinney, Francis F. *Education in Violence: The Life of George H. Thomas and the History of the Army of the Cumberland.* Detroit: Wayne University Press, 1961.

McPherson, Edward. *The Political History of the United States During the Great Rebellion.* Washington, D.C.: Philp and Solomons, 1865.

McWhiney, Grady. *Braxton Bragg and Confederate Defeat.* New York: Columbia University Press, 1969.

Monaghan, Jay. "Custer's 'Last Stand'—Trevilian Station, 1864." *Civil War History* 8 (September 1962), 245–58.

Morris, Roy Jr. "All Hell Can't Stop Them." *Military History* (February 1986), 34–40.

———. "Battle in the Blue Grass." *Civil War Times Illustrated* (December 1988), 15–23.

———. "A Bird of Evil Omen: The War Department's Charles Dana." *Civil War Times Illustrated* (January 1987), 20–29.

———. "Cavalry Blooded." *Wild West* (December 1990), 34–40.

———. "Eastern Ohio Quaker in Gray: Bushrod Johnson's Strange Career." *Blue & Gray* (March 1985), 52–57.

———. "I Am Dying, Egypt, Dying." *Civil War Times Illustrated* (October 1986), 24–31.

———. "The Sack of Athens." *Civil War Times Illustrated* (February 1986), 26–32.

Morrison, Elting E., ed. *The Letters of Theodore Roosevelt.* Vol. 8. Cambridge: Harvard University Press, 1954.

Morrison, James L. *The Best School in the World: West Point, the Pre-Civil War Years, 1833–1866.* Kent, Ohio: Kent State University Press, 1986.

Morsberger, Robert E., and Katharine M. Morsberger. *Lew Wallace: Militant Romantic.* New York: McGraw-Hill, 1980.

Mosby, John S. "Retaliation: The Execution of Seven Prisoners by Col. John S. Mosby—A Self-Protective Necessity." *Southern Historical Society Papers* 27 (1899), 314–22.

Murdock, Myrtle M. *Your Memorials in Washington.* Washington, D.C.: Monumental Press, 1952.

Nevins, Allan. *Grover Cleveland: A Study in Courage.* New York: Dodd, Mead, 1932.

———, and Malton H. Thomas, eds. *The Diary of George Templeton Strong.* 4 vols. New York: Macmillan, 1952.

Oates, Stephen B. *With Malice Toward None: The Life of Abraham Lincoln.* New York: Harper & Row, 1977.

O'Connor, Richard. *Sheridan the Inevitable.* Indianapolis: Bobbs-Merrill, 1953.

———. *Wild Bill Hickok.* New York: Doubleday, 1959.

O'Toole, G. J. A. *The Spanish War*. New York: W. W. Norton, 1984.

Parris, William E. "Fremont in Missouri." *Civil War Times Illustrated* (April 1978), 4–10, 40–45.

Parsons, Edwin B. "Sheridan." *War Papers: Commandery of the State of Wisconsin, Military Order of the Loyal Legion of the United States* (1891), 275–84.

Piatt, Donn. *General George H. Thomas: A Critical Biography*. Cincinnati: Robert Clarke & Co., 1893.

Pierce, Lyman B. *History of the Second Iowa Cavalry*. Burlington, Iowa: Hawkeye Printing Co., 1885.

Porter, Horace. *Campaigning with Grant*. New York: The Century Co., 1897.

Price, Willadene. *Gutzon Borglum: Artist and Patriot*. Chicago: Rand McNally, 1961.

Rable, George C. *But There Was No Peace: The Role of Violence in the Politics of Reconstruction*. Athens: University of Georgia Press, 1984.

Ramsdell, Charles W. *Reconstruction in Texas*. New York: Columbia University Press, 1910.

Reid, Whitelaw. *Ohio in the War*. Vol. 1. Cincinnati: Wilstach & Baldwin, 1868.

Richter, William L. *The Army in Texas During Reconstruction, 1865–1870*. College Station, Texas: Texas A&M University Press, 1987.

———. "The Army in Texas During Reconstruction, 1865–1870." Ph.D. dissertation, Louisiana State University, 1970.

———. "The Brenham Fire of 1866: A Texas Reconstruction Tragedy." *Louisiana Studies* (Fall 1975), 287–314.

Riddleberger, Patrick W. *1866: The Critical Year Revisited*. Carbondale and Edwards, Ill.: Southern Illinois University Press, 1979.

Rister, Carl Coke. *Border Command: General Phil Sheridan in the West*. Norman, Okla.: University of Oklahoma Press, 1944.

Robertson, John. *Michigan in the War*. Lansing, Mich.: W. S. George & Co., 1882.

Rowell, John W. *Yankee Artilleryman: Through the Civil War with Eli Lilly's Indiana Battery*. Knoxville: University of Tennessee Press, 1975.

Schmitt, Martin F., ed. *General George Cook: His Autobiography*. Norman, Okla.: University of Oklahoma Press, 1946.

Sefton, James E. *United States Army and Reconstruction, 1865–1877*. Baton Rouge: Louisiana State University Press, 1967.

Sheridan, Philip H. *Personal Memoirs of P. H. Sheridan.* 2 vols. New York: Charles L. Webster & Co., 1888.

Siepel, Kevin H. *Rebel: The Life and Times of John Singleton Mosby.* New York: St. Martin's Press, 1983.

Skoch, George F. "In the Shadow of the Valley: Lieutenant Meigs Dies." *Civil War Times Illustrated* (September 1984), 35–39.

Smith, Sherry Lynn. " 'Civilization's Guardians': Army Officers' Reflections on Indians and the Indian Wars in the Trans-Mississippi West, 1848–1890." Ph.D. dissertation, University of Washington, 1984.

Stackpole, Edward J. *Sheridan in the Shenandoah: Jubal Early's Nemesis.* Harrisburg, Pa.: Stackpole, 1961.

Stanley, David S. *Personal Memoirs of Major General D. S. Stanley, U.S.A.* Cambridge: Harvard University Press, 1917.

Starr, Stephen Z. "Hawkeyes on Horseback: The Second Iowa Volunteer Cavalry." *Civil War History* 23 (1977), 212–27.

———. *Jennison's Jayhawkers: A Civil War Cavalry Regiment and Its Commander.* Baton Rouge: Louisiana State University Press, 1973.

———. "The Second Michigan Cavalry: Another View." *Michigan History* 60 (1976), 161–82.

———. *The Union Cavalry in the Civil War.* 3 vols. Baton Rouge: Louisiana State University Press, 1981.

Stevens, Hazard. "The Battle of Cedar Creek." *Papers of the Military Historical Society of Massachusetts,* Vol. 6 (1907), 89–140.

Stevenson, Alexander F. *The Battle of Stones River.* Boston: James R. Osgood, 1884.

Stutler, Boyd B., ed. "Notes and Queries." *Civil War History* (June 1960), 192–93.

Swift, Lester. "The Preacher Regiment at Chickamauga and Missionary Ridge." *Lincoln Herald* (Summer 1970), 51–60.

Taylor, Joe G. *Louisiana Reconstructed, 1863–1877.* Baton Rouge: Louisiana State University Press, 1974.

Taylor, John. "With More Sorrow Than I Can Tell." *Civil War Times Illustrated* (April 1981), 20–29.

Thomas, Emory M. *Bold Dragoon: The Life of J. E. B. Stuart.* New York: Harper & Row, 1986.

———. "The Kilpatrick-Dahlgren Raid on Richmond." *Civil War Times Illustrated* (February 1978), 4–9, 46–48.

Trefousse, Hans L. *Andrew Johnson: A Biography.* New York and London: W. W. Norton, 1989.

Tucker, Glenn. "The Battle of Chickamauga." *Civil War Times Illustrated* (May 1969), 5–46.

———. "The Battles for Chattanooga." *Civil War Times Illustrated* (September 1971), 4–44.

———. *Chickamauga: Bloody Battle in the West*. Indianapolis: Bobbs-Merrill, 1961.

Turchin, John B. *Chickamauga*. Chicago: Fergus Printing Co., 1888.

Utley, Robert M. *Cavalier in Buckskin: George Armstrong Custer and the Western Military Frontier*. Norman, Okla.: University of Oklahoma Press, 1988.

———. *Frontier Regulars: The United States Army and the Indian, 1866–1891*. New York: Macmillan, 1973.

———. *Frontiersmen in Blue: The United States Army and the Indian, 1848–1865*. New York: Macmillan, 1967.

———. *The Indian Frontier of the American West, 1846–1890*. Albuquerque: University of New Mexico Press, 1984.

Van Deusen, Glyndon G. *William Henry Seward*. New York: Oxford University Press, 1967.

Van Horne, Thomas B. *History of the Army of the Cumberland*. Cincinnati: Robert Clarke, 1875.

Volpe, Edward L. *A Reader's Guide to William Faulkner*. New York: Noonday Press, 1964.

Walker, Aldace F. *The Vermont Brigade in the Shenandoah Valley*. Burlington, Vt.: The Free Press Association, 1869.

Walker, Robert S. "Pyramids at Chickamauga." *Chattanooga Times*, September 13, 1936.

Watkins, Sam R. "*Co. Aytch*". New York: Collier Books, 1962.

Weigley, Russell F. *The American Way of War: A History of United States Military Strategy and Policy*. New York: Macmillan, 1973.

———. *Towards an American Army: Military Thought from Washington to Marshall*. New York: Columbia University Press, 1962.

Weinert, Richard P. "The South Had Mosby; The Union: Maj. Henry Young." *Civil War Times Illustrated* (April 1964), 38–42.

Wert, Jeffry D. *From Winchester to Cedar Creek: The Shenandoah Campaign of 1864*. Carlisle, Pa.: South Mountain Press, 1987.

———. *Mosby's Rangers*. New York: Simon and Schuster, 1990.

———. "The Third Battle of Winchester." *American History Illustrated* (November 1980), 8–16.

Williams, John Hoyt. *A Great and Shining Road: The Epic Story of the Transcontinental Railroad*. New York: Times Books, 1988.

Williams, Robert A. "Haw's Shop: A 'Storm of Shot and Shell.' " *Civil War Times Illustrated* (January 1971), 12–19.

Williams, Samuel C. *General John T. Wilder, Commander of the Lightning Brigade.* Bloomington: Indiana University Press, 1936.

Wilson, George T. "Battle for Missouri." *America's Civil War* (January 1990), 27–32.

Wilson, James H. *Under the Old Flag.* New York: D. Appleton, 1911.

Wilson, John. *Chattanooga's Story.* Chattanooga: Chattanooga Publishing Co., 1980.

Wooster, Robert Allen. "The Military and United States Indian Policy, 1865–1903." Ph.D. dissertation, University of Texas, 1985.

Zeimet, Roger Thomas. "Philip H. Sheridan and the Civil War in the West." Ph.D. dissertation, Marquette University, 1981.

INDEX